MEXICO'S MERCHANT ELITE, 1590–1660

MEXICO'S

MERCHANT ELITE,

1590 – 1660

———————— Silver, State, and Society

Louisa Schell Hoberman

Duke University Press   *Durham and London 1991*

© 1991 Duke University Press
All rights reserved
Printed in the United States of America
on acid-free paper ∞
Library of Congress Cataloging-in-Publication Data
appear on the last page of this book.

To May Magriel and the memory of Irving Schell

Contents

List of Tables

List of Illustrations

Acknowledgments

In the course of writing a study of this scope, I naturally incurred many debts. Although this book is not based on a dissertation, I first want to thank the professors who guided my dissertation research and writing and who started me thinking along the lines which led to this project: Herbert Klein, Lewis Hanke, and Karen Spalding. I am grateful for the advice they offered and the high standards they set. John TePaske offered deeply appreciated encouragement and much valuable information over the years. I am very much indebted to William Taylor for his meticulous and perceptive reading of the manuscript. Murdo MacLeod provided a very well-informed critique. Among other scholars, I would like to thank Fred Bronner, Susan Deans-Smith, John Kicza, Asuncion Lavrin, Cheryl Martin, Fritz Schwaller, and Stuart Schwartz. As the footnotes to this book indicate, I have learned much from the stimulating works of Peter Bakewell, Woodrow Borah, D. A. Brading, Mark Burkholder, J. I. Israel, James Lockhart, Richard Salvucci, John Super, and Stanley Stein. Finally, I wish to remember my co-editor, Susan Socolow, and the other contributors to *Cities and Society in Colonial Latin America*, because editing their fine essays gave me greater insight into my own.

At the two major archives consulted, I want to acknowledge the assistance of Rosario Parra, director of the Archivo General de Indias in Seville, and Jorge Ignacio Rubio Mañé, director of the Archivo General de la Nación in Mexico City when this research began. The staff of these archives made them an enjoyable and fruitful place in which to work. In Seville, the able research assistance of Victoria Stapells-Johnson was very helpful. Conversations with José de la Peña and Enriqueta Vila Vilar there were most useful. I also appreciate the permission to consult their archives from the directors of the Archivo de Notarías and the Archivo Judicial del D.F. in Mexico City. In the United States, Peter Boyd-Bowman was kind enough to share with me unpublished data from the passenger lists of the Indies, and George Hough ran the SAS program, analyzing the shipping data. As a result of an enjoyable collaboration, John V. Cotter contributed the maps. Finally, I wish to thank the editors at Duke University Press for the care they took with the manuscript. Any errors are, of course, my own responsibility.

Financial support for research in Mexico and Spain was provided by the American Philosophical Society, Pomona College, and Wesleyan University. The Mary I. Bunting Institute of Radcliffe College offered a year of funding and of stimulating company for writing, and the University of Texas, Austin, and Boston University provided Visiting Scholar affiliations and office space for a year each. George Mason University generously made possible additional writing time.

This book would not have been begun without the scholarly example and affection of my parents, who instilled in me a love for historical research. Nor would it have been completed without the steadfast and informed encouragement of my husband. I am very grateful to them all.

Introduction

MERCHANTS AND THE EVOLUTION OF COLONIAL SOCIETY

This book is a history of the merchant elite of Mexico and of its influence on the development of the viceroyalty during the first two-thirds of the seventeenth century, a period which is still one of the country's most controversial and obscure epochs. In 1634 Viceroy Cerralvo asserted: "trade is the lifeblood of this kingdom, and from it flows the prosperity of the realm."[1] The best known trade of the era was the commerce in silver, the transfer of bullion and coin from the mines and mint of New Spain to the courts and markets of Europe. But this exchange generated a host of other transactions, and reinforced a distinctive approach to investment, which affected other sectors of the colonial economy than trade and mining. The purpose of this volume is to analyze the formation, behavior, and continued preeminence of the colony's merchant elite, the wholesalers of Mexico City, and to depict its impact on the evolution of Mexico. In so doing, I seek to present an introduction to the seventeenth century that will be of interest to general historians as well as colonial specialists.

Mexican society of the seventeenth century was shaped by the interaction of the diverse members of the upper stratum, often called the *gente decente*, with the heterogeneous and more numerous *gente plebea*. A book about *hacendados*, mineowners, skilled laborers, Indian farmers, or the urban criminal and unemployed would also provide insight into the social dynamics of the seventeenth century. But to address many of the controversial topics of that period—the alleged economic depression, the degree to which wealth promoted social mobility, the extent of New Spain's economic dependence on Europe and Asia, the political power of the colonists, and the relationship between Mexico City and the provinces—

the most promising approach seemed to be a study of the group intimately linked to such topics.

Historiographical Background

In 1975, Charles Gibson remarked that historians of seventeenth-century Mexico must write without a context in which to place their findings.[2] Since then, studies of fiscal trends, mining, civil-ecclesiastical politics, creole and *peninsular* rivalries, some branches of agriculture, religious attitudes, and rural Indian society have greatly illuminated areas of the seventeenth-century landscape, but a thorough knowledge of the terrain, comparable to our knowledge of the late colony, is still lacking. In this study I hope to contribute to the knowledge of that time by presenting information on two general topics. The first topic is the use of capital: its investment in different types of enterprises, the organization of credit, the major trade routes along which it traveled, the incomes earned, and, more broadly, the scale and pace of economic life. The second topic is the government: the value of different saleable public offices, the internal hierarchy of such branches of the bureaucracy as the mint and the *cabildo* (city council), the history of certain tax farms, and the great variety of informal political networks.

The merchants, for the most part, remain in the obscure zone of the landscape. With a few exceptions, the new social history has passed by the traders of the seventeenth century. Excellent studies are available of the merchants of the eighteenth century, a time when the growth in mining production, the attempted implementation of Bourbon reforms, an increase in migration from Spain, and new intellectual currents fostered striking changes in the commercial elite.[3] Historians of merchants in the sixteenth and seventeenth centuries, however, have focussed primarily on commercial institutions and broad economic trends rather than on social history.[4] There are some valuable accounts of merchants as a social group, but they are short treatments.[5] This book is the first in-depth study of Mexico's merchant elite during the first two-thirds of the seventeenth century.

Although this study takes colonial Mexican society as its context and center of gravity, the Conclusion places merchants in the context of the dependency and world systems interpretations. While the former is based on Latin American research, the latter emphasizes the European literature. World-systems writers and many dependency scholars assign to merchants and other owners of capital the motive force in the creation of a global economy in the sixteenth century, which resulted in an international division of labor in which northwestern Europe became the core region, Spain and Italy, the semiperiphery, and Latin America and Eastern Europe, the periphery. From this point on, these scholars differ. Some Latin American dependency writers believe that the entrepreneurs changed the organization of colonial production in a positive sense. They promoted the growth of wage labor, urbanization, and their correlaries the domestic and regional market.[6] This allowed the Latin American economy to achieve substantial autonomy and dynamism and furthered movement toward capitalism. Other dependency writers stress the primacy of commercial capital but are skeptical about the degree of autonomy attained. World systems theory, for its part, emphasizes the predominance of a capitalist economy worldwide and the progressive role of European merchants. (Although it acknowledges the continuation of feudal or noncapitalist elements, it insists that the overall context was still capitalist, a claim disputed by other Europeanists.) Sixteenth-century European merchants still counted on monopoly, high profit per unit sales, and a small, luxury market; however, they included traders who took a more modern, competitive approach to business.[7]

World systems scholars also assert that each world region is characterized by a particular type of labor system and state control, and for Latin America, these were forced or coerced cash crop labor and a weak imperial government. Thus, Latin America was fated to remain a dependent region whose merchants could not promote autonomy. This accords with another dependency approach which emphasizes Latin America's subordination to decisions made in the core regions. These scholars view Latin American merchants as a conservative, even parasitic, force, producing, if at all, for a small elite market and distributing products made by coerced labor rather than the wage or self-employed labor found in the core. Rather than challenging existing pre- or noncapitalist structures, they adapted to them. These writers also state that merchant behavior, the search for profits and circulation of goods, was less significant than relations of production.[8] In other words, they consider the emphasis on trade as a motive force in the transition from one type of society to another misplaced.

Because the combination of tributary, draft, share, and wage labor in colonial Latin America indicates the insufficiency of the standard European categories of feudal and capitalist, there have been calls for a theoretical framework more appropriate to colonial society, one acknowledging the coexistence of different modes of production.[9] In the Conclusion I will suggest that the European-derived categories are also inadequate for trade and merchants, which in colonial Mexico did not fit easily under either rubric.

Summary of Contents

Chapter 1, "Formation of the Merchant Elite: Commissions, Credit, and Dowries," begins with an analysis of the social organization of the Atlantic and Pacific trades. Scholars have not yet analyzed how many participants there were at different times, how much they invested, nor to what extent their behavior in the Atlantic and Pacific trades may have differed. This chapter provides such a context. It then discusses some of the ways merchants established themselves. Some methods of capital accumulation are relatively well known, such as reliance on family members for cash or credit. Other techniques, such as the merchants' involvement in many projects as commission agents, have not been much discussed. Chapter 2, "The Mexican Economy and Merchant Capital: Mining and the Mint," and chapter 3, "The Mexican Economy and Merchant Capital: Agriculture, Manufacturing, and Urban Real Estate," trace the importance of each of these sectors to the merchants and their influence—or lack of it—on each. All three chapters address one of the central themes of the book, the theme of monopoly and elite control, whether exercised in the economy, politics, or social life.

As a class, wholesalers occupied an ambiguous position in the social hierarchy. As Lockhart has noted, of all colonial occupations, the merchants are the most difficult to classify. Consequently, their status can illuminate the values and tensions of the *sociedad de castas*, a system of stratification based on socially defined racial categories. Some historians characterize the wealthy merchants of the eighteenth century as members of the social elite. Was this the case in the seventeenth century when birth rather than wealth may have been the chief criterion for entry? By race, wholesalers belonged in the white *español* category. But were there other obstacles to their acceptance by the elite, obstacles not faced by other wealthy, white groups? The prestige of the wholesalers' guild, and the high income of many members, helped open the most aristocratic ranks to certain merchants and may eventually have contributed to a more flexible social system. The plebeian origins of some merchants, however, and the stigma attached to the occupation of professional merchant, lessened their claim as a group to elite status in the eyes of contemporaries. A further complication for the seventeenth-century wholesaler was the influx after 1580 of Portuguese *converso* (New Christian) traders into the Spanish realms and their subsequent persecution by the authorities. The wholesalers' place in colonial society also requires a discussion of relations with groups beneath them in rank. They routinely had contacts with artisans, laborers, retailers, muleteers and carters, and lower-level public officials. Merchants acted as landlords and employers and sometimes as suppliers of raw materials. They might also be relatives by blood or *compadrazgo* (ritual co-parenthood). These relationships flesh out the picture of the merchants' peculiar social standing.

For many years the political history of colonial Mexico was written as the history of bureaucrats' efforts to enforce royal legislation. The emphasis was on the formal dimension, officials and the law. Now, scholars of colonial politics focus on relationships that originated outside the government in family ties, place of birth, or economic interests. Chapter 4, "Public Office and Private Gain," combines the two approaches by asking why public office was such an attractive investment to merchants and how much political influence the merchant elite exercised. Given that in this period the colony was more dynamic economically than the mother country, another question arises: did New Spain remain a political ward of Spain? Chapter 5, "The Mercantilist Mirage: Taxes, Trade, and Turmoil," analyzes two unpopular metropolitan policies of the 1620s and 1630s— tax reform and commercial restrictions—and the merchants' and other colonists' attempts to frustrate them. It first describes the traditional opposition tactics the merchant elite used in earlier years to lessen the impact of the import-export tax and the sales tax; it then traces how these tactics were applied to new, adverse royal policies. In politics, more than in any other sphere, the colonists, with whom the wholesalers identified themselves politically, appear to be the captives of a metropolis-oriented system. To what extent were they able to escape from the colonial cul-de-sac?

Chapter 6, "Progeny and Property," discusses the merchants' transition from a class whose income derived from trade to one reliant on diverse sources of wealth. The phenomenon of economic diversification by elites is familiar, but which sectors of the economy appealed to persons with capital at this time need consideration. Trade, public office, urban real estate, and finance appear to have been more attractive sectors than ownership of agricultural or ranching properties. The social ambitions of the merchants, of course, led them to place many of their children in non-commercial occupations. Chapter 6 documents this pattern for the first two-thirds of the century yet also shows that outmobility was offset to some degree by such factors as considerable endogamy among the merchants themselves and the retention of close ties among their descendants. This chapter considers the value of the wholesalers' estates, the size of their families, and the fortunes of their children and grandchildren. How long-lived were the achievements of the first generation? An answer is offered through the reconstitution of the history of several important families. The theme of social mobility within a hierarchical society informs this chapter.

The Conclusion addresses the controversy over the seventeenth-century depression by looking at new data generated by the study of the merchant elite. These conclusions are related to the political and social character-istics of the seventeenth century. In general, chapters 1 through 4 and 6 emphasize the continuities which integrated the period from 1590 to 1660. Many characteristics of the commercial elite and economic life were con-stant throughout these decades. Some changes occurred, however, and they are noted. Chapter 5 and the Conclusion have a chronological organi-zation; they emphasize the discontinuities, especially the break between the years before and after 1640.

NEW SPAIN IN THE SEVENTEENTH CENTURY

Why does a book on the seventeenth century begin in the 1590s and end in the 1660s? Although no set of dates is equally meaningful for all as-pects of historical change, in commerce, mining, the bureaucracy, Indian culture, and demography either one or both of these decades did mark discernible shifts. The period from 1590 to 1660 was the heart of the middle colony, succeeding the rapid innovations of the sixteenth century and laying the groundwork for new directions from the 1660s, or, as some might argue, the 1680s. This section of the Introduction is an overview of the distinct characteristics of the first two-thirds of the seventeenth cen-tury, some the further development of sixteenth century trends, others representing new developments.

Social Changes

Between 1590 and 1660, the transformation of Mexican society from an Indian to a mixed-blood population continued to progress. The measles epidemic of 1595 marked the last of the epidemics that nearly destroyed the Indians in the sixteenth century. Altogether they were reduced from 25 million in 1519 to about 1.3 million in 1646. From the mid-1650s, the Indian population reversed its long trend of decline, although the impact of this unexpected shift was not felt for several decades.[10] Although in 1646, 86 percent of the population was still Indian, the rapid growth of white, black, and mixed groups indicated the direction the socio-racial composition of the population would take. *Mestizos* (persons of Indian and white ancestry) and *mulattos* (persons of African and white or sometimes Indian ancestry) grew from 24,793 in 1570 to 79,396 in 1646. Whites rose from approximately 63,000 to 125,000. Persons of African descent, due to forced migration, multiplied from 22,600 to 62,400 during the same years.[11] After 1650, the overall population continued to rise, although probably more slowly. Following an interruption from 1640 to 1651, the slave trade resumed, especially after 1675, and there is evidence of continued increase of whites and mixed-bloods.[12]

Most major cities gained in importance and population. While 1520 through 1580 had been the era of town founding, the following years saw growth in already established centers. In the Viceroyalty of New Spain the urban population increased from 11,333 *vecinos* (householders) in 1580 to 36,170 *vecinos* in 1630. For Mexico City the trend toward urbanization is even more striking. The capital had 3,000 *vecinos* in 1580 and 15,000 *vecinos* in 1630. Hospitals, schools, religious institutions, and public works multiplied accordingly. In 1620, Mexico City had more architectural monuments per capita than any other city in New Spain. Between 1580 and 1600, building activity had shifted from being greater in the countryside to greater in the cities.[13] One result was a more sophisticated consuming public. In the cities the Spanish style of life was more pervasive than in the countryside. For the nonwhites, acculturation stimulated a demand for hitherto unknown or unavailable products, provided by merchants. Thus, urbanization was directly linked to a new type of market and a specific group of suppliers. Merchants made possible the material basis for a higher social status for all social groups.

Urbanization contained the seeds of fundamental social change, but from 1590 to 1660 they were relatively dormant. This was the heyday of the *sociedad de castas*, which fostered the status quo and discouraged mobility. On the one hand, poverty, enslavement, disease, and prejudice kept nonwhites from collectively challenging a social order in which they usually held the lowest occupations and status. Violence against elites was infrequent and localized. Urban social upheavals, such as the Mexico City riots of 1624 and 1692, were rare and effected no permanent changes. On the other hand, the spiritual and esthetic attractions of Christianity and the opportunities for advancement of a minority of nonwhites reconciled some to the status quo. The growing number of persons of mixed racial ancestry, in particular, and their gradual increasing tendency to marry and found legitimate families, were foretastes of a later, more mobile society. Nonracial determinants of social status began to carry more weight at certain levels, as with artisans whose skills, earnings, and connections might earn them a position not expected from their lowly birth.[14]

Within Indian society a viable consolidation of village life became possible, even on the smaller population base of the seventeenth century. Pre-conquest cultural traits had, by the 1640s and 1650s, evolved into a more Hispanic ethos, visible in part through linguistic changes. These included use of Spanish syntax and pronunciation, not just loan words, by Nahuatl speakers, and writings which projected colonial concepts onto the pre-conquest history of the community. More or less accompanying these was the replacement of forced labor drafts by "free" wage labor, and the substitution of the large monastery complexes decorated with indigenous symbols by small, Europeanized parish churches.[15] The identity of Indian villages was further strengthened by the foundation of hospitals and lay brotherhoods.[16] By retaining valued corporate social traits within Hispanic forms, some Indians reached a constructive equilibrium at midcentury, which lasted for the rest of the colony.

In a narrower sphere within the elite the most remarkable social development of the post-conquest decades, the eclipse of the *encomenderos* (recipients of grants of tributary Indians) progressed apace. The middle colony saw the continued rise of a new dominant group, which derived its wealth from a combination of rural properties, officeholding, mines, and trade. Access to the new elite, however, seems to have become more restricted as the century continued. The tendency toward monopoly control, the ownership of property by a small number of families in a given region, accelerated. For example, in the sixteenth century ownership of land in the Center and South of New Spain had been quite dispersed. In the North new mining strikes initially permitted a number of prospectors to stake their claims. In the seventeenth century, however, land became concentrated in fewer hands in several, although not all, regions of the viceroyalty. The spread of the hacienda exemplifies this trend.[17] Increasing monopoly did not necessarily mean increasing continuity within the elite. Established families lost their wealth, and new families replaced them thanks to the latter's greater business acumen, favorable local economic conditions, marriage, or royal favor. The *extent* of turnover within the elite varied, but the *existence* of intra-elite competition was a prime feature of seventeenth-century Mexican society.

The displacement of the first settler group led in the late sixteenth century to a literature bewailing the disinheritance of the conquest families, which contributed to an increasing awareness of a creole identity. Another factor was the growing prominence of the more successful creoles, which the *peninsulares* attempted to check politically or by denigrating creoles as lazy, racially impure, or mentally deficient. The result was fluctuating creole self-awareness. Among the literate, intellectuals such as Juan de Torquemada in 1615 interpreted New Spain's history as having its own meaning, separate from Spain's imperial history. The cult of the Virgin of Guadalupe, which in the mid-seventeenth century moved from a creole, Mexico City–based devotion to encompass many racial groups in the viceroyalty, gave New Spain its own religious symbol. Colonists' attachment to their hometown or region, an attitude originally imported from Spain, now became a loyalty to the same in New Spain.[18] But the other side of love of birthplace was an inability to act jointly with other cities to oppose injurious royal policy. The competition between Puebla and Mexico City, for example, prevented the latter from leading a unified resistance to new taxes in the 1630s. Also, creole identity was still just one facet of white self-definition; religious beliefs also linked the colonists to Spain as the defender of the faith, while allegiance to corporate or extended family groups divided creoles among themselves, and depreciation of the Indian past kept them distant from the Indians. Creole patriotism was still in a formative state.

Within the existing institutional framework, the seventeenth-century Church became more creole and wealthier, yet remained internally divided. The late sixteenth-century *Ordenanza del Patronazgo* had strengthened the partnership between Church and Crown, raised standards of clerical training and, perhaps, performance, and given the secular priests greater security through lifetime appointments. However, the goal of subordinating the regular clergy to the episcopal authorities met with much resistance. Repeated conflicts between friars and parish priests over such matters as jurisdiction over Indian parishes, right to determine competence in Indian languages, clerical morals, control of education, and payment of tithe were a distinct feature of this period. In Puebla in the 1640s this struggle led to sufficient violence to evoke royal concern.

Another dimension of competition was the disputes over the offices of the regular orders, where the creoles were usually a majority and able to outvote the *peninsulares*. Beginning in 1590 with the Dominicans, it was stipulated that leadership of the various orders alternate between the two groups, imposing a temporary artificial parity.[19]

The rapid acquisition of urban and rural properties by all branches of the clergy but especially by the newest order, the Jesuits, was another characteristic of the Church. Although the colonists benefited from clerical loans and themselves made donations of land or founded chantries on real estate, they resented the Church's dominant role in agriculture. The dedication and poverty of the missionary friars continuing their work in northern New Spain did not compensate for the negative image held by some colonists of their more established brethren. Royal decrees and colonial protests were unavailing, however.

An important expression of the Church at this time was the Inquisition, which gained prominence and income with its *autos de fe* of the late sixteenth and early seventeenth century. These included trials for moral and religious offenses such as bigamy and blasphemy respectively, as well as heresy. The trials of secret Jews which occurred between 1585 and 1601 began again from the mid-1630s to 1649 when they succeeded in destroying the *conversos* as an organized group. The public burnings and other punishments the Inquisition organized were a key element of religious life, as were the social norms it tried to impose and the outlet its encouragement of denunciations offered for unacceptable emotions.[20] Its secret proceedings, relative autonomy from Spain, periods of corruption, and efforts to direct the aberrations of a heterogeneous, dispersed society into acceptable channels reflect in extreme fashion many elements of seventeenth-century society.

Politics and Warfare

As with the Church, the system of government devised by the kings and viceroys of the sixteenth century showed few major changes in the seventeenth. Apart from the addition of a few fiscal offices and supernumery posts, its organization was the same. But the substance of politics and the character of leading political figures was altered. The council chambers of sixteenth-century Mexico had reverberated with the great arguments about the humanity of the Indians and the role of the new *conquistador-encomendero* (conqueror-tribute collector) class. The debate over the General Indian Court, established in 1592,[21] closed out the philosophical discussions of the early colony. The following century saw heated debate, but the controversies emphasized different aspects of colonial rule. Should the Crown or should private individuals provide credit to the high-priority, but perpetually capital-scarce, mining industry? Should Indian forced labor, now an accepted fact, be directed by private employers or by the State? How were new taxes to be raised? Should the land-rich descendants of some *conquistadores* be required to pay? The seventeenth century was an acutely political period, not the "deep sleep" attributed to it in past historiography. The issues were, on the whole, more prosaic than in the sixteenth century, but they were important.

The balance of power in the colonial bureaucracy had shifted. On the one hand, there were fewer distinguished men serving as viceroys. The period began with the conscientious rules of Velasco II (1590–95, 1607–11) and Monterrey (1595–1603); Gelves and Albuquerque later represented what was best in the tradition of royal service. However, Guadalcázar, Cerralvo, Escalona, Salvatierra, and Alva de Liste were not particularly distinguished, and the Conde de Baños (1660–64) was particularly deficient. Possibly, since the viceregal office represented the royal interest, this reflected the decline in the caliber of royal leadership in Spain.

On the other hand, the caliber of officeholders in the Indies probably declined due to the sale of posts. By 1591, the minor, fee-earning offices, such as *escribano* (notary), honorific posts, such as *alférez* (municipal standard bearer), and paid municipal posts, such as *regidor* (alderman), were officially put up for sale. These accounted for the majority of purchases. They were followed by the treasury offices in 1633, the district governor posts in 1677, and, finally, the high court offices in 1687. Moreover, in 1606, the Crown made all saleable offices renunciable, that is, able to be sold, by the owner. By paying one-half the purchase price to the Crown at the first sale, and one-third the purchase price at subsequent sales, the owner could transfer the office to whomever he wished. Also, some offices, such as the post of *corregidor* (district governor and magistrate) were illegally sold well before the official date. At the very least, this change in administrative policy permitted many more creoles and Spaniards who had lived for many years in the Indies to enter the bureaucracy than would have been the case had sale and renunciation not been allowed. At the most, sale of office allowed less qualified, probably more corrupt officials to govern the colony. It is generally agreed that by the mid-seventeenth century corruption had increased, and not only through the sale of office but also of titles and pardons.[22]

Colonial administration, therefore, manifested scant external changes, but sale lessened the efficiency of government at a time when administrators were expected to raise more money for the Crown. This situation persisted well after 1660. However, there were some glimmers of bureaucratic change at the end of the period. From the late 1670s, the royal government attempted to check the abuses of Castille's councils by limiting their number, suppressing purchased offices, and eliminating supernumery posts acquired by grace and favor. With district governor posts, sale meant that creoles secured fewer such positions. In 1682 and 1692, the Crown declared industrial and commercial occupations compatible with nobility and high officeholding.[23] Significant change, particularly at the viceregal level, had, of course, to await the advent of the Bourbon dynasty.

Sale of office was an expedient adopted to help pay for Spain's spiraling defense costs. Campaigns in Europe, culminating in the disastrous intervention in the Thirty Years War, and the attacks of Dutch, French, and English in the New World, required a costly military expansion. While sixteenth-century warfare was frequent and expensive but relatively brief, that of the seventeenth century became more prolonged, more threatening to the Empire, and more burdensome to the weakened metropolitan treasury. Public monies spent on war and defense rose from 25 percent of the funds disbursed from the Mexican treasuries from 1590 to 1599 to 37 percent from 1660 to 1669.[24] The sums went for fortresses, warships, troops, and supplies. In New Spain the seventeenth century was the great period of coastal fortification. On the Atlantic, the new fort of San Juan de Ulúa was finished and the site of the city of Veracruz was transferred to a location opposite the fort. On the Pacific, the castle of San Diego was built to protect Acapulco from Dutch assaults. The *Armada de Barlovento*, a squadron first proposed to patrol the Lesser Antilles and Tierra Firme coast in the 1590s and financed by the Mexican treasury, was established and expanded from the 1630s to the 1670s.[25]

Military expenditures led to escalating taxes and more frequent royal confiscations of private treasure than had occurred in the sixteenth century. Existing taxes were raised on the use of trans-Atlantic convoys, on playing cards, on import and export of goods, and on internal wholesale and retail transactions. The government tried to collect them, and taxes on land titles and mining production, more efficiently. New taxes were added. These were the *mesada* (payment of a portion of salary upon the assumption of ecclesiastical office) and the *media anata* (payment of one-half year's salary upon entering the civil bureaucracy). New government monopolies, on such items as *solimán* (bichloride of mercury), gunpowder, salt, pepper, and stamped paper, were other forms of taxation.[26] Were the new or higher taxes effective? The first two-thirds of the seventeenth century saw sustained colonial opposition to the new fiscal demands, some successful, some not. As in the previous century, however, colonists had little say in the decisions which prompted the new taxes.

The Economy

The trends in mining and trade most aptly define 1590 to 1660 as a distinct period. Impressive expansion characterized the years until the 1630s. Rising throughout the sixteenth century, silver and gold production reached its highest point yet of 42,693,471 pesos from 1591 to 1600; from 1611 to 1620 it rose to 53,646,127 pesos. At the Zacatecas mines, silver output began its longest upward climb from 734,825 marks (1590–95) to 1,173,601 marks (1620-1625).[27] Production of the other major exports, Indian cochineal and indigo (as well as Hispanic wheat and sugar for domestic consumption), also expanded in the late sixteenth century, establishing the contours of the colonial economy. At that time too, the key link to international markets, the Mexico City–Veracruz road, the *camino de los arrieros* (muleteers' highway), which went north out of the capital and passed through Jalapa on the way to the coast, was given official status.[28]

The growth of New Spain's exports was reflected in the Indies' trade cycles. Between 1592 and 1622, trans-Atlantic trade reached its highest level before the eighteenth century, and within this cycle, the period from 1593 to 1604 was the most dynamic. In each of the decades of the period from 1591 to 1620 more ships sailed, bearing greater weight and carrying more treasure, than before 1591 or after 1630. The flourishing of the Indies' commerce in the 1590s as a whole coincided with a relatively more rapid growth in the New Spain branch. By volume and value of goods, colonial Peru participated more extensively in the trade from 1540 to 1585, but leadership passed to New Spain from 1590 to 1630.[29] Institutional development accompanied economic development. In 1592, a *consulado* (merchant guild) was approved, and in 1594, it was functioning. Because most histories of merchants have dealt with the late colony, when the merchants of the periphery in colonial Guatemala City, Santiago de Chile, and Buenos Aires challenged the dominance of the older commercial communities, the fact that it took almost a century for the merchant elites of Mexico City and Lima to consolidate their privileged position can be overlooked.

This boom was followed by a depression whose scope and results are still disputed. Initially, Borah asserted that a decline in Indian workers, rapid after 1576 to 1579 and hitting bottom about 1650 at 1,500,000, caused a century-long depression which affected all branches of the economy. However, the twin institutions of the white-owned hacienda—the self-sufficient, extensively cultivated great estate—and debt peonage—the reliance on wage workers of various races bound to the owner by debt—allowed Hispanic agriculture to be reorganized with some success.[30] Chevalier's depiction of the geographic, demographic, legal, and cultural factors which promoted the allegedly self-sufficient hacienda and its dependent labor force developed even further the picture of a ruralized economy, cut off from many trade routes which previously had flourished. The Chaunus' painstaking documentation of the shrinking of the official trans-Atlantic trade after 1622 in terms of number of ships, tonnage of vessels, and amount of silver legally imported into Spain did for commerce what had been done for agriculture and demography. They also saw a labor shortage at the root of the decline, but believed the monopolistic policies of the Spanish state, foreign competition, and the glutting of the Mexican market for imports due to increased local production also destroyed the dynamism of the trans-Atlantic trade.[31]

Scholars of mining were the first to challenge effectively the depression interpretation. Bakewell for Zacatecas, TePaske and Klein, and Garner for all the mining districts have shown that there was no century-long depression in this sector, but, on the contrary, a modest rise in production throughout the century. The most striking revision was that silver and gold output rose or remained high every decade until 1641 to 1650, when it still exceeded the years before 1580. They also demonstrated that although total silver production did decline from the period 1641–50 to the period 1671–80, it was a decrease of 21 percent, significant but not catastrophic.[32] How we assess the decline depends on our perspective. For economic historians interested in the long term, it was a modest drop, but for social historians studying particular merchants and enterprises, it was a serious blow. Too, the impact on the districts of Zacatecas or San Luis Potosí does constitute an acute decline.

Noting the variety of illegal trades, Lynch and others have questioned the alleged collapse of long-distance commerce, but none has yet documented the volume of clandestine activity. (The routes and goods of these trades are described on pages 22–32). In the Atlantic, for example, smuggling on the fleets shot upward from the 1630s, so that the official statistics used by Chaunu, and for 1650 to 1700 by García Fuentes, correspond less to reality for that period onward.[33] In Europe, trade with Spain's enemies continued right off the coasts. There are many reports of Dutch, French, and English vessels transferring bullion under the eyes of the port officials. Contraband on the registered vessels and on illegal sailings, therefore, modify the picture of collapse. Yet, the drop in the number of registered ships and tonnage crossing the Atlantic was so great that not even the most energetic contraband could have compensated for it: it fell from 1,363 ships (1621–29) to 971 ships (1630–39) to 722 ships (1640–49).[34] In the Caribbean, smuggling with New Spain via the Greater Antilles or Cartagena by Portuguese and foreign traders, which had benefited from the suspension of most European hostilities from 1603 to 1621, kept some goods circulating. However, the resumption of Dutch attacks in 1621, the disruption caused by the Portuguese loss of the Spanish slave supply monopoly after the 1640 revolt, and the depradations during the 1650s of the buccaneers ensconced in their enclaves in Jamaica and Tortuga prevented much expansion of smuggling at the mid-century.[35]

Despite the restrictions placed on the Acapulco-Manila trade, it continued to be dynamic in the 1630s, but in the 1640s, adverse factors mounted: Dutch attacks resumed, fewer Chinese ships came to Manila, Portuguese trade from Macao declined, and the fall of the Ming dynasty affected silk production. Shortages of silver in China contributed to a depression there lasting several decades.[36] Even though the discrepancy between official and actual volume was higher than in the Atlantic, the galleon trade truly must have declined. Finally, there were the varied exchanges with Central America, Peru, and the Spanish Main. The dynamism and diversity of these trades is one of the most interesting recent findings about seventeenth-century history. Nevertheless, New Spain's importation of cacao from Guayaquil seemed to decrease between 1650 and 1680, and its importation of Peruvian mercury, wine, oil, and silver may have diminished also. Traffic with Central America, fed by local indigo, pitch and naval supplies, and livestock, decayed in the 1640s and 1650s due to an economic decline in the Isthmus.[37] Thus, there was a contraction of international and interregional commerce but not a collapse.

The view that there was a depression in seventeenth-century agriculture and manufacturing has also been challenged. Bakewell showed that the loss of Indian labor did not ruin mining and reminded us that Borah himself claimed that debt peonage provided adequate workers for some farms and *obrajes* (textile workshops).[38] Other studies have chipped away at Chevalier's notion of the self-sufficient hacienda or plantation. They note that many were efficiently cultivated and market oriented and that labor and landholding systems were more varied than previously thought. Textile enterprises spread into new regions of the viceroyalty. Nevertheless, we still know less about seventeenth-century agriculture than we do about mining and trade. Key features of the depression interpretation may well be correct, such as the low productivity of the Indian subsistence economy (due to population loss and other factors) and the continued difficulty of many creole farmers in obtaining labor. As McAlister and Israel noted, great regional variation existed in agricultural productivity. Certainly, as the depression hypothesis claimed, a few families or religious corporations dominated certain rural regions, as pasture land was converted into grain-producing haciendas and numerous small properties were grouped into large estates. A number of studies since the 1970s have confirmed this trend for the Valley of México, the Valleys of Metztitlán and Actopan, the Bajío, the Valley of Hueyapan, the Yucatán peninsula, and, to some extent, the Valley of Oaxaca, as well as the classic areas of the great estate in New Galicia and New León.[39]

From the 1660s, the colony began a modest but identifiable recovery. Mining production of the viceroyalty rose 30 percent from 1671–80 to 1691–1700, reaching 50,751,914 pesos in the last decade of the century and compensating for previous losses. Zacatecas nearly matched its early seventeenth-century levels in the mid-1660s: 726,874 marks (April 1665 to June 1670) to 1,238,424 marks (October 1675 to June 1680). Its output reached an unprecedented high of 1,238,424 marks for 1675 to 1680, although it fell off dramatically after that. The amount of treasure *legally* imported into Spain continued its century-long slide. The number of registered trans-Atlantic ships was: 412 (1650–59), 302 (1660–69), 433 (1670–79), 368 (1680–89), 328 (1690–99); but other sources question the verdict of continued decline. The *casa de contratación* (house of trade) records of exports of *fardos* (boxes of dry goods) from Spain to the Indies show a slow upward trend, and the shipbuilding industry exhibited symptoms of revival in the 1670s. Especially suggestive, the *servicios* (grants) and *indultos* (pardons), compensatory payments made by merchants to the Crown for the importation of smuggled cargo from the Indies, reinforce the hypothesis of a trade recovery. The payments rose from the 1670s: 713,350 pesos (1650–59), 505,764 pesos (1660–69), 742,000 pesos (1670–79), 1,417,867 pesos (1680–89), 5,940,110 pesos (1690–99). Beginning in the 1670s, New Spain again remitted more silver to Spain than did Peru, resuming the position it had occupied in the prosperous years of 1590–1630. The shift in roles of the two viceroyalties became permanent; New Spain was the world's major producer of silver.[40]

Finally, the 1660s signaled the definite demise of Seville's long effort to control the Indies trade through the fleet system, and its replacement by a Cádiz-based commerce, in which Dutch, English, and French smuggling played an even greater role. The Peace of Westphalia (1648) ended Dutch hostilities, while the Treaty of Madrid (1670) marked the decline of the buccaneers. From the 1670s, privateering gave way to contraband trade between the Spanish colonists and the new English and French settlements on Jamaica (1655) and Tortuga (1654), as well as the already well-established Dutch entrepôt of Curaçao (1634) and the European settlements on Barbados and the other Lesser Antilles (1624–35). Spain was no longer dominant in the Atlantic-Caribbean trade, but her merchants profited from the contraband which undermined the monopoly. Reflecting the new situation, in 1660 the Crown ended the payment of the long-evaded convoy and import-export taxes and charged a fixed quota on the merchants for payment of fleet protection.[41]

Thus, the view of the seventeenth century as "the century of depression" can be replaced with a less dramatic but more finely tuned characterization: continued growth from the 1590s to 1630s; a contraction from the 1640s until the 1660s or 1670s; and an erratic recovery until the end of the century, at least in mining and trade. Although the second third of the century could be called a depression, the term denotes structural changes which did not, in fact, occur: the long-term decay of the mining sector, the collapse of international trade and much market-oriented agriculture, and a widespread ruralization of social life. As we shall see in the Conclusion, there were some changes but they were not as sweeping. Thus, the terms contraction and downturn will be used instead. On the whole, seventeenth-century Mexico demonstrated the systematic flexibility, the intensification and decay which occurs within a persisting set of institutions, which is one of the striking features of the colony.

THE MERCHANTS OF
SEVENTEENTH-CENTURY MEXICO

Domestic, and, to a lesser extent, international trade was an important source of income across the social spectrum of colonial Mexico.[42] However, among the devotees of commerce, professional merchants enjoyed a more favorable position, years of mercantile training, and access to silver bullion in New Spain and to markets in Europe. Unlike public officials, some of whom were not supposed to trade in goods for gain, the merchant elite could give free, public play to its commercial instincts. And unlike the *hacendados*, professional merchants were represented by a guild—the *consulado*—which guarded their corporate interests. They were regarded, and they regarded themselves, as members of an important group.

The *consulado*'s functions as a court and as a lobby were the most significant, although it also had religious and philanthropic activities. Persons suing in the *tribunal de consulado* (guild court) were to present their cases orally and were to speak for themselves. Lawyers could be consulted, but they could not prepare written documents. The judges were merchants elected by their colleagues, familiar with commercial matters. Sentence was supposed to be passed by the next day, and although this deadline was rarely met, in the eighteenth century hearings were estimated to take a year compared to the four years necessary for suits heard by the *audiencia* (high court). The guild court heard all cases relating to trade to which a wholesaler was one party, whether or not the other party belonged to the guild. Jurisdiction included, therefore, nonresident wholesalers and any other person who was party to a suit with a wholesaler.[43]

While the *consulado* exercised its judicial functions on a routine basis, it acted as a lobby for commercial interests when taxes were increased, new regulations imposed, and fines levied. Because of the wealth of its members, the importance of long-distance trade to the imperial economy, and the glamor of many goods in which the wholesalers dealt, the *géneros nobles* (sugar, cochineal, and silk, for example), the *consulado* was one of the most influential of the colonial corporations. Its financial contributions to defense and public works, and its administration of the *avería* (convoy tax), and of the *alcabala* (sales tax) at certain periods, enhanced its position.

The *consulado* also contributed to the preeminence of the wholesalers within the commercial community of the viceroyalty. As with ecclesiastics and artisans, traders comprised an internal hierarchy of greater and lesser members. As with other groups, a small minority attempted, with a considerable degree of success, to monopolize the wealth and power which its activities generated. When the establishment of the guild was proposed, a telling debate occurred about its location. Groups in the capital who opposed the formation of a *consulado* tried to lessen its power by situating it in Veracruz, the Atlantic port of the viceroyalty. But the merchants of the capital vigorously rebuffed the suggestion. "The only residents of Veracruz," they asserted, "are our factors and agents, who come to this city two or three times a year to give account of their management and receive their commissions. It makes no sense that the subject be judge and superior of him whose business he manages."[44] Having thus dispensed with a site offering the possibility of competition, Mexico City wholesalers prevented the foundation of *consulados* in Veracruz or any other city of the viceroyalty until 1795. The lack of a guild helped keep the merchants of Veracruz, Guadalajara, Oaxaca, and elsewhere subordinate to their Mexico City confrères.

The census of Spanish-born residents of Mexico City in 1689 casts light on the stratification of the community.[45] Its categories are based, in part, on the distinction between *wholesaler* and *retailer*. Only the wholesalers (*mercaderes*) were allowed to join the guild. Traders to "the kingdoms of Castille, the provinces of Peru, the Philippine Islands, Yucatán, Guatemala, and all the other provinces of this New Spain," as they described themselves, they conducted business whose value and scope put them in a special category, confirmed by their guild membership. To join the *consulado*, they were to be independent traders or the *encomenderos* (agents receiving a commission) of independent traders, investing 2,000 pesos each year. They were to possess an estate worth more than 28,000 pesos, to reside in Mexico City, to be of good reputation, and not to act as a retail shopkeeper or a notary. The *mercaderes* might own a warehouse and a shop managed by another person. While wholesalers could thus also act as retailers by proxy, retailers could not also act as wholesalers nor could they belong to the *consulado*.[46] One object of the guild ordinances was to maximize *mercader* opportunities and protect their privileged position with respect to retailers. As the sales tax contract of 1617 between the guild and the Crown recognized, however, there were differences in wealth within the *mercader* group. It referred to representatives of "rich, middle, and poor merchants" determining the assessment of the tax. Most of the men studied herein were in the first category, an economic elite. Below wholesaler rank there was a sharp distinction between those who owned their stores and those who were managers on commission or employees on salary. The owners included traders at vastly different economic levels, such as *dueño de tienda* (shopkeepers), *cajonero* (stallowners), and *mesillero* (persons who sold wares at their small table). Nonowners also comprised different levels. The highest was the *factor*, the general manager who received a salary (or sometimes a commission) and expenses. Beneath him was the salaried *criado*, who did accounting, correspondence, and sales. Finally, there was the apprentice, who might receive a small salary. The term *cajero* was used for *criado* and apprentice.

The wholesalers were, of course, far fewer than the retail proprietors and employees. They comprised 31 percent (177 of 628) of the persons of Spanish birth employed in commerce at all levels in 1689.[47] Since there were many American-born retailers, whom this census does not include, the percentage of *mercaderes* in the commercial community was actually smaller. Nevertheless, the wholesalers exercised an influence out of proportion to their numbers, precisely because they were a small, integrated group. They were the viceregal bankers and the tax farmers; they figured prominently among the largest transoceanic shippers.

Theoretically, the *consulado* spoke for all traders on matters of common concern. However, if the retailers disagreed with the position of the guild directorship, they had no alternative spokesman. In addition, the *mercaderes* owed their power to informal factors such as wealth and social ties. They were in an entirely different income bracket from most retailers. *Mercaderes* commonly had fortunes of 50,000 pesos or more, while retailers' wealth ranged between 1,000 pesos and 15,000 pesos.[48] Patron-client networks subordinated the retailers to them, and elite disdain for retail trade reinforced the economic disparity. Such a situation did not preclude upward mobility among the retailers, nor did it prevent the successful shopkeeper from enjoying a comfortable standard of living. It did mean, however, that there was a clear division between the two categories.

The wholesalers studied herein are primarily men who appeared on the lists of electors of the guild and were, therefore, a political as well as an economic elite. The electors were the thirty men chosen every year who elected from among themselves the *consulado*'s officials: the prior, the two councillors, and the five deputies. They were the official leaders of the community. Additional names for the study came from ship's registries and fiscal sources to comprise the group of 177 wholesalers analyzed herein. These are individuals for whom information about trade was available. A smaller group also left record of their social and political activities.

The number of persons who called themselves wholesalers at any one point in time ranged from 252 in 1598 to 177 in 1689. In 1670, 176 persons paid the sales tax on goods imported from Spain, and in 1675, seventy-three persons shipped goods to the Philippines. The leading merchants were fewer. Those who voted in guild elections numbered from twenty-two to ninety-nine at a given time. In Seville between 1630 and

1697, the voting merchants numbered between seventy-one and ninety-nine people. To appreciate the distinction between wholesalers in general and the more influential wholesalers, we can also look at the late eighteenth century, when there were about two hundred wholesalers based in Mexico City. However, only forty-nine men served as guild officers during the second half of the century.[49]

The commercial community included the *conversos*, a term which embraced both converts who considered themselves Christians and converts who secretly continued to practice Judaism. Most persons called *conversos* were Portuguese. The royal permission of 1601, and the papal pardon of 1604, allowed the Portuguese New Christians to emigrate to Spain and the Indies, as did the pardon of 1627. This had already been occurring from the 1580s after the Union of the Spanish and Portuguese crowns. The suspected Jewish practices and wealth of some *conversos* made them a vulnerable and controversial group within colonial society.

Most of the merchants studied herein were not identified as *conversos*, in part because one means of identification was arrest by the Inquisition, and its interest in persecuting *conversos* varied across time. Because there were few arrests between 1601 and 1635, *converso* merchants active then escaped notice. At least one-fourth of the wholesalers who are the subject of this book shipped to known *conversos* in Seville even though they themselves were not described as *conversos*. This points to another aspect of the composition of the merchant community: *conversos* did assimilate, completely or in part, and one stimulus for this was their business relations with Old Christians.[50] Thus, there were more *conversos* or semi-*conversos* among merchant guild members than can be shown. It is also possible that *conversos* were intentionally excluded from guild office, but the other chief reason for the lack of more *conversos* on the electoral lists of the *consulado* is that the Old Christian community was more important than has been realized. Previous studies of seventeenth-century merchants emphasized the *conversos* found in Inquisition records and official correspondence about Jews, but the sources used here indicate the significance of the Old Christians. Boyajian puts the relationship in context. In the *conversos*' heyday between 1609 and 1647, he asserts, they contributed 50 percent of the monopoly banking contracts to the Crown and accounted for at least 20 percent of the volume of the Seville trade, excluding slaves and contraband.[51] Thus, Spanish and foreign Old Christians, as well as *conversos*, competed for the Indies trade. The 196 naturalizations to trade in the Indies granted by the Spanish Crown between 1621 and 1645, for example, included sixty-six to Portuguese, fifty-six to Flemings, twenty-five to Genoese, and sixteen to French. Scholarship on the *conversos* in progress should further clarify their position in the commercial elite.[52]

TRADE ROUTES AND TRADE GOODS

Mexico City was the center of a trading network which stretched the length and breadth of the viceroyalty, extended east to Seville, Lisbon, and Luanda, west to Manila, and south to Guatemala City, Lima, and Caracas. The city's legendary commercial primacy is borne out by the road maps, fiscal records, and population figures. "Mexico City," wrote a collector of the *alcabala* in 1636, "is the belly of this kingdom, for in it are consumed most of the cattle and sheep, wheat, corn, and other grains."[53] "Most" was something of an exaggeration, but, with 58 percent of the population of the densely settled *audiencia* district of Mexico in 1630, Mexico City was certainly the largest market in the northern hemisphere.

The city was supplied from a set of concentric circles. From the immediate surroundings, according to friar Antonio Vázquez de Espinosa in the 1620s, each day canoes carried bread, beef, game, fish, firewood, and fodder, while mules brought wheat, maize, and sugar. Farther off, Toluca supplied ham, lard, soap and cattle; Matlalzingo, maize, cattle, and other foodstuffs. From distant Tamiahua and Tampico came shrimp; from Soconusco and Guayaquil, cacao; and from Realejo, honey. The capital was not only a belly, of course, but also (to prolong the metaphor) a pair of hands, a producer of manufactured goods, cloth, processed foods, and the chief reexporter of goods produced elsewhere. Its sales-tax payments were much higher than any other center. In 1612, the capital paid an annual *alcabala* of 77,000 pesos; Puebla, the viceroyalty's second city, paid only 25,000 pesos. In 1632, Mexico City paid 180,000 pesos and Puebla, 50,000 pesos. The discrepancy between these centers and all others in the *audiencia* district of Mexico is quite striking: the closest was Veracruz, with 22,500 pesos, while San Luis Potosí owed 15,400, Tlaxcala, 12,400, and Celaya, 5,000 pesos. The *provincia* of Orizaba owed 600 pesos.[54]

The unique position of the capital derived in part from pre-Columbian administrative and religious practices. The Aztecs intentionally promoted the economic supremacy of Tenochtitlán at the expense of other valley and regional cities. Then, Spanish settlers and Crown further fostered its importance. Mexico City's unique economic supremacy, however, was

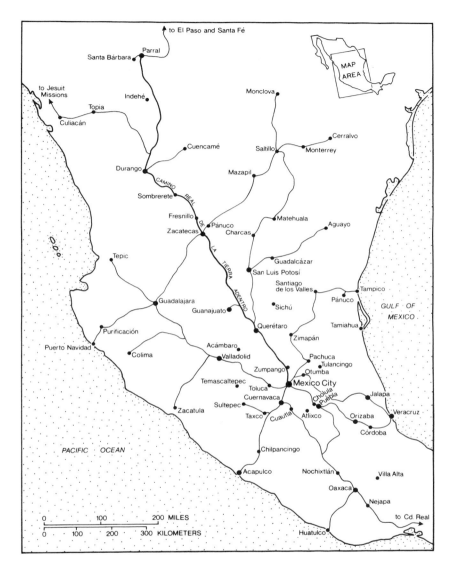

1. Trade Routes within New Spain to 1660

also a response to the obstacles confronting commerce in colonial Mexico: the difficult mountainous and desert terrain, the long distances between cities, and the existence of many regions which were self-sufficient at the subsistence level. These geographic and cultural obstacles could only be overcome by a centralized administrative and commercial network. Mexico City was the center of this network, and from it, its residents promoted the expansion of the colonial Mexican economy. The capital's preeminence was relative because it did not preclude some provincial cities from attaining a degree of independence and from acting as the hub of their own regional circle of trade. However, no regional centers surpassed the capital in commerce, finance, the professions, or crafts.

Regions of the Domestic Economy

A brief sketch of routes and the goods carried on them provides a view of the diversity of New Spain's trade, its economy, and its capacity for generating wealth. In the center of the viceroyalty lay the highland valleys of México, Puebla, and Toluca at 7,000 to 8,000 feet above sea level. Here, wheat and truck farming were carried out to provision the viceroyalty's two largest cities and the fleets. Wool, silk, and hides were processed into clothing. Tools and furniture were manufactured. Maguey, its derivative mescal, and charcoal were also important highland products. Outside of these three valleys, at varying altitudes, lay regions of warmer climate and rich soil with their own specialities. The valley of Morelos was famous for its sugar. The region around Orizaba and Jalapa produced sugar, rice, cotton, and tobacco. The Bajío began to challenge Puebla as the breadbasket of New Spain. Michoacán produced cotton and sugar in the lowland valleys, wheat, livestock, and leather goods in the highlands. Colima and Purificación near the Pacific grew high-quality cacao. Cochineal flourished in Puebla, Cholula, Huejotzingo, and Michoacán. Central New Spain was also the seat of several important mines: Taxco, Sultepec, Tlalpujahua, Pachuca, Zimapán, and Guanajuato.[55]

The south was more agricultural than the center. Its major cities were Oaxaca and Mérida. The Oaxaca region grew a tremendous variety of basic foodstuffs; it also cultivated sugar, cacao, cochineal, and livestock. The Yucatán peninsula was known for its exports of indigo, beeswax, honey, and cotton cloth. The Tabasco lowlands grew high-quality cacao. The north was the home of a flourishing livestock industry and many silver mines. The cattle herds of Sinaloa, Zacatecas, San Luis Potosí, Tamaulipas, Durango, and Chihuahua were famous. The regions along the northern highway and in the kingdom of Nuevo León specialized in sheep ranching. Irrigated wheat belts grew up around even the most distant mining and administrative towns, while selected locales in the otherwise arid north also produced citrus fruit, honey and preserves, and wine. To the north of the central plateau were the mining towns of San Luis Potosí, Charcas, Matehuala, and Mazapil, discovered in the last quarter of the sixteenth century. Extending from southeast to northwest on the eastern foothills of the Sierra Madre Occidental were Guanajuato (1550), Zacatecas (1546), Fresnillo (1566), Indehé, and Santa Bárbara (1567).[56]

Mexico's diversified domestic economy was sustained by a network of roads which reached throughout the viceroyalty. Only Yucatán lay outside this vast grid, but Yucatán was accessible by sea. The backbone of the road system was a rather crooked set of coordinates which intersected at Mexico City. There, a north-south highway, the *camino real de la tierra adentro*, met an east-west highway which departed from Veracruz on the Atlantic, passed along the *camino de los arrieros* through Jalapa to Mexico City, and then continued from the capital southwest to Acapulco. Although there were exceptions, silver and pastoral products usually flowed south along the *camino real* and were exchanged for agricultural and manufactured goods (imported and domestic) flowing north. The southern leg of the *camino real*, from Mexico City through Cuernavaca to Oaxaca and thence to Guatemala City, took final shape by the 1550s. The northern leg, however, continually extended itself northward as new mines were discovered in the Gran Chichimeca. In 1548, the *camino real* from Mexico City reached Querétaro; in the 1550s, Zacatecas; in the 1630s, Parral; and in the early eighteenth century, San Felipe de Chihuahua. By the mid-eighteenth century it terminated at Santa Fe. The northeastern branch now reached Nuevo Laredo.

The long-distance highways intersected with regional and local networks. Sometimes the exchange entailed supplying a provincial town with basic foodstuffs; on other occasions, local specialties such as pottery or sugar were traded. In some parts of the country the local roads preceded the arrival of the Spaniards; in other areas the local road system derived from the *camino real*. But in all cases the existence of better-regulated long-distance routes tended to limit the proliferation of regional routes. The local exchanges attained a degree of autonomy from Mexico City–based trade with regard to certain products. Oaxaca was a way station for Peruvian wine and Guatemalan cacao, but it also shipped its own hides, wheat, and silk to Guatemala, Puebla, and Mexico City.[57] The more diversified the functions of the provincial city and the more it attracted migration principally from its own hinterland, the more likely it could serve as a force for regional integration. The relative independence of these regional economies corrects the erroneous view that all economic life was centered in the capital, but their limits confirm that the capital remained unrivaled in certain areas.

A glimpse at the map indicates the great extent of this road system and suggests the length of time required to traverse it. By mule, the journey from Mexico City to Guadalajara took two months; from Mexico City to Parral, three to four months. The trip from Mexico City to Veracruz usually took one month, but during the rainy season could be delayed three months.[58] Such was the temporal and topographical context of trade by land in colonial Mexico.

Ties to the International Economy

When the dangers and length of interoceanic voyages just to reach New Spain are added to these internal transport times, the risky nature of business transactions becomes even more apparent. Goods converged on New Spain from the east, south, and west. The best-known transoceanic route is the *camino de Castilla*, which carried people and goods from the Iberian peninsula, other European countries, and Africa and its offshore islands. Europe shipped fine cloths, clothing, tools, paper, books, watches, furniture, iron, hardware, mercury, wine, oil, vinegar, and mercuric chloride to New Spain, and weapons, iron, East India cloths, alcohol, wax, and tobacco to Africa to obtain enslaved blacks. In exchange, seventeenth-century New Spain exported primarily silver bullion, cochineal, indigo, hides, wool, precious woods, cacao, and Chinese silks. The journey from Seville's seaport of San Lúcar to New Spain usually took two months or more, while the return trip from Veracruz took longer, about four and one-half months. The slave trade, carried on by Portuguese ships independently of the convoys, took from less than one year to as much as four years from the time of licensing at one of the European or Canary ports to arrival at Veracruz.[59]

The *camino de Castilla* had always included a legal intra-Caribbean trade to such cities as San Juan del Puerto Rico, Santo Domingo, Santiago de Cuba, Trujillo and Caballos in the Bay of Honduras, and ports on the Yucatán and Tabasco coast. But the illegal intra-Caribbean trade was more substantial. Spanish merchants on the fleets, merchants stationed at Havana and Santo Domingo (who included agents of Mexico City traders), and local *rescatadores* (creole middlemen) bought contraband slaves, cloth, and other European goods from foreigners and mingled the cheaper smuggled goods with the fleet goods or sent them separately to the mainland. The foreigners were first, the Portuguese; joined from the 1570s by the French; from the 1590s by the Dutch; and from the 1600s by the English, who competed and collaborated with their Spanish counterparts. Despite raids by corsairs of all nationalities, slaves and European goods, especially fine cloths, did reach New Spain by this route.[60]

The second major route converging on New Spain was the galleon trade across the Pacific from the Philippines to the west coast of New Spain, the *camino de China*. Part of the goods traded included Philippine cottons, cordage, wax, and some gold, but the bulk of the Pacific cargo came from China, and, in certain periods, from Japan and India as well. Manila had been an entrepôt for Far Eastern trade, just as Amsterdam and Seville were for European and colonial trades. Thus, in the Philippines, as in Mesoamerica, the Spaniards elaborated on trade routes which had preceded their arrival in the region. The Chinese brought an impressive variety of cloths and clothing from Canton or Amoy to Manila: silks of all types, including gauzes, velvets, and brocades worked into clothing, silken thread, bed and table linens, and church altarcloths. Gold; jewelry, cut and uncut; religious articles; porcelain, furniture, and trinkets also made up the cargo carried from China to Manila. From Japan also came silks, decorative boxes, and screens, cutlery, and weapons. From their strongholds in Goa, Malacca, and Macao, the Portuguese provided silks and furniture, Indian cottons and Persian rugs, musk, camphor, pearls, and amber. Spices from the East Indies and slaves from throughout the Far East comprised part of the cargo, too.[61] In return for this impressive array New Spain exported silver bullion in large amounts and chocolate, cochineal, oil, and Spanish wines in small amounts to Manila.

The galleon trade across the Pacific was the longest uninterrupted sea route traveled by Europeans in the sixteenth and seventeenth centuries. The westward leg was relatively safe and easy and took approximately three months. The eastward leg, on the other hand, was arduous and lengthy, beset by peril from the monsoons and hurricanes in the area from Manila to the Ladrones and by storms off the California coast. It averaged six months but sometimes took seven or eight.[62]

The trans-Pacific trade included the reexport of Chinese goods from Acapulco to Callao-Lima and to other ports on the Pacific coast. In the early seventeenth century the backbone of the Peru trade, as it was called,

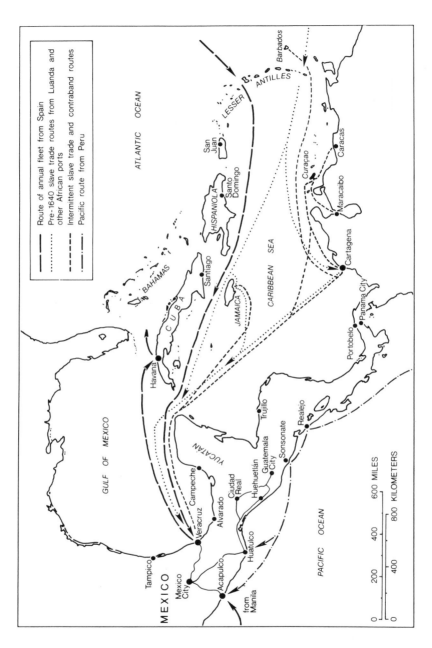

2. Interoceanic Trade Routes to New Spain

was the exchange of Oriental wares for Peruvian silver, without which it would have been quite different in character, less valuable and less controversial. The silk-silver trade, however, was complemented by the trade in colonial Mexican coarse textiles, furniture, and reexported European goods in exchange for Peruvian mercury and wine. Goods traveling the Acapulco to Callao-Lima route took two or three months between September and February, but as much as seven or eight months during the rest of the year. The return voyage required only one to one and one-half months.[63]

The Peru trade, which fed badly needed if adulterated silver coin into New Spain from the south, was closely connected to the third major external commerce conducted by colonial Mexican merchants. This trade could be called the American trade, for it consisted of trade with regions south and southeast of New Spain in goods that were produced there. To put it another way, while the American trade was stimulated by the reexport of China wares, it would have existed anyway because of the mutual need for the other exchanges involved. Unlike the European and Asian trades, the American trade included land and sea routes. Nearest to Mexico City was the traffic with colonial Central America. From the sixteenth century, New Spain exported silver, local textiles, slaves, horses, mules, and Chinese fabrics to the Central American districts and imported cacao and, after 1580, indigo, pitch and naval supplies, livestock, and cochineal. The cacao, then indigo, cultivated on the Pacific coast was shipped to Oaxaca, the chief New Spain transshipment point, then either to Puebla and Mexico City or to Veracruz. After Acapulco became New Spain's main Pacific port, Cuernavaca was also an important way station between the Pacific coast and the interior. The financial and trading center of the Central American merchants was Santiago de Guatemala. The land routes north required a journey of several months, the sea routes less.[64]

The other focus of the American trade was the Tierra Firme coast. In addition to slaves sent from Cartagena, Caracas in the early decades of the seventeenth century, and increasingly Maracaibo in the later decades, exchanged cacao for New Spain's silver, textiles, ceramics, and wheat at Veracruz or Campeche. Most of the Venezuelan cacao then reached Jalapa, Orizaba, Puebla, or Mexico City. Few merchants shipped it directly to other parts of the viceroyalty. The Caribbean cacao trade was important for New Spain because throughout the seventeenth century Venezuela was its major source of external supply. The other source at this time was Guayaquil. Groves there began production in the 1600s when

1. *Plaza mayor* of Mexico
City, 1768; *Portales de los
mercaderes* (at west side)

the Guatemalan plantations of Izalcos were reaching their final bloom. The Guayaquil bean was also of significance to the Mexican market, although after the 1620s, less so than the Tierra Firme supply.[65]

The lengthy travel times, the vast distances, and the risks of loss, damage, or arrival after demand had ceased imposed delays on return of capital and high transaction costs. Thus, only the wealthiest or most astute traders could survive. Unpredictable conditions form a piquant contrast to the minute regulations governing international and, to a lesser extent, domestic trade. The laws give an impression of regularity and security which circumstances frequently mocked.

By definition, the men studied herein were masters of the oceanic routes, first and foremost international traders. However, they also dealt in almost all the local specialities. They bought and sold cotton *huipiles* (overblouses worn by Indian women) as well as Oriental silks and satins. They raised and sold wheat and cattle. Certain merchants dealt regularly in the sale of tribute goods. Some spent their early career traveling the *camino real*, bringing cloth and hardware to the mining and agricultural towns along its route and dealing in local products along with silver. In the activities of the Mexico City wholesalers, the domestic and international economies met.

The illustration "The *Plaza Mayor* of Mexico City, 1768" depicts the commercial importance of the capital (plate 1). The central plaza was the same in the seventeenth century, except that the *Parián*, the cut stone trapezoid structure which housed retail shops (west side, in the plaza), had not yet been built. In the seventeenth century the whole plaza was occupied by the cruder, wood stalls, tables, and portable shops in the center of the painting.[66] Even without the imposing masonry *Parián*, however, we can appreciate how omnipresent was the commercial function of Mexico City. Although the procession of the viceroy (lower center) to the Cathedral is the main event in the picture and many interesting-looking spectators line the path of the viceroy and other high officials, the wide array of commercial activity is what catches the eye. From the flowers and caramel sweets sold in front of the *casa de cabildo* to the books, firearms, saddles, trunks, table services of silver plate, all manner of clothing, furniture, footwear, and riding gear sold in the wooden shops in the plaza, to the songbirds, ducks, chickens, and amazing variety of prepared foods and drinks proffered by Indian women seated behind their wares or by peddlers of all races walking through the plaza, the capital showed itself to be the greatest emporium of the New World.

CHAPTER I

Formation of the Merchant Elite: Commissions,

Credit, and Dowries

The purpose of this chapter is to examine selected aspects of how the merchant built his career in trade, looking at certain business practices and at the family connections which provided capital, information, and, of course, companionship. Consider the picture of the typical Mexico City merchant, which we now have, based primarily on eighteenth-century sources. Born in Spain, he was trained in a merchant house there or in Mexico City, often by relatives. The firm was one of a clique which controlled the Indies trade, with capital provided by naturalized foreigners, native Spaniards, Northern Europeans, or creoles. Once in Mexico City, the prospective wholesaler built up funds by saving part of his salary, by borrowing, by forming partnerships with local residents of various occupations, and sometimes by embezzling funds entrusted to him. He then began to trade on his own account, and by virtue of the high profits returned on international commerce, he was soon able to acquire the standing of independent trader. Marriage to an American-born woman, possibly a member of his employer's family, aided his ascent. While traditional accounts of the aspiring wholesaler emphasize his position as an employee of a peninsular house, recent studies stress the Mexican influences on his career.[1] How accurate is this picture for the commercial elite of seventeenth-century New Spain?

THE STRUCTURE OF INTERNATIONAL COMMERCE

The formation of Mexico's merchant elite took place between two poles of social organization. On the one hand, international trade was always in the hands of a small number of individuals, especially in the Pacific. On the other hand, the actual persons involved changed as new traders entered and established traders—for a variety of reasons—left. Although many merchants stayed in business for several decades, certainly there were opportunities for newcomers.

Given the limitation of legal trade to three designated ports, the fixed fleets, and the concentration of wealth in general, the view that the Indies trade was monopolistic is plausible, but the most complete evidence on which any conclusions should be based has not yet been analyzed. For the Atlantic trade, this evidence is the *libros de registro* (ships' manifest) preserved in the *casa de contratación* section of the Archive of the Indies. A manifest was prepared for each of the nine to fourteen vessels legally participating in fleets returning from Veracruz in the years studied (this number does not include the few ships from Honduras and Campeche). Each manifest consists of hundreds of *partidas* (entries), each stating the name of the Mexican shipper, the item shipped (silver or merchandise of some type), the consignee in Spain, the relationship of the shipper to the consignee, the value of the shipment for payment of the convoy tax, and, in some instances, the Spanish agents for the consignee, the place of residence of the shipper and the consignee, and the title of the shipper. One individual shipper might have more than twenty separate entries in each manifest; another might have only one or two. The value of entries was usually taxed as being worth 500 to 3,300 pesos. There are no summary totals for each shipper; in order to analyze the manifests for the present purpose, it is necessary to calculate the total for each individual shipper by vessel and then by year. To measure trends over time, five years were selected for analysis, based on the completeness of the manifests and on as close to a five-year interval as possible. The period covered, 1614 to 1639, includes the height and decline of the trans-Atlantic convoys. (The years 1615 and 1640 did not meet the criterion of completeness.)

It has been assumed that the organization of the Atlantic trade was similar to the Pacific, but no study has been made of the comparable (although not equivalent) archival material for the Acapulco-Manila commerce, the records of the import tax charged on the Philippine trade at Acapulco and registered in Mexico City, found in *contaduría* (treasury accounts). The tax was classified as "almojarifazgo de Filipinas a razón de 10%" (import tax from the Philippines at 10%) through 1611; thereafter, it was included under the heading "islas de Filipinas" (Philippine Islands), which also included freight and convoy taxes. Each entry for the import tax contains the name of the New Spain resident who owned the imported merchandise, the *encomendero* who received the shipment for him or her in Acapulco, and the amount of tax paid. Sometimes the record also includes the person in Manila who sent the cargo and a second recipient in New Spain. Occasionally, official titles and places of residence are included. Like the *libros de registro* used for the Atlantic trade, the import receipts consist of many individual payments, which had to be totaled. Unlike the documentation for the Atlantic, however, annual totals of the taxes paid on the cargo are usually available for the Pacific. However, these are not broken down by individual payers, and sometimes they include extraneous items such as the sum received for the purchase of a ship. So it is again necessary to calculate the total for each individual shipper. Because of the characteristics of the Philippine records, it is possible to take more years over a longer period, from 1595 to 1658. However, less information about each individual shipper is provided than in the Atlantic records. Thus, each set of data has its strengths and weaknesses. The structure of the Philippine trade was rather different and conforms more closely to the view of the international networks as monopolistic. The methodology used to analyze the tax records is discussed in appendix A for the Atlantic and appendix B for the Philippines.

The manifests show that the Atlantic convoy commerce was most certainly a monopoly trade, but they also suggest that it was not as monolithic and restricted as it has often been depicted. Certainly, its participants were few compared to the *vecino* population the trade served. The last column in table 1 presents the number of participants or investors, which ranged from about 457 in 1614 to 138 in 1639. (Because not all the cargo manifests for each year are extant, the actual number of shippers was somewhat higher; see appendix A and table 1, note d.) Bearing in mind that the *vecino* population of Mexico City alone in 1630 was 15,000, the shippers constituted a distinct minority of colonial residents.

If the number of large investors is considered, the impression of monopoly is strengthened. Table 1 divides participants into large, medium, and small investors. A large investor laded more than 7,000 pesos' worth of registered cargo, a medium investor, 7,000 to 1,500 pesos' worth, and a small investor, fewer than 1,500 pesos. These categories are based on the scale of trade found in notarial, fiscal, and inventory records. In the late sixteenth century a box of silver usually contained about 200 marks, or 1,620 pesos. The number of large investors was quite few, ranging from sixty-nine to nineteen persons, usually comprising between only 12.9 percent to 15 percent of all the investors.

Table 2 offers another perspective on monopoly; it indicates that the

Table 1. Distribution of Investment in the Atlantic Trade According to
Number of Shippers in Large, Medium, and Small Categories, 1614–39

Year	Number of Large[a]	% Large	Number of Medium[b]	% Medium	Number of Small[c]	% Small	Total Shippers[d]
1614	69	15.0	157	34.4	231	50.6	457
1620	52	12.9	132	32.7	220	54.4	404
1625	58	14.5	130	32.5	212	53.0	400
1630[e]	23	13.6	52	30.8	94	55.6	169
1639[e]	19	13.8	32	23.2	87	63.0	138
Average	44		101		169		314

Sources: AGI, Contratación, *legajos* 1823–29 (1614); 1859–63 (1620); 1880–84 (1625); 1896–99 (1630); 1926–28 (1639); each *legajo* may refer to one ship, part of one ship, or several ships.

[a]Large investors: persons who laded more than 7,000 pesos worth of registered cargo.

[b]Medium investors: persons who laded between 7,000 pesos and 1,500 pesos worth of registered cargo.

[c]Small investors: persons who laded fewer than 1,500 pesos worth of registered cargo.

[d]According to extant registers; see appendix A, table 1, column 8, note d.

[e]See appendix A, table 1, column 1, note e.

large investors always shipped more than half the cargo, between 68.2 percent in 1630 and 52.6 percent in 1639, to take the two extremes represented. Finally, figure 1 presents a visual perspective on the concentration of investment. It compares the percentage of large shippers with the percentage of investment for which they accounted. In 1625, 14.5 percent of investors shipped 65.2 percent of cargo; in 1639, 13.8 percent of investors shipped 52.6 percent. The pattern of concentration is noteworthy.

However, the term *monopoly* must be accepted with reservations because of other conclusions suggested by the cargo manifests for the Atlantic trade and because of the more extreme concentration presented by the Pacific trade. First, the manifests also show that the medium and small shippers were numerous and contributed a significant part of the value of the cargo (tables 1 and 2). Although as individuals they did not have the influence of a large shipper, as a group, the medium and small investors (including merchants shipping small cargoes) combined did place a substantial proportion of silver and goods. Thus, persons of small and moderate means from many walks of life played an important role in the Atlantic trade.

A reader of the cargo manifests is struck by the human dimension of

Table 2. Distribution of Investment in the Atlantic Trade According to the Percentage and Value of Cargo in Large, Medium, and Small Categories, 1614–39 (in Pesos)

Year	% of Cargo Invested by Large Shippers	Value of Cargo Invested by Large Shippers	% of Cargo Invested by Medium Shippers	Value of Cargo Invested by Medium Shippers
1614	63.1	1,797,078	24.0	682,870
1620	59.0	1,317,347	25.5	568,128
1625	65.2	1,693,435	21.9	571,937
1630	68.2	534,548	13.5	105,600
1639	52.6	419,489	15.0	119,326

Year	% of Cargo Invested by Small Shippers	Value of Cargo Invested by Small Shippers	Total % of Cargo	Total Value of Cargo[a]
1614	12.9	368,631	100	2,848,579
1620	15.5	345,542	100	2,231,017
1625	12.9	335,911	100	2,601,283
1630	18.3	143,401	100	783,549
1639	32.4	258,699	100	797,514

Source: see Table 1.

[a] According to extant manifests; see appendix A, table 2, column 9, note a.

these superficially dry lists of boxes; the vitality and scope of the Atlantic trade stands out clearly. Chocolate, cloves, and purges were sent in small amounts for personal use, as were religious items such as rosaries, statues of Christ, and silver articles for worship. There were boxes, valued at 100 or 200 pesos, termed "gifts." Then there were the sums sent back for the support of minor children in Spain or for the endowment of those who had reached their majority. Donations to religious organizations were another type of shipment. In 1620, secretary Gaspar Álvarez, former constable of the Holy Office in Manila, forwarded 7,200 pesos to a religious congregation in his hometown of Torrijos, while in 1639, the Convent of San Francisco in Mexico City consigned 2,936 pesos via Seville for the Holy Places in Jerusalem.

We also have a notion of the diversity of the participants in the Atlantic convoy trade by looking at their occupations, titles, and places of residence. The majority simply termed themselves a *vecino* of Mexico City, without indicating whether or not they were merchants. In 1614, 1620,

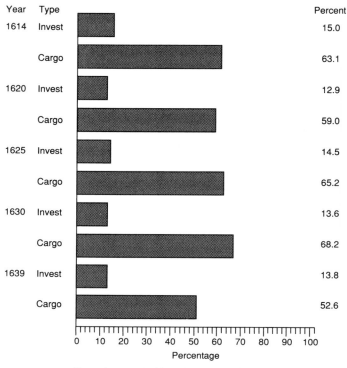

Figure 1. Monopoly in the Atlantic Trade, 1614–39.

and 1639, however, 16 to 20 percent of shippers identified themselves by an occupation or title other than merchant. Persons with military titles, especially captain, and university degrees were the leading group, followed by public officials, the clergy, and, finally, ships' officers; *pasajeros*, residents of New Spain who often went to Seville to buy merchandise to sell upon their return, were another important group. Once in a while, shippers from the provinces or Caribbean called themselves *mercader*. The proportion of shippers not from Mexico City increased from 19 percent in 1614, to 20 percent in 1625, to 31 percent in 1639. The highest number were from Puebla, followed by Veracruz, Oaxaca, Mérida, and Santiago de Guatemala. Residents of the mining towns apparently conducted their business through agents in the capital or in Veracruz. All of these cities were of commercial significance. Puebla, with New Spain's second-largest

Table 3. Distribution of Investment in the Pacific Trade According to
Number of Shippers in Large, Medium, and Small Categories, 1590–1659

Decade	Number of Large[a]	% Large	Number of Medium[b]	% Medium	Number Small[c]	% Small	Total Number of Shippers
1590–99	43	17.5	83	33.7	120	48.8	246
1600–09	26	10.5	82	33.2	139	56.3	247
1610–19[d]	8	44.4	9	50.0	1	5.6	18
1620–29	19	44.2	16	37.2	8	18.6	43
1630–39	29	34.1	34	40.0	22	25.9	85
1640–49	11	25.0	20	45.5	13	29.5	44
1650–59	3	37.5	3	37.5	2	25.0	8

Source: AGI, Contaduría, caxa de México, cargo, Almojarifazgo 10 percent or Islas Filipinas: 695A, 697, #2; 707, #3; 708, #1; 721, 725, #1; 728, #1; 728, #2; 729, #1;
729, #2; 731, #2; 733, 734, #1; 735, #2; 736, #1; 736, #2; 737, 739, 749, #1; 749,
#2. See appendix B for a discussion of the methodology used to analyze this data.
[a]Large shippers: persons who laded more than 7,000 pesos worth of registered cargo.
[b]Medium shippers: persons who laded between 7,000 and 1,500 pesos worth of cargo.
[c]Small shippers: persons who laded fewer than 1,500 pesos worth of cargo.
[d]Only one year during 1610–19 contains individual payments, thus the 1618 figure may
not be representative.

merchant class, helped provision the ships and was a source of capital
and a way station on one route to the port. Oaxaca was a transit point
for cochineal, Mérida and Santiago de Guatemala for indigo, and Veracruz was the official Atlantic port. These *vecinos* may have been agents of
Mexico City merchants. Still, their participation shows these provincial
centers had a direct connection to the port, and goods converged on the
fleet from diverse points of the viceroyalty.

In the Pacific the concentration was more pronounced. Considerably
fewer people were involved in the trade, and they were more likely to
be professional merchants. In the 1590s and 1600s, registered investors numbered about 246 persons—also a small group compared to the
overall *vecino* population (table 3). Subsequently, investors ranged from
eighty-five to a scant eight persons in a given decade. The number of large
investors was, therefore, extremely small, ranging from forty-three in the
1590s to three in the 1650s. Proportionately, they made up between 44.4
and 10.5 percent of total investors, depending on the decade. Not only
did large investors always ship more than half the cargo; in two decades,

Table 4. Distribution of Investment in the Pacific Trade According to the Percentage and Value of Cargo in Large, Medium, and Small Categories, 1590–1659 (in Pesos)

Decade	% of Taxes Paid by Large Shippers	Value of Taxes Paid by Large Shippers	% of Taxes Paid by Medium Shippers	Value of Taxes Paid by Medium Shippers
1590–99	67.0	71,554	27.2	29,070
1600–09	54.1	42,987	35.1	27,829
1610–19	64.1	13,858	29.0	6,255
1620–29	71.2	93,912	9.5	12,483
1630–39	87.1	141,546	11.3	18,419
1640–49	71.4	30,047	25.9	10,915
1650–59	85.3	8,970	13.5	1,417

Decade	% of Taxes Paid by Small Shippers	Value of Taxes Paid by Small Shippers	Total % of Cargo	Total Value of Taxes
1590–99	5.8	6,233	100	106,857
1600–09	10.8	8,577	100	79,393
1610–19	6.9	1,486	100	21,599
1620–29	19.3	25,512	100	131,907
1630–39	1.5	2,509	100	162,474
1640–49	2.7	1,142	100	42,104
1650–59	1.2	125	100	10,512

Sources: See table 3 and appendix B.

Note: In the 1770s, the role of the large shippers was similar to that in the 1620s, 1630s, and 1650s. In 1775, 1776, and 1778, they purchased 97 percent of the cargo at the Acapulco fair. Carmen Yuste López, *El comercio de la Nueva España con Filipinas, 1590–1785*, (México: INAH, 1984), 62, 89–91.

including the 1630s when private shipments peaked, they accounted for more than 80 percent of it (table 4).[2]

Comparing the Atlantic and Pacific trades to 1640 we can conclude that both were quite monopolistic and were dominated by Mexico City. In that context, however, the Atlantic was more broadly based. Even in the darker days of the convoys in the 1630s, they always had more participants, including more medium and small investors. The Philippine Hispanic community was small in number and not that diverse; it could not generate the varied relationships which Spain maintained with New Spain. The contrast is between a tie with an outpost and a tie with the mother country. Not surprisingly, the Manila trade was firmly under the thumb of the Mexico City merchants, who did not have to share their control with Spanish partners. Their agents in Acapulco strongly influenced the administration of customs there (see plate 2).

Usually, investment (silver plus merchandise) was higher in the Atlantic trade. Legally, five or more times as much private cargo was shipped in the Atlantic as in the Pacific. Unofficially, probably three or more times was sent to Spain between 1611 and 1629, and in the 1630s, more was actually sent to the Philippines. The latter estimates are based on a "fraud factor" which for the Philippine trade is calculated by comparing Tables 20 and 21 (pp. 218 and 219). Thus, fraud was two to four times the registered value from 1621 to 1630, and eleven times from 1631 to 1640. For the Atlantic, fraud rose greatly when the convoy tax was increased in the 1630s. Hamilton places contraband between 10 percent and 50 percent for the entire period from 1600 to 1650, while Kamen puts it as 100 percent above registered cargo from 1670 to 1700. Still, it was not as great as in the Manila trade.[3]

GEOGRAPHIC AND SOCIAL ORIGINS

The history of the groups involved in the transoceanic trades shows that within the limit of a monopolistic structure, there was much fluidity. Most men at the commercial pinnacle of colonial Mexico were Spanish born, but they came of varied occupational background and regions and had differing relationships to the established peninsular houses. Naturally, Seville was the one province which sent the greatest number of future merchants to New Spain. Combined with the two other maritime Mediterranean provinces, Cádiz and Huelva, they accounted for 35 percent (36 of 103) of the Spanish traders studied.

While more came from these Spanish southern maritime provinces than from any others, however, the majority of wholesalers were born elsewhere, in cities, towns, and villages throughout the central and northern provinces. Moreover, Seville-born merchants might themselves be sons of recent migrants to the city, some from quite far away. Exemplifying the importance of Italians in the trade was the Federegui family. Both parents had been born in Florence and migrated to Seville; one son, Stefantoni (often called Santifederegui in documents), went on to Mexico City, where he became the most prominent dealer in cochineal of his epoch. His brothers remained in Seville; Luis served as *alcalde mayor* (district

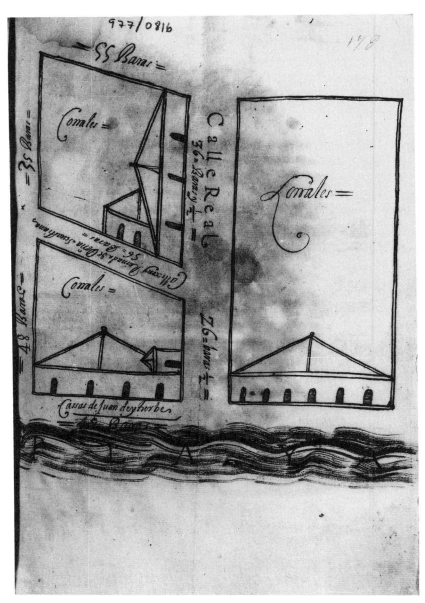

2. Customshouse at Acapulco, 1627.

governor), while Gerónimo was the senior constable. Juan de Astudillo, elector of the Mexico City guild in the 1590s and 1600s, was the son of a Seville trading family that had recently come from Burgos. Juan's brother, Gaspar, regularly welcomed his provincial relatives to his house in Seville. The origins of the Seville *consulado* merchants who received military orders also show the importance of migration in the family's recent history. Of the guild members who received military orders between 1628 and 1700, almost all were born in Seville. Their fathers' birthplaces, however, were fairly evenly divided among Seville, the Basque region, and foreign countries, especially Florence, Corsica, and Flanders.

The merchant houses of the city were a constant in Seville's economic and social life. Along with landed aristocrats, many of whom also traded, enobled merchants controlled the municipal government, occupying the posts of *ventiquatro* (noble alderman) and *jurado* (commoner alderman). Dealing in maritime insurance, sales credits, imported merchandise, and Andalusian produce,[6] their wide-ranging activities provided a model for their successors in the Indies.

The composition of this class shifted, however, most notably from one nationality to another. In the sixteenth century, native Spaniards, Italians, and Flemings were predominant. In the seventeenth century, Spanish firms continued to exist, but were much more dependent on foreigners, at first the Portuguese and the Dutch, the first "gens du Nord," then the French, and finally the English.[7] Apart from nationality, Seville's merchants, like all international traders, experienced upward or downward social mobility. A desire for noble status led many to abandon trade for investments in urban or rural real estate, and merchant daughters for other brides. The more prominent Genoese married Spaniards. The French seem to have been more endogamous; in Cádiz some dynasties lasted for several generations.[8] Sometimes royal confiscations of bullion, enemy attacks on shipping, gluts in the American market, and overextension of investments led to bankruptcies and loss of merchant status. In short, Seville was a dynamic community where fortunes were not secure, and where new groups entered and established houses left the commercial elite.

In conformity with the traditional view of the formation of New World merchant communities, Mexico City wholesalers came, in part, from the well-known Seville houses. Salvador de Baeza, prior of the Mexico City *consulado* in the early seventeenth century and an important lender to the viceregal government, belonged to the *converso* Baeza clan. The Baeza house was founded in Seville in the sixteenth century: Pedro, Gaspar, and Gonzalo Baeza were very large investors in the Atlantic trade in the first two decades of the seventeenth century. Another Mexico City wholesaler, Bernardino Justiniano, was an offshoot of one of the famous Genoese ennobled merchant families of sixteenth-century Seville, which sent its sons to the Philippines as well as to New Spain. Bernardino's career spanned the vicissitudes of the 1630s and 1640s; the Justinianos were still prominent Seville bankers in the mid-seventeenth century.[9] There were, however, many more migrants with mercantile ambitions than the established houses could possibly absorb.[10] Some parents worked their way up from lower-status occupations such as craftsmen or retailers, an upward climb that might have begun in the previous generation. Juan de Alcocer, one of the most important traders in this book, had a paternal grandfather, born in Cologne, who earned his living from a dry goods store in Seville. His father then became a wholesaler to the Indies.[11] Other parents were provincial landowners whose status may have been sufficiently high at home but whose sons went to Seville to enhance their family's income. The case of Martín Bribiesca Roldán, elector of the merchant guild in the 1590s, is striking. The scion of several generations of local officials and landowners of the town of Moguer in the Bishopric of Seville and the son-in-law of a druggist, he became not only a prominent trader, but also one of the largest real estate owners in Mexico City. Other wholesalers came from families residing in the villages and hamlets of central and northern Spain.[12] There was an unmistakable rural component in the geographical origins of the merchant elite.

When Mexico City wholesalers identified their fathers' occupations, they most commonly listed "merchant" (table 5). The second most common occupation was public official; the others included landowner, doctor, and artisan. Artisanal fathers may be underrepresented because practicing a craft was less likely to be brought up in documents stressing family achievements. No large landowners of the central provinces nor royal officials outside Seville are mentioned, indicating that these Mexico City wholesalers did not come from the highest groups in Spanish society.

The fundamental feature of commercial success was, as with so much of enterprise, the family. Each member promoted the welfare of the family unit, a situation which maximized opportunities for the group but also restricted the freedom of individuals. It was extremely common for father and several sons to be in trade together. Thus, future wholesalers usually appear first in the documentation as *encomenderos* of more experienced

Table 5. Occupational Background of Mexico City Wholesalers and Their Wives

Father's Occupation	Number of Merchants	% of Merchants	Number of Wives	% of Wives
Merchant	34	56	40	46
Public official[a]	13	21	11	13
Landowner[b]	6	10	24	28
Professional	3	5	5	6
Artisan	3	5	3	3
Textile manufacturer	2	3	4	4
Total	61	100	87	100

Sources: AGI, Escribanía de Cámara, Contratación, Audiencia de México; AGN, Inquisición, Bienes Nacionales, Tierras, Vínculos, Civil; Archivo de Notarías; Archivo Judicial.
[a]Nine of eleven of the wives' fathers who were public officials were high fiscal, judicial, or naval officers; all of the merchants' fathers were in lower categories.
[b]Thirteen of the wives' fathers who were landowners were of first-settler families.

relatives. As agents on commission, they bought and sold goods at the owners' risk. Less frequently, the young wholesaler-to-be is described as a *cajero*. The title *encomendero* was not limited to beginners; many merchants retained this function even when well-established, calling themselves *mercader y encomendero*.[13]

The father, uncle, or older brother was often stationed in the most desirable and important locations, Seville or Mexico City, while the younger brothers resided for many years in cities of lesser commercial significance, or traveled between Veracruz, Manila, and Cartagena, and Seville.[14] Traveling was less attractive than being what was called a stationary merchant, as is apparent from the Zuleta brothers. Cristóbal de Zuleta, a prominent Mexico City trader from the 1600s to the 1640s, had a long association with his older brother, Fernando. Both began as *maestres* (supercargoes) on the convoys. A *maestre* was an ideal post for a merchant in training, since he received 1 percent on each shipment he laded and could bring his own goods as cargo; he was also in an excellent position to smuggle goods. From 1588 to 1593, Fernando served as *maestre* on a number of vessels. He then became a major silver dealer based in Seville, while Cristóbal voyaged for a few more years, settled as an *encomendero* in Veracruz, and by 1607 moved permanently to Mexico City. Other silver merchants of Seville at this time, Gerónimo and Alejandro Zuleta, probably also were family members.

Pedro Jiménez Enciso the younger, an elector of the guild in Mexico

City in 1635, was one of a triumvirate of brothers trading to New Spain in the first half of the seventeenth century. Diego, the *ventiquatro* of Seville, was the senior and stationary member of the family. Sebastián and Pedro first served as *maestres* in the 1610s, traveling back and forth between Seville and Veracruz. In 1613, Pedro purchased his own ship with loans from senior merchants. A year later he was sued for nonpayment of the import-export tax and the convoy tax, after being caught smuggling 145 *arrobas* of wild cochineal, 18 *libras* of indigo, and pitch into Cádiz harbor in broad daylight. The two younger brothers formed partnerships in the next four years to ship wine and oil from Spain for hides and cochineal from New Spain, with Pedro receiving two-thirds of the profits, a common arrangement. Pedro made his last voyage as *maestre* in 1621; he then stayed in Seville while his brother Sebastián did the traveling. By 1635, Pedro had established himself in Mexico City, where he died a few years later.[15]

Gerónimo de Aramburu, an elector of the 1640s and 1650s, began as a *maestre* in 1636 and also served as an *encomendero* for Guillermo Bequer, one of the most important merchants in Seville at that time. Gerónimo had been preceded to Mexico City by his brother Pedro, who was supplying credit to miners in Zacatecas in 1616 but a few years later returned to establish himself in Seville. Gerónimo, his younger brother, eventually replaced him in Mexico City.[16]

Unless the older brother were incompetent or died young, his siblings could remain in the *encomendero* role, earning commissions during their travels, or in a less attractive city, for an extended period. One striking case was the somewhat pathetic history of the merchant Fernando Matías de Rivera. He stated: "I served the treasurer of the mint, my brother [Juan Luis de Rivera] for 40 years, and I helped him earn his living, travelling the highways and risking my life in Chichimeca country. Afterwards I came to this city [Mexico] and with the 28,000 pesos which I gave him from my own pocket, he began to coin silver in the mint and then bought the office of treasurer of the mint . . ." (The first stop for merchants journeying to the mines was at Cuautitlán, fourteen miles north of Mexico City; see plate 3). Fernando Matías was bitter because Juan Luis had promised to found a *mayorazgo* (entailed estate) for Fernando's son, don Alonso de Rivera, but failed to carry out the promise. Nevertheless, such was the strength of fraternal loyalty that Fernando in his will asked the disappointed don Alonso not to sue his uncle's estate for the *mayorazgo*.[17]

It could take ten years or more to move from family *encomendero* in

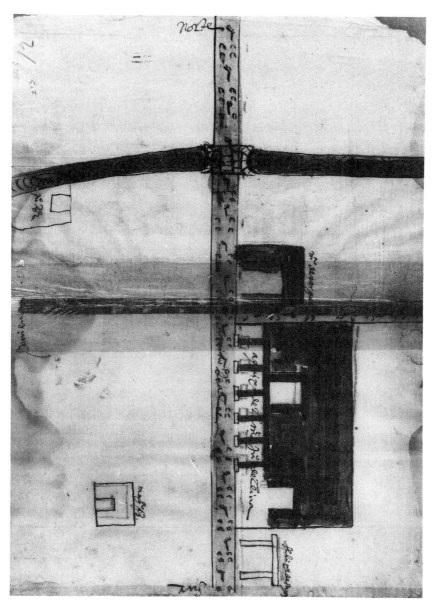

3. Inn at Cuautitlán, on the *camino real*, 1616.

Veracruz to *mercader y encomendero* in the capital. Melchor and Bernardino del Cuéllar, sons of a Cádiz physician, first served as *encomenderos* in Veracruz and Manila, respectively. Melchor spent ten years in the port before moving to Puebla, where he spent at least six more years, and then went to Mexico City. Bernardino, the junior brother, served in the Philippines, only moving to the capital after Melchor's death fourteen years later. The brothers Francisco and Matías del Castillo both began as *encomenderos* in Veracruz in the 1610s; in the 1620s, they became *vecinos* of Mexico City, and by 1635, both brothers were electors of the Mexico City guild.[18]

Men who became wholesalers acquired their initial capital from a variety of sources, but personal histories and cargo manifests show that the most important were, first, their earnings as *encomenderos;* second, short-term credit from fellow merchants, which enabled them to ship on their own account; and, to a lesser extent, partnerships, in which the younger man supplied the labor or travel, were important. Somewhat later, but still at a formative stage of the merchant's career, his wife's dowry played a significant role. The careers studied also suggest that the fabled profits of the Indies trade were not quite as high as has been depicted. Although some merchants started with next to nothing and made a killing from a few voyages, the experience of most points to a slower and more laborious accumulation of wealth.

THE IMPORTANCE OF COMMISSIONS

Commissions of 4 to 5 percent played an important role in the acquisition of commercial capital. They offered the great advantage of allowing merchants to profit without risking their own funds. According to the ship manifests, by far the highest proportion of the value of cargo shipped from New Spain to Spain was shipped by wholesalers acting as commission agents for other people. The value of all shipments sent by the merchants studied herein according to four categories that derive from the manifests is provided in table 6. Each category identifies a different relationship that the merchant had to the goods he was sending from Veracruz to Seville. Column 1, "Independent," refers to the value of the cargo that the merchant shipped on his own account, as sole owner. Column 2, "Agent," refers to the value of the goods the merchant shipped as a commission agent for a Spanish merchant. Column 3, "Partner," refers to the value of the goods the merchant shipped in partnership with his Spanish corre-

Table 6. Apportionment of Cargo Shipped to Spain by Mexico City
Wholesalers, According to Ownership (Percentages)

Year	Independent	Agent	Partner	Intermediary	Ownership Not Known	Total
1614	19.2	39.8	19.4	9.7	11.9	100
1620	29.3	30.8	14.0	22.9	3.0	100
1625	25.8	41.3	13.4	11.1	8.4	100
1630	27.6	49.1	7.6	12.4	3.3	100
1639	10.3	76.7	1.0	6.9	5.1	100

Source: AGI, Contratación, 1823–29, 1859–63, 1880–84, 1896–99, 1926–28.

spondent. Column 4, "Intermediary," refers to the value of goods owned by a third party in Mexico City or elsewhere, for whom the merchant and his Spanish consignee were acting as brokers. As *"Encomenderos"* and as "Intermediaries," Mexico City wholesalers received a commission.

Column 2 contains a higher proportion of the cargo than any of the other columns. In every year analyzed, therefore, the Mexico City wholesalers invested the most capital as *encomenderos* for Spanish correspondents. (In one of the five years analyzed, 1620, column 2 is rather close to column 1, suggesting that there was some variation by year. But the pattern is marked for the four other years.) Moreover, if column 2, "Agent," is combined with column 4, "Intermediary," the proportion of capital shipped on which merchants earned a commission rises higher.

A common view of a typical merchant's career was that he began as a commission agent but as he became wealthier, he relied less on this source of income and became primarily an independent trader. This progression holds true for some men, but it was more typical for the wholesaler to retain the *encomendero* function even when he changed his place of residence and rose in rank. The following examples are merchants who represent common patterns of commercial behavior; their careers and children will be discussed more fully in succeeding chapters.

Francisco Medina Reynoso was a merchant who progressively invested more capital on his own account, independent of his Spanish consignees. Throughout his life Francisco consigned cargoes almost exclusively to his relative (uncle or brother) in Seville, Jorge Reynoso. His relationship to Jorge, however, changed. In 1614, Francisco shipped only 32 percent of his cargo on his own account, but in 1625, shortly before he died, he was shipping 57 percent at his own risk. He also reduced by 67 percent the sums that he handled as an intermediary for third parties. Antonio de

Burgos, one of the wholesalers who specialized in exporting dyestuffs and hides, shipped 17 to 26 percent of his cargo on his own account in the 1620s, but 56 to 84 percent at his own risk in the 1630s.

The pattern of extensive lifetime commission shipping, however, was more prevalent. Andrés de Acosta, while serving as prior of the *consulado*, the highest commercial position in New Spain and after twenty-five years of residence there, shipped virtually nothing on his own account in the second decade of the century. Acosta shed some light on the high status of the agent when he proudly described himself as "the largest factor of the Portuguese slave merchants in New Spain from Angola, São Tomé, and Cabo Verde, having paid the Crown over 140,000 pesos in 12 years in sales taxes."[19] Because of his Portuguese birth, Acosta became involved in furious debate over whether he, a naturalized resident, should be allowed to be elected prior of the guild. (His father had been based in Lisbon and his two brothers in Luanda and Goa). But Spanish-born merchants had a similar reliance on commissions. Gonzalo Sánchez de Herrera, also prior of the *consulado*, shipped only 5 to 8 percent on his own account throughout his entire career. Francisco de Rossales, a large mint merchant investigated for fraud in 1611, at the time was shipping only 18 percent of his cargo at his own risk. Clemente de Valdés, who died at seventy-two after one of the longest mercantile careers in seventeenth-century Mexico City, in some years shipped no goods at all on his own account, in other years up to 46 percent. More goods were sent on commission in the 1630s, when some scholars have seen a movement to greater self-sufficiency in New Spain, than in earlier decades (table 6). Valdés was more, rather than less, active as an *encomendero* at this time. Pedro de Soto López and Juan Francisco Vertiz, who were bankers to the Viceroys Cerralvo and Cadereita in the 1620s and 1630s, were also primarily *encomenderos*.

THE SCALE OF TRADE AND ITS PROFITS

The income that could be obtained from commissions depended, of course, on the value of the trade. The convoy and import tax records permit examination for the first time of the amounts shipped by merchants as a group and of the differing sums individual merchants invested at successive dates. The sums invested, in cash or on credit, were large compared to the yearly salaries of other occupational groups. The money invested in transoceanic trade can also be placed in the context of the total assets held by the merchant to appreciate the relative importance of working capital and fixed capital.

In the Atlantic trade, the sums merchants invested ranged widely, from a mere 110 pesos to the very large amount of 95,000 pesos in a given voyage. The majority of merchants' investments were in a much closer range.[20] They naturally varied by year. In 1614, the majority placed between 5,103 pesos and 46,555 pesos; in the 1620s, the majority placed an average between 2,208 pesos and 31,402 pesos; in the 1630s, they laded an average between 2,875 pesos and 30,076 pesos. These sums are the registered shipments and, therefore, are minimum figures. For the 1630s, especially, the amounts were higher than the extant registers show.[21]

To turn from the behavior of the traders as a group to their behavior as individuals, the conditions of trans-Atlantic trade were sufficiently erratic that investments fluctuated tremendously. Merchants doubled or decreased by one-third or more the amount they had invested only five years before. The one discernible pattern was, as might be expected, that the majority initially placed small amounts and increased the value of their shipments as they grew older and more successful. They then might lower their investment, transferring it to other trades or other sectors. For example, in 1614, Melchor de Cuéllar and Gonzalo Sánchez Herrera were placing rather substantial cargoes (figure 2); they later raised them dramatically, to 41,000 pesos and 47,000 pesos, respectively. Their next investments were much lower. Juan Ontiveros Barrera took the same approach but invested less money. In 1614 and 1620 Clemente de Valdés laded close to 50,000 pesos of cargo, but in the latter year he shifted to the Pacific (figure 3), investing between 51 and 57,000 pesos for that decade and then returned to 6 and 10,000 peso investments in the Atlantic. Ontiveros Barrera made a similar shift from Atlantic to Pacific but in the 1630s. Although the decline in registered trade in the 1630s also contributed to lower Atlantic investments, there were merchants who increased shipments considerably in that decade. Stefantoni Federegui, for example, went from 6,575 pesos in 1620 to 58,505 pesos in 1639.

In the Pacific, merchant investments ranged from 106 pesos to more than 100,000 pesos for a given voyage. The bulk of investments, however, concentrated in a narrower range. To take a few decades, in the 1590s, most occupied between 1,525 pesos and 10,280 pesos; in the 1620s, the range was 5,422 pesos to 33,800 pesos; and in the 1640s, it was 2,255 pesos to 9,933 pesos. As in the Atlantic, there were dramatic rises and falls (figure 3). Another instance were the investments of Juan

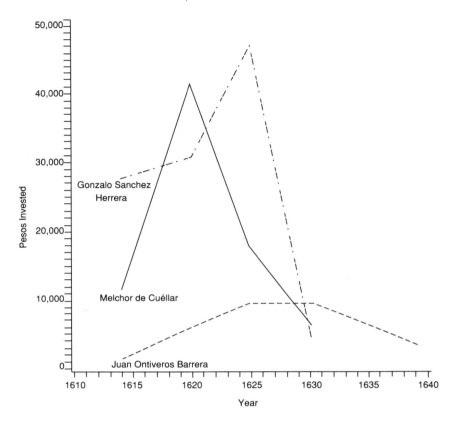

Figure 2. Patterns of Investment in the Atlantic Trade, 1610–40.

de Montemayor, whose sums were lower but also fluctuated greatly. In 1622, he placed 1,859 pesos; in 1626, 10,244; in 1629, 4,333; in 1631, 13,163; in 1636, 1,259; and in 1637, 726 pesos. As in the Atlantic, even in the crisis decades some merchants increased shipments. As figure 3 shows, Simón de Haro's increased erratically from 6,526 pesos in 1628 to 32,407 pesos in 1659. Another example were Luis Vásquez Medina's investments, which rose steadily from 963 pesos in 1633 to 11,630 pesos in 1652. Juan de Alcocer's pattern represents the declining investments, which appeared more often in the Pacific. Because the general range of investments and the individual patterns are based on registered cargo, they consistently show the Atlantic shipments higher or similar to the Pacific; in the 1630s, however, the unregistered cargo was higher in the Pacific.

These investments of 5,000–20,000 pesos or more represented large sums by the standards of the day. Salaries of most *corregidores* were between 200 and 300 pesos a year, while *audiencia* judges received just under 3,000 pesos, generals of the *armada*, 4,000 pesos, and military governers, 2,000 pesos. These were minimum incomes. Officials also received commissions for special tasks, bribes, and profits from investment in land or mines. Even tripling these salaries, however, put income below what many merchants invested in overseas trade in a given year.[22]

For the traders themselves, the merchandise they held—and the cash

Figure 3. Patterns of Investment in the Pacific Trade, 1590–1660.

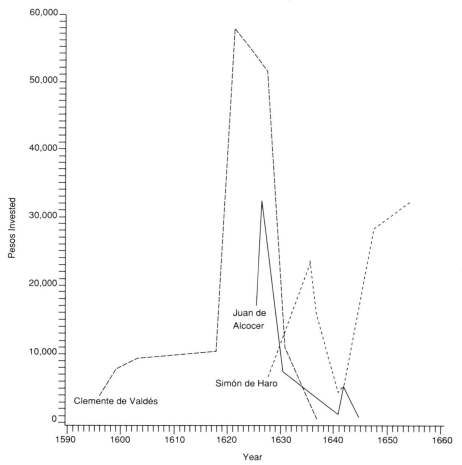

and credit used to purchase more of it—occupied a larger part of their estate than any other investment, just over half of their total assets, a conclusion based on an analysis of thirty-six inventories from Mexico City. Twenty were made at or after the merchant's death for the purpose of dividing his estate; most (fifteen) are from the years from 1630 to 1669 and were found in a variety of archives (table 7). The other sixteen inventories are the declarations of wealth by Mexico City traders, which the Crown ordered all public officials to submit in 1622, which have been analyzed by José de la Peña.[23] Most merchants were not public officials, so that those he includes are chiefly priors and councillors of the *consulado*. Thus, we have information about merchants who thrived both before and after the contraction of the 1640s. It is unusual to find so many inventories for seventeenth-century traders.

The merchants in table 7 invested overwhelmingly in movable goods and instruments of credit rather than in real property. Fifteen percent of capital comprised merchandise stored in traders' warehouses, while 6 percent was found in silver coin. Within the group of men studied, of course, the capital of some individuals was more heavily invested in merchandise and cash than others; the former might have merchandise alone which was worth 25 to 50 percent of their assets (and a few had no stock-in-trade at all on hand).

Seven percent of assets was spent on consumption: jewels, plate, home furnishings, and black house slaves, while 6 percent was devoted to settling children in their careers or marriages before their parents' property was divided at the merchants' death. Only 16 percent of the assets of the group as a whole were placed in real estate: 11 percent in urban houses and 5 percent in rural holdings. Finally, 3 percent was distributed in legally bought public offices; the figure does not include the appointments facilitated by bribes. The distribution of investments for de la Peña's sixteen men in 1622 is very similar.

Forty-six percent of the group's assets consisted of credits held by the merchant. They were extended to a wide variety of social groups. Some merchants lent primarily to other traders, miners, and landowners, while others included civil and military officials, priests, craftsmen, and notaries among their debtors. An impressionistic review of the inventories and notarial documents yields the conclusion that about one-third of their credits were in international trade, another third in provincial commerce (including to suppliers of trade goods, such as sugar), and the rest were given for purposes which did not relate directly to their business. Thus, we can say 52 percent of the group's assets (15.4 + 6.3 + 30 = 51.6 percent) were invested in movable goods, coin, and credits which served business. Thus, working capital comprised the majority of the merchants' assets. The conditions of uncertainty which, as Salvucci stressed, characterized the colonial economy made this portfolio a fairly rational one.

To reach a conclusion about the income from this scale of trade, it remains to consider profits. The shipments whose value is given in the tax records analyzed were later sold at a markup. Thus, the 20,000 pesos' worth of cochineal shipped from New Spain would be sold at a higher price in Spain, and the owner's profit was the difference between the final sale price and the expenses related to it. The *encomendero*'s commission of 4 to 5 percent was most likely a percentage of the wholesale value of the shipment. Markups could be 200 percent or more; not so profits.[24]

The fabled profits of the Indies trade have been a staple in the literature. Recently, however, at least for earlier periods, scholars have balanced high figures of 200 or 300 percent with other examples of profits which were 50 or 70 percent.[25] That is also the case herein; table 8 offers some examples of profits earned, or estimated earned, in different trades from 1593 to 1668. Variable, lower than might be expected profits, were often in the 30 to 70 percent range, suggesting that merchants acquired capital more slowly and experienced a less meteoric career ascent than has been thought. These profits of 30 percent or more were, however, higher than the 5 percent interest earned from *censos redimibles* (redeemable liens) or from other sources. For example, commissions received for collecting taxes ranged from 8 to 15 percent, while those received for serving as executor of an estate ranged from 6 to 25 percent, more frequently close to the lower figure. Collecting debts owed to another party usually brought a 4 to 6 percent commission. Profits from *obrajes* have been estimated at 9 to 10 percent, while those from some ranching properties were 5 to 20 percent.[26]

CREDIT

Serving as an *encomendero* was the most frequent way that a merchant conducted his business in the Atlantic trade. The second most frequent method was to ship goods independently, but this, in turn, usually involved obtaining credit, either merchandise shipped on credit or a cash loan to purchase goods. The reliance on credit was one of the fundamental

Table 7. Distribution of Merchant Assets, Mexico City, 1607–69 (in Pesos)

Name, Date Died	Offices	Houses, Shops	Rural Property	House Slaves, Number and Value	Merchandise	Cash
Alzega (1664)	—	16,654	—	1,450	27,730	13,40(
Arellano Sotomayor (1654)	—	—[a]	—	2,885	9,139	19,98!
Baeza del Río (1624)	—	20,000	59,500	—	—	—
Cárdenas Jaramillo (1659)	—	—	—	2 500	—	27!
Castellete (1638)	—	10,600	—	11 2,865	25,778	—
Chavarría (1647)	—	—	6,000	—	500	—
Guerra Chacón (1669)	—	12,000	—	4 1,350	21,270	11,00(
López Páramo (1636)	—	30,000	—	13 5,150	114,208	1,92(
Millán, A.	—[c]	22,497	88,374	5,000	80,438	12,90'
Montemayor Herrera (1648)	56,600	27,000	—	15 3,600	7,026	35,69!
Munabe, A. (1665)	—	—[a]	10,000	3 750	1,000	3,00(
Ossorio Soto, L. (1658)	—	4,740	—	2 500	2,516	7,00(
Pardo Agüero (1622)	—[c]	—	—	17 3,400	—	—
Rivera, J. L. (1607)	—[d]	110,000	—	—	117,369	—
Rodríguez de León, J. (1611)	—	13,010	13,600	—[a]	45,000	—

Plate, Jewels	Household Goods	Dowry Given	Debts in favor	Total Assets	Debts Against	Net Worth
6,139	2,362	—	25,613	93,354		93,354
2,611	2,340	—	168,380	205,340	92,630	112,710
—	250	12,000	10,000	101,750	72,265	29,485
155	1,436	—	1,065	3,431	11,702	−8,271
20,020[b]	20,020[b]	—	183,015	262,299	129,816	132,483
135	—	—	25,500	32,135	15,084	17,051
3,088	2,442	9,002	69,127	129,279	—	129,279
7,916	14,059	—	49,773	223,032	103,436	119,596
12,907[b]	2,706	—	213,987	438,816	236,082	202,734
9,766	4,658	50,500	83,424	278,266	41,037	237,229
—	—	—	6,800	21,550	5,000	16,550
8,900	18,234	—	6,850	48,740	7,204	41,530
8,712	1,680	14,600	27,500	55,892	7,400	48,492
—	606	—	234,851	462,826	90,053	372,773
—[a]	—[a]	—	55,004	126,614	85,600	41,014

Table 7—*Continued*

Name, Date Died	Offices	Houses, Shops	Rural Property	House Slaves, Number and Value	Merchandise	Cash
Ruíz de Ordunaña (1626)	—	12,000	—	7 1,750	22,000	—
Salcedo, G. (1619)	—	—[a]	—[a]	—[a]	15,645[b]	—
Santos Corral (1622)	—[c]	36,000	—	12 3,000	—	—
Toledo y M. (1631)	66,666	64,000	—	20 6,000	73,918	127,62
Urrea, T. (1663)	—	24,000	—	13 2,475	10,560	—
Totals	123,266	402,501	177,474	40,675	574,097	232,81
Percent of total assets (3,722,025 p.)	3.3	10.8	4.8	1.1	15.4	6.

[a]Has property in this category, but value not given.
[b]Sometimes categories such as "Plate, Jewels," "Household Goods," or "Merchandise" are give a combined value. In such cases, the value is divided between the two categories.
[c]Held office by appointment, not purchase.
[d]His office, treasurer of the mint, purchased for 130,000 pesos, was not included in his inventory it had been auctioned previously by the Crown. He had no heirs.

traits of the colonial economy. While helpful to the merchant starting out, reliance on credit also continued throughout his career. Contemporary observers remarked on the large transactions carried out without any money actually changing hands. In 1620, it was estimated that 3 to 4 million pesos of merchandise was sold at Puerto Belo, one-half of which was sold on credit to be repaid in installments. In 1652, the *consulado* of Seville emphasized that "the merchant more often uses credit than cash, and if he has 10,000 ducats on hand he can invest 200,000 pesos on credit." Joseph de Veitia Linaje, author of the definitive seventeenth-century treatise on the Indies trade, *Norte de la contratación de las Indias Occidentales* (1672), noted that the convoy vessels were provisioned on credit. Further indication of the crucial role of sales on credit is the concern of theolo-

Plate, Jewels	Household Goods	Dowry Given	Debts in favor	Total Assets	Debts Against	Net Worth
12,168[b]	12,168[b]	—	183,173	243,259	40,063	203,196
—	15,645[b]	150,411	246,793	428,494	—	428,494
800	4,640	—	41,800	86,240	69,580	16,660
5,658	20,601	—	66,363	430,833	237,622	193,211
6,420[b]	6,420[b]	—	—	49,875	28,000	21,875
105,395	130,268	236,513	1,699,018	3,722,025	1,272,574	2,449,451
2.8	3.5	6.4	45.6	100%		

Note: Mines and *obrajes* are omitted because no merchants listed owned them.

Where no entry appears under "Merchandise," it is sometimes because goods ordered have not yet arrived.

"Dowry given" to children which preceded the merchant's death is considered as an asset and is included here. The wife's dowry, which was deducted from the joint estate once debits were paid, is not part of the inventory of the merchant's property, hence, it is not included.

gians about the doctrinally illicit practice of earning interest on such sales by charging more for goods bought on credit than they would have cost if bought with cash.[27] Merchants were, thus, users as well as providers of credit. If we compare the group's debits to their total assets, we see that debits constituted 34 percent of assets. Because the focus herein is on how merchants acquired capital their role as borrowers is discussed. Their lending activity is discussed in succeeding chapters.

When merchants sought cash for trade, they most often borrowed in a writ of *obligación* an amount *en reales* (in silver coin) on a short-term basis. The quantity could be as low as 50 pesos or as high as 30,000 pesos, obliged to be repaid in a stated period of time in two or three installments. Often, sums of between 1,000 and 5,000 pesos were due in a year,

Table 8. Profits in the Indies Trades

Date	Destination of Shipment	Principal (in Pesos)	Percent Profit	Source
1593	Manila	—	33	AGI, Audiencia de México 22, 8 October 1593
1608	Seville	—	7	AGI, Audiencia de México 27, 1608
1608	Callao-Lima	—	10–12	Ibid.
1611	Seville	12,000	50	AJud, No number Juan Rodríguez de León
1623	—	10,000	60	AJud, Number 22 Toribio Fernández Celi
1628	Manila	101,411	33	AJud, Number 6 Gerónimo Calar de Irolo
1635	Manila	—	30–40	Antonio Álvarez *Extracto historial. . . , 3.*
1637	Cartagena	—	10–12	Ibid., 8
1637	Manila	4,000	200	AGN, Bienes Nacionales, 416, 11
1641	Seville	1,751	25	AN, López Ahedo, f.6
1660–68	Manila	16,325	74	AGN, Tierras, 1272, ff.49r–62r

while sums lower were to be repaid in six months or less, but because the return on money invested in transoceanic goods easily could take two or three years to be realized, the due dates were not necessarily met. Not all agreements were written down. Fernando Matías de Rivera refers to the "many thousands of pesos which I gave Juan Luis as a brother, without our keeping any accounts."[28]

These loans do not mention interest or collateral. However, interest might well be charged but disguised in order not to violate the Church's prohibition against usury. The Church allowed the creditor to charge more than the principal if he carried out a genuine sales transaction in which he assumed risks in recovering his capital. For example, if a merchant advanced silver coin to another merchant to be repaid in unminted silver, he assumed both the risk of possible loss of the silver bullion during the trip from the mines to the capital and the cost of transport. The lender, however, used the Church's doctrine to earn illegal interest on the credit advanced by exaggerating the risks and inflating the transport costs. Taking the deception one step further, the lender and borrower might even agree not to purchase unminted silver (or any other commodity specified in the contract). The contract would state the terms for such a sale, but all that transpired was that the lender gave the borrower a sum and received a higher repayment, which included the illegal interest passed off as charges due to costs and risk. The lender could also manipulate the Church's sanction of an increase above the principal due to varying exchange rates. The Church allowed dealing in bills of exchange because it considered that the lender took a risk because the rates for currency fluctuated according to time and location. However, if the creditor knew the rates, he did not take a true risk. A merchant could earn a profit by lending coined silver at the unofficial market rate for bullion but requiring that he be repaid at the official, higher rate.[29] These short-term loans, therefore, could include disguised interest.

For the merchant who had collateral or bondsmen, another method was to seek capital from a *depósito*, a short-term loan which was often extended. In this case, interest of 5 to 7 percent to cover risk was legally charged, and collateral in the form of jewels, plate, or slaves might be required. Long-term loans were a third source of funds. In this case, the merchant obtained a sum of money in exchange for paying interest of 7 percent, then after 1621, 5 percent to the lender. To guarantee his annual payment, the merchant imposed a *censo* or lien upon his city houses or rural property. Thus, such credit was available only to established merchants. Scholars have stressed the importance of capital from *censos* to the growth of the late colonial economy.[30] The merchants studied here used them principally to purchase or improve real estate, to establish chaplaincies or otherwise provide for children, or to finance other types of consumption, rather than for annual purchase of trade goods.

Short-term credit could be provided by anyone with a few hundred pesos to lend, but the largest proportion of these credits and cash loans came, in fact, from fellow merchants. For the beginner, therefore, support from colleagues was the crucial factor in his advance. The larger and longer-running *depósitos*, on the other hand, were offered by a variety of social types, merchants, naturally, but also wealthy landowners and officials, lawyers, or religious corporations. *Censos* were chiefly the province of the various branches of the Church, although there were aristocratic and commercial *señores de censos* (lords of *censos*) too.[31]

Although interest on *depósitos* was supposed to be 7 percent or less, here too the market could supplant doctrinal prescriptions. One way we learn about interest paid is through lawsuits brought by debtors who sought a reduction of interest or creditors seeking a higher rate. For example, merchant Juan Vázquez Medina charged 20 percent interest on a debt of 4,931 pesos owed to him by General don Fernando Zenteno Maldonado. In 1645, after hearing the suit of Zenteno's widow, doña Isabel Guzmán Carabeo, the *consulado* reduced the 20 percent to 6 percent and gave the balance of 14 percent back to her. A lawsuit between the executors of the estates of merchants Juan López Olaiz and Álvaro de Lorenzana revealed another twist. Lorenzana's estate was trying to recover a debt of 11,500 pesos. The sum represented the interest of 11.5 percent which Lorenzana charged on the 100,000 pesos he had given López Olaiz for the Manila trade but which López Olaiz had never invested because of a viceregal order forbidding López Olaiz, who was also an admiral, to trade. López Olaiz's heirs refused to pay, claiming that 10 percent was excessive; they asserted that the interest should have been only 5 percent and that Lorenzana had preferred to keep the debt unpaid so that he could charge exhorbitant interest. In the end, a ruling favoring Lorenzana was reached, and the heirs of López Olaiz were ordered to pay 9,000 pesos, or 9 percent, to Lorenzana's estate.

Uncollectible debts constituted a standard category in the merchants' estate inventories. This worked to the advantage of the merchant as borrower. Gonzalo Gutiérrez Gil had an irritating collection of bad debts when he died at seventy-three in 1624. One of Gutiérrez Gil's three writing desks, naturally under lock and key, was stuffed with a large number of these very old notes. One went back to 1590, many of the others were from the early 1600s. Increasing wealth did little to alter the situation. In Francisco López Páramo's 1630 inventory he held 14,645 pesos in good debts and 10,887 pesos in bad debts. In 1636, the former totalled 32,453 pesos, the latter, 17,320 pesos. In 1654, Francisco Arellano Sotomayor's credits included 168,380 pesos in collectible debts and 74,852 pesos in noncollectible debts, some twelve and thirteen years old.[32]

A merchant mindful of his credit rating could not postpone payment for too long, but then he could borrow again. Even experienced merchants were deeply in debt. Of the twenty whose assets are analyzed, nine had debts which exceeded their credits. Of course, these debts were not necessarily for commercial purposes.

COMPANIES

In addition to commissions and loans, forming a company was the other common strategy for acquiring commercial capital. The longest original agreement encountered here ran for **six years**, which may be compared with the tax collection contracts, a type of company, which lasted seven to nine years. The initial capitalization of the companies started by Mexico City wholesalers ranged between 1,109 pesos and 70,000 pesos. The latter figure was unusual; it refers to a silver minting company which Pedro Ruíz de Orduñana formed with Simón García de Becerril, another Mexico City merchant, for three years. Ruíz was to provide Becerril with 70,000 pesos, but in the first year he gave him only 44,765 pesos and the company ended with Ruíz's death the following year.[33] Remittances from the initial investment might take several years to reach New Spain. In 1630, Pedro de Toledo and don Lope de Monsalve de Armendáriz sent 10,000 pesos to their correspondent in the Philippines, licenciado Alonso García de León, archdeacon of the Cathedral of Manila. By 1634, he had returned only 7,697 pesos' worth of goods. The partners Antonio de Millán, a Mexico City wholesaler, and Diego de Palencia, a Manila trader, invested 16,325 pesos in a company whose remittances arrived over a period of eight years; all in all they earned 12,099 pesos' profit.[34]

Division of profits might be made *a perdidas y ganancias* (split equally), which usually occurred when both parties invested capital, or by a lesser and greater amount when a wholesaler provided the capital and a partner traveled and sold the stock. In this case the senior partner received 75 or 66 percent.[35] Profits were supposed to be proportional to risks—the risks of investing money not the risks to life and limb on the high seas or the Indian frontier of which the junior members later complained. Profits earned might be reinvested in the second and third years of the company. In 1645, Juan de Montemayor Herrera formed a company with his son, don Francisco, who went to the Philippines as a sergeant major and traveling partner. The father contributed 12,000 pesos, the son, 5,000 pesos. The next year Juan invested an additional 6,000 pesos, but his death terminated the agreement. Of course, profits were not necessarily forthcoming. Alonso Baeza del Río formed a company to buy gold and silver with doña Petronila de Meneses, the widow of *secretario* Alonso de Torres. It was to last from 1604 to 1608 and was capitalized by doña Petronila at 14,000 pesos. She was to receive two-thirds of the profits. As of 1606, doña Petronila had only recovered half of her initial investment. In 1608, Baeza del Río "retired from trade," and in 1618, he still had not paid the other 7,000 pesos. Interest of 10 percent was charged on the debt, and Baeza's heirs had to pay it.[36]

Company agreements tried to limit all possible fraudulent activity. In 1639, Juan Vásquez Medina formed a four-year company with José de Herrera. Herrera, the junior partner, agreed to work full time in the shop, selling at the best prices he could get, to live in the house of Vásquez Medina, and to issue credit of up to 1,000 pesos and only in consultation with Vásquez. In 1593 in Seville, the two Vera brothers, Diego Matías and Juan Lorenzo, formed a company to earn 8,000 ducats for their sisters' dowries. Both were repeatedly enjoined to obey their father in the conduct of the business. Diego, who left for Mexico City, was obligated not to deduct his living expenses from the company account, and Juan, who remained in Spain, was not to give gifts exceeding 50 reales in any one exchange.[37]

DAUGHTERS AND DOWRIES

Economic and social benefits were inextricably entwined in marriage. The dowry was an integral aspect of capital accumulation; two-thirds of the men studied received large dowries of 20,000 pesos or more. Marriage also offered an opportunity for social mobility and the perpetuation of the family line, two desiderata in colonial society.

Was the merchant likely to marry outside his occupational group or within it? There are two conflicting models of merchant marriage patterns during the colony. One is endogamous: the marriage of the impecunious, up-and-coming, Spanish-born nephew or man from the same home province to the daughter of a wealthy, established Mexico City merchant, the "nephew syndrome," first described by Brading. The other model is exogamous: the marriage of the wealthy, established, Spanish-born immigrant trader to a less well-to-do creole aristocrat. In this case the merchant could enter the landed-bureacratic elite. Each marriage usually involved a dowry, but in the second type of alliance, it was less valuable than the social prestige. The marriages of the Mexico City merchants illustrate the validity of both models and point to other combinations too, such as marriage to women in Spain and marriages to wealthy aristocratic creoles.

Unlike the rather large proportion of eighteenth-century bureaucrats who could not afford to marry, wholesalers of the years from 1590 to 1660 almost always married. There were a few prominent bachelors among them but not enough to be considered as exemplars of an alternative style of life. In the case of Juan Ontiveros Barrera, a famous bachelor, marriage was less necessary because, as the son of the wholesaler and rancher Cristóbal Ontiveros Barrera, Juan already had the wealth and social connections which a marriage partner could bring. His subsequent choice of the priesthood may have been influenced, in part, by this consideration. Another indication of the importance of marriage was the relatively high remarriage rate. Approximately one-fifth of the merchants had two or three spouses during their lifetimes. Although the needs for companionship and romance were also motives for marriage and compatible with practical considerations, this discussion will focus on the more tangible economic and social benefits.

The majority of the wholesalers improved or maintained their social position when they married (table 5). Two-fifths wed into landowner or bureaucrat families, thus experiencing a rise in social status. Almost one-half married into merchant families. Only a few married daughters of artisans or *obrajeros* (owners of textile workshops), occupations which were lower than *mercader* in social status. Both endogamous and exogamous unions occurred. How were wholesalers able to marry the blueblooded daughters of first-settler families such as the Lara Cervantes, Ávalos y Bocanegra, Velasco, and Maldonado Zapata? Either the in-laws suddenly needed capital or business relationships already existed with the merchant that would be solidified through marriage. The old, landed families did not regard wholesalers as social equals.

One interesting variant on the theme of the capital-rich merchant who marries the poor but noble landowner's daughter was the wholesaler whose marriage increased his already substantial fortune as well as improved his social position. Francisco López Páramo scored a matrimonial coup when he took an aristocratic and wealthy woman as his second wife. His first spouse, María de Contreras, was the daughter of Diego Contreras, a native of San Lúcar Barromeda. Her dower contribution is unknown, but by the time López Páramo remarried in 1630, he was a rich man with a net estate of 65,289 pesos. His storehouse contained 85,919 pesos' worth of merchandise. He then wed doña Beatriz Gómez de Ávila, a descendant of conquistador don Rodrigo Gómez and granddaughter of the founder of the Guerrero *mayorazgo*, don Juan Guerrero de Luna.

Doña Beatriz was rich as well as noble. She brought Francisco the large dowry of 30,000 pesos, one of the biggest received by a seventeenth-century merchant. He provided an *arras*, a gift to the bride in recognition of her virtue and upbringing, of 5,000 pesos. The dowry consisted of cash and household goods, for doña Beatriz was too far down the line to have inherited the family *encomienda* at Actopan, nor the houses at seven different sites in the capital. After the marriage Francisco paid 1,000 and 2,000 peso sums to his father- and brothers-in-law for expenses. During their six-year marriage Francisco and doña Beatriz had no surviving children, so that she was free to dispose of her dowry and joint property as she wished. Francisco's marriage to the creole aristocrat was financially and socially advantageous. Due to his "good treatment of her and his alleged financial troubles," doña Beatriz left one-third of her dowry, all rights to the *arras*, and the joint property to her husband; she bequeathed the rest of her dowry to her father. In 1637, Francisco married for a third time. His wife was the young daughter of *tesorero* (treasurer) Martín López Erunchen, Mariana Salmerón. At this moment Francisco's net estate was 119,596 pesos. His fortune had increased in the categories of merchandise, house furnishings, debits and credits; he acquired no new real estate nor did he have much in cash. He died two years later.[38]

The fact that so many merchants were endogamous suggests something about their own preferences as well as the exclusiveness of the higher social echelons. The Inquisition genealogies of merchants who wanted to become *familiares* (informers) tell of the long friendships between merchant families, relationships which extended back to Seville or even to the provinces in Spain. These give the impression that many merchants preferred to marry within their own circle. The geographical origins of merchants' wives does show two regional patterns. The majority were natives of New Spain, more often from the capital but sometimes from the provinces. However, a fifth were born in Spain and not members of the local creole group.

To return to the question of capital formation, What impact did the dowry have on the wholesaler's assets? Between 1591 and 1642, dowry information exists for thirty-two merchants. Three-quarters received dowries of 10,000 pesos or more; two-thirds received dowries worth 20,000 pesos or more. By the standards of the time, 20,000 pesos was the entire estate of a well-to-do person.[39] Another way to determine the wife's contribution to the merchant's assets at marriage would be to compare his *capital* (property) with his wife's dowry, but such information was infrequently given in the first two-thirds of the seventeenth century. The nine instances which do provide a comparison of *capital* with dowry show that the bride's assets either exceeded the groom's or equalled them. The only exception was when the merchant married for the second time and had already inherited half of the joint property from his first marriage.

The prevalence of large dowries does not mean that marriage immediately placed a chest of silver coins in the merchant's lap to use as he pleased. Dowries usually consisted of personal property, such as clothing, jewelry, silverware, and furniture as well as cash. In Puebla, in only

28 percent of the dowries did cash make up more than 50 percent of the value of the dowry. Merchants were more likely to have access to coin and bar. Cristóbal de Zuleta, interim treasurer of the mint from 1607 to 1617, received a 70,000 peso dowry, of which 12,600 pesos' worth were jewels and the rest was cash. Domingo de Cantabrana, one of the four or five minters of silver for the Crown in the 1640s and 1650s, received a dowry of 10,000 pesos; 3,000 pesos' worth were household effects and jewels, while 7,000 pesos were cash. The acquisition of personal property did save the merchant expense in furnishing his new home and in purchasing clothing for his wife.[40]

Because the dowry remained the wife's property, the merchant had to obtain her permission to employ it in his own ventures, but there were many transactions in which the wife is recorded as agreeing to the use of part of her dowry. For example, two of the official collectors of the *bulas de cruzada* tax (sale of papal indulgences), Juan de Alcocer and Antonio de Millán, received part of the bond they were obliged to post from their wives' dowries. The merchant was also required to return the dowry, or its equivalent value, to his wife or to her heirs upon his own death; suits of creditors against a merchant sometimes included the wife or her children, claiming the return of the dowry. In an interesting twist, García de Salcedo spent 8,585 pesos in court costs trying to hold onto the dowry bequeathed to him by his first wife against the claims of her three children.[41]

Not all fathers-in-law honored the dowry agreement. Juan Rodríguez de León successfully climbed the social ladder with his second marriage to Mariana Martínez, the daughter of doctor don Alonso Martínez, *fiscal* (Crown attorney) of the *audiencia* of Guadalajara, despite the "stain" of his Jewish ancestry. Rodríguez de León was promised a dowry of 23,000 pesos, 12,000 pesos from the cattle ranch, San Juan de Bribiesca, and 4,000 pesos from the house next to his father-in-law's. Ten years after the marriage Juan Rodríguez de León declared he had been the victim of a trick. The ranch sold for 3,700 pesos, and the Mexico City house for only 1,700 pesos. Rodríguez de León had supplied his father-in-law with *avío* (cash, credit, or goods) for the ranch. Other victims of incompletely paid dowries, whether due to deception or to bad luck of the father, were Melchor de Cuéllar and Antonio de Munabe.[42]

Despite these obstacles to the merchants' use of wives' dowries for their own business, it is clear that marriage did contribute substantial capital to merchants' estates. Precisely when in their careers each acquired a dowry varied. There are cases of merchants receiving capital through a dowry early in their careers. In 1611, Juan de Montemayor Herrera married at twenty-one with assets of only 1,800 pesos, while his wife, Leonor de Bañuelos, the daughter of an *obrajero*, brought a dowry of 20,099 pesos. Montemayor's name appears in the transoceanic shipping registers from the 1620s. By 1627, when he married his second wife, Luisa de Salcedo, the daughter of a fellow wholesaler, his estate was worth 115,805 pesos. Gerónimo de Arezti began as a *cajero* in the home of Simón de Haro. He married María Pérez de Angulo, daughter of merchant Bernardino de Angulo, in 1624, early in his career and received a dowry of 10,000 pesos. Only after his marriage did Arezti begin trading to the Philippines, and in 1636, he was chosen elector of the *consulado*.[43]

To be eligible for such largesse, however, the ambitious merchant had to offer his bride's family business ability or other prior connections. For example, Francisco de la Torre said he had been poor when he arrived in the Indies in 1606. He went to work for his *deudo* (relation), Pedro de la Torre, as assistant, then sole farmer, of the *cruzada* tax. The two men dealt in tribute goods—grain, cloaks, and cacao. Francisco then married Peralta's widow, doña Ana Amada, who brought him a fabulous dowry of 150,000 pesos, based primarily on her share of Gaspar's estate. Thus, Francisco benefited from Pedro's relationship with Gaspar to make a splendid match. In 1626, Juan de Alcocer had acquired a number of haciendas in Michoacán as well as in Tacubaya, and in 1634, he married doña Guiomar Ávalos y Bocanegra, descendent of an *encomendero* family based in Valladolid. In the 1640s, he was selling his livestock to Mexico City's contractor, an agreement his wife continued after his death.[44]

For some merchants, therefore, the dowry launched their first independent business ventures. For the majority, it added considerably to an already established income. When combined with capital earned from commissions and obtained on credit, dowries definitely helped propel merchants upward.

CONCLUSION

By *social mobility*, students of colonial Latin America sometimes mean the change from one income level to another, from one occupation to another, or from one region to another. In fact, all were involved in the formation of the merchant elite. The view that a person's position in colonial society was the result of a number of criteria, therefore, is confirmed here.

The passage from the beginning merchant earning 400 pesos a year to the *mercader y encomendero* with an income of 10,000 pesos, 15,000 pesos, or even more was not a smooth one. The great distance between these incomes represents a distance in years, type of business activities, place of residence, and style of living. Compared to other members of society, the beginner was by no means poor, but compared to what the elector of the Mexico City *consulado* could expect, he was definitely at the low end of the income scale.

The practice of recruiting a young relation or hometown resident from the provinces in Spain into the family merchant house in Mexico City, so well documented for other periods, was an important means of ascent. There were, however, other patterns, too. Brothers of nonmercantile background migrated from the provinces to Seville (with capital from agriculture or local office) and entered trade together. Retailer fathers backed aspiring wholesaler sons. One scion of an established merchant house in Seville carried on the family's commerce while his siblings followed other careers. There were several routes, but all involved the family at the point of departure.

After learning the fundamentals of international trade from a more experienced relative, the capital-hungry beginner typically built up assets through a combination of measures. First, there were commissions on goods he shipped as an agent. Given the scale of international trade in the Atlantic in the 1620s, he sold a typical 15,000 pesos of goods for a Spanish merchant and earned 750 pesos. To this, he added a commission, 710 pesos, on a lesser amount of 14,200 pesos in the Pacific trade. Second, the young merchant served as the junior partner in a company in which the senior partner invested 10,000 pesos, and he provided his labor. At a profit of 50 percent, the partners earned 15,000 pesos, and he received one-fourth, 3,750 pesos. From these transactions, therefore, he had an income of 5,210 pesos. Of course, it could take several years for the profits on these goods, sold chiefly on credit, to be returned. There might also be some adverse events, such as the failure of some provincial merchants to pay for what they received, royal seizure of silver, or a lack of demand for some of the goods. The merchant's income, therefore, should be considered income from over a three-year period. If he lived frugally at 300 pesos a year, however, he would still come out ahead with 4,310 pesos in assets over the three years.[45]

After twelve years of such activity, most of it outside of Mexico City, the merchant had about 17,240 pesos. He was well known, of good reputation, and possessed business correspondents in the major towns. He now had something to offer a bride and her family. He married and received a dowry of 20,000 pesos. His wife was the Mexico City–born daughter of a fellow merchant (or of a local landowner). One-third of the dowry was in cash, which his wife made available; she would, of course, benefit from an increase in their joint property. The merchant stopped renting his living quarters and bought a house in Mexico City, paying for most of it by continuing existing mortgages. The rest of the dowry was used to furnish the house, maintain his wife in the proper style, and produce some rental income.

Now that the merchant was a well-to-do, settled man, he had other means to increase his capital. He lent money at interest to a variety of people and received a commission as the executor for estates being settled. He also borrowed money on deposit and handled more valuable cargoes for merchants in Spain, with whom he retained close ties. Although he now shipped more cargoes as an independent trader or in partnership than he had before, he continued to derive most of his income in trans-Atlantic trade from commissions. During this second stage the merchant raised his standard of living, spending 2,000 pesos a year.

Finally, the merchant entered a third phase. His loans were larger and to such prominent people as sugar planters and high public officials. He purchased a summer house outside the capital. Chosen as an elector of the *consulado*, he was more a public figure, a role enhanced by his collecting of city and royal taxes. At the peak of his career he extended credit to and minted silver for the Crown, but he did not abandon his commercial activities. His household now required 5,000 or 6,000 pesos a year for living expenses.[46] The merchant was now at the pinnacle of his career.

CHAPTER II

The Mexican Economy and Merchant Capital:

Mining and the Mint

In 1598, Viceroy Montesclaros wrote to the Crown: "without silver, nothing happens in this kingdom."[1] In the late 1630s, when the production of other goods had increased in importance, Viceroy Cadereita stated that "without silver, which is the only thing that gives value to foodstuffs and merchandise, there is no trade."[2] In the colonial period, silver was by far New Spain's principal export to Europe, although the proportion of cargo it comprised fluctuated from year to year.[3] In 1639, the majority of the merchant elite shipping to Spain continued to rely on the export of silver to pay for European goods even when output had declined in Zacatecas, one of the chief centers of silver production, and new sources of supply had to be obtained elsewhere. And what was true for the Atlantic trade was even more true for the Pacific. Manila galleons remained virtual waterborne treasure chests, carrying upward of a million pesos of silver coin and bar across the Pacific.[4] Within the viceroyalty, silver was a crucial stimulant of interprovincial trade, the settlement of northern Mexico, and the creation of markets for local goods in those regions. Even areas whose economies were not tied directly to mining, such as Querétaro and the Yucatán, were indirectly influenced by the presence of mining elsewhere.[5] Coins might be imperfect due to variations in fineness, clipping of edges, and shoddy minting techniques. However, standardization was sufficient for precious metals to be prized as the main, although not the only, medium of exchange, as well as commodities of value in themselves. Thus, silver production and distribution occupied a special place in the viceregal economy, not only due to silver's high value but also because of its centrality to the operation of the economy.

MERCHANT PRODUCERS AND FINANCIERS

The production of silver bullion was the work of many social groups, from Indian pickmen and black refiners to white mineowners and their financiers, whether merchants, clerics, or *hacendados*. All these social groups were crucial to the mining industry, but merchants occupied a special position because of the volume of their investment and their multifunctional participation. First, as providers of merchandise (iron, steel, salt, mules, cattle, various kinds of cloth, and leather), coin, credit, and, illegally, mercury, to the miners, whether directly or through local agents, they enabled silver to be produced. Second, as purchasers of refined silver bar or coin on a large scale, they provided an important market for that product and then circulated it through the domestic and international economy. Finally, a smaller group of the merchant elite controlled the mint of Mexico City by occupying its highest posts. These men coined silver there, both for the royal account and for private individuals. The first two roles of the merchant in mining have received considerable attention, particularly for the eighteenth century; the third role, the activity at the mint, has been neglected. Mint merchants had considerable influence on the amount of specie available in the viceroyalty and on the proportion of silver that the royal treasury ultimately received. Other groups invested in mining, but only the merchants combined regular access to specie, a need for international trade goods, commercial expertise, and wide-ranging business contacts. They also had to find markets for their imports and for the domestic goods they might produce themselves or receive as commodity payments. For their part, provincial producers needed wholesalers to sell their silver or crops, especially overseas. The key to the relationship was the credit extended by the wholesaler. At the apex of the credit pyramid stood the Mexico City wholesalers, at the base, a wide variety of agents, ranging from the well-known example of the *alcalde mayor* to local retailers, priests, assayers, and muleteers. Through partnership, employee, and debtor relationships, which might be complemented by *compadrazgo* or other social ties, merchants cultivated connections with suppliers in the capital and provinces, extending the influence of Mexico City throughout the viceroyalty and beyond.

The merchants' position in the economy was enchanced by the State's delegation to the wealthy colonial elites of functions which in other societies have been carried out by the government. Compared to the laissez-faire model of nineteenth-century Britain and the United States, the Spanish State of the seventeenth century was, of course, highly interventionist. But despite the Hapsburg State's well-documented efforts to regulate economic life, the law left many areas open to private enterprise. With a few exceptions such as the royal monopolies of such products as mercury, playing cards, and stamped paper, and the attempted monopoly of cochineal, the Crown did not participate directly in the production of the colony's goods. Nor did it routinely provide entrepreneurs with badly needed credit, except by carrying debts incurred in the purchase of goods under the royal monopolies. The way was open to merchants, landowners, the various branches of the Church, and other groups to finance and direct economic activity.

SOME CHARACTERISTICS OF SEVENTEENTH-CENTURY MINING

Unlike other enterprises of colonial Mexico which used techniques or products familiar to pre-Columbian society, deep shaft silver mining was strictly a European import. Its early introduction into New Spain, and its rapid development in the sixteenth century, paralleled the early transfer of European culture to the viceroyalty. By the 1570s, silver mining was a dynamic, technologically complex, capital-intensive enterprise owned by a fairly small number of creoles or Spaniards, and it continued to be so. Although expansion is associated with the settlement of the north, and the mines of San Luis Potosí, Zacatecas, Sombrerete, Cuencamé, Topia, and Parral, central New Spain also contained many productive sites, a situation which was helpful to the Mexico City merchants. Pachuca, founded in 1551, had eighty-two stamp mills in the 1590s, more than any other mine in the viceroyalty. Taxco, Sultepec, and Cuautla were also still important in the seventeenth century. According to the distribution of mercury by region, 36 percent of mercury was received by central Mexican sites between 1630 and 1634 and again between 1665 and 1669.[6]

With the exhaustion of high-quality surface deposits and with the need to increase production to compensate for the inflationary effect of previously exported specie, in the 1570s deep-shaft mining of lower-grade deposits predominated. Fortunately, the earlier introduction of refining by amalgamation of ore with mercury made it possible to exploit these deposits profitably and vastly increased the productive potential of the mining industry. As the seventeenth century progressed, however, drainage and excavation costs rose, the silver yield of the amalgamated ore fell, and the capital requirements of mine ownership became more onerous. Miners had to purchase more mercury to produce the same amount of silver. However, because the Crown expected 1 *quintal* (101 pounds) of mercury to produce 100 marks of silver (1 mark equaled 65 reales), and distributed mercury on the basis of previous production, smaller owners, who could not produce at the official ratio of silver to mercury, went bankrupt. The overall number of mines, therefore, tended to decrease as those who worked low-grade ores which could not produce at this ratio went bankrupt.[7]

The large capital investments in equipment, buildings, mercury, and labor required for amalgamation helped limit the number of owners. The mining enterprise was "as distinctive as the more commonly known agricultural hacienda . . . [containing] stamp mills, washing vats, patios for incorporation, sheds for machinery, store rooms, stables for horses and mules, rooms to house workers and their families, a dwelling house for the owner, and a chapel."[8] The mines at Tecoyuca display many shafts, as well as houses, stamp mills, foundries, and churches (see plate 4).

Workers numbered from eighteen to eighty-five per mine. A large mine at Pánuco with four mills sold for 50,000 pesos in 1607. In 1620, a *hacienda de minas* (mining enterprise) in San Luis Potosí, containing fourteen smelters, two refinery areas, one stamp mill with ten hammers, and thirty slaves, was worth 70,000 pesos (not counting ranches and grazing sites). Mines in Zacatecas in the seventeenth century as a whole cost between 10,000 pesos and 50,000 pesos, depending on size and condition.[9]

Thus, mineownership became concentrated in relatively "few hands," as contemporaries liked to say. Around 1600 in Pachuca, the most productive district, there were only fifty-eight mines. In New Spain as a whole it is estimated there were some 370 refineries, according with the scholarly observation that by the end of the sixteenth century large enterprises tended to dominate the industry. The system of distributing the mercury itself was also centralized. Decisions about the apportionment were made yearly by the *junta de hacienda* (council of finance), composed of the viceroy, senior *oidor* (high court judge), the *fiscal*, treasury officials, and the senior accountant of the tribunal of accounts. According to the miners of New Galicia, this system deprived them of their fair share.[10]

Although excellent information exists about the total output of mining districts in the seventeenth century, little is known about the volume of production of individual mines during this period. A *visita* (royal inspection) of Zacatecas in 1668, however, provides the production figures of

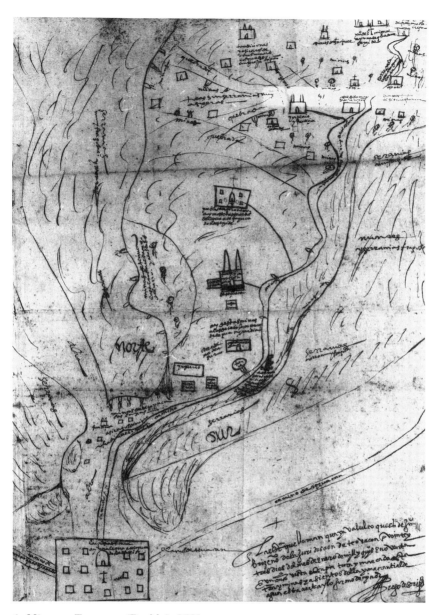

4. Mines at Tecoyuca (Puebla), 1591.

forty-three mines from 1658 to 1667, when production had risen from its trough of the early 1660s and was about to enter the boom of 1670 to 1690. Of the forty-two mineowners (one man owned two mines), eighteen produced a total of 10,000 marks or more during the decade from 1658 to 1667; nineteen produced 1,000 to 9,999 marks; and five produced fewer than 1,000 marks. The large producers, that is, 43 percent of the owners, accounted for 452,515 marks, or 82 percent of total production. On an annual basis, production ranged from the high reached by General Bartolomé Bravo, who mined an average of 8,693 marks (70,587 pesos) a year to the low of the *licenciado* (holder of masters degree) José Ruíz, who mined an average of 33 marks (268 pesos) a year. Most large producers had an annual average output of between 1,000 to 2,000 marks (8,120 to 16,240 pesos). The number of refineries in Zacatecas (forty-three) from 1658 to 1667 was about the same as it had been in 1603 (forty-five) and 1625 (forty-two).[11] Among a rather small number of mineowners, the men and women who accounted for the bulk of production in mid-century Zacatecas was even smaller.

BANKERS TO THE MINING SECTOR

Silver was the sine qua non of wholesaler merchant activity. Although not all wholesalers dealt in cochineal or indigo, the second and third major exports, all dealt in silver. All advanced credit at one time or another to individuals at different social levels in the silver-producing regions. The merchants themselves emphasized their role as financiers of the viceroyalty's major industry. In 1653, Simón de Haro claimed that he founded 250,000 marks (2,031,250 pesos) in the mint each year, about 55 percent of average annual registered production in that decade. The volume of silver bar he purchased from miners, and the prompt payment he made to them, Haro asserted, made him the mainstay of the mining provinces.[12] The correctness of Haro's claim allowed him to bargain successfully with the Crown for tax reductions and other favors.

As the description of the *hacienda de minas* suggests, the routine financial requirements of the industry were exigent. To take examples from periods of decline, in 1647, the *alcalde mayor* of San Luis Potosí regularly provided the miners of that city with clothes worth 40,000 to 50,000 pesos, and in the early 1650s, Pachuca mineowners needed 2,000 pesos of credit each week, or more than 100,000 pesos a year to run the mines. In 1673, 600,000 pesos' worth of merchandise was sent to Parral and other towns of New Biscay.[13] The penury of the mineowners was a constant theme in the policy debates of the seventeenth century. How should the problem be resolved? Debate focussed on the two major sources of credit: *alcaldes mayores* and merchants. Viceroy Monterrey proposed a royal monopoly. In 1598, he described the miners as caught in the grip of local merchants, forced to buy clothing for their Indian laborers which the wholesalers could not sell in the cities. He recommended that the Crown assume responsibility for the supply of vital goods and sell them for a reasonable price through contractors or through the *alcaldes mayores*, who in any case were already using royal funds to trade. The view that the Crown should provide essential supplies in addition to the mercury already under royal control was also put forward by Alonso de Oñate, legal representative of the miners of New Spain. In 1600, he proposed that in each fleet the Crown ship 4,000 quintales of iron, worked and to be worked, and 500 quintales of steel to be sold at the mines at cost without freight charges.[14]

The government, however, declined to become more active. Failing such intervention, the industry continued to rely on credit from private sources, chiefly merchants or royal officials acting in a private (illegal) capacity. Contemporaries saw a distinction between the two types of creditors and debated which of the two exploited the miners less. In 1618, the Pachuca miners complained of the abuses of the *alcaldes mayores*, who tried to exclude the merchants from their districts, harassed those who remained with lawsuits, and charged three or four times the value for supplies. The miners asked that the prohibition against *alcaldes'* trading be enforced and that merchants be ordered to live in the mining towns and provide supplies and credit. Viceroy Guadalcázar opposed the petition, probably because his power to appoint most local governors was a cherished source of viceregal patronage which he wanted to remain attractive to clients. Despite repeated royal discussion of enforcing the prohibition, or of eliminating the office of *alcalde mayor*, these officials continued to trade with the miners.[15] The need for credit and supplies was such that in 1625, the *cabildo* of Mexico City favored the miners receiving aid from either the merchants or the *alcaldes mayores*. It noted in 1636, however, that the former were discouraged from lending to miners because of the difficulty of collecting their debts, while the latter did not have as much money to lend. In 1651, Viceroy Conde de Liste noted that both merchants and *alcaldes* exploited the miners, who continued to need more credit than the local governors could provide.[16]

The distinction between local merchants and *alcaldes mayores* may seem artificial, since both were often sponsored by the Mexico City wholesalers, but it was, in fact, valid because there was competition in the mining centers between them. It was difficult to reform such a complex credit system, whether complexity is measured in terms of the number of regions included, social types involved, or the multiplication of lending agreements at the local level. Capital for the mines was generated locally to some extent, but the contribution from Mexico City wholesalers is evident from the numerous loans in the notarial records and inventories of Mexico City merchants to persons living in, or traveling to, the *reales de minas* (mining towns). There were no mining centers to which the merchant elite did not supply credit; those with sufficient capital reserves diversified their regional ties considerably. García del Salcedo extended credit simultaneously to residents of Zacatecas, Durango, Topia, Cuencamé, Zaqualpa, Culiacán, and Fresnillo. Others made loans in two or three different *reales de minas* at the same time.[17] Scholars of particular regions have also noted mineowners' reliance on capital from outside the area. In the mid-seventeenth century "many of the large general stores in Parral seem to have been operated by commercial agents of Mexico City merchants," and a large amount of merchandise was sold by the traveling merchants who were also their agents. Mexico City financing was quite prominent in Zacatecas in the 1650s; Guadalajara was another provincial center which received credit from the capital in the seventeenth century, although it was not itself a mining town. "In Guadalajara," inspector licenciado don Jines Morote Blásquez Dávila remarked in 1661, "the majority of the merchants whose shops bordered the central plaza were backed by silver merchants and travelling merchants sponsored by Mexico City wholesalers."[18]

Merchant-bankers in Mexico City routinely granted loans, usually from 2,000 pesos to 10,000 pesos each, or advanced merchandise, to several local agents residing in a number of mining towns, usually to be repaid within four months to a year. In 1652, Franco Alfonso lent 2,200 pesos *en reales* (in cash) to two local merchants of San Luis Potosí to be repaid within one year. Some transactions were small: Gregorio Pérez Passos lent 110 pesos in coin to Pedro Ramírez Jofre, a canon of the Cathedral of Durango, to be repaid in bar within four months' time. Debts of more than 10,000 pesos were usually the accumulation of several loans over a number of years. Inventories list the uncollectable debts, often twelve or fourteen years old, from mining towns; Captain Lucas Blanco of Durango owed García del Salcedo 6,082 pesos for eighteen years.[19]

Because royal policy was not to press miners unduly to pay debts to the treasury, and because the *alcaldes mayores* who had advanced credit naturally preferred to have debts owed them repaid first, the wholesalers of the capital could wait years before settlement. In addition to such better-known factors as mercury debts to the Crown which hindered repayment, there was another. Local retailers used the goods or cash advanced to them to establish their own local credit network. For example, when Captain Lope Ossorio Soto, a Mexico City wholesaler, died in 1637, he was owed 8,617 pesos by two Zacatecas merchants for China goods he had sold them over a period of time. They could not repay him because one of the merchants, Pedro de Jérez, had lent 5,705 pesos of the money he had received from sales of the China wares to two miners, Andrés Fernández Pan y Agua and Francisco Roldán de Arenas, to purchase supplies for the *hacienda de minas* they rented at Pánuco. Jérez could not repay Ossorio Soto because the miners could not repay Jérez, and he lost his store and became a tailor.[20]

The identity and relationships of these local agents are interesting. The *alcalde mayor* had a special importance for the wholesalers because, unlike other local agents, he held unique powers granted by the State. Among them, in the mines located within the district of the *audiencia* of Mexico such as Taxco and Pachuca, he was the sole legal provider of mercury. In the northern mining towns within the district of the *audiencia* of New Galicia, this function was performed by the *oficiales reales* (royal treasury officials) or by the *receptores de azogues* (officials receiving the royal mercury allotments). Like the local *cabildos*, the district governors could set prices of foodstuffs and enforce labor legislation; they could grant miners stays in the collection of debts. In the Indian towns the *alcaldes* administered the *repartimiento de comercio* (forced sale of goods). Because district governors were political appointees, they might have powerful friends in the capital who could be useful to the wholesalers. In the *visita* of *licenciado* don Diego Landeras de Velasco (a general investigation begun by him in 1606 and concluded by another official in 1611 and using records dating back to 1585), the *ensayador de minas* (official assayer) of Chichigapa, Francisco Mejía de Salazar, described the indebtedness of the miners to the district governor, Francisco de Torres. Torres acted as a *rescatador de plata*, buying unrefined silver ore from miners and sending it to his brother-in-law, Pedro de la Torre, the *secretario de gobernación* (viceregal secretary) in Mexico City. De la Torre, in turn, sold the silver to a merchant in the capital.[21] Finally, the *alcaldes* could help their merchant sponsors by allowing the silver owed by local *rescatadores* (middle men) to pay the royal mining tax at the *diezmo* (one-tenth) rate for miners rather than the *quinto* (one-fifth) rate for middlemen, or by pocketing silver received in payment for mercury and passing it along to their merchant backers.

The choice of other types of local agents was as ingenious as it was effective. Naturally, many were merchants lower down in the commercial hierarchy, including the notorious *rescatadores de plata*. Contemporaries were quite sensitive to the mercantile lines of command and distinguished the "stationary" merchants, who "sat in their shops in Mexico City, Puebla, and Veracruz,"[22] from the local correspondents. The local traders were either long-standing residents at a *real de minas*, who had an established relationship with a Mexico City wholesaler, or they were departing *vecinos* of the capital, sent out to the provinces to manage a retail outlet, obtain silver, and collect debts. The resident provincial might then establish his local credit ties, adding to the complexity of the tie which originated in the capital. For example, Pedro Díaz, a *vecino* of Zacatecas, was an agent for the Mexico City wholesaler Pedro Torres Castroverde, to whom Díaz delivered silver bar. Díaz lent Francisco Ruíz, another Zacatecas resident, part of Torres Castroverde's advance for the silver, and in 1641, Ruíz still owed 100 pesos of it to Díaz. Juan Fernández de Castro was a trader in Durango, who had purchased 800 pesos' worth of merchandise on credit from the capital wholesaler García de Salcedo. Later on, Fernández de Castro served as a bondsman for Enrique de Mesa, a Mexico City resident whom Salcedo sent out to the mining town of Topia to open a store for Salcedo. The company agreement between Mesa and Salcedo included the stipulation that Mesa receive 2,886 pesos in coin from Salcedo, to be returned in bar of full value within four and one-half months.[23]

Traveling merchants were an important category in the credit hierarchy. Called *mercaderes viandantes*, many of these agents were residents of Mexico City who made periodic trips to mining towns on their backers' behalfs to collect debts and sell merchandise. They were not the peripheral figures that the term implied in the late eighteenth century, for they were sent to major centers and entrusted with large sums. In 1621, Medina Reynoso empowered Gaspar Serrano to collect 5,180 pesos owed by residents of Zacatecas. In 1630, the wholesaler Tiburcio Urrea lent Captain Francisco de Montoya 20,000 pesos to buy merchandise to sell in the mining town of Cuenca. Sometimes provincial *vecinos* served as collection agents.[24] Traveling merchants might rise to stationary merchant status eventually, as did Gonzalo Aransemendi and Fernando Matías Rivera. Later it was Rivera who employed one Juan Pretel Gallego to go to Fresnillo and Zacatecas to collect the approximately 11,000 pesos owed to Rivera and return to Mexico City in four months. The resident provincial merchants and the traveling merchants were described as being in competition with one another on the local level, with the traveling merchants secretly underselling the resident merchants.[25]

The *visita* which began in 1661 identified all figures who marketed silver in the regions of Guanajuato, Guadalajara, San Luis, Zimapán, and Zacatecas. The findings accused these individuals of numerous violations against the miners and the royal treasury, such as passing off silver liable to the *quinto* as *diezmo* silver and smuggling untaxed silver out of the viceroyalty as tableware. The report emphasized the network of correspondents which linked the mining towns to Mexico City, Puebla, and Veracruz. The provincial *rescatadores de plata* were singled out as the worst offenders, a judgment which included the local merchants because the same man might perform both functions. The *receptores de azogues*, who were also often the local *alcaldes mayores*, were other villains. They were accused of forwarding untaxed silver to Veracruz for a very high commission, where "there were more than 12 persons who loaded it onto ships with the connivance of the ships' officers. The generals and supercargoes received a commission of three to four percent."[26]

Other parties accused of using illegal methods to obtain silver for merchants included carters and muleteers. Certainly these people were important agents. In 1651, Tiburcio Urrea bought 2,705 pesos' worth of silver coins from a muleteer of Guadalajara. At the death of Francisco Arellano Sotomayor, a wholesaler, he was owed 6,000 pesos for the purchase of silver by the wagonmaster Francisco de Ávila. Merchants might be bondsmen or *compadres* of their wagonmaster. Francisco Medina Reynoso's lending practices illustrate the existence of credit lines to various mining towns at one time. In the year of 1621, Francisco Reynoso, resident of Culiacán, owed Medina Reynoso money, as did Bartolomé Álvarez de Prado, the *factor* (royal business agent) of the treasury of Zacatecas, and don Alonso Tello de Guzmán, *alcalde mayor* of the mines of San Luis.[27]

Then there were the regular and secular clergy, who "with scandal take gold and silver from the miners and keep it in their houses and cells."[28] Sometimes the clergyman was an investor, other times, he was the mineowner himself. García de Salcedo formed a company with padre Esteban Rico to purchase silver for Salcedo from a miner in Sinaloa. As a typical provider of *avío*, Salcedo also sold tools to padre Francisco Antonio de Vergara, a Mercederian, for the working of the friar's mine in Zaqualpa.

In 1635, the wholesaler Melchor Terreros brought a lawsuit against padre Juan de Vigil, a priest of San Luis Potosí, for a balance of 250 pesos owed to Terreros for 490 pesos' worth of bar. Vigil claimed he was not obligated to pay because the suit had to be heard in the Bishopric of San Luis, not the Bishopric of Mexico. His contention was rejected, however, and he pledged three slaves as security for payment to Terreros. A vicar and miner of Zacatecas was charged with bribery during the *visita* in 1665. To the *alcaldes mayores* and *oficiales reales*, the merchants of different types, the wagoneers and the priests, and the *rescatadores de plata*, the inspectors added such other figures as the owners of smelters, the officials who separated gold from silver, the assayers, and the silversmiths.[29]

Miners themselves were not the subject of investigation at this time, but, of course, miners were also an important source of silver for wholesalers. They had to provide a bondsman for the mercury advanced to them by the royal treasury. This might be the origin of a long-term business relationship. Juan Luis Rivera, merchant and director of the mint, advanced large sums to miners: 34,261 pesos to a miner of San Luis and 24,025 pesos to a miner of Fresnillo. Typical were the smaller loans of Juan de Castellete: 6,879 pesos to Antonio Rodríguez Becerra in Sombrerete and 3,030 pesos to Alonso Hidalgo in San Luis Potosí. Andrés de Acosta, the major slave trader of the first quarter of the century, sold slaves to residents of San Luis and Zacatecas. His credit ranged from 150 pesos to 665 pesos. Unlike in the eighteenth century, merchants rarely owned mines themselves. When they did, it was because a miner could not repay the merchant and the mine was the only property on which the merchant could foreclose. In 1624, Agustín Medina Orozco acquired a *hacienda de minas* in Zacatecas when Cristóbal Tostado, a mineowner and local *cruzada* farmer, could not pay the 3,945 pesos he owed Medina. The mine was foreclosed, and Medina empowered his local agents to rent it. Tomás de Santos Corral acquired a mine in Tlalpujahua in a similar fashion upon the death of its owner, his debtor, in 1643, and he appointed an administrator to run it.[30] Direct investment in mining, however, does not appear to have been typical of Mexico City wholesalers. Given the many sources of silver bar, the wholesalers did not need to own the mines themselves. The credit pyramid enabled merchants to conduct their business without such involvement.

MERCHANTS AND THE MINT

The final stage in the production of silver was its coinage at the Mexico City mint. The institution of the mint, and the individuals who operated it, stood at the top of the silver industry in colonial Mexico. They influenced the monetary structure of the viceroyalty in several ways. First, because the coinage of silver bar was restricted to the Mexico City mint, it determined the money supply, defined as the amount and the quality of specie which would circulate domestically and abroad. Second, the mint influenced the proportion of silver which would circulate illegally. Illegal silver was bar or coin which had not paid the decreed taxes at some stage in its production. For example, mint officials could coin silver which had paid the *diezmo* rate rather than the legal *quinto* rate or which had not been taxed at all. In this manner, the mint defrauded the Crown of the income that the mint had been established to provide. Finally, the mint enriched a very small group of persons, who used part of their gains to advance their own position and who also provided investment capital to the mining industry and other branches of the economy. This group included officials of the mint, most of whom were Mexico City merchants or their sons, and a category of traders called *mercaderes de plata* who supplied the mint with the silver bar to be made into coins. These merchants were at the pinnacle of the credit hierarchy. By varying the discount rate on bar, by coining silver on a very large scale, and, illegally, by evading foundry and mint fees, these mint merchants became wealthy and wielded a great deal of influence.

The Crown ordered the mint established in 1535, and the following year it was in operation. Although it was periodically proposed that a mint also be set up in northern New Spain, such a step was not taken until the end of the colonial period. Before the reforms of 1728, the mint contained two sections: the *casa de fundición* (foundry) and the *casa de moneda* (mint). The former carried on the same assay activities as similar institutions at the royal treasury offices in the different cities of the viceroyalty. The latter was unique and contributed to the preeminence of the Mexico City merchants. In 1600, there were ten types of mint officials (table 9). There were six *oficios mayores*, posts sold by order of the Crown. This group included both the high-level *ministros* (ministers) and the lower-level *oficiales* (officials). Below the *oficios mayores* were the four *oficios menores* posts sold by order of the viceroy whose occupants were all called *operarios*, although some were manual workers and some were not. There was

Table 9. Income and Hierarchy of Mint Officials
in the Late Sixteenth Century (in Pesos)

Title of Post	Number of Posts	Purchase Price	Annual Income	% of Purchase Price Represented by Annual Income
Oficios mayores[a]				
Ministros				
Tesorero				
(Treasurer, director)	1	130,000	12,000–14,000	9–11
Ensayador y fundidor				
(Assayer)	1	56,000	7,000	13
Balansario				
(Weigher)[b]	1	7,000	1,600–1,700	23–24
Oficiales				
Tallador				
(Die cutter)	1	80,000[c]	5,000–6,000	6–8
Escribano				
(Notary)	1	8,000	1,600	20
Guardas				
(Guards)	2	—	1,600	
Oficiales menores				
Negros				
(Laborers)	20	—	—	
Capataces				
(Bar cutters)		—	500–600	
Monederos or				
Acuñadores				
(Coin fashioners)	20		About 400	
Alcaldes ordinarios				
(Magistrates)		—	120	
Alguaciles				
(Constables)		—	120	

Sources: Aiton, "First American Mint," 210–11; AGI, Audiencia de México 23, 26 November 1597, ff. 1–4.

[a]These posts were sold by the Crown, the others were sold by the Viceroy.

[b]There was also an *apartador de oro*, who separated gold from the silver bar, but he does not seem to have been part of the mint hierarchy in 1597.

[c]This was the price fetched somewhat later in 1611, although the office did not change hands until 1619.

also an *apartador de oro* (assayer of gold). The *oficios mayores* often had *tenientes* (lieutenants) attached but they were not formally part of the mint hierarchy.[31]

The *tesorero de la casa de moneda*, assisted by a *teniente*, was the chief administrator who oversaw both the foundry and the mint (figure 4). In the foundry the *ensayador y fundidor* assayed, that is, determined the quality of the bar and had it brought to the correct fineness. The *balansario* (weigher) then weighed it and had the foundry foremen remove the *quinto* or *diezmo*, the royal tax, from each bar. Some silver had already gone through this process at the provincial foundry. The bar then left the foundry stamped with a number, its grade, and its weight. In the mint the *tallador* (die cutter) stamped the bar with the royal die. All silver then had the *señoreaje* (royal minting charge) and *braceaje* (mint director's charge) deducted. The *capataces* (bar cutter) then cut the bar into coins and the *acuñadores* (coin fashioners) molded and imprinted them correctly. Both settled accounts with the treasurer and his lieutenant at periodic intervals.[32] The other staff at the mint was that found in many bureaucratic agencies: constable, notary, guards, civil magistrate, and black slave laborers. Only silver coins of different denominations were produced at this time. Gold was taxed but not allowed to be coined until 1675. Copper was coined initially, but since the Indians for whom the small denominations were destined did not accept it, its coinage was discontinued after 1541.[33]

Such was the bureaucracy at the Mexico City mint. The four men who were the treasurer, assayer, weigher, and die cutter controled the coinage of 3 or 4 million pesos a year. During 1590 to 1660, the four high-level posts were held by fourteen people. Nine were merchants or their sons, while two were aldermen of landed family background (a father and son), and two were of unknown occupation. One post was also donated to a convent by a merchant. The cost of these offices was so high that only a person with access to considerable liquid capital could purchase them. In 1585, the office of treasurer of the mint fetched 130,000 pesos plus 20,000 pesos' worth of slaves and tools. In 1629, the treasuryship cost 275,000 pesos. The post of assayer cost 140,000 pesos in 1609, and 160,000 pesos in 1633. The offices of die cutter and weigher cost less but were still expensive compared to other offices (chapter 4). The former sold for 80,000 pesos in 1619 and 100,000 pesos by 1632. The latter went for 13,000 pesos in 1611 and 20,000 pesos in 1620 and 1639. Merchants had both the motive and the means to occupy such posts. From 1608 to

Table 10. Sums Coined by *Mercaderes de Plata* at Mexico City Mint, 1585–1607 (Annual Average during Years Indicated, in Marks)

Merchant	1585–89	1590–94	1595–99	1600–1604	1605–7
Duarte	25,872	31,358	3,088		
Enríquez				20,522	22,962
Fernández Celi				59,492	38,895
Gutiérrez Çarfate, D.	34,035	97,383	101,257	70,651	37,607
Gutiérrez Çarfate, P.				46,186	38,478
Gutiérrez Gil	39,170	59,171	5,897	42,422	36,433
Leardo			97,293	62,259	
Miguel [a]					
Montemolin				36,730	39,584
Oñate		25,920			
Pacho					33,397
Rodríguez Soto	31,523	34,608	37,769		
Rossales			85,244	63,105	38,658
Ruíz				23,198	37,109
Vilches					23,755
Totals	130,600	248,440	330,548	424,565	346,878

Source: AGI, Escribanía de Cámara, 272A, *piezas* 2–6, and 272B, *piezas* 7–15.
[a]The entries for Miguel are incomplete.

1660, two sons of wholesaler Diego Matías de Vera, don Melchor and then don Juan, held the treasuryship. Don Pedro de Toledo y Mendoza, and then his son, filled the post of die cutter from 1630 to 1665. The López Erenchun family held the position of weigher from 1611 through 1653.[34]

Mint officials received the silver bar to be coined from the *mercaderes de plata*, an elite group of traders within the elite of Mexico City wholesalers and silver dealers. The process of transfer, which began with the local *rescatador*, miner, storekeeper, or *alcalde*, culminated in the acquisition of bar by a strikingly small number of men who could be called mint merchants. A select group supplied the mint with the silver bar from which all the colony's specie was produced: nine or ten in the first decade of the century, seven in 1617, six or seven in 1631, two to four in 1651, and four in 1661. Each of these men coined very large amounts of silver. Table 10 lists the sixteen *mercaderes de plata* who were active at different times between 1585 and 1607. From 1590 to 1594, for example, five merchants coined an annual average of 248,440 marks (2,012,364 pesos). From 1600 to 1604, nine merchants coined an annual total of 424,565 marks (3,438,977 pesos).[35] It is hard to imagine a more monopolistic situation.

The mint bureaucracy and the mint merchants were closely intertwined. Officials usually had served as *mercaderes de plata* before they purchased their posts, and they continued to have financial dealings with the silver traders. Director don Juan de Vera, who held the post for thirty-one years, was directly indebted to the seven *mercaderes de plata* who enabled him to acquire his treasuryship. These *compañeros* (partners) co-financed don Juan's purchase of his brother's post in 1629, each member of the company putting up 20,000 pesos. Subsequently, some of the shareholders sold their portion to other merchants to obtain ready cash (chapter 6). But *mercader de plata* connections to the mint were not limited to the top posts. They extended credit to silversmiths, who also sometimes acted as lieutenants, to bar cutters, and to coin fashioners. In each decade certain merchants made loans of 300 or 400 pesos to these personnel. In the 1600s, it was Fernando Matías Rivera; in the 1620s, it was Juan de Castellete and Francisco Medina Reynoso; and in the 1650s, it was Antonio de Millán. The silver traders' influence at the mint was a subject of comment by contemporaries, who may not have known about the loans but who did see the merchants present at the mint on a routine basis. The mint merchants were "up at the crack of dawn," one critic put it, supervising the refining carried out by the workers, guarding the silver while it was checked by the assayer, and handing the bar over to the die cutter to be coined.[36] Silver traders and mint officials did not always work together harmoniously. In 1618, the seven *mercaderes de plata* brought suit against the *ensayador*, the wholesaler Melchor de Cuéllar, for charging them 2 reales for every 10 marks assayed instead of the stipulated one real for every 10 marks, a dispute resolved in Cuéllar's favor.[37] But such occasional conflicts were characteristic of intra-elite relations and did not alter the fact that a commercial and bureaucratic elite controlled the mint.

These close ties enabled both officials and *mercaderes de plata* to amass large fortunes. The officials gained income from State-sanctioned fees and from bribes; table 9 presents the considerable income from legitimate fees in 1597. The treasurer is in a class by himself. Two other *oficiales mayores* also had incomes higher than the salary of a high court judge, the most prestigious office after the viceroy. The similarity of incomes of the weigher, guard, and notary, positions of very different status, is also of interest. It is noteworthy that the supervisors of manual laborers (*capata-*

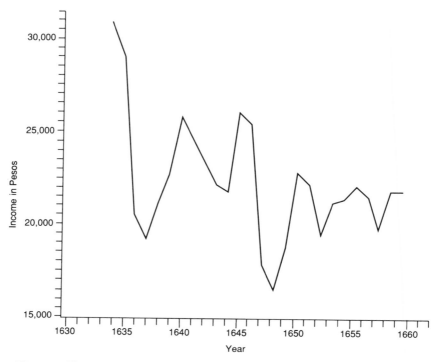

Figure 4. Two-Year Moving Average of Income of the Treasurer of the Mint, 1634–60. *Source*: AGI, Vínculos 284, ff.350r–351r and 460r–471r.

ces and *acuñadores*) earned so much more than the justice and constable, a post so poorly paid that "nobody wants it."[38]

Of course, income fluctuated with the amount of silver minted, as the range given in table 9 indicates for the posts of treasurer, die cutter, and weigher; for example, the die cutter earned between 5,000 and 6,000 pesos in the late 1590s. The *tesorero de la casa de moneda*'s income fluctuated considerably ranging from 36,893 pesos in 1630 to 14,741 pesos only six years later as figure 4 shows.[39] (The percentage which the mint official received as commission remained the same throughout the period.) When the assayer Melchor de Cuéllar was, like all public officials, ordered to declare his income to the Crown, he stated that since he had purchased the post in 1610, his income ranged from 13,000 pesos to 14,000 pesos, but that in the year 1622, it was 10,000 pesos. Cuéllar's assertion about his income before 1622 is more or less confirmed by the records of the lawsuit brought against him. In 1615 he earned 13,858 pesos; in 1616,

15,232 pesos; and in 1617, 12,565 pesos.[40] In addition to considerable year-to-year variation in silver production, incomes were higher in the first three decades of the seventeenth century than in the late sixteenth century. The treasurer's earnings in the 1580s had ranged from 12,000 to 14,000 pesos, while the assayer's predecessor earned 7,000 pesos earned in 1597.

These lucrative offices allowed their owners to acquire much capital. Don Melchor de Vera and Pedro de Toledo y Mendoza had fortunes of close to 200,000 pesos, and Melchor de Cuéllar declared his assets to be 400,300 pesos in 1622. The *mercaderes de plata* also benefited. One of the principal mint merchants of 1606 to 1608 was charged with making a fortune of 300,000 pesos, which gave him an annual income of 10,000 pesos.[41] In 1618, an observer asserted that all the mint merchants had grown rich because "in addition to the earnings being very large, the business was completely without risk."[42]

Silver traders speculated in the silver market, just as *hacendados* speculated in grain or beef. In 1598 and 1602, Viceroy Monterrey complained about the shortage of coins, which he attributed to the small number of mint merchants. The merchants could also pay a lower price for the bar when it was more plentiful and only conform to the official valuation of a mark as 65 reales when it suited them. When silver traders purchased bar from provincial suppliers, whether miners or other persons, they charged a commission known as the discount rate. The higher the discount, the lower the price the seller received for the silver. The discount rate was commonly 1 real per peso (of 8 reales), or 8.1 reales the mark (of 65 reales). The ratio was the same for each denomination. In other words, the merchant paid the miner 8 coined reales for 9 reales of taxed silver. Such a discount gave the merchant a commission of 12.5 percent, a rate that drew continual unfavorable comment from critics at the time. Twelve percent was high compared to the interest of 5 percent received on *censos* or *depósitos*, but it was similar to other types of commissions such as that for serving as executor of an estate or for collecting a tax. Certainly, a 12.5 percent commission allowed silver merchants who dealt in large volumes to gain substantial incomes. The situation was, however, not simply a question of applying the standard discount to the volume traded. It was more complicated, offering the merchant both greater opportunity for gain and for loss, because both the discount rate and the fineness of the silver bar fluctuated. "Merchants bought silver bar with discount at 2 or 3 reales the mark more or less than the usual 8 reales, *depending on the abundance or scarcity of reales*."[43] It is not surprising that the discount rate charged reflected the bargaining position of the two parties involved. When more coin was available, silver merchants collected a higher, more favorable discount. In times of silver scarcity, the discount dropped; merchants cited the lower rate of 7.8 reales the mark in 1648 and 7.5 reales the mark in 1661.

The other variable was the fineness of the bar. Through the early seventeenth century a mark of taxed silver was officially valued at 65 reales. Because silver produced by amalgamation was of higher fineness, however, a mark of it was actually worth 67 or 68 reales. In 1607, for example, Juan Luis Rivera dealt in some silver marks valued at 67 reales. Contemporaries acknowledged the considerable variability in the value of bar. In 1620, the miner Juan de Zavala referred to the difficulty of assessing his estate because of the fluctuation in the fineness of the silver. In 1700, the official valuation was changed to 70 reales the mark, while discount rates were cited at 7.5 reales and 8 reales.[44] Given this proportion, the rate had fallen over the seventeenth century. The fluctuation in fineness of the bar meant that until 1700, a merchant could pay the miner for a bar of silver officially valued at 65 reales but actually able to produce 67 or 70 reales. This discrepancy was an important source of mercantile profit.

From the discount rate the merchant charged, he had to deduct his costs: foundry and mint fees, freight and storage charges, new advances to producers, and other expenses. The final profit returned to the merchant, therefore, could be less than the 12.5 percent discount rate, depending on what he made. However, merchants whose rate of profit was low but who traded a large volume of silver could still reap impressive gains. Assume the mint merchant netted only 5 percent for each purchase. Between 1595 and 1599, Cristóbal Rodríguez Soto coined 37,769 marks a year as an annual average (table 10). If he obtained a 5 percent profit, he received 1,888.5 marks, or ($\times$ 65 r. = 122,749 r. divided by 8) 15,344 pesos, annually as net gain, more than the treasurer of the mint received from fees. Between 1605 and 1607, Francisco de Rossales coined 38,658 marks as an annual average. If 5 percent equals 1,933 marks ($\times$ 65 r. = 125,645 r. divided by 8), he realized a 15,706 pesos profit. Other years the amounts were higher.

To these legal methods of making money, the silver traders added tax evasion and smuggling. By not paying the *diezmo* or *quinto* taxes, the mint merchant reduced his costs by 10 to 20 percent. Because it was risky to trade this contraband silver bar, merchants had an incentive to smuggle it out of the viceroyalty by way of direct trade with foreigners in the Caribbean, or by shipping it hidden on the fleet to Spain. In the *visita* of 1606 to 1611, the sending of *plata de rescate* (untaxed silver) to Castille or to China was a standard accusation. The export of contraband silver is thought to have grown rapidly from the 1630s; in 1651, one-third of the silver that reached Spain from Mexico was thought to be contraband.[45] In 1661, Viceroy Conde de Baños wrote of the export of untaxed silver "originating in the mining towns and protected by the most powerful people in the Indies."[46]

Mint merchants also coined contraband silver. Landeras de Velasco's investigation concluded that between 1585 and 1607, most mint merchants defrauded the Crown in this manner. One offender was Gonzalo Gutiérrez Gil, who during twenty-three years at the mint coined 842,599 marks of silver, 26,936 marks (3.2 percent) of which were untaxed. Gutiérrez Gil's illegal 26,936 marks equal 218,855 pesos. Over twenty-three years, on the average, therefore, he coined 9,515 pesos' worth of untaxed silver bar a year. Another mint merchant, Toribio Fernández de Celi, coined 297,460 marks of silver during five years, 5,143 marks (1.7 percent) of which were untaxed. Because 5,143 marks equal 41,787 pesos, Fernández Celi coined 8,357 pesos of untaxed silver on the average each year. During three years of coining, Rodrigo Ruíz coined 111,327 marks of silver, 8,136 marks (7.3 percent) of which were untaxed. Because 8,136 marks equal 66,105 pesos, Ruíz was coining 22,035 pesos *a year* of contraband silver on the average.[47]

Other abuses charged included devaluing silver coins in various ways. After the bar was assayed, the mint merchant might reduce the fineness it was declared to have by mixing lower-grade silver, sometimes from Peru, into the bar. He might persuade the weigher to false weight the bar, or the notary to record less bar than the merchant actually presented.[48] As with any official inquiry of powerful people, the amount of fraud uncovered was only the tip of the iceberg. The proportion of untaxed silver that Gonzalo Gutiérrez Gil and his colleagues coined illegally, therefore, was probably higher than the Landeras de Velasco *visita* revealed. The most significant information the investigation provided is its description of the structure of relationships at the mint that allowed mint merchants to make illegal profits there. By occupancy of key posts, by extending credit to their associates in the top-ranking positions and to lower-level bureaucrats, and by their physical presence at the foundry and minting process, a small group of the silver traders exercised control.

A final source of revenue for the mint merchants was the commission some received for minting royal silver. Every year it was usual for four or five men to be charged with converting into coin the silver bar the Crown received for taxes. The coins were destined for the royal treasury in Madrid, for the payment of public officials in New Spain, and for defense costs in New Spain, the Philippines, and the Caribbean. The mint merchant paid coin to the treasury of the district of Mexico in exchange for a specified amount of royal silver bar, received as taxes; he then supervised the coinage of the royal silver bar at the mint. Within a set period, usually four months, the merchant turned the new coins over to the treasury and received his commission. For example in 1606, Pedro Gutiérrez Çarfate handed over to the treasury 3,346 pesos in coin and received 382 marks of taxed silver of standard fineness in order to return it in coins within four months.[49] The mint merchant received a commission of 26 maravedís the mark, or 1.06 percent, for his work. One-half of the commission was paid by deducting it from the coins the merchant handed back to the treasury office from the royal share. In other words, one-half of the commission was paid by the Crown. The other half was paid by the *oficiales mayores* of the mint. This activity went on throughout the year; each month the mint merchant received new bar and returned to the royal treasury part, or all, of the coin he had minted out of the previously received royal bar. The merchant received allotments of bar worth varying amounts. The bar might be worth 2,000 or 3,000 pesos' worth or as much as 135,000 pesos at a time. The 1.06 percent commission, therefore, might provide as few as 20 pesos or as much as 1,350 pesos per allotment.[50]

The Crown's reliance on the silver traders to perform this crucial function is another example of the State farming out duties intrinsic to its operation. It is difficult to imagine a more sensitive government function than coinage. The government's attitude enabled a powerful private interest group, the elite of the *mercaderes de plata*, to gain great influence.

CONCLUSION

Mining was central to the colonial Mexican economy because silver was always the principal export and provided a stable medium of exchange within the viceroyalty. Credit backed by silver was what made the Hispanicized economy work. It also affected part of the Indian economy through the *repartimiento de comercio* and the sale of tribute goods. Mining, the provision of credit, and the money supply were all knit together through the activities of Mexico City's merchant elite. Although it is known that some merchants in the capital financed mining enterprises, the breadth of their involvement and the connection they provided between the first stage (mining the silver) and the last (minting the coins) has not yet been sufficiently appreciated.

The requirements of the silver industry dovetailed nicely with economic preferences of the merchant elite. Capital intensive and dominated by large enterprises, mines needed outside credit, and only the merchants and *alcaldes mayores* (many backed by merchants) were willing to offer it on a regular basis. Credit originating in the capital was channeled to the mining towns, where a wide range of people used it to finance silver production. The State disliked the fact that mineowners were overcharged by their creditors but it was unwilling to provide royal funds, and so this important sector continued to operate privately, except for the mercury monopoly.

The government also surrendered autonomy over the production of coin. The Mexico City mint was controlled by a bureaucratic-commercial elite of officials who were or had been merchants and by the *mercaderes de plata*. A few men minted hundreds of thousands of pesos each year. They determined the amount and quality of coin and the proportion which circulated without paying taxes. In so doing they made fortunes for themselves because although silver production fluctuated year by year, the general trend was upward between the late sixteenth century and the 1630s. Typical of trade at this time, much of officials' and mint merchants' incomes derived from commissions. Because the industry was monopolistic and a few persons dealt in large volumes, even a low commission (gained through official fees for minting privately owned silver, the discount rate paid by mineowners, or the percentage received from the Crown for minting its coin) could provide high income. These transactions were entirely legal. However, mint officials and *mercaderes de plata* also illegally evaded taxes and adulterated coin. The mint officials did not have the status of such bureaucrats as high court judges, but they probably made more money and were important to the viceregal economy.

Mining was the ideal enterprise for a merchant investor because it produced goods of high value per unit, was heavily capitalized, was located near Mexico City or on commonly used transport routes, and was easily subject to a monopolistic system of finance and distribution. If the merchant elite had simply reinvested its mining and trade profits, it would have had a significant impact on New Spain's economic evolution. In addition, however, wholesalers financed, owned, or leased plantations, farms, artisan shops, ranches, and urban real estate. Thus, their influence was broader, for better or for worse, than it initially appears.

CHAPTER III

The Mexican Economy and Merchant Capital:

Agriculture, Manufacturing, and Urban Real Estate

In 1651, the *visitador* Pedro de Gálvez, struck by the large debts owed to the royal treasury, concluded: "In this realm the chief source of wealth is trade, and there is no real property which can be relied on to produce wealth as in other regions."[1] Risky as trade was, the profits from agriculture, ranching, and manufacturing were even more elusive, in part because they were generally lower. Yet Mexico's merchant elite did invest in these branches of the economy, and in the more secure areas of urban real estate and public office. This chapter will present an overview of the main branches of the Hispanicized economy and trace wholesalers' differing relationships with each. On the assumption that merchants were rational actors, their investment preferences, affected by location, volume, value, and profits to be made, are a rough guide to the characteristics of the different sectors in the first two-thirds of the seventeenth century.

AGRICULTURE VERSUS TRADE?

Agriculture and trade were distinct types of economic activity. According to the traditional European historiography, the figures of large landowners and long-distance merchants were also distinct, and, in some respects, competitive social types. Landowners, agricultural specialists, derived income from cultivating a region's characteristic products and selling them nearby. Merchants, with their mastery of foreign currencies and trade routes, traveled frequently, dealt in international markets, and did not directly participate in local agriculture. This view of the trader's relationship to the land definitely applies to the Mexico City wholesalers in one respect. As a group, they remained primarily a mercantile and financial class. In general, the majority did not buy rural estates—although they certainly had the means to do so—and preferred to obtain their articles of trade through credit relationships with nonmerchant producers.

Such a conclusion does not tell the whole story, however, for it omits the fact that a segment of the merchant class did purchase haciendas and plantations and thus merged with an agricultural class. Much recent research on other regions and periods of Latin America has emphasized that urban-based capitalists acquired rural properties for social status; to diversify their sources of income; to produce, as well as trade, particular goods (vertical integration); and to obtain collateral for loans. This was certainly true for an important group within the merchant community in the first two-thirds of the seventeenth century. A comparison of the dates merchants traded and the dates they owned land indicates that 60 percent continued to trade after purchasing their rural properties. Despite the high social value placed on landowner status, wholesalers did not abandon their old occupation to become full-time *hacendados*.[2] Their caution was a function of the continued profitability of trade, even when at a lower level.

SUGAR PLANTATIONS

Thomas Gage, the English Dominican friar who traveled widely in Mesoamerica from 1625 to 1637, enthusiastically praised the dainty and luscious preserves which he ate on his journeys.[3] *Dulces de tierra* were great favorites among all ranks of society, and sugar was the requisite ingredient. In the seventeenth century the market for sugar was primarily domestic. At the beginning of the period there were approximately fifty to sixty *ingenios* (water-driven mills) and large *trapiches* (animal-powered mills) in New Spain and its dependencies. It has been estimated that a mill produced from 3,000 to 4,000 *arrobas* to 20,000 *arrobas* each year, that is, a minimum of 150,000 to 240,000 *arrobas* (at twenty-five pounds per *arroba*) for the whole region.[4] Since the price of sugar was often 4 or more pesos an *arroba*, using the lowest estimate for production and number of mills, this meant that sugar production was worth at the very least 600,000 pesos a year in the early seventeenth century. The high value of this sector may be appreciated by comparing it to production of another commodity, cochineal, the second most important export of New Spain. In 1620, exports of cochineal were worth 1,239,502 pesos.[5]

Sugar was a revolutionary crop. Its cultivation spread rapidly in the last decades of the sixteenth century and affected the regions where it was introduced so dramatically that the Crown tried to curtail its production. Its diffusion was part of the commercialization of agriculture in general, which occurred in the wake of the *matlazáhuatl* (disease with typhus symptoms) epidemic of 1576, the depopulation of Indian lands, and the growing Hispanic demand for foodstuffs. By the early 1600s sugar had taken root in four major areas: the Cuernavaca-Cuautla basin, the Atlixco-Orizaba-Veracruz crescent, the Valley of Miahuatlán in southern Oaxaca, and the province of Michoacán. Over the century production also spread widely—to Córdoba, San Luis Potosí, the Huasteca east of San Luis, Huachinango, the region west of Guadalajara, and other far-flung areas of the viceroyalty.

This rapid advance was all the more remarkable because sugar production was a demanding enterprise. It required a work force able to perform differentiated tasks, many requiring special skills. One sugar plantation lists sixty-one different job titles.[6] Government opposition to the use of Indian labor in sugar mills expressed in the decrees of 1599 and 1601, although not always effective, frustrated sugar entrepreneurs, as did the more basic problem of Indian population decline. The answer until the mid-century was imported black slaves, who were, in addition, believed to be harder workers and more easily trained than Indians. After the 1650s in Morelos, creole black slaves, Indians, and mulattos became the predominant groups on the plantations; a similar pattern developed later in Córdoba and this was probably typical of the evolution of the work force from slave to wage elsewhere. However, the high cost of slaves, usually 250 to 300 pesos for an adult male, constituted a heavy burden on the owner's resources. Many plantations had 80 or 100 slaves, and there were even some with 200.[7]

Irrigation canals and, in some cases, dams and aqueducts were another expense characteristic of sugar cultivation. Requiring water to power the more productive water mills and to irrigate the canefields, planters consistently faced expenses which other cultivators did not necessarily have. Efficient utilization of existing waterworks prompted acquisition of more land to plant cane. But, obtaining additional land was a complex procedure. The owner of Atotonilco, with its canefields and water-powered mill, sought more lands (see plate 5). Receipt of viceregal *mercedes* (royal grant of land or office) and purchase or forcible removal from Indian owners were two common methods, which could be challenged by competitors.[8]

In addition to workers, water, and land, planters needed refinery equip-

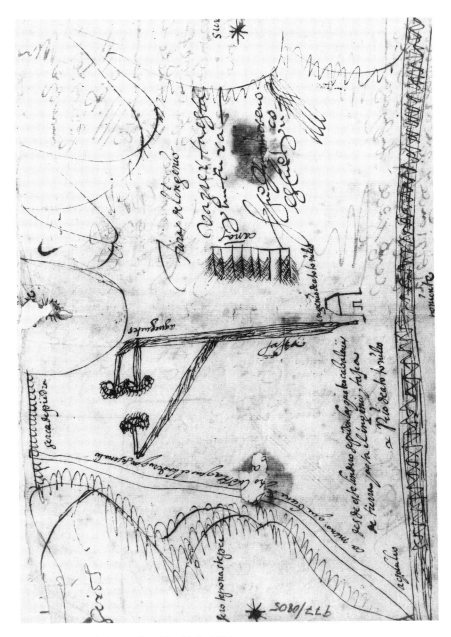

5. Sugar Mill of Atotonilco (Puebla), 1614.

ment, livestock, and buildings. Thus mills were extremely expensive enterprises. Of twelve mills between 1606 and 1654, six sold for between 30,000 and 82,000 pesos and five for 100,000 pesos or more.[9] De la Peña considers values of 50,000 to 75,000 pesos typical. Examples of lower prices come from the late seventeenth century, when these mills had deteriorated. Theoretically, capital could have been generated internally through profits, but, in reality, plantations were voracious consumers of outside credit. Scholars have stressed the role of different branches of the Church and merchants in capitalizing sugar cultivation.[10] Here, the close relationship between wholesalers and plantations in Morelos, Puebla, and some other regions will be substantiated using data from the Mexico City side. I will also show that merchants owned and rented, as well as financed, these mills. Indian *cajas de comunidad* (Indian community treasuries) and local *hacendados*, of course, as well as the Church also played a role.

There was definitely a very neat fit between the needs of sugar planters and the capacities of the merchant class. Planters required not only credit and coin but also imported goods such as iron tools. Black slaves were crucial. Planters needed the viceregal distribution network operated by the merchants from Mexico City, the chief market for the Cuernavaca-Cuautla sugar region. For other regions, they sold also to the merchants in the nearest city, such as Puebla, Veracruz, Oaxaca, or Jalapa, who might well be correspondents of Mexico City traders.[11] The timing and volume of shipments to major centers of consumption was important. Wholesalers, for their part, were attracted by the industry, in part because much of it was located near major trade routes and in part because—given the limited number of mills—cane processing was quite centralized. This made it easier for merchants to control overall supply, a strategy they tried to use in all their dealings. Another method was for wholesalers to influence supply by becoming planters themselves. Finally, profits in the sugar sector could be high because the State did not set prices for sugar as it did for basic foodstuffs. Sugar provided some of the viceroyalty's major fortunes in the seventeenth century.[12]

The Morelos Connection

The long history of Mexico City merchant participation in sugar cultivation, and the practice of individuals rotating through owner, renter, and creditor roles, are illustrated by the history of the principal mills of the Cuernavaca-Cuautla region in the late sixteenth and seventeenth centuries. These enterprises also show the trend of clerical acquisition and the central role of the Marqués de Cortés's holdings in this part of the country. In 1600, Barrett asserts, there were twelve *ingenios* and *trapiches* in the Cuernavaca-Cuautla region.[13] Other mills were founded later in the century, but the importance of the former may be inferred from the fact that all remained in operation at least until the end of the seventeenth century. Of these twelve mills, in the early part of the century five were owned by Mexico City merchants, two were founded and continued by ecclesiastical institutions, one was part of the Marquesado domain, and the rest belonged to officials or landowners. Over the century, three of the wholesalers' mills remained in merchant hands while the other two passed to the clergy. Two mills previously owned by officials were sold to clerics, and another to a Mexico City merchant. The Marquesado mill remained in the Cortés estate. A brief sketch follows of the interlocking ownership and rental of these plantations.

The *trapiche Santa Ana Amanalco*, one of the oldest mills in New Spain, was founded by Bernardino del Castillo in 1531 on land granted by Cortés. In the 1580s, it was purchased by the Mexico City merchant Diego Caballero, Castillo's son-in-law. Caballero, an important figure in the Valley of Cuernavaca, also owned the *ingenio Santa Inés Las Amilpas* in Cuautla. In the early seventeenth century he donated Santa Inés to the convent of that name that he and his wife founded. Between 1599 and 1612, the debts incurred by Santa Ana Amanalco forced Caballero to sell it.[14] He was one of the minority of merchants who had ceased his trading activities after purchasing land. The purchaser of Santa Ana Amanalco was Andrés Arias Tenorio, another wholesaler, who at this time had dealings with another important planter of Cuernavaca, the Marqués del Valle, owner of the *Tlaltenango* mill. In 1613, Arias Tenorio was processing cane from the Tlalcomulco fields of the Marqués; a few years later Pedro Cortés granted him six *caballerías* (630 acres) for *his* Amanalco mill. From 1625 to 1634, Arias Tenorio obtained the lease of the Tlaltenango mill, so that he acted as owner and renter at one time. Then, in 1632, he purchased *San Nicolás Pantitlán* at auction for 60,000 pesos. San Nicolás had been founded about 1599 by Lucio Lopio Lampertengo, a *vecino* of Mexico City who was probably a merchant of Italian descent. It evolved from small amounts of land purchased from Indians and from several viceregal grants, as had Caballero's Santa Inés estate.[15]

Andrés Arias Tenorio's sons Francisco and Melchor inherited Santa Ana Amanalco and San Nicolás Pantitlán (along with its Hacienda Michiapa) from their father. Their holdings, however, were confiscated by the Inquisition in the 1640s, and ownership passed to the family of their chief creditor, the merchant Antonio Millán and his son Félix, who paid off the 88,000 pesos of accumulated debts. The family held both mills, Santa Ana and San Nicolás, at least until 1696. Santa Ana and possibly San Nicolás as well then passed to the Aranda (or Araña) family. This clan also owned *Nuestra Señora Concepción Temixco* and the *trapiche* Nuestra Señora Guadalupe, which was active from 1626 to 1660 and then from the 1670s (which does not seem to have been included in Barrett's count). N.S. Concepción began with viceregal *mercedes* in 1607 and *censos perpetuos* in the 1620s granted by the Cortés estate, and in the 1610s had passed to Captain Gaspar Yáñez Osorio. By 1670, it was owned by the Mexico City wholesaler Pedro de Eguren and then his cousin, Antonio de Aranda. Aranda, a Puebla merchant and alderman, was also co-lessee of the Cortés Atlacomulco mill and the uncle of the Mexico City merchant Antonio de Munabe. Aranda's daughter married a wholesaler, Francisco García Cano, who also owned Nuestra Señora Guadalupe.[16] Thus, for many years of the seventeenth century a succession of Mexico City merchants either owned or leased five of the Valley of Cuernavaca's twelve major mills.

A sixth mill had the same type of ties to the merchant elite. *San Pedro Mártir Casasano* was founded in the 1570s by the *contador* (accountant) of the treasury of the district of Mexico, Gordián Casasano, son-in-law of the wholesaler Toribio Fernández de Celi. Sometime between 1599 and 1624, the mill passed to merchant Tomás de Zuaznavar y Aguirre. In 1639, his son Juan inherited it and continued to operate it in the 1660s. The mill was still in existence in 1746.[17] A seventh mill, the *trapiche San Nicolás Tolentino* by the late 1680s was owned by a priest, *bachiller* (holder of bachelor's degree) Felipe Pérez Delgado, who rented it for a time to Captain don Antonio Millán, a nephew of the don Félix Millán who owned Santa Ana Amanalco.[18]

Clerical institutions owned sugar estates in the valley from the late sixteenth century, when the Order of San Hipólito began to develop the holdings which became *Hacienda Hospital*, and the Convent of Santo Domingo began acquiring land for *Santo Domingo Cuahuixtla*. *Xochimancas* had been founded in 1614 by Juan Fernández de la Concha, secretary to the Viceroy Guadalcazar, acting as an intermediary. In 1634, his widow doña Catarina de Diosdado y Meneses married Diego de Coca Rendón, a prominent merchant of the capital, who added two *caballerías* to the property.

Five years later, she sold the mill to the Jesuits, who made it into one of the four major Jesuit mills in the kingdom.[19] If merchants sold to the clergy, so did lay first-settler families. *San Nicolás Coatecalco* was owned by the Villanueva Sandoval Zapata family, a conquistador clan, from 1618 through 1660, when it passed to the Colegio de Cristo. The twelfth mill, the *ingenio* of *Guajoyuca* was also founded by the viceregal secretary Fernández de la Concha in 1616 and then held by his heirs.[20]

The Marquesado mills were often administered by merchants. The contract of Andrés Arias Tenorio, gives an idea of the power and responsibilities of renters. It stipulated that he pay in advance 4,666 pesos annually for nine years to the owner. He was to be provided with workers and food but had to pay all taxes and wages and repairs to the mill. If an adult slave died during his tenure, he had to replace him or her. Arias Tenorio also had exclusive rights to the Marquesado's sugar store in the capital. Similar arrangements were made at other mills. The renter received a commission on sales, usually 11 or 12 percent, and/or the right to a certain amount of sugar to sell on his own account. Sometimes he had to pay with commodities such as wine as well as a sum in cash, as was the case with the wholesaler Juan Pedrique Montero, renter of the San Hipólito Camatitlán *trapiche* in Cuautla in 1652.[21] The key element was the exchange of cash in advance for exclusive rights to the harvest.

Renting presented less risk than purchase, but because of the value of the crop, it still represented a serious financial commitment that only persons with access to liquid capital could make. Rentals varied greatly by value of crop and by period, but all involved several thousand pesos. The largest known rent was for the Santissima Trinidad complex, which fetched 50,000 pesos a year in 1619. The rent of the merchant Diego Caballero's Santa Inés Las Amilpas mill fluctuated considerably over the first half of the seventeenth century. In the early 1600s, it was leased for 24,000 pesos; by 1629, it declined to 7,000 pesos; and by 1644, it was renting at 10,500 pesos. In 1660, San Nicolás Pantitlán and Santa Ana Amanalco owned by the merchant Antonio de Millán rented for 9,000 pesos and 4,700 pesos, while in the 1670s, the Hospital mills rented for 29,032 pesos.[22]

Financing the mills involved offering *depósitos* and *censos redimibles*, some as small as a few hundred pesos but usually between 2,000 and 15,000 pesos, very large sums. In 1629 and 1630, for example, the Santa Ana Amanalco mill received 17,810 pesos from the merchant Francisco Esquivel Castañeda, 3,240 pesos from Gabriel López Páramo, and 8,313 pesos from Álvaro de Lorenzana—a total of 29,363 pesos. From an individual merchant's standpoint, such a loan to a plantation was a substantial commitment, sometimes the largest single credit on his ledger. Such was the case of Simón de Haro, who was owed 26,500 pesos by the *ingenio* San Francisco in Cuautla in 1655. In 1636, Juan de Castellete placed an immense *censo* of 40,000 pesos, the largest in his accounts, on the *ingenio* Nuestra Señora de Concepción belonging to Captain don Sebastián de la Higuera Matamoros. The debt was still outstanding in full in 1646.[23] The merchant Pedro Sedeno Benítez had sunk 28,000 pesos into the Marabatio *trapiche* in Michoacán, which he left to his son-in-law to try to collect. Even clerical institutions received some financing from merchants. In 1636, the Hospital mill of the Order of San Hipólito borrowed 46,000 pesos of *censos*, of which 14,000 (or 30 percent) were provided by laymen. Mexico City merchant financing of the Hospital complex increased during the century. In 1652, the wholesaler Felipe Navarro y Atienza placed a 1,500 peso *censo* on the Jesuit plantation Xochimancas.[24]

Why did seventeenth-century planters borrow so much money? Some reasons concerned expenditures on a lavish life-style, on pious works, and the loss of income in years of drought or low prices for sugar; another reason was to finance acquisition and development of new lands in anticipation of greater profits. Planters increased their holdings and borrowed money to develop them and defend them against competitors. Tomás de Zuaznavar y Aguirre, merchant-owner of San Pedro Mártir in Cuernavaca, for example, already had forty *caballerías* under cane in 1624, "so that his mill would be continually supplied" at a time when an eleven-to-twelve *caballería* plantation was considered large. In the 1630s, Zuaznavar borrowed from a fellow millowner, Miguel Rodríguez Acevedo, to add new properties of one to four *caballería* lots.[26]

One expense related to expansion that has sometimes been overlooked was the cost of lawsuits. By the mid-seventeenth century in regions such as Cuernavaca, Orizaba, Veracruz, and Oaxaca, much productive land was already in the hands of white or Indian owners. Acquisition of new canelands was, therefore, a slow process, occurring only when existing holders wanted to (or had to) sell. The merchant Diego Caballero offers a case in point. He sought to obtain more water for his Santa Ana mill in 1596 and was opposed, unsuccessfully, by the Indians of the village of Zumpango de las Amilpas and by two other millowners, the Convent of Santo Domingo and the *contador* Gordián Casasano. The Convent of Santa Inés, proprietors of Caballero's former *ingenio* Las Amilpas, attributed part of the decline in the rental value of the mill to the costs of lawsuits. To meet these expenses, the nuns had to impose a 4,000 peso lien on the property.[27] Tomás Zuaznavar, a wholesaler, had to defend himself in court on three occasions when neighbors encroached on his properties. However worthy the motive for borrowing may have been, the result was increased indebtedness, which plagued the sugar sector, especially in the regions first cultivated, as the century progressed. Until the 1670s, the profitability of the crop seems to have been sufficient to sustain sugar cultivation, but from then until the mid-eighteenth century, at least in Morelos, many venerable plantations were in a state of collapse because of debt servicing and lower prices.

The cycle of debt-expansion-debt had the potential for decline or increase in earnings. As an instance of the former, the Millán complex earned 11,950 pesos' profit a year in the 1680s, but after mortgages, pensions, and renter's commission of 12 percent were deducted, only 1,717 pesos remained to the owners. The history of another large mill, the San José in the Valley of Atrisco, however, showed that debt-financed expansion could increase productivity and earnings, provided prices were adequate and other favorable conditions prevailed.

The Ingenio San José

The history of the *ingenio* San José (*jurisdicción* [administrative district] of Izúcar) in the southern sugar crescent is a rare account of the expansion of a lay sugar plantation in the seventeenth century and sheds light on the relation of trade to agriculture. The San José was a major enterprise, producing more sugar on an annual basis than the better-known mills of the Jesuits and the Marquesado. There was a considerable degree of continuity in ownership; possession of the mill alternated in a roughly twenty-year cycle between the Pastrana family (1599–1618, 1643–61), a merchant clan with diverse investments in an *obraje*, a mine, and a wheat hacienda, and the Toro Muñoz, a family with merchant ties eventually connected with New Spain's aristocracy, the Luna y Arellano (1618–43). Toro was Pastrana's *compadre*, but this did not prevent a bitter battle over the mill.

The San José expanded its plant from 1599 to 1643, which suggests that the owners thought they could sell more sugar. The tradeoff for expansion, however, was increased indebtedness. They initially relied on religious institutions and Indian towns for credit, but as the century continued the owners turned to merchants from the capital, to whom they had

Table 11. Changes in the Sources of Financing
for the *Ingenio* San José, 1618 and 1643 (in Pesos)

1618		1643	
Religious:			
(Censos)			
Mexico City Cathedral	14,000	*Censos* of 1618 still out-	
Sor María de Jesús,		standing	36,400
Convent of Santa Clara,		Convent of N. S. Encarnación	
Villa de Carrión	1,400	(location unavailable)	3,000
Convent of Santa Clara,			
Villa de Carrión	1,000		
Capellanía	2,700		
Capellanía	2,800		
Convent of San Agustín,			
Villa de Carrión	1,100		
Convent of N. S.			
Concepción, Puebla	6,000		
Colegio and Convent of San			
Gerónimo, Puebla	1,500		
Indios cantores, Church of			
San Francisco, Villa de			
Carrión	1,600		
Convent of San Juan			
Penitencia, Mexico City	4,300		
Total	36,400		39,400
Indian Towns:			
San Francisco Huilango	6,000	1618 debts still outstanding	
Tepexoxuma	600		
Total	6,600		6,600
Spanish Laymen:			
Juan García Barranco,		1618 debts still outstanding	7,450
former standard bearer,		Simón de Soria[a]	12,000
Puebla	7,000	Diego de Serralde[a]	6,057
don Juan Ochoa de Lexalde	450	Juan Navarro Pastrana[a]	7,000
		Mateo Cepeda Martínez[a]	15,000
		Juan de Acevedo	615
		Miguel Carrillo and José	
		Crespo Carrillo[a]	2,764
		Total outside financiers	50,886

Table 11—*Continued*

1618		1643	
		Debt of present owner Toro to former owner Pastrana	58,164
Total	7,450		109,050
Owed to Employees	0		9,917
Owed to Crown	0	*Composición de tierras*	3,000
		Condenación de aguas	18,000
Total owed to crown	0		21,000
Total unspecified	0		2,050
Debts:	50,450		188,017

Source: AGI, Escribanía de Cámara, 171A, ff.170r–176r and 1131r–1358r.
[a]Mexico City wholesaler.

marital and economic ties (table 11). Amounts lent ranged from 2,764 pesos (Crespo Carillo) to 21,400 pesos (Millán) per merchant in a given year. Although credit was available to the San José under the two different owners, Pastrana and Toro had clashes over repayment and eventual possession of the mill, which led to a 1,500-page lawsuit.

The *ingenio* San José was founded in 1599; Cristóbal Pastrana, his son Juan, a *vecino* of the capital, and Francisco Robledo Bernardo, a resident of Puebla, formed a company to build an *ingenio* on some lands they had near the town of Tepexoxuma in the valley. They financed the project by imposing a 14,000 peso mortgage on Cristóbal's Hacienda San Bernardo and *Obraje* La Fresnada in favor of Mexico City's Cathedral Chapter, the ecclesiastical council which governed the diocese.

Juan, also a merchant, served as administrator of the *obraje*, and after his father's death became owner of the San José mill until 1618. His business associates included relatives such as Hernando de Pastrana and *obrajero* Melchor de Pastrana, residents of Puebla and Mexico City, respectively; *contador* Francisco Carrasco; and the merchants Juan Martín Seufino, Diego de Torres, Pedro de Gómez, and his brother-in-law, Alonso Muñoz de la Torre (not Toro). Under Juan's ownership, the value of the mill rose from 40,000 pesos in 1599 to 148,000 pesos in 1618, when he sold it to Alonso de Toro Muñoz, a resident of Izúcar. The indebtedness of the San José had also risen from 14,000 pesos to 50,450 pesos.[28]

Toro borrowed even more from merchants. In the 1620s, Roberto Malcot and Pedro Bali del Valle, representatives of famous Seville firms, were Toro's agents; don Álvaro Rodríguez de Acevedo, son of merchant Miguel, and Cristóbal de Pastrana, son of Juan, were two of his administrators. Between April 6, 1620 and February 11, 1621, Toro borrowed 21,400 pesos from the wholesaler Antonio de Millán and 2,160 pesos from Diego de Mesa for the *avío* of the plantation. An additional 12,800 pesos was obtained from Francisco Sáenz and 3,000 pesos from Manuel Álvarez, totaling 39,360 pesos by 1622. By 1639, Toro had repaid 26,000 pesos of the sum but incurred new debts. In 1643, his mill owed a total of 188,017 pesos.

Toro's largest creditor was Juan de Pastrana himself, who was owed 35,931 pesos of the original purchase price from 1618 that Toro never repaid. Toro also owed 10,000 pesos for principal and interest for money borrowed before 1639, and Juan's son Cristóbal claimed an additional 12,233 pesos incurred between 1639 and 1643, when he administered the mill and lost money. The total was 58,164 pesos.

Part of Cristóbal's liquid capital, in turn, had come from the family of his father-in-law, the merchant Francisco Esquivel Castañeda. In 1644, doña Margarita de Covarrubias, Francisco's wife, listed the money she had previously lent to her four sons-in-law. In addition to a dowry, which Cristóbal owed to doña María, her daughter, he also owed her 4,280 pesos and interest on a 6,000 peso mortgage which he had placed on his house. Indeed, through his marriage to doña María, Cristóbal strengthened his Mexico City contacts. His new brothers-in-law, Juan Crespo Carrillo, Francisco de Salcedo, and the *converso* Sebastián Báez Acevedo, were all prominent merchants of the capital. At the same time, Cristóbal extended his ties to the sugar industry, for his mother-in-law, doña Margarita, was also the trustee of don Manuel Casasano, the son of Gordián Casasano and heir to the *ingenio* San Pedro Mártir.[29] Thus, the line of credit to the *ingenio* San José proliferated from Pastrana through two other merchant families.

The large claims of the Pastrana family against the San José enabled Cristóbal to purchase the mill for 270,999 pesos in 1643, at Toro's death. One of Cristóbal's brothers, Nicolás, left the store in Mexico City to become administrator. After Cristóbal's death, ownership passed to his widow, doña María, who became the fifth owner of the mill. The purchase was bitterly contested by the Toro heirs: doña Isabel Álvarez Luna y Arellano, Toro's second wife; Captain Fernando Rojas y Vargas, *alcalde mayor* of Cholula, her second husband; and Captain don Josefe Luna y Arellano, Isabel's son by Toro. They failed to regain ownership but were awarded a compensation of 7,983 pesos.[30]

The crux of the dispute was whether the *ingenio* San José had been profitable during Cristóbal Pastrana's tenure as administrator (1639–43) and, by implication, earlier. If it had not been able to turn a profit under Toro family ownership, the chances that creditors would ever be repaid were nil. They therefore had a right to recoup their losses by placing the mill in more able hands, namely, their own. As the Pastrana's lawyer put it: "Experience shows that it has not been possible to repay the debts and current interest with the fruits of the mill, as is evident from the fact that in 25 years Alonso Toro could not repay the debts he incurred when he bought the mill, on the contrary it became more indebted. . . . Future fruits depend precisely on the creditors' supplying *avío*, especially slaves, and with profits uncertain and costs certain, there cannot be any *avío* nor repayment of debts."[31] If, on the other hand, the mill had been profitable, Toro's failure to repay the Pastranas was due to his use of the money for other purposes, and Cristóbal's assertion that, as administrator, he had had to run the mill at a loss was false. In that case Cristóbal's claim to ownership in 1643 was untenable. There were three aspects to the debate: the amount of sugar produced, the value of the plantation, and the profits it earned the owner.

Tithe records show that the mill's production in 1620, two years after Toro bought it, was 8,802 *arrobas* of sugar (figure 5); molasses output was usually between 100 and 150 *arrobas*. Volume declined for a few years, then rose dramatically in 1627 to 12,818 *arrobas* of sugar and stayed above 10,000 *arrobas* every year between 1627 and 1642 except for 1639, the first year of Cristóbal's administration. From 1643 to 1651 volume declined somewhat, but, with the exception of a few years, it was still much higher than in the early 1620s. When these figures are compared to two other important mills, the Tlaltenango *ingenio* of the Marqués del Valle and, somewhat later, the Cuautepec mill of the Jesuits, one can appreciate Pastrana's and Toro's achievement. The former was producing 1,793 to 4,234 *arrobas* in the early 1620s; the latter about 9,000 *arrobas* in the mid 1680s.[32] The San José's general history of incremental growth in production from the late 1620s suggests that the market for sugar was expanding.

Higher output occurred because of the expansion of the plantation, as reflected in the inventories of 1618 and 1643, and the increased value

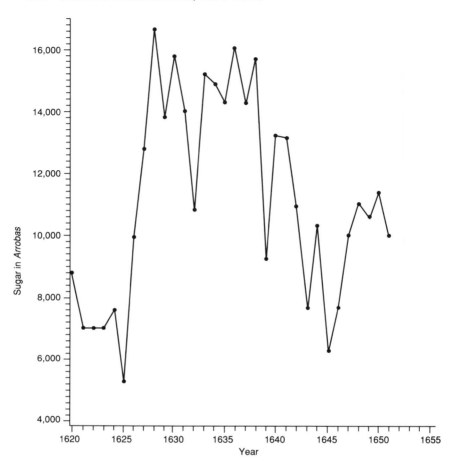

Figure 5. Sugar Production at the San José Mill, 1620–51.

of the mill. The *ingenio*'s area increased from twenty-four *caballerías* to forty-five *caballerías*; oxen increased from 1,000 to 1,300, mules from 30 to 150, and horses from 100 to 646. There were 294 cows and bulls. The sale price rose from 40,000 pesos in 1599 to 270,999 pesos in 1643, in part because the plant was improved. The greater number of draft animals shows that the mill grew intensively through greater application of power, as well as extensively by acquiring more land. In 1643, San José also had 220 slaves. Thus, Toro, the second owner, was able nearly to double his output only ten years after he bought the San José. In 1620, the mill produced 8,800 *arrobas*, while in 1628 it produced 16,600 *arrobas*.

Was it also profitable? Probably, yes. One set of figures is provided by Pastrana, who was arguing that the mill was losing money and that he, as chief creditor, would never be repaid. He presented accounts which showed that from April 7, 1639 to December 3, 1641, he received 98,568 pesos from the sale of 26,562 *arrobas* and paid 110,802 pesos for expenses, incurring a debit of 12,234 pesos. From June 15, 1642 to February 18, 1643, he received 43,199 pesos from the sale of 5,283 *arrobas*, took in 50 *arrobas* as his rather low commission and 14,020 pesos in *avío*, and paid 40,705 pesos in expenses, incurring a profit of 2,494 pesos. The profit from 1642 to 1643 was too small to offset losses from 1639 to 1641. The Toros challenged Pastrana's accounts and presented the figures from the tithe, which supports the Toros' claim that the sugar produced was greater than Pastrana stated. For example, Pastrana asserted that the mill could not make 10,000 *arrobas* a year, but the tithe shows that production exceeded 10,000 *arrobas* in many years. For 1642 and 1643, Pastrana insisted he had made only 5,283 *arrobas*, but according to the tithe, the amount was actually 7,650 *arrobas*.[33] He also declined to give the requisite account of his administration every six months, "as he has been too busy."[34] Pastrana was able to make his version prevail, however, because of his informal power in the district. This *hombre mañoso y caudaloso* (a rich and cunning man) intimidated Toro's widow, bribed her son-in-law, Juan Ramírez Arellano with 4,000 pesos, and falsified the accounts presented to the *audiencia*.[35] Despite the valuation of the San José at above 411,711 pesos in 1635, Pastrana managed to buy it for only 270,999 pesos.[36]

Pastrana's position does appear to have merit with regard to the indebtedness of the *ingenio*. Under Toro, debts rose more rapidly than the value of the mill. From 1618 to 1643, debts as a percentage of value increased from 35 percent in 1599 and 1618, to 68 percent in 1624 and reached 75 percent in 1643. Not all this debt was the result of Toro's expansion. Of the 188,017 pesos due in 1643, 35,931 pesos were outstanding to Pastrana from the 1618 sale and 50,450 pesos were debts Toro inherited from Pastrana. Nevertheless, servicing these growing debts suggests a decline of profits. Considering how hard Pastrana fought to regain ownership, how he sunk more money into the mill, and that his widow retained it at least until 1661, the mill remained attractive. Pastrana was so eager to obtain the San José that, according to Toro's widow, "he and Nicolás [his brother] seized it before Toro had hardly breathed his last."[37] If the prospects of profits were as poor as Pastrana claimed in his suit, he would have chosen a bankruptcy settlement instead of pressing the Toro heirs to sell. Therefore, it is plausible to conclude that the *ingenio* San José was profitable at the mid-century because of expansion of capacity, demand, and good prices.

HACIENDAS

One of the most characteristic institutions of colonial Mexico was the hacienda, whose formation, at least in the central provinces, occurred in the seventeenth century. Any overview of the hacienda in the seventeenth century must be tempered by the recognition that great variation existed among even those in the same region and that they coexisted with smaller-scale ranches, farms, and Indian plots. Nevertheless, we can define a hacienda as a mixed ranching and agricultural enterprise, considered large by local standards, which provided foodstuffs to cities, served as centers of population in sparsely settled regions, and were another source of aristocratic fortunes of the time.

The composition of the work force usually included some mixture of resident laborers, daily hands who came from nearby settlements, and extra workers hired to meet seasonal demands. Payment was in money, food, and the right to cultivate part of the hacienda's land in exchange for labor. Forced labor drafts also contributed to the hacienda work force, even after 1633 when they were illegal for agriculture. Important changes in labor practices occurred during the century. Debt peonage developed, but whether these debtors were victims of the *hacendados* or beneficiaries of credit the *hacendado* could ill afford remains controversial. The average amount owed on several large estates in the early seventeenth century was 50 pesos per person, while the number of these resident Indian workers ranged between thirty-six and ninety, a substantial number. Reflecting the broader demographic trends of particular parts of the viceroyalty, the socio-racial composition of the hacienda workers was changing, increasingly including *mestizos* and, on more properties than was previously realized, black slaves as well as Indians.[38] Finally, as many interesting studies of rural regions have shown, the population of haciendas included a number of occupational categories other than owners, cowboys, and field workers: managers, foremen, renters, carpenters and blacksmiths, other artisans, and household help.

Although the haciendas of the seventeenth century included some valuable properties, what is known about their cost indicates that they were labor, rather than capital, intensive. There were, to be sure, estates such as the huge ranch and hacienda complexes of don Juan Saavedra Guzmán in Soconusco, which included two hundred thousand cattle, twenty-six slaves, more than twenty grazing sites, and many *caballerías* of farmland; it was worth 150,000 pesos.[39] In addition to estates valuable because of the size of their lands and herds, others were made costly by elaborate buildings, expensive irrigation facilities, distilleries, dairies, tanneries, or *obrajes*, but, on the whole, the hacienda consisted of a main house, granaries, stables and corrals, shacks for a few permanent workers, a few tools, draft animals, and sometimes a church. The greater part of the value of the hacienda derived from its arable land, its stock, and the money advanced to its laborers.[40] More is known about valuable estates because they were more likely to be entailed; two examples suggest the more common range. In 1596, an eight-*caballería* hacienda in the fertile valley of San Pablo near Puebla was sold to the Jesuits for 8,000 pesos, while in 1660, a hacienda complex in the province of Tehuacán containing thirty *caballerías* of agricultural land and fifty-one grazing sites for sheep and cattle was worth 30,000 pesos.[41] All the haciendas owned by Mexico City merchants were less than 20,000 pesos in value.

Lower in value and less heavily capitalized than other enterprises, haciendas were also the most dispersed geographically. Maize and beans, cattle, mules, small farm animals, and magüey were found on almost all of them, while wheat, European fruits and vegetables, and sheep were more localized. Despite the concentration of rural property holding which occurred by the mid-seventeenth century in most parts of New Spain, there were still far more haciendas than sugar plantations. In 1622, it is estimated that the Valley of Mexico had 116 haciendas; by 1632, the Valley of Atlixco contained 90; by 1643, there were 41 in Oaxaca, to name only three regions in the first half of the century. Haciendas were a regional institution that arose in response to local demand, and the low per-unit value of its grains, beef and mutton, wool, grease, candles, cheese, and mules would, in any case, have prevented paying high transport costs to ship them long distances. Basic foodstuffs were subject to State regulation and price ceilings in the public interest, even if the definition of public interest often rested with the private producers. Finally, the returns were not spectacular, at least compared to trade. The entailed estates, those most likely to be diversified and to include fertile land, on the average produced annual profits of 5 and 6 percent in the early seventeenth century.[42]

All of these factors ran counter to the merchants' preference for a capital-hungry, high-profit enterprise whose products they could monopolize. For their part, the *hacendado* depended less directly on merchants than did planters or miners. As Florescano has emphasized, *hacendados* did rely on the merchant class for credit and distribution, and there is no doubt that the hacienda needed outside capital to survive bad years of low demand or decreased output due to natural disasters; to continue interest payments and cover labor costs; and to support the conspicuous consumption in which the owner was expected to engage.[43] For the seventeenth century, however, this capital did not come as extensively from Mexico City merchants. Local sources, ecclesiastic and lay, were quite important; their funds might have originated in dealings with the wholesalers of the capital but did not come directly from them. At least, this is the repeated impression from the merchants' list of debtors, where the names of miners, planters, and provincial traders stand out more than the *hacendados*, although these, especially the large landowners, do have a place. As for merchants' role in marketing, there was also less need. Agents of the *hacendado* could sell his produce in the provincial cities of Valladolid, Oaxaca, Guanajuato, Zacatecas, and Guadalajara, where, he or his relations were likely to occupy a place on the city council which set food prices.

There was, nonetheless, a group of wholesalers who diversified by acquiring or financing these landed estates. Relatively inexpensive anyway, purchase could be financed by assuming existing mortgages, and a manager or renter could handle daily administration of the property. Merchants who made loans to the viceregal or royal government were likely to find their requests for *mercedes* favored, and their access to credit fostered expansion. Then, there was the social cachet of owning a hacienda, even if it was not overwhelming.

Three Merchant Hacendados

One form that merchant purchase of agricultural properties took was exemplified by Gonzalo Gutiérrez Gil, the mint merchant (chapter 2) who became one of the merchant-landed magnates of the early seventeenth century. Gutiérrez Gil gradually developed a large hacienda complex in one of the most desirable regions of the viceroyalty, a complex he owned until his death. In 1603, he received a *merced* in Tacuba, west of Mexico City, and by 1624 he was calling the property a hacienda. By 1613, Gutiérrez Gil had purchased from Álvaro de Loso a sheep hacienda containing ten thousand sheep of both sexes, three mules, five slaves, and some male Indian shepherds and female Indian cooks, as well as a nearby site for an *estancia* (pasture) for sheep and three *caballerías* of farmland. All this property was near the village of Coacualco (*jurisdicción* San Cristóbal Ecatepec) north of Mexico City. Gutiérrez Gil asked for and received sheep pens in the jurisdictions of five different Indian villages; in 1616, he bought a house and forty yards of land in the town of Coacualco from the Indian Diego Juan, possibly to supervise the estate. The combination of acquisition through land grant and through purchase was common, although the distinction might be more apparent than real, as when Gutiérrez Gil was accused in the 1590s of buying land grants outright in collusion with treasury officials.

Gutiérrez Gil was as ready to profit from fellow Spaniards as from Indians. In 1611, he snapped up the urban property, including five houses and seven shops, of the bankrupt merchant Luis de Quesada for 18,000 pesos. In 1622, he was sued by Antonio Martínez de Villagra, a resident of Cuautitlán, for selling him the property near Coacualco for 15,500 pesos. The property was close to worthless: the 10,000 head of sheep were sick, 3,000 of them dying after the sale; the farmland and pastures were of poor quality; and the lot not worth more than 8,000 pesos. By 1624, Gutiérrez Gil had also acquired a hacienda and cattle ranch at Istapalapa; by 1619, a hacienda at Tulancingo that rented for 40 pesos a year and a nonirrigated hacienda in the village of San Ignacio near Tepexi del Río (*jurisdicción* Tula). He purchased the second from the leading Indians of the town.[44] This purchase and sizable debts owed to Gutiérrez Gil by Indian towns reflect the steady white occupation of lands originally held by Indians, one of the typical processes of seventeenth-century rural development.

Another agricultural role the merchant might play was that of hacienda administrator. Alonso Picazo Hinojosa, when *mayordomo* (administrator) of a hacienda complex in Texcoco, had lent 4,262 pesos to Juan de la Torre, its owner. Unable to collect the debt, Picazo purchased for 9,500 pesos the two irrigated haciendas and the pasture site for *ganado menor* (sheep, goats, and hogs) near Capulalpa (Texcoco) and the two plots of land in Tlaxcala, which Torre had rented.[45] Unless the property was very close to Mexico City, as was Texcoco, however, it was not practical for a merchant to serve as resident manager while he was carrying on mercantile activities from the capital. Merchants also speculated in land, acquiring properties only to sell them at a favorable opportunity. They received land grants in the 1590s that do not appear in their later inventories because they, like other recipients, held them only for a short time.[46]

The one-third of the merchant *hacendados* who made a complete break with their commercial past could face ruin. Alonso Baeza del Río was one of the merchants who viewed acquisition of landed property as the beginning of a new means of livelihood and social status. He made a point of stating that he had left trade to become a landowner. In 1608, after thirty-three years as a merchant, he ceased to trade and purchased rural properties in and near the Valley of México. Both purchases noted were from Spaniards, although for a brief period Baeza del Río rented several breeding pens from the Indians of the town of Xaltocán. The more important property included the Hacienda San Gaspar, which in the bankruptcy settlement of 1637 contained 9,650 sheep, and the Hacienda Jilotzingo—which contained thirty large and small mares, four old oxen, and eleven used plows—in adjoining jurisdictions of Zumpango and Pachuca. There were also agricultural and pasture lands in these jurisdictions. The other property was a hacienda near the town of Coyoacán.[47] By 1613, Baeza del Río was already experiencing cash-flow problems. He was sued by one of his sons-in-law, don Lorenzo de Herrera y Baeza, *relator* (preparer of reports) of the *audiencia*, for failure to pay 4,333 pesos and interest on the 12,000 peso dowry of don Lorenzo's wife, doña Rafaela. In 1622, Baeza del Río said that his haciendas were running at a loss, with debts exceeding assets by 18,490 pesos.

In 1638, after he had died, the Zumpango and Pachuca properties, which in 1622 had been worth 23,450 pesos, were auctioned for 11,000 pesos. The *casas principales* (the mansion which is the main family dwelling and sometimes the place of business), which were originally worth 20,000 pesos, were auctioned for 15,000 pesos to pay Baeza del Río's outstanding debts. The *casas principales* were all that was left of the four sets of houses which Baeza del Río had once owned. The auction was bitterly protested by his daughter, doña Rafaela, and her five children, who had lived in the house since 1619 and who had spent what she received of her dowry on repairing it. The family estate had declined to the point that after don Lorenzo's death, doña Rafaela rented the second floor as well as some single rooms at ground level facing the street.[48]

Thus, investment in rural property did not prove a good choice for Alonso Baeza del Río. Despite the proximity of his holdings to the Mexico City market and his cultivation of a saleable crop, wheat, the investment detracted rather than added to his wealth and ultimately led to the loss of his urban properties too. A number of factors contributed to Baeza del Río's debacle. Conflict with the Jesuit College at Tepotzlán over his breeding pens points to one type of problem, and the heavy mortgages—which in the case of the hacienda complex totaled 8,000 pesos—and Baeza del

Río's loss of income from trade also seem important. Of the 28,305 pesos which the total estate owed in 1637, 16,975 pesos (60 percent) was owed from mortgages and back interest.[49] His difficulties—litigation, indebtedness, and family feuds—were shared by many landowners and reflect the risks of investment in agriculture at this time.

The career of a more successful merchant *hacendado*, Álvaro Rodríguez de Acevedo, suggests that it was useful for the new landowners to continue receiving income from commerce and to maintain social and economic ties to other Mexico City merchants. If these circumstances were present, haciendas quite distant from Mexico City could still take advantage of selling to its lucrative market and because of profits earned from sales to the capital, the haciendas could remain in the hands of the same family for three generations.

Álvaro Rodríguez de Acevedo owned two ranching complexes: San Lorenzo (*jurisdicción* Huachinango) and Isla del Espíritu Santo (*jurisdicción* Pánuco) just to the north. In 1619, the properties included haciendas, ranches, fallow farmland, corrals, herdsmen, bull pens, cattle, mules, horses, and slaves. The senior Álvaro (who used the *don* on some documents and not on others) entailed the property for his eldest son, don Álvaro, who inherited the ranches when his father died in 1613. He, in turn, passed them to his son, don Francisco.

The Rodríguez Acevedo estates served two functions: first, they purchased newborn and older mules, and to a lesser extent cattle and young bulls, from other ranchers. From 1616 to 1618 don Álvaro purchased from residents of Tampico (*jurisdicción* Pánuco), Guaxutla (*jurisdicción* Huexutla), and Chicontepec (*jurisdicción* Guayacocotla), all provinces neighboring don Álvaro's holdings.[50] Second, the estates sold various kinds of livestock to Mexico City residents. One such agreement was the contract between the widow of Álvaro, doña Melchora Pellicer, and Pedro de Ayllón, a temporary resident of Mexico City. Ayllón agreed to remove three breeds of bulls from doña Melchora's estates and to bring them to the Venta de Carpio, four leagues from Mexico City for sale, at doña Melchora's cost and risk. The first 3 pesos per head would go to doña Melchora's children, and any amount in excess of 3 pesos would be split between the two parties. Ayllón brought 550 head to Mexico City, thirty-eight of which were lost and the rest sold to Jacome Vela, a resident of the capital, by the agency of the merchant Francisco Medina Reynoso at 7 pesos, 1 tomín per head. The children's share, after losses, totaled 4,040 pesos, while Ayllón received 1,144 pesos.[51]

One of the merchant *hacendado* Álvaro's business associates was this

powerful silver trader, Medina Reynoso, who lent Álvaro funds and provided goods to his ranch, as well as helped him sell livestock. The arrangement continued after Álvaro's death in 1613 by adding marital to
financial ties. Medina Reynoso became the guardian of Álvaro's children, managed their business affairs, and his daughter Isabel married don
Álvaro, the eldest son who received the entailed ranches. In 1620, don
Álvaro empowered his father-in-law and his brother-in-law, don Fernando
de Angulo y Reynoso, *regidor* of Mexico City and commissioner of the
slaughterhouse, to buy and sell quantities of cattle, sheep, mules, and
horses for him.[52] The city council let a contract to one supplier to stock
the city's registered meat markets, and the supplier purchased livestock
from a variety of sources. Trade to urban markets in basic foodstuffs was,
therefore, one source of income for the merchant *hacendado*.

The senior Álvaro had made money in the Philippines and slave
trades.[53] Don Álvaro, his son, did not follow his father's profession and
whether due to the loss of income from trade or to other reasons, found
himself with a debt problem that grew worse under his son, don Francisco.
In 1619, don Álvaro agreed to pay Medina Reynoso the substantial sum
of 17,481 pesos to settle their accounts. By the 1640s, the ranches were
operating at a loss and threatened with sale to meet claims of creditors.
After Medina Reynoso died, other Mexico City wholesalers replaced him
as financier, and to these men don Álvaro owed a great deal. His chief
creditor, the merchant Martín de Chavarría, was owed 25,046 pesos by
don Álvaro and 4,753 pesos (in addition) by don Francisco. Although
Rodríguez Acevedo agreed to repay Martín over the next five years, by
1645 nothing had been received. Martín sued don Francisco, and the
court ruled that the profits of the estate, although not the estate itself,
pass to Martín. Don Álvaro appealed the sentence, claiming his nobility
made him immune from seizure of property. The *audiencia* confirmed the
sentence. However, since don Álvaro and Martín had been *compadres*
and "accounts are more securely settled by mutual agreement than by
litigation," Martín agreed to reduce his claim to 23,000 pesos to be paid
in installments over ten years, with the first payment not until five years
from the date of the sentence.[54] Thus, from the 1590s to at least 1650, the
northeast Mexican ranches remained in the Rodríguez Acevedo family,
but by the latter date the family's hold was slipping badly. Some of their
debts may have been due to expansion, but there is no discussion of this
in the records.

The experiences of merchant *hacendados* illuminate some features of hacienda ownership which may have deterred more merchants from purchasing farms and ranches. As the example of Gutiérrez Gil indicates, political connections were necessary to obtain needed grants. Gutiérrez Gil was successful in obtaining *his* sheep pens, but another merchant might lack ties to the viceroy's circle which offered the *mercedes*. The location of available land was another factor. If a merchant bought in the north, he, like Rodríguez Acevedo in far-off Huachinango, had to bear transportation costs and the need to maintain good connections in Mexico City to dispose of his stock. The majority of merchant *hacendados*, in fact, held property in the present-day states of México, Puebla, Toluca, and Morelos; only sixteen of the sixty-four held property outside of the central zone. However it was here that competition for land was more severe because the central zone estates were consolidated first. Baeza del Río's litigation with the Jesuits was one example of the problem. Tomás Zuaznavar y Aguirre offers another. Tomás, owner of the huge San Pedro Mártir sugar mill, also owned haciendas at Atzcapozalco and at Tacuba, as well as a controversial mill site nearby. The site had been granted to one *licenciado* Juan Guerrero in 1612, over the opposition of both the governor of the Marquesado del Valle and of the Indians from the neighborhood of Tepotalco near San Agustín de las Cuevas. Their claims were denied, and Guerrero sold it to Zuaznavar. When Zuaznavar's son, *licenciado* don Salvador, sought to build a mill and dam at the site in 1656, he too was opposed, this time by don Diego Martín de Riego, owner of the Santa Ursula hacienda, whose water supply the mill would reroute. Don Salvador went ahead, built without permission, and then succeeded in obtaining it after the fact from the *audiencia*.[55] The possibility of indebtedness was also a deterrent. Baeza and Rodríguez either lost, or were threatened with the loss, of their holdings because of their debts.

In addition to noting the problems of the merchant who did buy rural estates, one can look at those who chose not to. Some declined to acquire land even when they had a prime opportunity, either as a creditor who foreclosed or as the executor of the owner's estate, when land had to be sold to pay creditors. Domingo de Barainca declined the opportunity to purchase the wheat hacienda in Otumba, which belonged to a long-standing business associate and for which he was the executor; it was sold for 12,000 pesos. Barainca is not known to have owned other rural property, but Chavarría owned a hacienda and firewood yard in Coyoacán. However, he declined to acquire the haciendas founded by Álvaro Rodríguez de Acevedo when they were later auctioned, preferring to collect his 25,046 pesos' debt in cash. Even Juan de Ontiveros Barrera, son of the cattle magnate Cristóbal mentioned by Chevalier, decided against purchasing a foreclosed cattle and wheat property (*jurisdicción* Istlaguaca) when it was sold for the low price of 1,110 pesos. In yet another example, Domingo del Puerto had the opportunity to acquire some of his uncle's pasture sites in Nuevo León but instead sold them for 4,000 pesos.[56]

THE SPECIALIZED CROPS: COCHINEAL, INDIGO, AND CACAO

An important branch of agriculture in colonial Mexico was the cultivation of highly specialized crops: the dyes cochineal and indigo; nonessential foodstuffs such as cacao, honey, and forest spices; and other products such as beeswax and pitch. All these items were used in pre-Columbian society. Indians were the original cultivators or gatherers, although they placed different value on the items than did Europeans, a greater value for cacao, a lesser value for indigo. (An exception to Indian origins of specialized crops was, of course, sugar.) Mexico City merchants had little interest in many of the regions where these items were produced, but the high per-unit value of cochineal and indigo, and the high demand for the less costly cacao, prompted traders to develop credit networks which reached out to what they saw as marginal areas. As with mining, they perfected their role as financiers and distributors. Mexico City merchants rarely became landowners in the rich agricultural districts of Oaxaca, Campeche, Tabasco, and the Yucatán. Rather, they remained in their classic and often-criticized position of intermediaries between producers and consumers.

With regard to Indian specialty agriculture, therefore, the history of the merchant elite shows how a small group with capital could redirect an indigenous system of production to new markets for new uses by, in a sense, remote control. The existence of a bureaucracy which extended the length and breadth of the country and whose members could serve as local agents, the need for specie and credit in the provinces, and the untapped potential of the European and domestic market for dyes and other raw materials enabled merchants to change the organization of this branch of agriculture and link it to the capital and to the cities of Europe.

The beautiful, high-quality dyestuffs were the second and third most valuable exports of seventeenth-century Mexico. Cochineal, a scarlet dye produced by placing insects on the prickly pear cactus and then drying them, had been used as dye, paint, and tribute article in pre-Columbian society. In the first years of the colony cochineal cultivation was concentrated in the Mixteca, Oaxaca, Puebla, and on the outskirts of Huejotzingo and Cholula. By the 1550s, it had become more intense in these regions and had spread elsewhere: to Michoacán, Purificación, and the Atlantic and Pacific coasts. From the beginning of settlement, colonists and friars had encouraged Indians to grow the insects for the export market and for the domestic silk industry. From the 1570s, expansion of the dyestuff became a State priority. Viceroy Enríquez, through the *alcaldes mayores*, compelled the Indians to raise the insects in those regions suitable for cultivation.[57]

Indigo, a plant that yields a violet blue dye, gained prominence a few decades later than cochineal and was concentrated in fewer regions. Although cultivated in Yautepec in the 1560s, it took hold most vigorously in Yucatán and Guatemala. In the 1570s, *encomenderos* in Yucatán were forcing their village Indians to raise it, but soon it became a Spanish-owned industry. Its processing was more complicated than that of cochineal, requiring a water supply, large fermenting vats, wheels with blades, and drying basins or tables. Both crops were extremely important to the cloth industries in both New Spain and in Europe. By the seventeenth century cochineal from the New World had a monopoly of the European market; it was sometimes worth more than the fabric on which the dyer worked.[58]

Cacao had been a prized elite drink in pre-Columbian Mexico and a form of currency. As with cochineal and indigo, its regions of cultivation and its market expanded after the conquest. It first became a popular beverage among all ranks of Indians, later among the creoles, and, by the 1630s, among European middle-class consumers. Within New Spain cacao was grown near the Pacific coast (Colima, Purificación, Acapulco, Huatulco, Zacatula), southern Veracruz, Tabasco and northern Oaxaca, and in Soconusco, which, after 1556, formed part of the *audiencia* of Guatemala. By the 1570s, however, the chief centers of Mesoamerican production had moved southeast in Guatemala to Izalcos. From the 1610s, Guayaquil began export of the bean, to be followed by Venezuela from the 1620s, so that cacao's role in the colonial Mexican economy was in part as a domestic crop, in part as an import.

Once the marketability of these crops had been demonstrated by the late sixteenth century, their cultivation became Hispanicized to different degrees. Either the *encomendero* or *alcalde mayor* forced the Indians to cultivate it on their own lands, or they grew it on their own initiative using traditional methods, which applied to cochineal and, in some cases, cacao (see plate 6). Sometimes Spaniards set up heavily capitalized indigo mills with European machinery on their own land, thus changing the method of production; or the colonists retained nonmechanized, pre-Columbian techniques but planted groves on non-Indian land and employed wage laborers, as with cacao plantations.[59] Whatever the method, the object was to accommodate the Indian economy to the European one.

The result of this shift was to permit production on a scale which generated considerable wealth by the early seventeenth century. In 1593 and 1595, 5,035 *arrobas* and 11,121 *arrobas* of cochineal, respectively, were exported and were evaluated as worth 390,716 pesos and 669,484 pesos each. For the early seventeenth century there is some serial data. Between 1604 and 1610, 4,376 *arrobas* were exported annually, evaluated at 552,689 pesos. Although volume of exports was lower during these years, the value was greater because of a rise in price in the European market. From 1611 to 1620, an average of 3,781 *arrobas* were exported annually at a value of 630,671 pesos. There are no extant export figures for indigo for New Spain in the 1590s. From 1606 to 1610, 7,106 *arrobas* were exported yearly, evaluated at 273,581 pesos. From 1614 to 1616, 10,873 *arrobas* were exported yearly at a value of 371,857 pesos.[60] Because some cochineal and indigo was used by the textile industry in New Spain, and because some was smuggled out, the actual value for these years would be higher.

The high per-unit value of these dyes can be appreciated by comparing the price per *arroba* fetched by cochineal and indigo with that received for sugar in the early seventeenth century. Royal officials assigned the value of cochineal (cultivated and wild) and indigo for taxation at Veracruz before being exported; values were taken at five different dates in the seventeenth century. Rounded off, they indicate that prices for cultivated cochineal ranged from a high of 149 pesos the *arroba* in 1614 to a low of 110 pesos the *arroba* in 1620. Prices for indigo ranged from a high of 34 pesos the *arroba* (138 pesos the *cajón*) in 1614 to a low of 20 pesos the *arroba* (79 pesos the *cajón*) in 1639. Both dyes, therefore, declined in value between 1614 and 1620. Cochineal, however, was always more valuable than indigo. Now, consider the price obtained for sugar. In the 1610s it ranged between 2.5 and 5 pesos the *arroba*. In the 1630s it was a minimum of 4 pesos the *arroba*. During the early decades, therefore, cochineal was worth sixty to thirty times an *arroba* of sugar; in the 1630s,

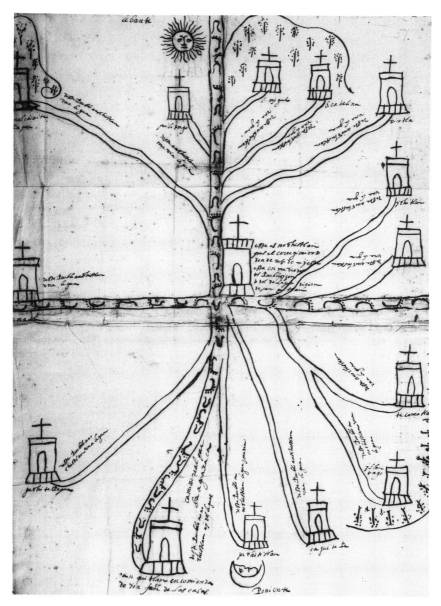

6. Nochixtlán and surrounding Indian villages (Oaxaca), 1602.

Table 12. Cacao Prices in New Spain, 1588–1654

Year	Price per Arroba (in Pesos)[a]	Origin	Source
1588	1.5	Sonsonate	AGI, Contaduría 693, Almojarifazgo nuevo
1591	2.5	Sonsonate	AGI, Contaduría 694, Almojarifazgo nuevo
1594	1.1	Campeche	AGN, Bienes Nacionales, 132, 39
1607	2.5	Unspecified	AGI, Aud Méx 4 (Oficial Real, Veracruz)
1617	5.3	Guatemala	AN, Pedro Santillán, 14 December 1617, f. 166
1618	5.1	Soconusco	Ibid., 13 February 1618, f. 196r
1621	3.8	Unspecified	
1624	5.0	Guatemala	AN, Pérez de Rivera, 7 December 1624, f. 22
1626	3.2	Tancítaro	AJ, 1626, no. 52
1631	1.2	Unspecified	AGI, Aud Méx 32, (Quiroga)
1633	2.2	Maracaibo	AN, López de Rivera, 23 March 1633, ff. 17–18
1635	1.2	Unspecified	AC, Book 30:81
1635	1.8	Unspecified	Ibid.
1652	1.6	"Criollo"	AN, Cobián, 17 September 1652, f. 62
1654	1.2	"Criollo"	AJ, 1654

[a]Prices for cacao are usually given in *cargas* (1 *carga* equals 12 *arrobas*). These prices may be compared with MacLeod, Figure 37, "Some Cacao Prices in Mexico City," *Spanish Central America*, 250.

when cochineal was 115 pesos, it was twenty-nine times the value of sugar. A comparison of the value of dyestuffs to the value of cacao yields similar conclusions about the high value of the former. Prices for different types of cacao in the first quarter of the seventeenth century ranged from 1 peso the *arroba* to 5 pesos the *arroba* (table 12). Sugar and cacao producers, therefore, had to produce in much greater quantities to make these items as valuable a branch of agriculture as was the cultivation of dyestuffs.

In early seventeenth-century Mexico, sugar production was worth more than 600,000 pesos a year and possibly as much as 1 million pesos later. Production estimates for cacao are not available, but trade figures exist for the 1630s. At that time contemporaries called the cacao trade the largest in the kingdom, an assessment that was not strictly accurate but which does indicate its importance.[61] Cacao was one of the goods which the Crown tried to tax from 1636 to 1638 (chapter 4). Because the tax records for the coastal trade, the *almojarifazgo* of 5 and 2.4 percent (and the coastal trade included much of the cacao traffic because not much was exported to Europe from New Spain at this time) are fragmentary, the volume of cacao imported into the viceroyalty cannot be determined. In 1638, however, Viceroy Cadereita asserted that in previous years the cacao trade through Mexico City, the chief entrepôt, had been worth 525,000 pesos a year, and that in 1638 it was worth 950,000 pesos a year.[62]

Hispanicization of the Specialty Crops

Producers needed capital to set up indigo processing plants or to advance credit, either to Indian cochineal or cacao growers or to the colonists who controlled their labor. Because these three crops required distribution to consumers overseas or regionally, information networks were very important. Prices in Mexico fluctuated dramatically, as Gómez de Cervantes put it, "according to news of the demand in Spain of the harvest here."[63] In one year, considerable shifts in price could occur. In 1618, for example, the price fluctuated for the same type of cochineal from 125 pesos the *arroba* to 130 pesos the *arroba*. In 1634, the price varied from 130 pesos the *arroba* to 140 pesos the *arroba*.[64] Prices also changed over the years. Wholesalers of the capital, with their correspondents in Guatemala, Peru, Spain, and Italy, were in the best position to follow these price movements, even though their calculations were not always successful.

Merchants were attracted to the high value per-unit dyes, but also to the cacao trade, which was large enough during many years to compensate for its lower retail value. Although the wholesalers were the elite among traders, they scorned no product which turned a profit. The most prestigious merchants sold cacao: Antonio de Millán, farmer of the *cruzada* tax; Pedro de Soto López, legal representative, of the city of Manila; Pedro de Toledo, *tallador* of the mint; Juan Francisco Vertiz, *regidor* of Mexico City; Francisco Medina Reynoso and Stefantoni Federegui, chief bankers to the Crown in their respective epochs; and Antonio Urrutia de Vergara, confidant and *maestre de campo* of Viceroy Cerralvo.

Thus, cochineal and cacao presented a challenge to monopoly-oriented merchants because these crops were originally grown by large numbers of Indian smallholders who alone had the requisite expertise. Cochineal remained less Hispanicized than cacao. Of the two types of cochineal, domesticated and gathered wild, the vast majority of shipments by the wholesalers was of the former, but these still included several grades, depending on the region of origin. In the seventeenth century the cultivation and drying of the insects which produced the dye was an intricate and demanding process which was still carried out by thousands of Indians on their own lands using Indian techniques. *Grana cochinilla* was grown in plots adjoining their houses or on community lands. By the end of the sixteenth century each family was responsible for twenty of the cactii on which the insects fed. The late sixteenth-century legislation forbidding blacks or Indians to trade in cochineal suggests that many growers did trade and posed a perceived threat to the wholesalers.[65] As for cacao, in the sixteenth century it had been grown by Indians on their own land, but by the 1590s, it had become Hispanicized in certain areas. In Tabasco, Indian-owned groves, both large and small, coexisted with creole-owned plantations, while on the Pacific coast creole plantations seem to have dominated production. In Guatemala, MacLeod has shown how creoles took over the crop in demographically exhausted regions, while Indians and persons of mixed descent were the chief growers in the newer areas.[66]

In this situation the merchants relied on their usual local agents such as public officials, priests, and provincial merchants, to obtain cochineal and cacao, but they also had direct contact with the Indians themselves. The credit network was, therefore, more fragmented at the production level than it was for mining and sugar. Using the traditional approach to obtaining far-off goods, Tiburcio de Urrea, trading in the late 1630s, acquired from the new *alcalde mayor* of Guaxuapa (*jurisdicción* Mixteca Baja) eight *arrobas* of cochineal. Urrea then shipped these and five and a half more *arrobas* to his correspondent in Seville, Manuel de Neve, who like Urrea was a native of the famous textile center of Toledo (chapter 4). When Antonio de Millán became the farmer of the *cruzada*, his agents officially collected the tax and unofficially obtained cochineal, cloaks, cacao, wax, honey, and pitch for Millán.

Provincial merchants also served as agents. The capital wholesaler Francisco Arlanzón obtained his fifty *arrobas* of cochineal in 1609 from Gerónimo Termiño, then a merchant and *vecino* of Oaxaca, but later to become a *vecino* of Mexico City and an elector of the merchant guild. Francisco de Rossales, a capital wholesaler who shipped indigo in the 1610s, used a traveling partner, Captain Sancho de Meras, to purchase 88 *arrobas* of indigo in Guatemala and bring it to Veracruz by way of Oaxaca without passing through the capital. Another elector, Francisco Solarte, originally served as an *encomendero* in Tabasco, trading cacao. Finally, priests in frequent contact with Indian parishoners could be local representatives. In 1594, the Mexico City merchant Martín Bribiesca Roldán filed suit against Gabriel Pacheco, a parish priest, for the 1,200 *arrobas* of cacao Pacheco promised Bribiesca in exchange for merchandise.

Indian agents were also part of the credit network; the *converso* merchant, Tomás Treviño de Sobremonte had close relations with his Indian correspondents.[67] Between 1622 and 1624, Treviño had sixteen local agents, most in the villages of Nejapa, Villa Alta, and San Idlefonso Amatlán. They purchased cochineal on his account and kept him informed about local market conditions. Two Indian correspondents in the town of San Pablo even warned him of forthcoming confiscations of his property by the Inquisition.

The Hispanicization of the cultivation of cacao also meant the growth of the influence of Mexico City in the producing regions. Consider events in Tabasco. Between 1607 and 1609, the *alcalde mayor*, Juan de Miranda, backed by Juan Francisco de Vertiz and two other merchants of the capital, conducted a commercial reign of terror against independent businessmen of the district. Using the 5,160 pesos' worth of merchandise advanced to him by his *aviadores*, Miranda forced sales at three times the true value on the small-scale Indian cacao growers, ran them into debt, and, when they could not pay up in cacao, effectively sold them into slavery on nearby creole plantations. Not content with acquiring debtors of his own, Miranda bought up all the chits held by *español* traders living in the district against these petty Indian growers, some chits going back twenty years! He drove large-scale Indian growers out of business by such tactics as fining them uncollectable sums for small offenses and auctioning off their groves in recompense. Creole retailers also suffered; they were victims of Miranda's wine monopoly. When questioned about this state of affairs, Juan Francisco de Vertiz denied any association with Miranda, despite the fragment of a letter which showed that they were in business together. Miranda seems to have gotten off scot free.[68]

By these fair and foul means, therefore, the wholesalers of the capital acquired the cacao and cochineal of the provinces. In 1618, the *consulado* stated that cochineal merchants obtained the stock in their warehouses through numerous small purchases. Likewise, the *cabildo* observed in 1635, that cacao's sale and resale passed through "many hands" but that "a few persons" dominated the trade. Two cochineal magnates stood out, Melchor de Cuéllar in the 1610s and 1620s and Stefantoni Federegui, who succeeded Cuéllar in the 1630s. When the king sought to purchase 2,000 *arrobas* of cochineal on his own account in 1618, only Cuéllar was consulted in Mexico City and three men, Gaspar de Cháves, Francisco de Vitoria, and Juan de Cueto, in Puebla. Of the 1,115 *arrobas* sent to the Crown in 1618, nearly half, 505 *arrobas*, were purchased in Puebla from only six merchants.[69] Cuéllar built an economic empire from his cochineal business. An agent of such Spanish commercial notables as Miguel de Neve, Oracio Levanto, and Pedro de la O, Cuéllar was active in the cochineal trade for more than thirty-three years. He used his profits to diversify. In 1610, he purchased the *ensayador y fundidor* post at the mint for 140,000 pesos. By 1619, he was active in the Philippine trade; in that year he lent 10,000 pesos to the Crown for the dispatch of the Manila galleon. In the 1620s and early 1630s, he placed registered sums of 52,460 pesos, 19,859 pesos, and 41,785 pesos in the trade. Cochineal remained important, for in 1630 he sent 6,165 pesos' worth to Spain, but as one of several investments.[70]

The pattern of investment that emerges from the *libros de registro*, inventories, and bills of sale reinforces the impression of contemporaries that the specialty crops trade was quite monopolistic. Only one-third of wholesalers traded in cochineal and indigo; clearly there were specialists in the dyestuffs trade. While all members of the merchant elite shipped silver, only this third shipped dyes. Furthermore, only one-half of the indigo shippers dealt in cochineal too, so that there was specialization between dyes. One trader accounted for nearly one-fifth of the cacao imported from the Pacific in the mid-1630s. Antonio Báez Acevedo was charged with smuggling in from Guayaquil on one journey 42,000 *arrobas* (worth 49,000 pesos) at a time when 240,000 *arrobas* were generally imported from "Peru."[71]

One intriguing aspect to the history of specialty crops in the seventeenth century was the State's effort to exercise more control over their production, an effort which the Mexico City merchants and their correspondents in Puebla and Oaxaca repulsed successfully. Crown intervention to force Indian cultivation of cochineal was, naturally, welcome, but two other measures were not. In the 1570s, the government introduced inspection of the quality of exported cochineal, which provoked the indignation of the Mexico City wholesalers. They successfully countered with a less rigorous inspection procedure, to occur in the merchant's warehouse rather than in a central warehouse. Then, between 1608 and 1618, the Crown imposed a new tax of 14 pesos the *arroba*, a measure which resulted in a sharp decline of registered cochineal exports.[72] Unlike all other crops, cochineal was also the object of an often-discussed and once-attempted royal effort to establish a semimonopoly on it and to sell cochineal on its own account or through a licensed contractor. The government first proposed the idea in 1568 and returned to it in 1596, 1607, 1624, 1634,

1636, and 1638, but it was always rejected by the viceroys. There was one exception: between 1618 and 1622, the Crown established a partial royal monopoly intended to replace the 1608 tax. Merchants resisted and hid their stores, only offering them at auction as required after they had been confiscated by public officials, and then at exhorbitant price.[73] Merchants also misled royal agents about the quality of different types of cochineal. Lacking the expertise of the merchants, officials could not administer the tax: "The dealers in cochineal are crafty and far more knowledgeable than we."[74] The initial 2,000 *arrobas* to be purchased was reduced to 1,000 *arrobas*, and in the sale in 1621 proved a loss. Even Viceroy Gelves, partisan of royalist fiscal measures, welcomed the repeal in 1622.[75] Thus, the attempt to challenge the mercantile grip on the cochineal trade failed.

Cacao was never a Crown monopoly, but the government unsuccessfully did attempt to tax it and to restrict its trade to Mexico City from Guayaquil and Lima (chapter 6). Mexico City merchants were active in the Pacific Coast trade in cacao with Guayaquil and Lima after 1634, precisely when all trade between the two viceroyalties was prohibited. Lope Ossorio Soto, and his two brothers Juan and Lucas took turns traveling back and forth to Guayaquil and Lima in the 1630s, selling China goods for Peruvian silver and Guayaquil cacao. On one such trip Lope fathered a natural son, who tried to obtain some of the profits made on these travels as his inheritance. One of the Ossorio Soto brothers' debtors in Peru was the merchant Juan Cárdenas Jaramillo, who owed them a balance of 1,245 pesos. Cárdenas Jaramillo had begun trading from Seville, moved to Mexico City where he joined the *consulado* in the 1630s, and then settled in Lima, where he sold shipments of 188 *cargas* of cacao and owned but did not manage a retail store. Sebastián Báez Acevedo, Cristóbal Bonilla Bastida, and Antonio Urrutia de Vergara also made large investments in the Pacific cacao trade in the 1630s.[76] Private interests were too strong, however, for the State to gain control over these lucrative businesses.

TEXTILE PRODUCTION: ARTISANS, MERCHANTS, AND *OBRAJEROS*

Types of Enterprises

Textiles—from the silken cloths and *paños de 24*, the highest-quality woolen cloth, to the coarser sackcloth and friezes—were another important branch of New Spain's economy. In 1602, the *cabildo* placed the annual value of *obraje* production alone at more than 400,000 pesos.[77]

Although textiles (yarns, cloth, and made-up clothing) were the colony's major imports, along with hardware and furniture, quite a variety of cloth goods were produced right in the viceroyalty. Despite its importance, less is known about this sector than about mining and agriculture. What types of establishments produced textiles, and where were they located? How were they staffed and capitalized? More generally, did colonial Mexico come to clothe itself, as by the late sixteenth century it did come to feed itself, and reduce importing fabrics from Europe and Asia?

New Spain's textiles benefited from drawing on both indigenous and European traditions. Cotton cloth had, of course, been an important pre-Columbian article of household use, trade, and tribute; its manufacture, usually (although not exclusively) on backstrap looms in the countryside, continued in the seventeenth century to be in the hands of Indian or other small farmers. Shortly after the conquest, Europeans had introduced different blends of wool and silk. Although the cultivation of raw silk had declined by the 1590s, silk goods were still being made up by artisans in the mid-seventeenth century with raw silk imported from Asia. In general, woolens of differing quality were produced by three types of enterprises: the traditional artisan's shop; the factorylike *obraje*, and the *trapiche*, which shared features of both.[78]

The artisans' shops were family concerns that operated in a building which included living quarters, workshop, and a retail store. They usually involved one or two looms and three or four craftsmen at different levels of skill, as master, journeymen, or apprentices. Workers were obtained voluntarily, by parents placing their sons or daughters as apprentices to a particular master. Although blacks and mixed bloods were legally excluded entirely or from master rank from many artisanal guilds, in fact they participated widely. Some reached the highest position of master; however, this rank was more likely to be filled by whites. At the other extreme of production, the *obrajes* used six to ten looms and more and housed average work forces estimated at twenty for Tlaxcala in the late sixteenth century, a hundred for Puebla in 1588, and forty-four for Texcoco in the early seventeenth century. Some *obrajes* had many more; one in Puebla had 257 in 1610. In 1660, the work force of three merchant-owned *obrajes* in Coyoacán was 45, 114, and 125 persons, respectively.

Workers included free persons and indentured apprentices, but many were there as a result of coercion because they were slaves, convicts, vagrants, or orphaned individuals whom law or custom forced into the *obraje*. Another method, debt peonage, increased in the eighteenth century, and general indebtedness reached 50 pesos per individual. As with sugar plantations, authorities tried to end the abuse of Indian workers, and as a result of legal pressure and demographic changes, the ethnic composition of the labor force shifted in the seventeenth century from Indians to black slaves and persons of mixed white, Indian, and black ancestry. *Obrajes* were more centralized than artisanal workshops. Among the latter, such operations as spinning, weaving, and buttonhole making were performed by different shops, but in the *obrajes* all operations were more likely to be carried out under the same roof. The heart of the *obraje*'s resident labor force were the specialists: the weavers, dyers, and finishers (fulling, shearing). The *trapiches* were an intermediate enterprise, which Salvucci describes as half an *obraje*, using nonfamily wage labor but with fewer looms and workers and legally limited about which fabrics it could make.[79]

Textile production, therefore, was a heterogeneous affair with a great diversity of enterprises supplying part of the colonial market. It is tempting to contrast the traditional artisanal sector with the apparently more modern *obraje* and *trapiche* sector and to look for evidence of the latter supplanting the former. But this overlooks changes in seventeenth-century artisanal production such as the increase in unlicensed workshops and a gradual loosening of the guild's regulatory efficiency, as well as the conservative features of the *obraje*. As Salvucci argues, the *obraje* was a capitalistic, but not a protoindustrial, enterprise. Its reliance on a State-coerced labor supply, the high ratio of working to fixed capital, and its increasing technical backwardness meant that it was not a forerunner of the modern factory.[80] Did *obrajes* edge out artisans' shops? In 1620, the sales tax assessments for guilds producing apparel (tanners, glovemakers, capmakers, doubletmakers, silkweavers and spinners, and shoemakers) and for *obrajes* (woolen cloths, hats, and cotton cloths) were the same: 2,950 pesos, or 147,500 pesos total value. Even in the late eighteenth century, Kicza points out, artisanal weavers and hatmakers "lived in uneasy coexistence with these nascent industries."[81]

To illustrate the coexistence between artisan shops and *obrajes*, the Mexico City wholesalers were involved in both types of manufacture. Despite their fame as importers of fine cloths, they played a variety of roles in domestic production of both fine and coarse fabrics.

Merchants and Artisans

In 1607, the Mexico City wholesaler Juan de Castellete formed a company with Fernando de Padilla, a master silkmaker, to manage a store for him and supervise the production of silk clothing there. Castellete contributed 2,500 pesos' worth of silks and merchandise to the store, and Padilla, "mi persona y trabajo" (myself and my labor). Five conditions were listed: (1) Padilla was to trade as profitably as he could with the merchandise; (2) he was not to offer goods on credit; (3) he was to supervise the silkmakers who worked in the shop; (4) he was to receive a salary of 72 pesos a year; and (5) he was to pay Castellete 874 pesos for the merchandise of 2,500 pesos, a clause which made him a partner in the business.

Castellete's activities illustrate the potential for vertical integration in the cloth trades. He was from Toledo, his father had been a merchant, and he knew many silk weavers and spinners from Spain. In the 1610s and 1620s, at the early stages of a commercial career which lasted until his death in 1638, Castellete made diverse investments in the clothing and cloth trades, foreign and domestic. He imported and reexported Chinese silk, sending 5,883 pesos of it to Seville in 1614; in the same period he extended between 80 and 1,600 pesos of credit to capmakers and tailors in Mexico City. Castellete also dealt in shipments of cochineal from Guatemala via Chiapas and had a number of debtors in Guatemala.[82] Finally, he hired silk artisans to finish cloths with his own dyestuffs in shops like the one managed by Padilla, to be sold abroad and in New Spain.

His social ties to artisans from Toledo and his application of his Spanish experience to the New World clothing trades was also true of other merchants in Mexico City. Francisco de Esquivel Castañeda, a merchant of the first third of the century, was the son of a guild-certified silkmaster and trader from Granada. As records taken when his son applied to be a *familiar* of the Inquisition, show, Francisco's family circle was composed of silkweavers, dyers, and merchants. He established himself in Mexico City by exporting cochineal and indigo to Seville. His specialization in the trade was such that he was one of the few whose exports of dyes exceeded his exports of silver. He also reexported Chinese silk to Spain.

Migration to the New World was one way that Spanish artisans could change into merchants, upward mobility through geographical change. Francisco Sánchez Cuenca, another wholesaler, was of artisanal origins and kept up ties with the silk trade. His parents, both silk spinners, were natives of Toledo, and his father-in-law was a silkmaster from Torrijos. In 1639, Sánchez Cuenca was employing a silkmaster and renting living quarters to him. It was natural to link investment in the Chinese silk trade with finishing silk in New Spain. The merchant Pedro de Brizuela imported Chinese silk thread, lent money to a dyer, and exported Chinese silk cloth to Spain. Gabriel López Páramo, also born in Toledo, was the son of a raisin and almond merchant whose associates included several silkmasters and a weaver. In the 1630s, Gabriel traded to the Philippines, extending credit to a Mexico City dyer. Pedro de Toledo, another wholesaler who sent large shipments to Manila, was a creditor of two weavers in the 1630s.[83]

Finishing and selling imported silk goods was quite compatible with trade in, or production of, wool cloth for the domestic market. Juan de Montemayor Herrera invested heavily in the Philippine trade in the 1640s and 1650s. He also advanced credit to a dyer and exported both silk and cochineal to Spain. In 1645, he paid sales tax of 120 pesos on 1,600 cotton cloaks from Nejapa, which he distributed. At the tax rate of 6 percent, his domestic transactions were worth 26,666 pesos, an amount which shows the importance of the local cloth trade to certain Mexico City wholesalers. In the 1650s, Francisco de Arellano Sotomayor, a Manila trader, dealt in 2,867 pesos' worth of coarse woolen cloth from Querétaro and advanced credit of 1,050 pesos to a dyer. Loans to silkmasters (as well as to *obrajeros*) appear in the accounts of other merchants as well.[84]

Merchant financing of artisans was an old story. The trader might provide the wool or silk to the spinner, the spun yarn to the weaver, or the dye to the finisher—all on credit. For the craftsman working up clothes, he could offer gold and silver threads and exotic buttons and trim imported from abroad. To meet food and other expenses, he could offer cash. And in Mexico City, some merchants were major landlords who rented rooms to craftsmen. Then, the merchant could sell the wares more widely, to his correspondents in the provinces.

Merchants have been depicted as undermining the guild system, which was well established in New Spain by the mid-sixteenth century. In 1565, the Crown applied all existing legislation for the Spanish textile industry to the Indies. Yet, as Borah points out, artisans and merchants already were competing for silk yarn produced in New Spain, the latter buying raw silk in the countryside and having it worked up by their own employees.[85] Of course, these employees might be guild certified, as the title "silkmaster" which appears next to the name of several merchants' debtors suggests. By working free-lance for merchants, however, they constituted an alternate form of production, that challenged the self-employed masters of the guild system. Even these, however, relied on merchant advances to varying degrees and, as was the case with farm laborers who could benefit from landowner credit, artisans could benefit from merchant credit.

The Obraje *in the Seventeenth Century*

Compared to the artisanal workshop, the *obraje* was a large-scale, highly capitalized business; compared to the sugar plantation on the one hand and the hacienda on the other, it would be called a middling establishment, whether because of its value, its annual sales, or the extent to which ownership was concentrated in a few hands and regions. The geography of the *obraje* reflects the shift of production from one region to another, which makes it so difficult to determine total output. In the mid-seventeenth century, it began to migrate from its earliest areas of establishment—the Valley of México and the Puebla-Tlaxcala axis—to the Bajío. By the beginning of the seventeenth century there were 110 *obrajes* in central Mexico according to a report prepared by the Crown, in addition to "many others" both in and outside the Valley of México. The chief centers mentioned were Mexico City; the five leagues around the capital, which included Azcapotzalco, Tacuba, Xochimilco, and Texcoco; Puebla; and Tlaxcala. Other centers about which the Crown had not received information when the report was prepared were Cuautitlán, Querétaro, Tecamachalco, Guachindeo, the city of Valladolid, the town of Carrión, and Coyoacán. By the early eighteenth century, San Miguel, Acámbaro, and Querétaro were the centers. Haciendas were also *obraje* sites, but it is not possible to enumerate these. At their height in the seventeenth century, there were probably 135 *obrajes* in New Spain; they were to decline to 39 in 1793.[86]

The high value of *obraje* sales in the seventeenth century was reached by the moderate per *obraje* output of numerous owners. According to the *alcabala* records, the sales of Mexico City's *obrajes de paños* were 80,000 pesos in 1602. If all thirty-five *obrajes* in the capital had been *obrajes de paños*, the annual sales value of the average *obraje* was 2,286 pesos— not a large sum compared to the annual value of production of individual sugar plantations or mines. There are also sales tax records for a number of individual *obrajes* in 1662. They are:

> Antonio de Ansaldo, Coyoacán, 132 pesos of *alcabala* on 2,200 pesos of sales
> don Baltasar Martínes, Azcapotzalco, 99 pesos on 1,650 pesos of sales
> Juan de Olivera, Coyoacán, 32 pesos on 533 pesos of sales
> Diego de Pasalle, Texcoco, 345 pesos on 5,750 pesos of sales
> Andrés de Urrutia, Tacuba, 99 pesos on 1,650 pesos of sales
> Pedro de Sierra, Mexico City, 276 pesos on 4,600 pesos of sales.[81]

Given that taxes were generally underassessed, we might be closer to the truth by doubling these figures, but even so, the middling value of annual sales per *obraje* is still apparent.[87]

Obrajeros earned a modest income from such a volume of business. Assuming profit of about 10 percent[88] on 6,000 pesos of sales, their income of 600 pesos was decent but no more. Perhaps this is why, as a group, Mexico City merchants in the first two-thirds of the seventeenth century were not that interested in owning *obrajes*. In addition to unspectacular profits, the position of *obrajero* did not confer prestige. In such provincial cities as Puebla or Querétaro, *obrajeros* enjoyed a high status, but not in the capital. Within the merchant elite there was a clique that acquired *obrajes*, however, and through them can be glimpsed the workings of the enterprise.

An interlocking group of merchant families dominated the *obrajes* in Coyoacán for most of the seventeenth century. (Between eight to ten *obrajes* were in the suburbs of Tacuba and Coyoacán, and these families owned at least six of them). Of the Coyoacán *obrajeros*, the Díaz de Posadas family owned their *obraje* for more than twenty-six years (1636 to after 1662); the Contreras family for sixty-five years and at least four generations (1627 to after 1692); the Ansaldo family for at least forty-eight years (1647 to 1692); and the Sierra family for at least twenty-eight years (1632 to 1660). Considering that in eighteenth-century Querétaro sixteen years was the longest period of ownership, this is noteworthy. The Coyoacán merchant *obrajeros* intermarried, lent money, and sold slaves to one another, indicating that they were a close-knit group. In addition, they were linked to a larger circle of wholesalers who supplied the merchant *obrajeros* with credit over a period of years.[89]

The history of the *obraje* of the wholesaler Antonio de Ansaldo reveals several characteristics of mercantile ties to the textile industry, probably characteristic of other *obrajes*. Between 1598 and 1692, their *obraje* complex at San Gerónimo and Miraflores passed through four merchant families of the capital. Until 1598, it belonged to Cristóbal Escudero and his wife doña Leonor de Figueroa; after Cristóbal's death, his widow and son Francisco operated it together. At this time the *obraje* at San Gerónimo included seven looms, seven oxen, eight *caballerías* of land, one skilled slave, six shearing scissors, a napraiser, a fulling mill, and an unspecified number of dying vats. At Miraflores there was a fulling mill, a wheat mill with three grinding wheels, and an unspecified number of farmland, slaves, and living quarters. The Escuderos financed their operations with loans, chiefly from religious institutions (see table 13); they also used the

Table 13. Changes in the Sources of Financing for the *Obraje* Complex,
San Gerónimo and Miraflores, Coyoacán (in Pesos)

1590s		1657		1692	
Religious:					
Censos		*Censos*		*Censos*	
Hospital de los Indios [a]	5,000	Redeemed			
Convent of San Juan de la Penitencia	1,400	Redeemed, then reimposed	4,400	Still outstanding	4,40
Capellanía (for bachiller don Juan Zerezo)	2,800	Still outstanding	2,800	Still outstanding	2,80
Censo unspecified	5,700	Redeemed			
		Convent N. S. Limpia Concepción (for madre María de San Francisco)	5,000	Still outstanding	5,00
		Capellanía (for bachiller Manuel de los Reyes)	2,100	Still outstanding	2,10
				Capellanía (for María Ana de Santa Inés, Convent San Joseph de Gracia)	5,25
				Capellanía (for bachiller Francisco de Almazán, presbitero)	5,00
				Convent of Santa Isabel	3,00
Total	14,900		14,300		27,55

Table 13—*Continued*

1590s	1657	1692	
		Lay[b]:	
		don Nicolás de Rosal y Frías	4,000
		Heirs of Capitán don Félix Millán	2,400
		doña Mariana de Cantabrana	3,500
Total	0	0	9,900
Debts	14,900	14,300	37,450

Source: AGN, Civil, 355, 1, ff.6, 29r, 31, 38–39, 52r.

[a]This *censo* was offered together with the merchant Juan Rodríguez de León, so it is one-half religious and one-half lay financing. All institutions listed here are in Mexico City.

[b]All three were the children of wholesalers.

obraje to establish *capellanías*. These chantry funds were pious endowments established for a cleric by a private party; interest from a mortgage imposed on the donor's property supported the device. The *obraje*'s indebtedness reached 17,200 pesos in 1598. In that year doña Leonor sold the complex to Juan Álvarez, who by 1603 had redeemed 9,600 pesos of the previous mortgages but had imposed new ones, also from ecclesiastical institutions, so that by 1608 the *obraje* owed 15,600 pesos. Subsequently, the *obraje* was sold to Baltasar de la Barrera, another wholesaler, and then in 1647 to Antonio de Ansaldo, the husband of doña Ana Covarrubias y Contreras, sister of another merchant *obrajero*, Tomás de Contreras. Antonio's uncle (or brother) Bartolomé wed another sister in the Contreras family, doña Juana. After Antonio's death about 1665, his widow and her son Francisco managed the *obraje*, just as doña Leonor had done with her son in the early seventeenth century.

When Antonio acquired the *obraje*, it carried 7,200 pesos of ecclesiastical mortgages dating from before 1603. Over the course of forty-five years Antonio increased the total indebtedness to 37,450 pesos: 27,550 pesos owed for *censos* and *capellanías* to ecclesiastical institutions and 9,900 pesos owed for loans to the heirs of three merchants. Antonio, therefore, leaned more heavily on merchant financing than his predecessor in the

1590s had done, but the bulk of his debt still consisted of long-term eccle-siastical mortgages. Meanwhile, the rental price of the mills had more than doubled. It rose from 2,000 pesos a year in 1598 to 4,866 pesos a year in 1692. Yet by 1668, the establishment had financial problems and was sued by creditors for not paying interest. They wanted doña Ana Ansaldo to sell, but she hung on through 1695 at least, in part through appealing to the family feeling of her creditors. As don Nicolás de Rosal y Frías put it, "considering that we are all related and from the same family line," her creditors granted a series of postponments of the interest due. Doña Ana's brother, Tomás de Contreras, made interest payments for her on two occasions; her son Francisco lent her money; and her nieces and nephews, who claimed interest owed by doña Ana to their father, accepted renegotiation of the debt. Thus, in 1695, Francisco, who rented the *obraje* from his mother, was able to pay creditors 1,000 pesos out of the 4,866 pesos annual rent. Doña Ana attributed her difficulties to a shortage of wool and its high cost, the deaths of her slave labor force, and a shortage of maize (a consequence of the famine of 1695).[90] She did not mention her debts nor any diminution in demand for clothing.

The merchant financier was the more common figure. The Mexico City wholesalers and clerical institutions were the chief suppliers to *obrajeros* in the valley, while those in Puebla and Querétaro acquired some capital locally.[91] Credit was first supplied to build or purchase the physical plant. *Obrajes* were quite costly. Ansaldo's can be estimated at 48,666 pesos in 1692, when it was at its most valuable, while two others in the Coyoacán group were worth 25,000 pesos and 24,934 pesos.[92] Long-term loans (*censos* from religious organizations) were acquired at this stage. Then there were the operating expenses: purchasing of raw wool, dyes, slaves, and the supplies such as hides, cacao and sugar, and household goods for the owner. These were financed by *censos* or by short-term instruments. The *obraje* of Baltasar de Sierra, a relative of merchant *obrajero* Pedro de Sierra, indicates the high value of the buildings, equipment, and land: 17,944 pesos, or 72 percent of the total (table 14). This *obraje* was a well-integrated enterprise with sites in Mexico City (weaving and dying), Coyoacán (fulling), and Mexicaltzingo (food supply). The value of the slaves, 5,975 pesos, was considerable in an absolute sense, although only 24 percent of the total. Normally, the *obrajero*'s operating expenses (raw wool and fabrics in various stages of production) would have comprised a higher proportion of assets than in Sierra's case, his inventory having been taken several years after his death when some of these were sold.[93]

Table 14. *Obraje* of Baltasar de Sierra, 1679 (in Pesos)

Mexico City site:	
Principal buildings, next to the Convent of San Diego, plus nearby and more distant lots	8,817
5 looms to manufacture *paños 18*, plus 1 more at the fulling mill in Coyoacán, plus 1 to manufacture *paños 24*	180
2 dying cauldrons	500
Other equipment, storage areas, and furniture, including 1 warehouse of clean wool	747
21 slaves	5,975
Total	16,219
Coyoacán site:	
Building which houses fulling mill and water channel	3,000
Fulling mill with conduits and 2 basins	2,000
Surrounding lands and garden	700
Assorted garments and equipment, including 6 *arrobas* of iron for chains	418
Total	6,118
Mexicaltzingo site:	
1 hacienda, "La Estrella," and a quarry, with tools, livestock, and farm implements	2,000
100 pesos en reales collected by Sierra from his workers who went to serve in other *obrajes*	100
Diverse types of fabric	497
Total	2,597
Total value of Sierra *obraje*	24,934

Source: AGN, Tierras, 1056, 5, ff. 15r–19v.

Finally, the Mexico City trader supplied cash and bills of exchange as well as information about prices and taxes. For the provincial producer who sold outside his home region, the Mexico City connection was important.

Thus, merchants had a hand in *obraje* production. Peninsular background in the cloth trades, a use for woolens to stock their provincial stores, and a decent profit rate in selling domestic cloth drew them into the business. The capital needs of the *obrajero*, although lower than those of a sugar mill or mine owner, made outside financing, merchant and ecclesiastic, necessary. As a group, however, more wholesalers offered credit to artisans than to *obrajeros*, perhaps because there were more of the former to whom to lend money. It also may mean the greater importance of handicraft production in the seventeenth century. Finally, some merchant families had roots in both traditions of production.

In 1627, Diego Contreras, the father of the merchant *obrajero* Tomás de Contreras, had asked the Mexico City *cabildo* to allow him to place a seal on the cloth (*paños 24*) which Diego made in his *obraje* in the Mexican town of Magdalena. The seal was to contain the name of Juan Busta-mante, Diego's own father to whom the *obraje* had originally belonged, and the name of the town of Magdalena "as is the custom in Segovia." The grandson, Tomás, was able to reach the status of *obrajero* wholesaler, and his great-grandson, captain don Diego de Contreras, followed *his* father's career, higher up but still in the cloth business. In 1682, don Diego was embroiled in a lawsuit because he sold woolen cloth which did not meet guild standards.[94]

Did the *obraje* and the other types of domestic production promote import-substitution, pointing New Spain in the direction of greater self-sufficiency? It depends on the type of fabric. With regard to coarse woolens used for "tents, sacks, horse blankets, . . . religious habits, military uniforms, and the clothing of the urban poor"—yes. Although some believed the quality of such goods was poorer than comparable European wares, they were widely used and definitely cheaper.[95] *Obrajes*, and, of course, artisans' shops also manufactured fine woolens, and the latter, silks, taffetas, and damasks as well. Of the five types of cloths produced in Puebla in 1597, 96 percent were the high-quality wool *paños 24* or *paños 18*, but because Puebla was the most specialized center, its greater production of fine cloths rather than the coarser woolens and baize fabrics was probably atypical.[96] Some import substitution logically occurred for fine fabrics, but consumers who could pay more—and in the case of China wares, it was not always necessary to pay more—preferred imports. The increase in demand for clothing, therefore, was met in part by local, in part by imported, fabrics.

URBAN REAL ESTATE

One of the most valuable assets of the colonial Mexican economy was the buildings and lots of its major cities. The buildings of the capital were estimated by Juan Díez de la Calle in 1646 to have been worth 20,500,000 pesos in 1607 and 50,000,000 pesos in 1635.[97] The wealthiest members of society were willing to invest thousands of pesos in the hundreds of houses, shops, ecclesiastical buildings, and rooming houses that occupied the urban landscape. Investment in urban real estate and in public office have been seen as the traditional, safe investments of the elites of early modern societies. For the small group of individual residents who owned their houses in the city, status and practicality were more pressing motives than a high return on capital. To conduct one's business affairs and shelter one's household in style, a *casa principal* was a necessity, and ownership of one or more of these multiroomed structures conferred prestige indispensible to upper-class standing. Not only did the merchants aspire to the noble ideal of a *casa poblada* (established household), but they also needed rooms for their warehouse and retail stores, as well as the clerks, apprentices, and artisans whom they may have employed. They also shared enthusiastically the civic pride which characterized residents of the greatest metropolis of the New World. Particularly in the early seventeenth century, the merchant elite substantially influenced the physical development of Mexico City by building houses on empty lots and expanding and beautifying existing structures.

Homeowners and Landlords

The merchant elite invested in three types of urban property. First, all for whom residence information is available (ninety-four) owned their own home and ground-floor shops, which they described as a *casa principal*, or sometimes as a *casa principal y tiendas* (mansion and shops). Even where there was no specific reference to stores, the *casas principales* often had shops on the ground floor. Second, a large number of the wholesalers owned rental property. These buildings ranged from houses adjoining the family mansion and worth similar amounts, sometimes described as *quatro pares de casas, incluyendo la casa principal* (four sets of houses, including the chief dwelling) to a variety of rental units scattered throughout the city. Finally, a smaller number held mortgages on property owned by other people. Thus, the merchants played various roles in the real-estate sector, as they had in the agricultural sector.

Ownership of a mansion that had stores on its lower floor and was located on streets running off the central plaza or in other select spots was the goal of all wholesalers, but the goal took them a while to reach. A merchant would typically begin business while living with a relative or renting accommodations from an ecclesiastical landlord or from the city.

In 1607, Pedro de la Barrera lived in the house of Juan Luis Rivera, treasurer of the mint, but by 1620 Barrera had his own house on prestigious Doncelles. Luis Vásquez Medina lived in the home of his relative, the merchant Nicolás Patiño Dávila. This building was next to Luis's brother's *casa principal* on Pilaseca. When brother Juan died in 1663, Luis inherited his house. The wholesaler might also rent a separate store, until he bought his own. From 1619 to 1621, Juan López Zarate rented a store for 290 pesos a year, but by 1636, he owned two sets of houses with stores on Perpetua. Alonso Picazo Hinojosa likewise rented a store from 1619 to 1621 for 220 pesos; in 1643, he had his own mansion on La Concepción. The records of two sets of desirable rental properties, the thirty-seven houses, stores, and small shops on Celada and San Agustín owned by the city council, and the stores owned by the Hospital Nuestra Señora de la Concepción, demonstrate the movement of merchants from rental to ownership and the gradualness of the traders' ascent to merchant elite status.[98] Most *casas principales* were costly, ranging from 8,000 pesos to 25,000 pesos in price,[99] but the merchant might reduce the expense by assuming the existing mortgages or inheriting a mansion.

The next step, which nearly one-half of the merchants took, was to become a landlord. The majority were central city landlords who owned a few large houses and shops near their own residence, thus strengthening the already existing concentration of wholesalers, retailers of imports, and artisans around the central plaza. Most of these properties fell in *quarteles* (subdivisions) 1 and 2 and the western sections of 3 and 4 of the 1793 García Conde map on which many studies of the colonial capital are based. A smaller number of merchants were citywide landlords who possessed many buildings in the choice central zone and also in other neighborhoods and rented to a heterogeneous population. Specialists in urban real estate their activities affected many of the capital's predominantly rental population. One prime location was the houses on the streets west of the *portales de los mercaderes*, the masonry buildings that housed stores along the west side of the central plaza and were fronted with an arcade. In the early seventeenth century a number of these buildings were owned by three merchant real estate moguls. Martín Bribiesca Roldán held ten or more houses and shops, which in 1623 were auctioned for 155,000 pesos. Next to his property was that of Baltasar Rodríguez de los Ríos, whose holdings, including his *casa principal,* were worth 100,000 pesos in 1607 and 125,000 pesos in 1622. Francisco de la Torre owned 112,000 pesos' worth of real estate, including twenty sets of houses and shops on San Juan in 1621.[100] These were, of course, immense investments in urban buildings by the standard of the time. They show that the merchant did not necessarily limit himself to owning one or two mansions.

Other wholesalers had numerous buildings also. Francisco Medina Reynoso had at least ten buildings, some on del Parque, worth more than 49,200 pesos in 1622, including his own home. Gonzalo Gutiérrez Gil owned more than twenty-five houses and seventeen shops at varied sites throughout the city, including *casas bajas* (one story, poorer houses). Alonso Ortiz Arévalo also owned at least fourteen houses and shops which brought in a total of 11,000 pesos a year in rent in 1622. They included a mansion on elegant San Agustín, which rented for 250 pesos a year, and a smaller *casa baja* in the southern neighborhood of Monserrate which rented for 50 pesos a year. Juan Luis Rivera had at least sixteen houses and shops in 1607. One set, containing three of each, was located at the *tianguis* (Indian market) of San Juan and was worth 12,500 pesos. His total investment in city buildings was 88,000 pesos. These examples are from Mexico City, but merchants owned houses in the provinces too. Rivera had 5,000 pesos' worth in Zacatecas, where Agustín Medina Orozco and Juan Pérez Gallardo also owned property. Several merchants also invested in Puebla, Veracruz, and San Luis Potosí as logical extensions of their commercial activities.[101]

The third type of investment was for the wholesaler to offer credit to other homeowners in the form of *censos*. Chevalier concluded that the Church derived more income from its mortgages on other people's property than it did from its own holdings. Was the same true for merchants, the other major source of liquid capital in seventeenth-century New Spain? Wholesalers preferred rental property because despite the custom of charging only 5 percent of the property's value as rent, rents could be raised, especially if the owner improved the building. *Censos*, on the other hand, were fixed at 5 percent after 1621.

There were some mortgage holders of princely proportions among the merchant elite. One was Juan Castellete, the trader also involved in textile production. His mortgage principal totaled 60,670 pesos, of which 40,000 pesos had been placed on the Higuera Matamoros's Orizaba sugar mill and 20,670 pesos on houses in Mexico City. In 1608, when in his twenties, Castellete began investing in *censos* and continued to do so until his death in 1638, when nineteen mortgages were still outstanding. His *censos* ranged from 300 or 400 pesos to 1,500 pesos on houses owned by persons of diverse occupations including merchants and artisans. Cas tellete had very little rental property. An even greater mortgage holder was merchant García Salcedo, who had offered *censos* worth 98,600 pesos. These included 9,000 pesos on the Colegio of San Pedro y San Pablo, 10,000 pesos on the *propios* (income from municipal land) of Mexico City, 10,000 pesos on the goods and rents of the Cathedral, and 6,900 pesos on property of eighteen individuals, including fellow merchants. Of particular interest is Salcedo's mixture of institutional and individual debtors, the latter, however, borrowing more. His inventory shows that his mortgages ranged from 400 pesos to 25,000 pesos, with 3,000 pesos the more common amount.[102]

Thus, urban real estate was an important investment for all merchants because the value of their *casa principal* alone usually was fairly high. It was also important because homeownership identified the merchant to his colleagues as an established trader and to other members of the elite as a member of the city's upper class.

Impact on Urban Development

Although the rebuilding of Mexico City commenced immediately after the end of Cortés's siege, there were still vacant lots and much construction underway in the early seventeenth century. Some merchant-landlords deserve to be called developers in the positive sense of the word because of the contribution they made to the physical splendor of the city. Thus, Francisco Medina Reynoso declared to the *cabildo* in 1605, that he had constructed fine buildings for the embellishment of Mexico City, and his son Fernando continued to do the same in a different neighborhood in 1620. Merchants, such as Juan Luis Rivera in 1607 and Juan de Rossas in 1616, put up their *casas principales* on the lots granted to them by the *cabildo*. Later, Alonso Ramírez Vargas constructed his houses on Acequia Real by 1643, while Pedro Ruíz Orduñana occupied his in 1624.[103]

Juan Ontiveros Barrera, the merchant turned clergyman, was another type of builder; he renovated existing property. In 1616, he bought from the Convent of San Gerónimo two houses in need of repairs on the calle de Celada for only 2,600 pesos. These became the nucleus of four properties he owned on this street, one worth 12,000 pesos in 1622. Clemente de Valdés, the perennial prior of the *consulado*, made a similar purchase of existing buildings. His holdings have an interesting history. Valdés owned more than forty-six rental houses and shops, many in the Alcaicería of the city west of the *plaza mayor*, which provided income for himself and his widow, who, ten years after his death was renting them out to merchants, silversmiths, barber-surgeons, druggists, priests, weavers, and blacksmiths. The Alcaicería had originally been built on a garbage dump by *regidor* Cristóbal de Molina with a *censo perpetuo* (unredeemable mortgage) from the Marqués del Valle. Molina claimed he had spent more than 200,000 pesos on it, to the "great adornment and good order of this city," and that in 1620 more than eighty *vecinos* (not counting their families) lived there. Valdés's rents in the Alcaicería in the 1640s ranged from 30 pesos to 300 pesos, but most were 200 pesos a year.[104]

The example of Ontiveros Barrera indicates that property values could rise if improvements were made. Baltasar Rodríguez de los Ríos acquired and improved his urban holdings quite systematically, beginning in 1597 with the purchase of a 5,000 peso property and acquiring additional properties in 1604, 1607, and 1613. He spent 6,900 pesos building new houses. Of his *casa principal* with its four shops and four columns and their arcades on the *plaza mayor*, his son stated that it cost 25,000 pesos but that he had improved it by the time of his father's will in 1618 to the value of 50,000 pesos, by building one new store and improving the others to increase their rental value. Mateo Barroso and Pedro Sánchez Olivera offer similar examples.[105] There is only one instance of a merchant's house decreasing in value.

Certainly, there were factors which threatened investments in city buildings. The most extraordinary were the periodic floods which occurred in 1604, 1607, and from 1629 to 1634, which caused much havoc to houses in the capital. Complaints of flood damage appear in the judicial and notarial records of the period, some genuine, others were the usual attempts to stall creditors. The stone buildings in the central zone of the city suffered somewhat less from flood waters. Even without flood, however, the location of the city on a former lake bed meant that subsidence of the soil was an ongoing problem which required rebuilding floors. Other types of common repairs were replacement of doors, retiling of roofs, replacement of rotted wood beams, replastering of walls, rebricking of rooms, recovering of floors, and rebuilding of shop counters. One merchant's children sold his house because they claimed they could not afford the repairs.[106] Some clerical institutions were reluctant to acquire urban property in the seventeenth century for these reasons. As with owners of other types of property, merchant houseowners required outside capital to expand or simply to maintain their real estate. Some of their properties were quite burdened with mortgages. Bribiesca Roldán had 135,000 pesos of *censos* on his 155,000 pesos' worth of houses and stores. More often the merchant imposed mortgages ranging between 6,000 and 10,000 pesos on one or several houses.

Even taking all these disadvantages into account, however, the pattern of merchant investment in urban real estate did not change during the seventy years studied in this volume. The only difference between the early and the mid-seventeenth century is that more merchants owned many rental properties in the earlier period. Urban property was not free of risk by any means, but it was not subject to abrupt price fluctuations or glutted markets. There seems to have been an adequate labor supply for urban construction. The period when Díez de la Calle asserted that the capital's real estate more than doubled in value included the years when the most serious flooding occurred.

As might be expected, considerable continuity of ownership existed among merchant homeowners, as well as a tendency to buy and sell to one another. Living in the same neighborhood, training the next generation in their own homes, intermarrying, and—perhaps most important— earning sufficient income to keep up their mansions and shops—it was quite natural for merchants to keep properties within their own group. Juan de Ontiveros's buildings passed through the hands of six different merchants. Receiving mortgages from colleagues encouraged this practice. Pedro Ruíz de Orduñana bought his house through an interesting arrangement, as a result of a house swap. The previous owner, captain Juan Espinosa Montero, a *regidor* of Manila, had exchanged his houses there for houses in Mexico City owned by Terencio Galli. Ruíz de Orduñana then purchased Espinosa's building. All of the tax collectors of the sales tax on houses and mortgages in the period from 1618 to 1640 were merchants, most connected with the slave trade.[107]

CONCLUSION

Merchants influenced a broad range of colonial Mexican economic activities, primarily as financiers but also as owners and renters. They had close ties to agriculture but of different sorts. Wholesaler interest in the sugar plantations was remarkable. After mining, the largest individual credits on mercantile ledgers were granted to the mills. As owners and lessees, merchants also established a presence in the major producing region, the Cuernavaca-Cuautla Valley and, to some extent, elsewhere throughout the viceroyalty. They were exclusively financiers, however, when it came to the specialty items of cacao, cochineal, indigo, honey, or forest products. By using local agents—*alcaldes mayores*, priests, *caciques* (Indian nobles), and others, they could obtain desired goods. Here the participation of the Mexico City merchant elite meant both the extension of the influence of the capital into the provinces and the extension of the Hispanic economy into the Indian subsistence economy.

More merchants purchased haciendas than any other type of rural property, and the merchant *hacendado* was definitely a social force of the period, illustrating the merging of urban and landed elites. The convergence was only partial, however, because the majority of merchants did not own haciendas. Ranching and basic agriculture were profitable, and certain individuals did become prominent landowners even in the far north, as Chevalier emphasized. They were not typical of the merchant elite, however. Geographically dispersed, producing products of low per-unit value, and not heavily capitalized, the hacienda was less appealing than other types of agriculture.

Merchants influenced textile production more directly. Any wholesaler had to know the cloth trade because textiles, along with hardware, were the chief goods he imported. Moreover, some merchants were the sons and relatives of weavers and spinners from Spain. A number of Mexico City merchants competed with Spanish suppliers by promoting the *obrajes'* fine and coarse woolens. Even more intervened at some stage of artisanal manufacture of silk cloth. Examples of vertical integration exist; for example, financing the growing of cochineal or indigo, dying cloths, and selling them in New Spain or abroad. Judging from the number of merchants involved or the amount of credit they extended, there was less interest in domestic textile production than in silver or sugar, however.

Any account of merchant investments would be incomplete without emphasis on the sums they poured into the buildings of their admired capital city. They were members of a small elite of homeowners and landlords who contributed to the elegance of the city and to the housing of its predominantly rental population. They did not dominate urban real estate, but they held a substantial share and even gave mortgages to clerical institutions. Lacking a complete housing census for the period, the best source of information about ownership are the requests for *datos de agua* (water allotments) that *vecinos* made to the city council. They were reserved for persons who added luster or were useful to the city; only wealthy people could afford these allotments which were periodically taxed at 250 pesos a year. Between 1603 and 1643, 25 percent (31 of 124) of requests by individuals (as opposed to institutions, mainly ecclesiastical), were made by wholesalers. The rest of urban property was owned primarily by the established landholding families and individual clerics—certainly the case in the late colony.[108]

Historians have long been interested in assessing the dynamism of different branches of New Spain's economy. One fruitful approach is to look at the tax revenues generated by different sectors; TePaske and Klein conclude that mining was the most productive. Two other methods are introduced here. Chapter 1 notes common rates of profit for different economic activities; rates were highest in trade and short-term lending. This chapter considers where merchant investments tended to concentrate, assuming that merchants were fairly rational users of capital. Money earned in trade was most commonly plowed back into commerce, lent to producers of silver, sugar, and specialty crops, and used to purchase urban real estate and, as chapter 4 will show, public office. Less often, it purchased sugar plantations, was lent to textile producers, used to buy *obrajes,* and invested in general purpose loans. Finally, it was used to buy the classic hacienda.

Finally, two other features of New Spain's economy from 1590 to 1660 deserve note. Although the State succeeded in drawing a significant surplus through taxes on mining and its mercury monopoly, in the case of agriculture its role was quite reduced. The government attempted to regulate draft labor and intermittently collected small taxes on land and water, but it rarely tried to control prices (except for basic foods) and it stayed out of production. The chief outside burden on agriculture was the Church tithe. This was, therefore, definitely a private-sector economy. It was because the State's participation was limited that wealthy groups like the merchants acquired such economic power. Second, merchants fostered a characteristic colonial entrepreneurial style to finance expanded production through borrowing. Enterprises grew, but at the risk of bankruptcy. Along with other groups, merchants extended credit to enterprises which did not use profits to retire all debts. The result was a more productive and diversified economy but one also vulnerable to disruptions in one of its chief sources of credit: profits from international trade.

CHAPTER IV

Public Office and Private Gain

The government of colonial Mexico has long evoked interest from institutional historians because of its intricate organization and because of its ability to contain conflict in a potentially violent society. The contrast between the high-minded ideals which informed the administration and the self-serving behavior of many of its members has also intrigued observers for some time. Social historians brought a different perspective to the study of the Spanish imperial government. They saw formal structure—the hierarchy of officials, their prescribed duties, and the policies of the Crown—as strongly influenced by an informal structure of relationships, originating outside the administration in family ties, place of birth, or economic interests. They tended to depict the State as relatively weak, dependent on elite groups, and they downplayed its importance as a causal factor. However, the view that the State acted with its own dynamic and autonomy has received renewed acceptance. Fiscal historians call attention to its directive role in the economy, even if some feel that role had a negative impact on productivity. Some view the State's relinquishment of power to local elites as a shrewd retrenchment in a difficult situation.[1]

The purpose of this chapter and the next is to explore how much political power the central government ceded to local elites in the first two-thirds of the seventeenth century. Was the mother country, in the throes of economic decline and political confusion at home, forced to relax its grip and permit considerable independence? And if so, did the colonists accomplish this by challenging the royal government or by other means? More theoretically, these chapters will consider the nature of the political process in colonial Mexico: Were seventeenth-century politics merely struggles between "ins" and "outs," or did fundamental conflicts divide the Empire and the colonists? The basis for this analysis is the political actions of the wholesalers, one of the colonial elites that exercised both formal and informal power with regard to the State and other groups. (*State* refers to the King, agencies in Spain with jurisdiction over the Indies, bureaucrats in America, and royal legislation). This chapter, organized topically, will consider the merchants' position within the administration and how its functions affected them. It will also discuss their informal influence on routine operation of government. Chapter 5, organized chronologically, will analyze merchant impact on fiscal and commercial policy and its implementation. Both chapters will stress the merchants' and other colonists' use of favorable legal provisions as the most characteristic expression of their power. The Conclusion will link topical and chronological approaches. In addition to explaining the relationship between merchants and government, both chapters present new material on the tax system, patronage, loans to the State, and on the purchase of office.

Colonial Mexico was a transitional polity in which both bureaucrats recruited by universalistic standards and local notables and corporations legally had a role. In cities, where there were more public officials, the formal structure naturally had more influence, it provided a context in which informal struggles were played out. The formal government ultimately drew its strength from its legitimizing function, which the elites certainly recognized. Just as silver stood behind the credit network in economic life, the monarch stood behind the bureaucrats in political life. Neither might be visible, but each gave meaning to a respective system.

Government also encompassed a legal role for informal groups. The viceroys or the *cabildo* routinely consulted with nongovernment interest groups on matters of defense, taxes, or Indian policy. Merchants posted bond to assure that royal officials would meet their responsibilities; they provided credit to the royal treasury, types of extraofficial cooperation which were legal. The Laws of the Indies, however, proscribed other connections. Viceroys who sold nonpurchaseable offices to friends or clients were wrong by the standards of the system. Merchants who smuggled goods or had their silver taxed at the lower *diezmo* rate rather than the *quinto* rate acted outside the law. Even so, contravention of these rules did not necessarily result in severe punishment because the government also allowed violators to make amends by payment of a fine or some other restitution. Although elites frequently broke the law, their behavior carried monetary and sometimes other penalties which were preferable to minimize.

Merchants' activities illustrate different types of elite formal and informal power. They held a few high posts in all branches of government, but they clustered in fiscal and administrative branches and at the middle and lower levels, including valuable clerking posts whose impact on how government functioned should be better appreciated. The merchant middle- or lower-level official was as much a stock figure of the time as the dignified judge or the resplendent viceroy. Their great wealth, control of vital goods, key role in fiscal structure, access to commercial information, and interprovincial contacts also made them powerful behind the scenes. Nevertheless, merchants were not allowed to wield the power their fortunes and other contributions would logically have permitted. As a group, the majority held no office; their political impact was not commensurate with their wealth nor comparable to other elite groups.

THE FORMAL ORGANIZATION OF GOVERNMENT

The colonial administration evokes admiration in part because of the scope of its concerns and the complicated allocation of the tasks of government among a variety of officials. While to eighteenth-century reformers (not to mention twentieth-century historians) the Hapsburg system looked inefficient and confusing, in seventeenth-century terms it was one of the more rational, well-articulated elements in colonial society. The system of checks and balances, the high qualifications required for most important posts, the graded salary scale, the guidelines governing promotion, and the philosophical rationale behind the whole system all testify to its sophistication.

The chief branches of civil government in colonial Mexico were the executive (viceroys and military personnel), the central judicial (the *audiencias* in Mexico City and Guadalajara, the General Indian Court, and the Inquisition, which although not a civil body was staffed at lower levels by civil members), the fiscal (tribunal of accounts, royal treasury offices, tax collectors, known as tax farmers, and the mint), the provincial judicial (local governors and magistrates), and the administrative (aldermen and ex-officio officers such as postmaster general and city magistrates).[2] Classifications require caveats, and two are in order here. First, because officials often performed more than one kind of function, branches of government and members' duties did not neatly correspond. District governors, for example, were primarily judicial officers but also acted in executive and administrative capacities. Second, all persons in some sense employed by the government, whether salaried or not, whether temporary or permanent, will herein be considered public officials. Thus, tax farmers, treasurers and paymasters of specific public works, and notaries employed by the courts are included.

Let us consider briefly the ways in which public officials affected commerce and made political allies a prerequisite for mercantile success. Among the responsibilities of the viceroy, the chief military and civil officer, was the right to appoint most *corregidores,* the district governor-magistrates notorious for their illegal commercial activities. He also granted land to deserving colonists, apportioned "voluntary" loans among wealthy subjects, contracted services required by the government, and legislated within the limited sphere allowed by the Crown. The famous system of checks and balances stipulated that most of these powers be shared with the *audiencia,* whose judicial authority especially affected economic life when it heard cases on appeal from lesser judicial authorities such as the merchant guild, the district magistrates, city magistrates, and the treasury officials. The other court of particular interest to traders was the Inquisition. Its trial of persons suspected of practicing Judaism made it a source of commercial information and an opportunity to acquire confiscated goods, cash, and notes.

The duties of fiscal bureaucrats obviously had a sharp impact on merchant activity. Fiscal policy could only be made in the *junta de hacienda,* but treasury officials collected, recorded, and spent the King's revenues, sold the goods received as payment for taxes or confiscated as contraband, and bought supplies needed by the State with little interference from above. They also heard lawsuits regarding taxes and supervised the smelting and taxing of all precious metals. The members of the tribunal of accounts audited all treasury officials and tax farmers. Mint officials registered gold and silver, coined silver, and collected mint fees; the centrality of the mint to merchants is described in chapter 2. Finally, the tax farmers collected such taxes as the imposts on playing cards, gunpowder, or the *cruzada.* They had fewer formal powers than the treasury officials because they were not permanent, salaried employees; nor did they sit with the *junta de hacienda;* nor (with the exception of the *cruzada* farmer) were they called *juez oficial* (an official with judicial powers). As they came to collect more revenues in the seventeenth century, however, their actual importance grew.

The district judicial and administrative branches performed many similar functions, but the former had more power. Because the local magistrate collected tribute, sold mercury to miners in certain districts, and sold merchandise to the Indians under his jurisdiction, his actions vitally affected commerce, especially outside of the cities which were *audiencia* seats. The *cabildo* affected the lives of merchants both as traders and as urban residents in many ways. Its members set prices of certain goods, licensed craftsmen and regulated production, allocated water and maintained public works, regulated the city's grain and meat supply, heard local lawsuits with the *corregidor*, and passed local ordinances.[3]

There was another distinction within the bureaucracy. Within each branch officials were classified either as *ministros superiores* or *ministros inferiores*. Historians of the colonial bureaucracy have not paid as much attention to *ministros inferiores* because they were not in policymaking positions. The lower ranks of the government were significant, however, in part because of the high value of the office, and in part because they determined the impact of many laws on the citizen. The *ministros superiores* performed the function most characteristic of that branch of government, while the more numerous *ministros inferiores* held police or clerical positions to be found in any branch. In the *audiencia*, for example, the *oidor, alcalde de crimen* (judge of the criminal chamber) and *fiscal* were the superior ministers. The inferior ministers included the *alguacil de corte*, the constable who executed fines or imprisonment; the *relatores*, who prepared reports and summaries of cases for court proceedings; and the *receptores*, who collected fines.[4] After 1606, these positions could be bought and renounced. Second, the *ministros inferiores* had their own internal hierarchy. Some offices were much more valuable and prestigious than others. Indeed, some were more expensive than the higher-ranked *ministros superiores*. Table 15 presents the cost of offices, first between 1603 and 1624, and then between 1627 and 1663. The offices appear in the order of their cost, the most expensive first, the least expensive last. Among the *ministros inferiores* certain offices were expensive and led the others in that category. The *secretario de la gobernación* (viceregal secretary) at 126,000 pesos was twelve times the value of the *secretario de entradas de la cárcel de la ciudad* (secretary of the income of the municipal jail) at 11,000 pesos. The office of *receptor general de penas de cámara, estrados y gastos de justicia* (general manager of high court fines and expenses) at 80,000 pesos was worth thirty-one times the value of one of the ordinary *receptores de la real audiencia* (collectors of the high court) at 2,600 pesos. The more costly and prestigious "inferior" posts, therefore, were more important than the term describing their function, such as *secretary* or *collector*, suggests.

Table 15. Cost of Selected Purchaseable Offices
in Mexico City, 1603–24 and 1627–63

Title of Office	1603–24		1627–63		Increase (+) or Decrease (−) in Value
	Cost	Date	Cost	Date	
Tesorero de la casa de moneda (chief administrator of the mint)	250,000	1607	300,000	1663	+50,000
Ensayador y fundidor (assayer of the mint)	140,000	1609	160,000	1633	+20,000
Alguacil mayor desta ciudad[a] (senior constable of the municipality)	—		97,500	1627	—
Secretario de la gobernación (vice-regal secretary)	126,000	1619	72,000	1627	−54,000
Alguacil mayor desta corte (senior con-stable of the high court)	115,000	1611	70,000	1631	−45,000
Receptor de penas de cámara[b] (collector of fines of the high court)	80,000	1622	50,000	1630	−30,000
Tallador (die cutter of the mint)	80,000	1611	100,000	1632	+20,000
Correo mayor (post-master general)	58,000	1603	46,000	1654	−12,000
Contador de cuentas (accountant of the tribunal of accounts)	not yet sold		22,000[c]	1651	—
Depositario general (public trustee)	44,000	1607	50,000	1628	+6,000
Escribano mayor de cámara de lo civil (chief notary of the high court's civil chamber)	63,000	1617	40,000	1658	−23,000

Table 15—*Continued*

Title of Office	1603–24		1627–63		Increase (+) or Decrease (−) in Value
	Cost	Date	Cost	Date	
Escribano del juzgado de bienes de difuntos (notary of the tribunal of intestate property)	17,089	1614	12,000	1645	−5,089
Balansario (weigher of the mint)	13,000	1611	20,000	1639	+7,000
Escribano de las entradas de la cárcel real desta corte (notary of the income of the high court jail)	8,000	1609	—		—
Regidor de la ciudad de México (councilman of Mexico City)	6,000– 11,000	1602– 1618	6,000– 7,000	1636– 1643	−4,000
Secretario de entradas de la cárcel de la ciudad (secretary of the income of the municipal jail)	11,000	1624	6,300	1630	−4,700
Escribano de provincia (provincial notary)	6,000	1609	7,000	1643	+1,000
Escribano de registros de la real audiencia (notary of high court records)	4,000	1609	—		—
Escribano mayor de cámara de la sala de crimen (chief notary of the high court's criminal chamber)	—		4,600	1660	—
Receptor de la real audiencia (collectors of the high court)	2,620	1609	3,200	1645	+580

Table 15—*Continued*

Title of Office	1603–24		1627–63		Increase (+) or Decrease (−) in Value
	Cost	Date	Cost	Date	
Procurador de la real audiencia (attorney for the high court)	2,000	1615	2,400	1643	+400

Sources: tesorero moneda: AGI, Audiencia de México 260 (hereafter Aud Méx); AGN, Vínculos 284; *ensayador:* AGI, Aud Méx 261; Contratación 2754; *alguacil ciudad:* AGI, Aud Méx 75; *secretario gobernación:* Ibid.; *alguacil corte:* Díez de la Calle, 49rv; AGI, Aud Méx 75; *receptor cámara:* AGI, Aud Méx 75; *tallador:* AGI, Contaduría 722; AJ 1631; *correo mayor:* AGI, Indiferente general 77; AC Book 20:217–21; *contador de cuentas:* Guijo 1:175; *depositario general:* AC Book 22:125–32; Book 26:274–91; *escribano civil:* Díez de la Calle, 49v; AGI, Registro de Oficios, México 1098, 32; *escribano difuntos:* Díez de la Calle, 50r; *balansario:* Ibid., 51r; AGI, Registro de Oficios, México 1095, 22; *escribano cárcel corte:* AGI, Aud Méx 325; *regidor:* AC Books 15–22:30–33; *secretario cárcel ciudad:* AGI, Aud Méx 75; *escribano provincia:* Ibid.; Díez de la Calle, 50r; *escribano registros:* AGI, Aud Méx 325; *escribano crimen:* AGI, Registro de Oficios, México 1098, 32; *receptor audiencia:* AGI, Aud Méx 325; Díez de la Calle, 50v; *procurador audiencia:* Díez de la Calle, 50r.
[a]Offices which lack prices for one of the time periods are included to show the prices fetched for these types of posts.
[b]Díez de la Calle states that the price of this office decreased from 40,000 pesos in 1626 to 24,300 pesos in 1645.
[c]For supernumerary position.

MERCHANTS IN THE GOVERNMENT

Only about one-third of the merchants studied held public office. What accounts for this limited degree of participation? To begin with the incentives, officeholding was advantageous because officials intimately affected the conduct of business. Salaried posts provided a secure income, although at the lower levels it was a modest amount. For high officials (aside from viceroy) the legal salary ranged from 2,941 pesos (*oidor*) to 1,287 pesos (provincial *contador* of the royal treasury), but salary was supplemented by illegal income. In 1620, for example, the treasury officers at Veracruz were accused, at least, of collecting bribes of 12,000, 16,000, and 20,000 pesos from smugglers, and at Acapulco, a 8 to 10 percent cut on incoming merchandise. In 1670, the viceroys of New Spain, who received a salary of 27,000 pesos, were said also to obtain 375,000 pesos from the illegal sale of *corregimientos* and *alcaldías mayores*.[5] Purchaseable posts were an asset in themselves, and many provided lucrative fees. One reason many merchants purchased a *receptor* or *contador* office or sought appointment as *corregidor* or treasurer of the *cruzada* was that the first two gave access to cash and silver bar, while the latter was an entrée to tribute goods, dyes, cacao, or mercury.

Prestige and legal immunity for seizure for debt were other motives for obtaining office. Occupants received the much-desired title of office, marched in processions with their colleagues, and enjoyed a degree of status in accord with the rank of the office they held. In 1660, the Council of the Indies wrote to the Crown, stating, "those who buy posts for sale for 8,000 pesos are for the most part rich merchants who do so to benefit their business and defraud royal rents," because in the Indies "only the appearance of a royal office is necessary for the owner to enjoy immunity from prosecution."[6] Logistically, the high number of posts right in the capital was convenient for merchants aspiring to office.

More merchants would have pursued a dual occupation as merchant bureaucrats if not for three obstacles. Most important, intense competition existed with other groups for a finite number of posts, particularly those carrying jurisdiction, such as the treasuryships or as *corregidor*. Without a doubt, the official sale of the former, beginning in 1633, and the illegal but common sale of the latter from the 1620s opened the door to numerous wealthy merchants and to their children who previously would not have been able to enter the hallowed bureaucratic halls. Contemporaries and historians repeatedly commented—usually unfavorably—on the influx of merchants once royal policy or viceregal corruption led to the widespread sale of offices that conferred jurisdiction.

From the standpoint of observers of the bureaucracy, the entry of traders into the level of government conferring jurisdiction was a striking innovation of the seventeenth century. From the standpoint of the merchant community, however, the majority did not occupy the high public offices proscribed to them. Although merchants were wealthy, many other office-seekers had sufficient funds and good connections and also pursued a limited (even if growing) number of positions. The fifty-three posts in the civil bureaucracy (and the Inquisition) in Mexico City for which merchants might qualify were also avidly sought by *peninsular* clients of the viceroys, upwardly mobile bureaucrats, the prosperous landed elite in New Spain, not to mention the famous impecunious descendents of the first settlers such as Gonzalo Gómez de Cervantes, who complained—possibly incorrectly—that settlers' children and grandchildren did not receive their share of royal patronage.

Another obstacle to greater merchant participation was the legal norms and social values of Hispanic culture. According to the tenets of Spanish political thought shaped by the Thomistic belief that the world was organized hierarchically in higher and lower spheres, public service and business were two incompatible and unequal activities. Officeholding was a higher profession than trade, although both were necessary to the general good. The higher the public office, therefore, the more inclusive were the laws forbidding trade, ownership of real estate, or other business. Even aldermen and city magistrates, and after 1619, chief notaries and court recorders, who were able to own property could not trade without royal permission. These strictures reflected both the object of removing public officials from conflicts of interest to which their business activities might lead and the prejudices of a society with aristocratic values.

These proscriptions were, of course, violated frequently, but they did have some impact on the composition and activities of the bureaucracy, even after sales. For example, Viceroy Cerralvo was criticized for appointing Antonio Urrutia de Vergara as *maestre de campo*, for Urrutia "had come to this city with a consignment of wares and married a merchant's daughter. . . . He was *seen trading* [italics added] just like a public merchant."[7] Finally, distance from Madrid, the center of royal patronage, had the same deleterious effect on merchants aspiring to posts not sold at public auction as it did on the aspirations of other colonials. As a result of these constraints—competition, social prejudice, and distance—wealth and ambition did not translate into officeholding for most merchants, even when, as in the seventeenth century, it was possible to purchase most posts. Such rich and prominent wholesalers as Pedro Ruíz de Orduñana, Francisco Medina Reynoso, Simón de Haro, Clemente de Valdés, and Alonso Guerra Chacón held no major posts outside the guild.

The merchants who did combine trade with a formal government position were scattered throughout all five branches of government. In eighty-nine posts, they were more prevalent in the fiscal and administrative branches; they were also found in the central judiciary (table 16). Within these branches were departments where merchants concentrated and where their influence was marked. In the fiscal branch they controlled the tax farms and the mint; in the administrative they were influential in the *cabildo*; and in the central judicial branch, in the Inquisition. Most of these were lower-level sections of the government.

Merchant ownership of city council posts is of particular interest because the council was the only policymaking body in which local elites

Table 16. Merchant Participation in Government, 1590–1660

Branch	Number of Posts Held by Merchants Who Occupied No Other Offices	Number of Posts Held by Merchants Who Also Occupied Other Offices[a]	Total Number of Posts Occupied by Merchants
Executive[b]	4	5	9
Judicial (Central)			
High Court	1	3	
Inquisition	6	9	19
Fiscal			
Treasury[c]	8	7	
Mint	5	2	22
Judicial (Provincial)			
Mexico City	0	1	1
Other cities	4	11	15
Administrative			
Mexico City	6	13	
Other cities	1	3	23
Total	35	54	89

Sources: AGI, Audiencia de México, including Registro de Oficios y Partes; Contaduría (Azogues, Bulas, Naipes, Alcances); Actas de cabildo; AGN, Inquisición, Vínculos; Gregorio M. Guijo, *Diario, 1648–1664*, 2 vols. (México: Porrua, 1952); Antonio de Robles, *Diario de sucesos notables (1665–1703)*, 3 vols. (México: Porrua, 1972).

[a]Twenty merchants held two or more posts, so the total of merchant officeholders was fifty-five.

[b]Includes viceregal and military offices.

[c]Includes Tribunal of Accounts and Tax Farms.

routinely served and because the social origins of the members of the Mexico City *cabildo* have been a subject of dispute. Although the *cabildo* was a weak body compared to the treasury or the *audiencia*, it did articulate local interests with varying degrees of effectiveness. It was long thought that the city council was dominated by first-settler families,[8] although it actually included a mix. It was composed of first settlers, of course, such as the López, Cervantes, and Valdés; as well as landowner or bureaucrat clans who became prominent in the late sixteenth century, such as the Nuñez Prado y Córdoba, the Rivadeneyra, and the Molina; merchants like Alonso Díaz de la Barrera; and the sons or grandsons of merchants, such as the Pacho Mexía, Angulo Reynoso, and López de

Zarate.[9] The *cabildo* was neither controlled by merchants, nor were they excluded from it. The types of office in the city council were *regidores*, *alcaldes ordinarios*, treasury officers and the tax farmer of the *cruzada*, and occupants of special posts—the *correo mayor* (postmaster general), *depositario general* (public trustee), treasurer of the mint, and *alguacil mayor de la ciudad*. The *alcaldes ordinarios* were usually not merchants, the treasury officials, rarely. Between 1590 and 1660 the merchant members of the city council varied from a low of 5 percent in 1590 to a high of 25 percent in 1610. They consistently held two of the four special posts, the offices of postmaster general and public trustee. The treasury of the mint was held first by merchants Juan Luis Rivera and Cristóbal Zuleta. From 1608 to 1663, it was owned by sons of the merchant Diego Matías de Vera, while the *alguacil mayor* was occupied by the son and grandson of the trader Baltasar Rodríguez de los Ríos.[10] Depending on the family, some sons and grandsons continued to trade or retained connections with the merchant community, whereas others were fully transformed into agriculturalists and bureaucrats and were in no sense merchants. The city council generally supported the merchant guild's demands, but most of the issues it raised addressed the interests of the colonial landed elite.

The Inquisition employed a noteworthy proportion of Old Christian merchants in the middle-level posts. Of the eight *alguaciles mayores* who served from 1590 to 1660, four were professional merchants and a fifth was the son of one. Three of the six *receptores generales* were merchants and a fourth was the brother of a wholesaler. Merchants also held the posts of *contador*, *ayudante del secreto* (assistant of the tribunal of the Inquisition), and *alcalde de las cárceles secretos* (officer of the tribunal prisons). Many of the familiars of the Inquisition were merchants, such as Juan Esteban Real[11] (see plate 7).

As these titles suggest, merchants were to be found primarily where offices could be bought, where no higher formal education or previous administrative experience was required, and where their own expertise in accounting was useful. If their posts are ranked on a scale of 1 to 100 based on the salary or purchase price of the office, the prestige accorded it in contemporary documents, and the importance of functions performed, it is apparent that the great majority of offices held by wholesalers (94 percent) were in the middle and lower ranks of government, defined as having a score of 50 points or fewer. By and large, the merchant officials were the accountants, secretaries, and constables; a fair number were provincial *corregidors*, but rarely those of the major cities.

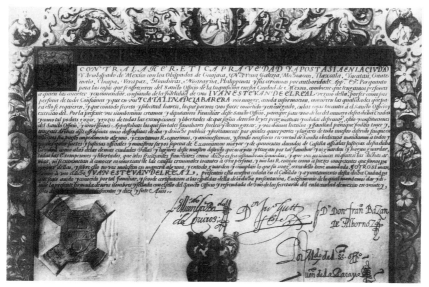

7. Appointment of merchant Juan Esteban del Real
to Familiar of the Inquisition, 1617.

A few brief biographies of merchant officials indicate the limited positions usually available to traders. At one extreme was Francisco de Córdoba y Villafranca, one of the few wholesalers to occupy a regular post in
the treasury branch as *contador mayor de cuentas* (senior accountant in
the tribunal of accounts) and only after these posts were put up for sale.
In the 1640s, Córdoba supervised the repairs on Mexico City's causeways
and dikes and participated in many visits to the *desagüe* (drainage canal
of the Valley of México) after 1650. He was also *alférez* and then captain of one of the city's infantry batallions. Not surprisingly, he held the
office of councilor and then prior of the merchant guild. In 1647, Córdoba
was appointed *alguacil mayor desta corte de México* (senior constable of
the high court); in 1648, he reached the powerful post of *corregidor* of
the capital but only as an interim appointee, and, more typically, he also
served as *juez de obrajes* (supervisor of the *obrajes*) of Mexico City. From
1650 to 1673, Córdoba held the senior accountant post, but even then,
however, he continued such characteristically mercantile commissions as
temporary administrator of the playing card monopoly, superintendant of
the sales tax, and supervisor of diverse flood repairs.

Most wholesalers stayed at the level that Córdoba reached in the 1640s, even though they were wealthy men. Juan de Alcocer illustrates the typical pattern. He began as a tax farmer and, eventually, became a *regidor*. In 1609, Alcocer administered the new tax on wine for the *desagüe* and then rented the playing card farm between 1618 and 1626. Since gambling was a popular diversion, this tax farm was lucrative. In the 1620s and 1630s, he made repairs on the aqueduct of Santa Fe. In 1627, he reached the post of *contador* of the Inquisition. In 1636, he served as alderman in the *cabildo* of the capital, but he also continued his tax farming, acting as administrator of the *cruzada* from 1636 to 1647. The career of Andrés de Acosta, the Portuguese-born slave trader, represented the other extreme from Francisco de Córdoba. Acosta overcame the opposition to his serving as councilor of the *consulado*, but he did not occupy higher posts. He held such offices as collector of the convoy tax imposed on slaves, *receptor* and *pagador* of the Cathedral of Mexico City, and *pagador* for the causeway repairs. The highest office he attained was one of the *receptores* of the *audiencia*.[12]

TAX FARMING

The branch of government where merchants were most influential was the section of the fiscal bureaucracy comprised of the tax farms. Taxes in the Empire were collected directly by royal treasury officials (*en administración*) or indirectly by granting the collection to a corporation or individual outside the government (*en asiento*). In the second case the tax farmer agreed to pay the government a fixed yearly sum in specific installments. The *junta de hacienda* had to approve the farm, and, in the case of the *cruzada* tax, the ecclesiastical commissioner and the supreme council did also.[13] In exchange, the farmer appointed his own agents, kept his own accounts, and retained as profit the excess above the sum owed.

Five commodity taxes were administered by private individuals or corporations in the viceroyalty from 1590 to 1660: the *cruzada*, playing cards, *solimán* (biochloride of mercury), gunpowder, and *alumbre* (alum). The tax on paper, instituted in 1638, was collected directly by the treasury officials during this time. Of these five farms, the first two were by far the most important. In the 1620s, the *cruzada* farm was let at 195,000 pesos a year and the card farm at 80,000 pesos and then 100,000 pesos a year, while the *solimán* farm fetched only 7,500 pesos; later, the *alumbre* farm was let at 600 pesos.[14] All the tax farm posts were occupied by merchants or the sons of merchants. From the government's standpoint, merchants were suitable farmers because they had more cash on hand than any other group and were willing to make it available. For the wholesalers, the contracts were attractive because the farmer could make a profit and could use the provincial agents as commercial employees. In the case of the *cruzada* tax, they also could sell the goods received in payment for the indulgences. Finally, the tax farmer had a title, and this carried a certain amount of prestige; merchants tried to upgrade the status of the office. The case histories of four merchant farmers, Juan Ontiveros Barrera, don Francisco de la Torre, Juan de Alcocer, and Mateo Barroso, illustrate the benefits and drawbacks of this typically merchant fiscal activity.

Features of the Tax Farm Contracts

In January 1626, Ontiveros Barrera was granted the right to collect the *cruzada* tax for eleven years. He agreed to pay the Crown 195,000 pesos annually in three installments. This was the crux of the agreement, but there were many other aspects to Ontiveros's obligations. He promised to pay for a notary, constable, and clerking supplies and to have the decrees sent to the provincial treasurers once the indulgences reached Mexico City, an agreement that included the documents' shipment from Manila to villages in the Philippines! The tax farmer was also a banker to the Crown. Ontiveros agreed to offer the government an advance of 100,000 pesos in cash to be sent on the fleet of 1626. In addition he agreed to pay *libranzas* (letters of credit) drawn by the ecclesiastical commissioner on *cruzada* funds as long as he, Ontiveros, was credited with the amounts. In *casos fortuitos* (unexpected events), such as war, disease, or flood, he was obliged to provide the funds at his disposal if requested by the viceroy. The posting of bond was a crucial element in these contracts. Ontiveros promised to post 150,000 pesos, a very large sum, although he actually posted 164,000 pesos, which was contributed by forty-two individuals.[15]

In exchange for these considerable responsibilities, Ontiveros received benefits which help explain the appeal of tax farming to wholesalers. First, he was to receive a *premio* (commission) of 11.5 percent to cover administrative costs and an additional 6 percent as profit. It was customary to distinguish the commission which covered collection expenses (*administración*) from the commission which covered profits (*intereses*). Other *premios* requested ranged from as much as 23 percent of the tax to 17.5 percent.[16] The *cruzada* farmer made his money because of the huge size of the farm; 6 percent of 195,000 pesos was 11,700 pesos—and that was only the legal earnings. Conversely, the tax farmer could petition to reduce what he owed when the *casos fortuitos* occurred. The farmer's claim of losses was not accepted automatically, but it was not easy for the government to prove him wrong.

In addition to the profits agreed upon in the contract, merchant farmers earned money because of the increase in the consuming population of the viceroyalty. The growth in the market for their "products," such as playing cards, was not immediately reflected in the terms of the tax farms, which were usually fixed for nine or more years without the government increasing the sum due. So the farmer sold more cards but owed the government the original, lesser sum. Between 1591 and 1617, the merchants who ran the card farm paid almost the same annual amount, between 60,814 pesos and 70,000 pesos. After 1618, the sum due was 80,000 pesos, then 100,000 pesos yearly until 1632 (table 17). Meanwhile the farmer collected more and more money from a higher volume of sales and kept the difference.

As with many offices, the tax farmer benefited also from the opportunity to trade. In 1597, for example, *cruzada* farmer Luis Núñez Pérez received payment for indulgences in the form of 3,366 *varas* (about 3,142 yards) coarse wool cloth. He sold the fabric, paid 631 pesos to the royal treasury, and retained the balance for himself. When don Francisco de la Torre took the farm, this practice was legalized. De la Torre obtained the right to trade with *cruzada* commodity payments under certain conditions, an extension of the trade he already carried on. For example, don Francisco's predecessor and then partner, don Pedro, had dealt in maize, cloaks, and other tribute goods before becoming a *cruzada* farmer. In 1612, don Pedro's treasurer in Puebla, Juan de Coca Gaytan, was paid for the indulgences in indigo; Coca Gaytan sold the dyestuff and forwarded 4,774 pesos to don Pedro for the royal treasury.[16] It is probable that he also retained a private profit from the sale. The de la Torres and Ontiveros Barrera were also permitted to retain the proceeds from the farm and use them in their own trade if there were no fleet that year on which to ship them to Spain.[17] The merchant might then resell the goods to his own clients. Ontiveros Barrera, for example, supplied *avío* to the hacendado don Juan de Samano Tercios of Tenacantepec (*jurisdicción* Istlahuaca). In 1629, Ontiveros sold Samano two boxes of cloaks from Campeche received for indulgences for 775 pesos.

The *cruzada* farmer Antonio de Millán had a contract with his provincial treasurer in Campeche, a prominent local merchant named Antonio

Table 17. Tax Farmers of the Playing Card Monopoly, 1591–1661

Name of Tax Farmer	Dates of Contract	Amount Owed (in Pesos)	Source
Tomás de Escocia*	1591–96 Originally to 1600 [a]	60,814 at 5 real rate	AGI, Aud Méx 22, 4 March 1591; Escribanía de Cámara, 169A, f.11r
Alonso Ramírez de Vargas*	1597–1600	60,814 at 5 real rate	AGI, Contaduría 703, Naipes
Alonso Fernández de Flandes*	1600–1609	66,500 at 5 real rate	AGI, Aud Méx 24, 20 April 1600
Luis Moreno de Monroy*	1609–17	70,000 at 5 real rate	AGI, Aud Méx 31, 3 November 1632
Juan de Alcocer*	1618–26	80,000 at 5 real rate	AGI, Escribanía de Cámara, 220C; Aud Méx 28, 24 May 1617
Alonso de Zubián*	1627–28 Originally to 1636 [b]	100,000 at 5 real rate	AGI, Contaduría 727, Naipes
don Francisco de la Torre*	1628–32	100,000 at 5 real rate	AGI, Aud Méx 31, 3 November 1632 and 10 January 1634
Mateo Barroso*	1633–34 and 1634–37 Originally to 1642 [c]	120,000 at 6 real rate 150,000 at 6 real rate	AGI, Aud Méx 31, 3 November 1632, 10 November 1634
Álvaro Paz*	1637–39 Originally to 1646? [d]	195,000 at 8 real rate	AC 32:14; AGI, Aud Méx 33, 27 July 1637
Juan de Alcocer*	1639–40 [e]	45,000 (the new 2 reales only)	AC 32:12
don Nicolás de Salcedo[†] with don Antonio Urrutia de Vergara*	1643–51	90,000 at 6 real rate	AGI, Registro de Oficios, 1096, book 27

Table 17—*Continued*

Name of Tax Farmer	Dates of Contract	Amount Owed (in Pesos)	Source
don Antonio Rendón‡	1652–61	70,000 at 6 real rate	AGI, Aud Méx 37, 19 January 1652

*Indicates occupant was merchant.

‡Indicates occupant was son of merchant.

aEscocia died before completing his contract; it was continued by Ramírez de Vargas.

bZubián administered the tax farm briefly for de la Torre, who described Zubián as "*personero mío.*"

cDe la Torre ceased to administer the tax farm after the rate was raised to 6 reales the deck in 1632 (chapter 4). Barroso ran the farm for the last year of de la Torre's contract and then continued under a new contract of 1634.

dPaz acted for Barroso, who actually continued to manage the tax farm, which went bankrupt in 1639.

eAlcocer was appointed by the city council as interim administrator of the additional 2 reales which had been imposed for the *Armada de Barlovento* in 1636 and took effect in 1637. These new 2 reales were suspended in 1640; the other 6 reales were in abeyance between 1640 and 1643.

Maldonado de Aldana. By the terms of this 1653 agreement, every two years Maldonado was to remit 36,000 pesos from the proceeds of the bulls to Millán, one-half in silver and one-half in local goods of Millán's choosing, which Millán would then sell in Mexico City. In addition, Maldonado was to invest an additional 7,000 pesos of Millán's in Campeche wares. The reach of such arrangements is indicated by a similar contract which Millán made with Diego de Palencia, the provincial treasurer in the Philippines, a long-time business partner of Millán's.

A particularly attractive feature of the *cruzada* farm was that goods traded from it were exempt from the sales tax. This was advantageous enough, but Millán tried to stretch his exemption to cover sales he made before he became tax farmer. The *consulado*, which was collecting the sales tax for the Crown, challenged Millán's exemption. Millán appealed to the Bishop of Michoacán, in whose district he owned property. The guild appealed to the council of the *cruzada* in Spain, which ordered Millán placed under house arrest. Millán's request that his administration of the farm be renewed in 1659 was rejected because of the "exhorbitant conditions" he set. Given these practices, it is not surprising that at his death owed 150,000 pesos to the *cruzada* rent.[18]

Tax farming also offered the merchant benefits which were noneconomic. Ontiveros Barrera obtained the right to appoint all the provincial
treasurers and some minor officials in the tribunal. These officials received their own commission, typically 8 or 5 percent. They were subject
to approval of the same body as the general farmer, and they had to post
bond but beyond that they were beholden only to Ontiveros. These appointees, who came from Mexico City, sometimes met opposition from the
local authorities, who resented their competition. Thus, patronage of fiscal offices was an important benefit for the farmer. Second, the general
farmer and the provincial farmers gained status. They were to have the
title of *juez oficial real*, the same title as the royal treasury officials, and
to be seated with them in public and at city council meetings because
the office of *cruzada* farmer is "so important that it requires all honor and
respect." Other signs of privilege were allowed: the slaves of the general farmer could carry swords and daggers, he and his provincial agents
could wield the staff of royal justice, and his appointment was signed by
the Crown.[19]

While the experience of the tax farmers between 1590 and 1660 was
not invariably advantageous, occupancy of such a post was instrumental
in the increase of many merchant fortunes, both through the commission
and the opportunity to trade. The problem for some farmers came when
they were audited at the end of their contract or during a general inspection and when the findings of the audit were enforced by unsympathetic
officials. One indication of the appeal of tax farming was the *cabildo*'s
desire to administer the *cruzada* itself in 1619.

Tax farming was not an activity for the beginner, however. The contractor had to have the funds to make the *prometido* (cash advance) to the
Crown to obtain the farm and to offer an advance on an annual basis thereafter. In this manner the merchant extended credit to the royal treasury.
For example, for the playing card farm, the wholesalers Tomás de Escocia
and Alonso Fernández de Flandes each advanced 10,000 pesos on the
card rent in 1591 and 1600. Luis Moreno de Monroy advanced 50,000
pesos in 1609, and Juan de Alcocer, 100,000 pesos in 1618. Don Nicolás
de Salcedo offered a *prometido* of 20,000 pesos in 1643 (table 17). For
the *cruzada* farm, Ontiveros Barrera offered 100,000 pesos in 1625, and
Alcocer provided 60,000 pesos in 1636. The farmer also had to extend
credit to the provincial treasurers, credit which might not be repaid for
many years. While running the card farm, Alcocer sold don Tomás Morán
de la Cerda, the *alcalde mayor* of Tlalpujahua, 473 packs of cards at

6 reales each (354 pesos) on credit. Although Alcocer ended his farm in 1626, de la Cerda was still paying him back in 1645. Fernando Ortiz, Alcocer's treasurer in Oaxaca, still owed him 10,418 pesos, while Antonio Gómez de Paz from Puebla still owed 14,862 pesos.[20]

By the time the merchant farmer bid for the farm, he needed to have established a network of colleagues who would provide bond for him. Farmers paid more bond than most other officials because the tax they collected was so high. Such large sums could only be obtained from other merchants. Of Ontiveros's forty-two bondsmen, fourteen offered 6,000 pesos each, a larger than usual amount of bond for the time. With the exception of don Melchor de Vera, the son of a merchant, all Ontiveros's bondsmen were merchants. So were the majority of the backers of the *cruzada* farmer don Gerónimo de Soto and the card farmer Mateo Barroso. Álvaro Paz, Barroso's agent, then successor, posted 112,500 pesos' bond but he had as many as sixty-seven bondsmen who gave smaller amounts of 1,000 to 2,000 pesos. These lower-than-average sums reflect the fact that by 1637, when Paz took the contract, the card farm was in deep trouble. Wealthy men did not want to risk the high bond they had provided in the past for a losing cause. Thus, Paz's backers atypically included some bureaucrat settlers such as don Juan and don Carlos de Samano and don Rafael de Trexo.[21]

Another method of financial backing which merchant farmers obtained from their colleagues was capital provided through a partnership. Tomás de Escocia, the card farmer from 1591 to 1600, established a formal company with other merchants to bid for the farm. One of his co-bidders, Alonso Ramírez de Vargas, assumed the administration of the contract after Escocia died in 1596, half-way through the agreement. The card farmers from 1643 to 1651, don Nicolás de Salcedo, the son of a merchant, and don Antonio Urrutia de Vergara, merchant and *maestre de campo*, were also partners. When Salcedo bid for the farm, Viceroy Salvatierra declared him a suitable candidate but pointed out that since his wealth was entailed and not alienable, he should seek a partner to put up the cash and persuaded Urrutia de Vergara to do so. Other partnerships were those between Alonso de Zubián, who held the card farm for don Francisco de la Torre from 1627 to 1628, and Álvaro Paz, who did the same for Barroso from 1637 to 1639.[22]

Merchants did not invariably support one another. They were competitors as well as colleagues. A lawsuit between don Luis Moreno de Monroy, card farmer from 1609 to 1617, and his successor, Juan de Alcocer, who held the contract from 1618 to 1626, illustrates business rivalries and other aspects of wholesaler participation in the farms. Moreno brought suit against Alcocer for manufacturing cards five months before March 18, 1618, when Alcocer's contract was to begin. Moreno *claimed* that Alcocer planned to dump ten thousand decks on the market, 625 dozen of which had already been sent to Guatemala City and the Province of Soconusco. Alcocer responded that the market was glutted by a great number of counterfeit cards and by the excessive number issued by Moreno. Alcocer's only hope of meeting his payments was to manufacture cards under a new stamp and send them out by the time his contract took effect. Moreno's real complaint was that he wanted Alcocer to buy up his unsold cards, just as Moreno had done with Escocia, but that Alcocer refused to do this.[23]

The career patterns of the merchant farmers of this period indicate that most of them did benefit from their stint as tax contracters. It is important to distinguish between the condition of the farm and that of the farmer. The royal rent might fall into arrears, but the farmer himself rarely went out of business. First, although yearly accounts were supposed to be taken and payments were due annually, the *contaduría* records show payments by tax farmers for a particular year considerably after that installment was due. The Crown's attitude was that as long as the debits were not too great and the merchant farmer sent an advance on the next year's payment to Spain, no action would be taken against him. Meanwhile, the contractor used the sum he withheld for his own purposes. Or, he might be himself waiting for payment from the provincial treasurers. At the end of the tax farm period came the final reckoning, and now the bondsmen were pressed to pay their pledges and the tax farmer's estate was supposed to be seized and auctioned toward the arrears. Second, however, was the fact that merchant farmers were adept at hiding some of their assets from the authorities, as shall be seen in the histories of de la Torre and Barroso.[24] Finally, the Crown preferred a compromise with the powerful merchant group, provided the government recovered some of the debits. The Crown did not want to alienate its chief financiers.

The Careers of Some Tax Farmers

The vicissitudes of don Francisco de la Torre illustrate the fortunes and reputation which might be made through tax farming and the ability of a contracter to postpone the day of reckoning with the government. Don Francisco openly claimed that he made his fortune by farming the *cru-*

zada, which he administered with don Pedro from 1606 to 1619 and by himself from 1619 to 1624. He asserted that his assets increased from nothing in 1609 to 220,000 pesos in 1622. Don Francisco also received other benefits, such as the right to be seated with the *oficiales reales* in the *cabildo*.[25]

Don Francisco's problems began with his alliance with Viceroy Gelves, who ruled New Spain from 1621 to 1624. After Gelves was overthrown, his coterie was vulnerable to the revanchist tendencies of the victorious *audiencia*. In 1624, don Francisco bid for a new *cruzada* farm, but his offer was rejected by the *fiscal*. In 1627, however, don Francisco bid successfully for the card farm, obliging himself to pay 100,000 pesos annually for nine years.[26] Profits from this quarter were reduced by a *caso fortuito*, the great flood of 1629 and 1631. From 1630 on, don Francisco refused to pay the sum promised, claiming that losses due to the flood reduced his intake to only 60,000 pesos a year. *Fiscal* don Juan González Peñafiel, who heard suits related to the tax, would have none of it, however. "It is contrary to reason," he stated, "that anyone would suffer a loss of 40,000 pesos a year [100,000 pesos minus 60,000 pesos], least of all don Francisco de la Torre, thrifty manager of his wealth and very mindful of his legal rights."[27] The extent of don Francisco's losses were difficult to ascertain. What exactly was the effect of the flood on card playing? Don Francisco insisted that the distress suffered by those householders who remained in the city so saddened them that they stopped engaging in one of their favorite pastimes. "On the contrary," asserted the *fiscal*, "since the flood prevented their usual diversions of promenading on the Alameda, people took to playing cards even more than before."[28]

To make matters worse for don Francisco, in 1632, Viceroy Cerralvo increased the price of cards by 1 real, bringing the total to 6 reales per deck to raise money for the *Unión de Armas*, the defense force to be funded by all the kingdoms (chapter 5). It was to add 20,000 pesos to the 100,000 pesos which don Francisco had originally promised to pay. He claimed the increase was illegal. Don Juan, for his part, retorted that the contract did allow an increase of one-seventh. (This was less than the one-fifth increase actually decreed.) Moreover, "contracts were subordinate to general dispositions." Don Francisco replied perceptively that the king would lose more by setting aside a contract than he would gain from the increase.[29]

Don Francisco continued to resist, and Viceroy Cerralvo decreed a compromise solution, a typical approach of the government to challenges. Don Francisco could pay the additional one-seventh, or 14,286 pesos a year, or he could without penalty withdraw from the farm, which would then be auctioned to another bidder. The new farmer would assume responsibility for the whole term of don Francisco's farm (to 1636) in addition to whatever time he bid for himself. If the *audiencia* did rule that don Francisco had suffered losses from the flood, the new farmer would reimburse him. If, on the contrary, it found that don Francisco had profited, as was likely despite his "bankruptcy," he would reimburse the new farmer. This, Cerralvo pointed out to don Juan González Peñafiel, took the burden off the royal fisc to make up the arrears. Don Francisco refused to cooperate, insisting that the accounts he needed to draw up the new farm were lost—another atypical situation for a man of business to be in, the *fiscal* pointed out—and continued to protest his rights.[30]

Don Francisco ignored Cerralvo's order to choose between continuing on a new basis or withdrawing from the card farm. Only over his objections was the farm given to another merchant, Mateo Barroso. In 1634, don Francisco was ordered to pay 6,000 pesos per year for the rest of his contract, which prorated amounted to 14,285 pesos, plus the sums due from the period before 1632. He protested this judgment also, claiming money was due *to* him not *from* him, and through 1645, when he received permission to send a representative to Madrid to take his case to the Council of the Indies, he continued lawsuits defending his position.[31] The amount don Francisco actually owed and the amount he paid is difficult to unravel because statements about his case vary. The *audiencia* judged him worth a million pesos in the 1630s; in 1644, he was able to bid 70,000 pesos for the new card farm, a bid which meant a cash advance of that amount to the Crown.[32] In 1648, Viceroy Salvatierra asserted that the high court had not been able to determine de la Torre's wealth, but the viceroy believed de la Torre had hidden his estate, "because he is very rich and has not suffered losses, and what proves this more than anything else is the great care and expense with which he has conducted his lawsuits."[33] Don Francisco never did pay the Crown what it claimed he owed. The government attempted to collect it from his bondsmen and from his estate after he died. In 1658, some of his houses were sold at auction, and 74,582 pesos passed to the royal coffers.[34] Thus, the career of this card farmer did better than the tax farm which he administered.

Juan de Alcocer, who managed the card farm between 1618 and 1626 and the *cruzada* farm between 1636 and 1647, illustrates the experience of the contracter who profits from his farm while it is in operation but suffers after the final audit is conducted. In Alcocer's case the audit coincided with his death, so that it was his heirs who paid the price. Juan de Alcocer was one of the few guild merchants born in New Spain. His father, Alonso, had been a wholesaler and had farmed the city wine tax on several occasions. By the time Juan took over the card farm, he had been an associate of the merchants Cristóbal de Zuleta and Simón de Haro in several commercial ventures. He later was one of the *compañeros* who purchased the treasuryship of the mint for Juan de Vera. By the time Alcocer completed the card farm he had been chosen an elector of the *consulado* and had held the post of *contador* of the Inquisition. He also owned haciendas in Michoacán and Tacuba, sources of beef and wheat, respectively, for the capital, and two mills at the village of Santa Fe outside Mexico City.[35]

Alcocer began his *cruzada* contract in 1636, in a strong position, therefore, but by its end its debits threatened to chip away at the property he had assiduously assembled. Again, exactly how much Alcocer personally owed the farm is difficult to determine. In his will of 1649, he insisted that he owed money from the last of six collections only and that the sum would be paid by his debtors. Viceroy Salvatierra, however, claimed in May 1647, that Alcocer owed 130,000 pesos from the sixth collection plus other sums from the previous ones. In April 1648, the viceroy stated that Alcocer owed much more: 400,000 pesos.[36] Salvatierra sought to avoid judicial action which would force the sale of Alcocer's hacienda because attaching Alcocer's property would frighten future farmers of the tax and would, in any case, fetch only one-third the value of the hacienda "since one never finds buyers for haciendas who pay cash."[37] At that time Alcocer did pay 52,100 pesos, and he may have handed over additional amounts in 1649. He still owed considerable sums to the *cruzada* farm, however. After his death, the *visitador general* of the tribunal of the *cruzada*, the Bishop of Michoacán, granted one of Alcocer's executors, his brother-in-law *contador* don Martín de Rivera, a delay of twenty years in the collection of the debt so that it could be gradually repaid from the *rents* of Alcocer's haciendas. His widow retained the properties at least until 1655, but by 1666, don Antonio Urrutia de Vergara had bought them from the tribunal of the *cruzada* for 91,500 pesos.[38] By then, however, Alcocer's sons had long been established in the careers their father's tax farming profits had made possible.[39]

Juan de Ontiveros Barrera, *cruzada* contracter from 1626 to 1636, had unblemished success as a tax farmer. Trade to the Philippines and Spain and shrewd investments in urban real estate had earned him a favorable description by the chronicler Gregorio de Guijo when he bid for the farm.

Guijo called him wealthy and highly respected, with very secure bond and a courteous manner toward all. Unlike don Francisco de la Torre, Ontiveros sided with the winners in the political wars of the 1620s, the rebellious *audiencia* and Viceroy Cerralvo. By the end of Ontiveros's administration, *visitador* Pedro de Quiroga described him as a man of unencumbered wealth.[40] When Ontiveros died in 1652, Guijo stated that he did not owe one cent to the farm and that he left 300,000 pesos in assets.

Luis Moreno de Monroy and Antonio de Millán also faired well as farmers of the playing card and *cruzada* taxes respectively.[41] There were two tax farmers whose terms appear to have been unsuccessful, but the appearance is misleading for the second. Don Gerónimo de Soto, *cruzada* contracter from 1600 to 1610, was criticized by Viceroy Montesclaros for having been "inimical to the rent."[42] When Soto died in 1607, he left the farm in disarray, with 170,790 pesos in arrears and insufficient bond to cover it. Soto's personal estate may have been substantial, however; information is lacking on this point. Much more is known about the most celebrated tax farm disaster: Mateo Barroso's management of the card farm. The career of this wily administrator shows how a shrewd businessman first could profit from a farm and then survive its collapse. Barroso presided over the card contract during the 1630s and 1640s, when the Crown twice declared an increase in the cost of cards. This pressure caused the farm to collapse in 1639; in 1641, it owed the royal treasury 434,456 pesos, not the final chapter for either Barroso or for the card farm.

Following the pattern of other tax farmers, Barroso was already a well-established merchant and financier when he undertook to manage the card farm in 1633. Beginning by trading livestock in the Celaya region, he was shipping to Seville by 1611.[43] In 1630, he served as executor of the estate and tutor of the daughter of a Manila *vecino* named Miguel de Urbiola.[44] His livestock sales grossed more than 17,350 pesos a year, while the credit he extended to silver miners in Guanajuato and other towns, brought him 3,000 pesos in annual profit. Barroso's other sales and loans earned him at least 12,500 pesos a year. When he began the card farm, he had assets of more than 80,000 pesos of his own, plus outstanding credits owed by others.[45]

Barroso married the daughter of merchant Tiburcio de Urrea and bought two houses and shops made of cut stone bordering the Church of Espíritu Santo and the Acequia Real in Mexico City, formerly the property of other merchants and worth 36,000 pesos in 1636. The houses were an investment as well as a residence and place of business. Barroso and two associates bought a total of six houses and shops for 23,000 pesos, financed the purchase by replacing a mortgage held by the Convent of San Gerónimo of 16,500 pesos with a mortgage of 21,000 pesos, and together spent 40,000 pesos, a huge sum, on repairs on all the houses.[46] In 1635 and 1637, he was chosen elector of the *consulado*.

Between 1633 and 1637, the administration of the card farm brought Barroso at least 10,000 pesos a year profit; this amounted to 6⅔ percent of his annual quota of 150,000 pesos. When he contracted for a new farm for 1634 through 1642, Barroso had agreed to pay the 214,000 pesos owed from de la Torre's farm and to pay 150,000 pesos annually thereafter. He offered an advance of 60,000 pesos and posted bond of 112,500 pesos.[47] Barroso's problems began in February 1637, when the viceroy and the city implemented the rise in price from 6 to 8 reales the deck to meet the Crown's demand for funds for the *Armada de Barlovento*, the squadron to patrol the western Caribbean (chapter 5). The increase was expected to provide between 45,000 and 60,000 pesos more each year. With cards costing 60 percent more than they had in 1631 (from 5 to 8 reales), demand fell from ten to twelve decks a day to four decks a day. The Crown seemed to have killed the goose that laid the golden eggs.

When the increase was first imposed, Barroso appealed to the *audiencia*, asking it to uphold his original contract, or, if the 2 real increase were confirmed, to order a reduction of 50,000 pesos in the amount Barroso owed each year to compensate for the drop in sales at the higher price. For technical reasons, however, the *audiencia* was prevented from hearing Barroso's suit, and it passed to the *cabildo*. In April 1637, the *regidores* in charge of collection went to Barroso's house and insisted that he post bond for the increase. When Barroso refused, he and his two associates were imprisoned and fined 1,400 pesos; some of his slaves were sold to meet the fine. Although released shortly afterward, he was denied access to the card factory. Then, the *cabildo* offered him a deal: 2,000 pesos a year for himself if he would continue to administer the farm at the 8 real price. He refused. *Regidor* Francisco Castillo took over the factory and hid the royal seal needed to make the cards from Barroso.[48]

At this juncture, in a manner typical of merchant practices, Barroso was temporarily rescued by two associates, the registered broker Álvaro Paz and the constable of the high court don Nicolás de Bonilla. They bid successfully for the farm in 1637 at the sum of 150,000 pesos plus 45,000 pesos for the new 2 real tax on the condition that criminal charges against Barroso be dropped and that he not appeal to any other courts. Then, contrary to the wishes of the viceroy, they handed the actual management of the farm back to Barroso. The damage both to Barroso's credit and to the market for cards had already been done, however. For the first time in the history of the card farm no new decks were produced because of lack of demand for the high-priced cards. Barroso could not make the triennial payments and claimed he lost 70,000 pesos in eight months. By September 1639, 311,000 pesos were owed, and treasury officials began to embargo Barroso, Paz, and Bonilla Bastida's goods. The farm collapsed.[49]

Fortunately for Barroso, this disaster coincided with Bishop Palafox's *residencia* (end of term evaluation) of Viceroy Cadereita. In January 1641, Barroso placed a claim against Cadereita's estate. He asked for the enormous sum of 217,000 pesos to cover the damages he had suffered. Although Palafox took the extent of the losses he claimed with a grain of salt, he believed Barroso was due some recompense, and he ordered Cadereita's estate to pay Barroso 20,000 pesos plus legal expenses. Palafox also supported Barroso's right to appeal the increase of the 2 reales in the 1637 contract to the *audiencia*.[50] Later, the *cabildo* was also fined 8,000 pesos for its conduct. Thus, the Crown, through its representative Palafox, reversed the policy imposed by Cadereita, also its representative, illustrating once again that the relationship between the merchant official and the State was highly sensitive to personalities and events.

With respect to the losses sustained by the Crown, it chose not to prosecute Barroso and Paz, but, typically, to compose the huge debt of 434,456 pesos outstanding in 1643. The debt was reduced by the *junta de hacienda* to 121,585 pesos and repayed. The advance of 60,000 pesos that Barroso promised when he signed the contract of 1634 was applied to the debt and paid by his bondsmen. Barroso transferred the 20,000 pesos he had charged against Cadereita to the Crown. He made 10,300 pesos' worth of his personal credits and 20,595 pesos of the card farm's credits over to the government as well. The *cabildo* was to pay its 8,000 peso fine over four years' time. Most of this was eventually repaid, with only 13,750 pesos outstanding in 1663.[51]

The bankruptcy of 1643 was a temporary bankruptcy of the card farm. When a new contractor assumed it at the lower rate of 90,000 pesos, it began to function again at a more realistic level. Nor did Barroso suffer a definitive reversal. As the bankruptcy settlement shows, he personally only paid 10,300 pesos; his bondsmen, the tax farm, and the city council paid the bulk of the debt. Barroso left jail for sanctuary and, after that, freedom. Moreover, Cadereita's *residencia* revealed that while the debt was being settled, Barroso had salted away 42,000 pesos (and probably more) by making them over to his father-in-law Tiburcio de Urrea. Thus, in 1640, Barroso was still trading to the Philippines. In 1641, he made a new bid for the card farm, but it was rejected as being too low.[52]

INFORMAL RELATIONSHIPS

From Bond to Business

Merchants' influence in government went considerably beyond occupancy of the formal positions in the five branches of the bureaucracy. To some extent, they simply shared in the influence which any wealthy group exerted on the administration and performed two functions indispensable to the operation of government. They posted the bond which most public officials had to present before taking office, and they provided the loans which the royal treasury needed to function while awaiting the arrival of tax revenues. The difference was that wholesalers specialized in these activities, which although legitimate often led to other forbidden arrangements. Such practices involved the merchant as financier and the official as deliverer of some type of illegal favor.

Historians have sometimes depicted both parties to such arrangements as clever manipulators of the system to their mutual advantage. In fact, however, these illicit deals were fraught with risks, the risk of detection for both sides and the risk that the official would renege on his promises to the merchant. A noteworthy difference between formal and informal power in colonial Mexico was that the rewards of the former were certain, whereas rewards of the latter were not.

Merchants had much to gain from friendships with members of all branches of government. Scholars have stressed the *alcalde mayor*–merchant tie, noting that merchants bonded the *alcaldes* and then extended credit to them so that they would provide the merchants with trade goods produced in their districts or with monopolies on the sale of imported goods. The bondsman-turned-partner of a provincial *alcalde mayor*, however, was only one variant on the theme of informal relationships.

Wholesalers of the capital provided bond and credit to public officials from the viceroy down to provincial notaries. Their financial services were in demand at every level of government. The bond required varied according to the office, naturally. For *alcalde mayores* or *corregidores* in New Spain, eight to ten persons often contributed 2,000 pesos to 4,000 pesos each, for a total of 16,000 to 40,000 pesos. The official was beholden to a number of *fiadores* (bondsmen), therefore, and the bondsmen limited their risk. Many, although not all, of the bondsmen of *corregidores* and treasury officials were Mexico City merchants. For example, Juan Ontiveros Nava, *alcalde mayor* of Sultepec and don Juan Espinosa Mondragón, *alcalde mayor* of Zaqualpa, in the 1620s were bonded primarily by merchants. Gonzalo de Córdoba and Andrés de Balmaceda, *regidores* of Mexico City, however, were also among their *fiadores*. *Factor* of the royal treasury at Acapulco, don Diego Torres y Sosa, was bonded by merchants but also by don Francisco López de Peralta, scion of a settler family.[53]

Posting bond was not without its risks. In 1631 and 1632, nine Mexico City wholesalers who had contributed bond for treasury officials of Veracruz had to pay their arrears in amounts ranging from 6 pesos to 270 pesos per merchant.[54] On the other hand, bondsmen could sometimes recoup their losses by purchasing the property of defaulting public officials. Sugar mills, haciendas, and slaves could be bought, if desired. Merchants might post bond for several officials at one time. Juan Bautista Guemez was bondsman for the *alcaldes mayores* of Gualpa, Tetela, and Guadalcázar. Between 1625 and 1628, Blas de Pedrossa bonded the *alcaldes mayores* of Pachuca, Zaqualpa, Guanajuato, Cuautla, and Sultepec.[55] Many references exist to merchants receiving power of attorney from officials of different ranks, an arrangement which could originate in their provision of bond. Captain Juan de Olin acted for the *alcalde mayor* of Chichigapa in 1651, while Juan Caro de Mallen was the agent of captain Juan de Vargas, first when he was *alcalde mayor* of Jalapa and then when he moved to *alcalde mayor* of Pachuca. Not surprisingly, the *alcaldes mayores* of Veracruz and Acapulco were of special interest to merchants.[56]

By requiring government officials to post bond, the Crown established a system which introduced trade into a network originally set up for administrative purposes. Thus, the wholesaler Juan Rodríguez de León posted bond for the *depositario general* of Mérida. He purchased cloaks, wax, and honey from Mérida for nearly thirty years with silver, some obtained from another official he bonded, the *alcalde mayor* of the mining town of Tlalpujahua. Rodríguez de León also obtained Chinese fabrics from his bureaucrat debtor in Manila. Another merchant, Simón de Soria, extended credit to the residents of the mining towns of San Miguel and Casulla and of Sichú and San Esteban de Albuquerque; he was also an agent of the Bishop of Oaxaca, who may have been a source of cochineal for Soria.[57] Sometimes wholesalers succeeded to the office of the people they bonded or represented. In 1601, Juan Pardo de Agüero acted for Francisco Calderón de Vargas, *alcalde mayor* of the mining center of Temascaltepec; Calderón de Vargas then moved to the same post at Cholula. (By 1625, he had left it to become *alcalde mayor* of Chichigapa.) Meanwhile, the merchant Pardo de Agüero had been busy. In 1603, he served as *alcalde mayor* of Teposcolula, where he invested money in the purchase of *huipiles* which he then sold in Guatemala. In 1619, he had become *alcalde mayor* of Cholula and now empowered wholesaler Clemente de Valdés as his agent.[58]

Loans from merchants to officials could be princely. The merchant turned senior accountant Francisco de Córdoba lent Nicolás Bonilla Bastida 21,000 pesos when he left to become *alcalde mayor* of San Luis Potosí.[59] The *alguacil mayor* of the Inquisition in Manila had borrowed 54,000 pesos from Baltasar Rodríguez de los Ríos for merchandise, while the merchant Francisco Arellano Sotomayor had lent the *alcalde mayor* of Orizaba 18,000 pesos, still outstanding at Arellano's death in 1654. Of course, officials like the notary public of Chalco or Guazaqualco did not receive credit on this scale. They were more likely to obtain 1,000 peso loans.[60] Whatever the amount, however, wholesalers provided the cash lubricant that greased the wheels of State and maintained the transit of goods and favors to the merchant elite.

Bankers to the Viceroys

Another type of legitimate informal involvement in government by merchants was the loans they made to the royal treasury during those months when expenses had to be met but royal revenues had not yet arrived. Public, legal loans were made to send additional funds back to the Crown, to provision ships and pay soldiers and sailors going to Seville or Manila, to pay the salaries of *audiencia* judges and other officials, and, in time of enemy threat, to send soldiers to the coast or outfit a warning vessel. These loans were for needs which arose frequently. No mention of interest appears in the records of these public-sector loans. Lenders requested and, contrary to our impression of Hapsburg finance, usually received prompt repayment, sometimes within two weeks, usually within a year; lenders also received appointments to office, membership in military orders, and favorable tax assessments.

These loans by merchants and other wealthy citizens to the treasury should be distinguished from the better-known "gracious gift and loan" requested by the king from his subjects on various occasions during the colonial period. Many more people subscribed to these loans and gifts. They were not financiers but rather public officials, *vecinos* of provincial towns, and corporations whose public position required them to contribute. Indeed, it was a way of taxing people exempt from direct taxes in the Empire. Although their contributions were useful, people who subscribed to gracious gifts and loans on an occasional basis did not occupy the same central role as merchants who repeatedly lent to the treasury and could be more or less counted on for assistance on an annual basis. In addition to merchants, frequent lenders included public officials and important landed families, but far more merchants lent than individuals from these other groups. Merchants could be called professional financiers.

Most loans to the treasury were at least 2,000 pesos, and many were 10,000, 20,000 or even 50,000 pesos. There was a central group of financiers, from two to seven individuals in most years, twelve to twenty in some years. The number of lenders tended to be fewer after 1630, when only two individuals lent all the money borrowed in that year. In addition to individual lenders, there were also institutional lenders, corporations, and even different branches of the treasury, which provided money where the government needed it. These institutional lenders were very important until the second decade of the century. After that, they were few and far between, and the treasury relied almost completely on individuals. Each generation produced its little group of financiers to the Crown. In the early seventeenth century, the merchants Francisco de Rossales, Álvaro Rodríguez Acevedo, Baltasar Rodríguez de los Ríos, and Francisco Medina Reynoso were among the most important, lending 8,000 or 20,000 pesos to the government on several occasions. Others, such as Andrés de Acosta and Gaspar de Peralta, lent smaller sums of 2,000 to 3,000 pesos but with greater frequency. In the 1620s and 1630s, Cristóbal Bonilla Bastida, Melchor de Cuéllar, Clemente de Valdés, and Cristóbal de Zuleta were prominent. In the 1640s and 1650s, five men dominated public banking: Simón de Haro, Esteban Molina Mosquera, Álvaro de Lorenzana, José de Retes, and Joseph de Quesada. In 1650, Molina Mosquera lent the government 32,000 pesos to dispatch the Manila galleon, while Simón de Haro provided 20,000 pesos for the galleon, 60,000 pesos for the fleet, and 19,681 pesos to pay salaries. In 1654, he lent 25,000 pesos for the fleet and 46,000 pesos for salaries. In 1655, he provided 100,000 pesos for the dispatch of the Manila galleon![61]

By relying on Mexico City wholesalers for short-term credit to meet government operating expenses, the Crown made more likely alliances between the officials who requested the loans and the merchants who provided them. Among the entourage which surrounded every viceroy and some high court judges was a small group of wholesalers "in his confidence" who lent him money for his personal needs, provided capital and cover for trade ventures in which the official was forbidden to participate, and ran shady operations of different kinds. In return for cash and goods, merchants received a variety of benefits, some stemming from the patronage powers of the viceroy and the *oidores*, others from their judicial attributes. More attention has been paid to the former. Viceroys could appoint their merchant allies to offices, to military commissions, and to the three military orders. Less noted but also important, the viceroy and *oidores* heard appeals from the lower courts regarding tax assessments and tax arrears. They could compose fines levied on smugglers, embezzlers, hoarders, and price-gougers. Or, they could confirm the original fine but postpone its collection.

The *visita* of Diego Landeras de Velasco, who had a reputation for honesty, uncovered bribes and business deals during the terms of Viceroys Monterrey (1595–1603) and Montesclaros (1603–7) between high court judges and merchants. Baltasar Rodríguez de los Ríos lent money to the *oidor* Juan Balderrama Maldonado to ensure favorable judicial rulings, and Pedro de la Barrera formed a partnership to trade with the *oidor* Santiago Riego. Viceroy Guadalcazar's tenure in office (1612–20) was synonymous with widespread corruption, but because no *visita general* occurred during it, little documentation remains. During the term of Viceroy Cerralvo (1624–35) there was, it was alleged, a charmed circle of six to eight merchants whose sales and import-export taxes were waived by the viceroy, whose lawsuits received favorable attention, and who were allowed to exceed by one-third the prices temporarily fixed by the city council on such scarce imports as linen goods, olive oil, paper, and iron. Stefantoni Federegui, the cochineal king during these years, was a member of this group. In 1624, he had, in a sense, invested in the viceroy by posting 8,262 pesos of bond with the *casa de contratación* against Cerralvo's traveling expenses. He was accused of creating a shortage of vanilla in 1635 by shipping quantities to Spain and causing the price in Mexico to rise from 2 pesos to 16 pesos the *libra*. Other confidants of Cerralvo included Cristóbal Bonilla Bastida, who concealed the viceroy's trade goods, and don Antonio Urrutia de Vergara, who was accused of acting as Cerralvo's broker in the sale of offices of war and justice. The bribes (or sale prices) charged by Urrutia de Vergara ranged from 7,000 pesos for the *alcalde mayor* of Nejapa, occupied by the son of merchant Clemente de Valdés, to 28,000 pesos for the governorship of the Philippines.[62]

Viceroy Cerralvo was, of course, deeply involved in illegal partnerships with merchants, but such transgressions occurred to some degree under every viceroy, though less so under Gelves. Gelves, however, had his own favorite, Tomás de Zuaznavar y Aguirre, *alguacil mayor* of the Inquisition and captain of the Basque Regiment, who was kept in his post by Gelves. The highest level of government was so honeycombed by these arrangements that *visitador* Landeras concluded that he would have little success prosecuting officials unless he granted their merchant partners immunity from prosecution if they testified. Viceroy Cadereita (1636–40) sold corregidorships before it became legal to do so in 1677. One was purchased by don Álvaro Rodríguez de Acevedo, son of the merchant Álvaro Rodríguez de Acevedo (chapter 3). Don Álvaro, already holding the post of *receptor de penas de cámara*, bought the *alcalde* mayorship of Huachinango, where he had his haciendas, for 20,000 pesos. The Conde de Salvatierra (1642–48) reduced Urrutia de Vergara's tax assessments. Viceroy Albuquerque (1653–60) was said to have stored 130 mule loads of his Philippine goods in the warehouse of the merchant Juan Vásquez Medina, who then distributed them for him.[63]

The experience that Álvaro de Lorenzana, one of the most important and respected lenders to the treasury in the 1640s and 1650s, had with two viceroys illustrates the risks that these relationships might entail. In 1640, Lorenzana lent the immense sum of 50,000 pesos to Viceroy Escalona. By the time of the viceroy's dismissal in 1642, he had not repaid Lorenzana, who asked Bishop Palafox, the official conducting Escalona's *residencia*, to seize Escalona's goods so that Lorenzana could be repaid. This was impossible, however, for Escalona had hidden the goods and claimed that the repayment date had not yet arrived. The outcome of Escalona's default is not known, but in another instance Lorenzana again came close to being outwitted by his viceregal associate. Lorenzana enjoyed a "close friendship" with one of Escalona's successors, Viceroy Alva de Liste, a friendship that Lorenzana used to intimidate those who traded with him. The viceroy had borrowed 22,000 pesos from Lorenzana. Although Alva de Liste had not yet repaid him, when Lorenzana was ill, the viceroy visited him and asked Lorenzana to leave something for Alva de Liste's heirs. Lorenzana refused. After he died, Alva de Liste tried to claim a share of the merchant's estate, based on the lack of any heirs. The executor of Lorenzana's estate did agree to forgive Alva de Liste the debt, but the *corregidor* reversed this arrangement, for he was determined that the viceroy must repay, and that 22,000 pesos revert to the royal treasury in payment of Lorenzana's overdue taxes.[64]

Under Viceroy Baños (1660–64) at least twelve merchants were charged with providing capital for diverse illegal operations. Domingo de Cantabrana distinguished himself. Not only did he lend the *alcalde mayor* of Villa Alta 117,000 pesos, but he also sent 70,000 pesos to Acapulco to invest for Baños in Philippine wares. Cantabrana also charged fees for Baños's sales and even renewals of office and placed his relatives in important district governorships, such as that of Mestitlán de la Sierra.[65]

The long *visita* of 1662 through 1685 showed the pervasiveness of these illegal merchant-official connections. The members of the *tribunal de cuentas* (tribunal of accounts) were charged with sixteen counts of illegal actions, chiefly failure to collect debts owed the treasury and to require reports of the officials under their supervision.[66] The miners of Zacatecas owed 454,905 pesos to the treasury there, but by 1669, only 94,297 pesos had been collected.[67] The *tribunal* officials were not entirely to blame for the deficit their lawyers pointed out, but what are we to make of the fact that they used a prominent merchant to bribe one of the *visitadores*, *contador* Francisco Lorenzo de San Milián and that San Milián had formed a company with the brothers Sebastián and Francisco Gómez Rendón, "well-known *rescatadores* in Zacatecas, Sombrerete, Mazapil, Charcas, and Fresnillo"?[68]

CONCLUSION

Local elites clearly gained power at the expense of the State in seventeenth-century New Spain. The government had already entrusted some of its essential functions such as coinage, the production of the economy's most important good (silver), and much of mainland defense, to private interests. In the seventeenth century the tendency increased, especially after the Crown sold higher offices and farmed out more royal taxes. Moreover, because government itself was defined to include the participation of extra-governmental groups, local notables had a legitimate voice in rule.

How we assess the outcome of this trend depends a great deal on our frame of reference. If we compare the power exerted by formal authority at this time to that envisioned by the monarch and the Laws of the Indies, most certainly the actuality does not measure up to the ideal. If we compare State power in seventeenth-century Mexico to that in the late eighteenth century (or to the European governments at the later time), the Spanish state was indeed weak. If we look at the State in comparison to other organized groups in seventeenth-century New Spain, however, our conclusions are otherwise. Formal government was a partner in the unacknowledged contract between the State and the upper levels of society, but it was an indispensible and unique partner because it originated outside colonial society, had a greater degree of continuity than the shifting local alliances, and had the symbolic authority of the king behind it.

Local elites knew they benefited from a stable and prestigious State. They wanted to turn it to their own purposes without challenging its unique attributes, and in many respects they succeeded. They gained great economic benefits, which some have defined as the right to exploit the non-elites with a free hand.[69] The licit incomes of state officials were sometimes large and usually secure, and they also received important noneconomic rewards of honor, influence, and mobility through office. The tax farming contract illustrates the mix of benefits obtained by the merchants. With regard to social control, the State upheld the hierarchy of the *sociedad de castas*, which the elites deemed essential. In return, government servants carried out their executive, judicial, or administrative tasks with varying degrees of effectiveness and honesty and publicly supported the authority of the Crown.

For its part, only the State could legitimize a society born of conquest and perpetuating many inequities. It also had broad theoretical powers, which under a vigorous viceroy or regalist *audiencia* it could make effective. Few areas of economic life were exempt from the heavy hand of attempted State regulation, as was the case with the merchants. It was essential for them to be on good terms with at least one faction within the bureaucracy in order to conduct business.

Another advantage was that the State had fewer offices available than there were aspirants. Elites competed, therefore, for a limited number of formal posts and informal types of influence. Among the merchants, the mix of corporate solidarity and individualistic rivalry made each interest group dependent on State favor. Merchants supported one another's political ambitions by pooling capital for offices, but they also undermined one another in lawsuits.

Furthermore, the State alone had the right to set qualifications for office, including those of education, experience, social status, and wealth. In the seventeenth century the financially straitened government accorded wealth increasing weight in making appointments. Thus, merchants bought numerous offices and were to be found in all five branches of government, especially at middle- and lower-level clerking posts. These latter *ministros inferiores* have not received much attention in studies of the bureaucracy, but they were lucrative posts and could affect the implementation of fines, trade restrictions, and contracts. Despite such merchant penetration of government in the seventeenth century, the State still had the option of enforcing the laws that prohibited high officials from trading. Merchant political ambitions were checked, in part, by legal norms and social prejudice which held commerce to be a lower form of activity than officeholding.

The problem for the State was that in an early modern polity such as colonial Mexico's, the informal influence of local elites was·legitimate up to a certain point, and when the State was under financial duress this already established influence grew dangerously. For example, the reliance of the viceregal government on loans from merchants to pay annual expenses was legal but threatening to State power. From such connections grew the illegal trading partnerships and sales of offices and *mercedes* which so undermined the authority and dignity of the State from 1590 to 1660. Nevertheless, the State's special role in the unwritten contract persisted.

CHAPTER V

The Merchantilist Mirage; Trade,
Taxes, and Turmoil

Despite the fact that in the seventeenth century Spain experienced its worst military-political crisis to date, which provoked sweeping new fiscal burdens as well as changes in patronage and commercial policies in the Indies and Spain, there has been no scholarly debate about politics comparable to the debate about the economy. One object of this chapter is to promote such a debate by identifying different approaches to politics and testing them against the new evidence presented here about two issues during the period from 1590 to 1660: the restrictions on interregional trade and the imposition of new taxes. The other object of this chapter is to show the political and legal actions taken by merchants and other colonists and assess their political power.

One historiographical approach is to assume that politics came closer either to a conflict or a consensus model. The conflict model is sometimes implicitly identified with a rational-legal structure of government and with a more modern society; the consensus model is more frequently associated with a patrimonial, traditional society. In the past, historians wrote about New Spain's politics as a fundamental conflict between metropolis and colony. The efforts of a viceroy and a few like-minded officials and friars to implement royal policy provoked the opposition of local landowners, miners, merchants, and clergy, who thought primarily of their own interests. Recent scholars updated and broadened the conflict approach, depicting two political groups with enduring differences. A "bureaucratic" party comprised of officials, *caciques*, and friars and usually corresponding to the *peninsular* group fought a "settlers' party" (generally creoles) comprised of the secular clergy, landowners, and merchants on such matters as the continued administration by friars of Indian parishes, the use of the *repartimiento* (forced labor draft) in agriculture, the closure of the

Peru trade, and the payment of new taxes. These historians also brought to light the rich political literature of pamphlets and petitions through which the parties urged their viewpoints.[1]

Social historians, on the other hand, downplayed the peninsular-creole rivalry and stressed the common interests which bound together all members of the elite and the colony to Spain. Intermarriage, long residence in Mexico, and joint participation in economic activities blurred political antagonisms. The division between *peninsulares* in the high bureaucracy and creoles in the *cabildo* were smoothed over by family ties; in fact, *peninsulares* purchased municipal office precisely to integrate themselves into local society. Outside the elite, *compadrazgo* and other patronage relationships mitigated social conflict.[2] Such conflict that occurred was transient, a conflict between "ins" and "outs" rather than among interest groups with fundamental differences.

This chapter will demonstrate that a political culture and genuine conflicts existed, but that conflicts were checked, in part by close social ties among the elites and in part by the existence of legal channels of redress and conscious royal policies designed to retain colonial loyalty. The best way to analyze politics from 1590 through 1660 is to distinguish three different levels of conflict: metropolis-colonist, intraelite, and elite-mass. In the first case, the fiscal demands, trade restrictions, and other policies of the Crown provoked repeated opposition to the government, beginning in the 1590s, increasing between 1624 and 1638, and continuing to 1660. Resistance was directed against particular policies or bureaucrats, not against the Crown itself, however, so there was consensus about the need to preserve the imperial relationship.

In the second case, the experience of the merchants indicates that clear divisions existed within the elite. Merchants owed the State a higher percentage of their income than their economic peers because they were liable for *alcabala*, *avería*, *almojarifazgo*, internal customs, and taxes on certain trade goods, as well as for involuntary loans. Fiscal structure reflected social structure and perceptions. Merchants were wealthy enough to pay—and sufficiently ignoble to merit—the burden. They clashed repeatedly with other elite groups on their share of taxes, the prices of imported goods, and the judicial prerogatives of the merchant guild. In addition, merchants were different because of their close economic ties to Spain and their peninsular origins. However, wholesalers drew close to agricultural and bureaucratic interests in several ways. They fully supported colonial demands for more posts in the civil bureaucracy, the clergy, the admiralty, and the militias in New Spain and the Philippines. In turn, the creoles supported them by calling for the reopening of the Peru trade (after 1631) and increasing the maximum on the Philippine trade. And, if we go beyond formal politics, merchant marriage and career patterns show considerable integration into the creole elite.

The unity of the upper groups was most apparent when confronting the non-elites. At this third level of conflict, the unusual riot of 1624 presented telling lessons. Groups, including merchants, hostile to Viceroy Gelves's reformist attack on privilege encouraged Archbishop Serna's mobilization of lower-class rioters to drive the viceroy from power. However, one of the first acts of the victorious colonists and officials was to organize eight infantry companies to repress any further popular commotion. There were few long-term benefits to the lower classes, who had rioted in support of Serna.[3] Elite-mass tensions in Mexico City more typically took less extreme forms, including boycotting products whose cost rose due to new taxes. Although urban popular groups did not form an active consensus with the elites, the positive and negative checks on conflict prevented group violence most of the time.

A historiographical issue related to the metropolitan-colonial conflict is the degree of success which colonists achieved in this contest. To what extent, if at all, did the elites translate growing economic strength into political independence? Historians generally agree that colonists could not change the broad outlines of imperial policy.[4] Yet, their efforts to do so merit more attention than they have received. Beginning in the 1590s, *cabildo* and *consulado* repeatedly fought the Crown on particular issues. This chapter will trace the struggle, which shows the strength of their efforts as well as a few victories.

Political actors drew on philosophical assumptions which have been neglected in the history of the period. Political theory and custom in Castille, whose institutions were, by and large, the model for the Indies, sanctioned periodic meetings of a semirepresentative body, the *Cortes*, to offer or to deny approval to royal measures. Scholastic thinkers propounded the idea that the people originally held the power to govern themselves but that they voluntarily conferred this power upon the ruler in the early stages of human history. Although some writers used this concept to justify such checks on the king as the *Cortes*, most theorists argued that the restraint provided by "original consent" was superseded by the king's obedience to natural law (the knowable reflection of divine law) and by his innate benevolence and sense of justice, which led him to promote the common good. Even those who asserted that an ongoing contract existed saw it as an agreement between unequal parties in which reasons of State might supersede corporate rights.[5] The philosophical traditions of the colonists were not monolithic by any means, but the sixteenth and seventeenth centuries saw an increasing emphasis on the powers of the monarch. Attempts of corporate bodies to resist this trend constitute a significant chapter in the history of colonial Mexico.

If *de jure* independence were limited, *de facto* independence grew. Historians concur that in the seventeenth century local elites gained at the expense of the royal government,[6] but it remains to be determined how far this autonomy went. This chapter analyzes in more detail and over a longer period than did previous studies the colonists' reaction to the *almojarifazgo* and *alcabala* taxes and the Philippine and Peru trade restrictions. Through aggressive bargaining and the proffer of money, merchants and other colonists mitigated the impact of many unfavorable policies. Although scholars have repeatedly pointed to examples of outright disobedience—such as smuggling—resistance was more frequently expressed by taking advantage of favorable legal provisions, that is, by negotiating with Crown representatives for more favorable treatment. Merchants exemplified this approach, bidding successfully to collect several important taxes (such as *cruzada*, playing card, sales) and underpaying their share. They used the courts to appeal the amount of taxes assessed; petitioned executive authorities for postponements of payments due; and generated enough resistance to certain taxes for the viceregal government to reject them. Through the liberal use of two devices, *composición* (compromise) and pardons, the authorities accepted a grey zone of partial compliance with the law as legitimate and yet did not lose face. This enabled the colonists, who did have a strong, if self-interested, attachment to "legality," to resist particular measures successfully and yet not challenge the Crown outright. Consequently, the Spanish imperial government was able to contain much of the conflict that its exploitation of the American realms naturally provoked.

MANIPULATING THE LEGAL SYSTEM: *ALMOJARIFAZGO* AND *ALCABALA*

The Almojarifazgo

The first major impost on trade was the import-export tax. Ordered collected in New Spain in 1528, it was well entrenched by the mid-sixteenth century, and its legitimacy was not challenged. After 1566, the *almojari-*

fazgo was 15 percent on goods shipped from Spain to the Indies (5 percent payable in Seville, 10 or 12.5 percent payable in Veracruz) and 17.5 percent on goods shipped from the Indies to Spain (2.5 percent payable in Veracruz and 15 percent payable in Seville). The inter-American trade paid 2.5 percent on outbound goods and 5 percent on inbound goods.[7] The *almojarifazgo* for trans-Atlantic trade was, therefore, a heavy tax. The proportion was justified—taxes were supposed to be just—by three arguments. Merchants were the chief beneficiaries of the Atlantic trade, and they could well afford to pay; besides, "the wholesale merchants are the least [noble] of this Republic. . . ."[8] Throughout the sixteenth century the Crown attempted to tighten the administrative apparatus for collecting the *almojarifazgo*. It often accepted underpayment, postponment of payment, or appeals for lower assessments in return for a loan or some other favor to the King, however. In this manner the royal government received at least a portion of the tax due, obtaining "with forbearance . . . what it could not obtain with justice and force."[9]

The official assessment procedure was the first legal concession to traders. Explicitly after 1557, merchants were to pay tax on the value of the goods they sent as declared by themselves rather than on the value as determined by official inspection. Boxes and bales were not to be opened.[10] Having conceded this favor, the Crown attempted to regulate more closely the next stage of *almojarifazgo* assessment, but other aspects of due process interfered with more stringent collection.

Once goods reached their destination, their value increased, but by how much? The amount of increase obviously affected the amount of tax the merchant had to pay. From 1554, treasury officials were to determine the increase on the basis of "the generally accepted value of things in that region."[11] But this arrangement apparently allowed merchants to reach understandings with treasury officials or to appeal treasury assessments successfully to the *audiencia*. Thus, in 1591, Viceroy Velasco II informed the Crown that the *audiencia* was notoriously prone to reduce the assessments made, having lowered the 30 percent increase in value to an 18 percent increase. In 1593, the viceroy was given a supervisory role, but the new system did not bring the desired results. In 1595, the treasurer of Veracruz, Pedro Coco Calderón, complained to the king that the *audiencia* reduced the fines imposed by his colleagues. In 1600, Viceroy Monterrey wrote to the king that merchandise in the Indies that year was worth 40 percent more than in Spain, but that it had been evaluated at only 20 to 13 percent more in order to favor the merchants. Some appeals to the courts even reached the Council of the Indies.[12] Procrastination was another technique which gained a certain legitimacy. It was customary for viceroys to grant postponements of one-third or one-fourth of the *almojarifazgo* due, pending royal approval of particular cases. A glut of goods left over from the previous year's shipment, the failure of ships from connecting routes to arrive, or a lack of specie were all reasons for a postponement.[13]

Merchants who smuggled goods outright were operating outside the law entirely. However, even in this instance there was a way back to legality for the repentent offender: the payment of a fine. Decrees against some aspect of smuggling were issued almost every year, especially after 1550. The jurist Juan de Solórzano asserted that the Indies had more legislation on the subject than did any other region. Methods of smuggling were as ingenious as they were widespread. The tax exemption of certain articles such as books and the personal effects of clerics constituted a loophole through which goods slipped that were supposed to be taxed. Other devices involved falsely turning back to port or emergency landings, and officers sometimes "wrecked" their ships close to port in order to disembark nondeclared cargo.[14] Such tactics met with considerable success, but what happened when offenders were caught?

From the earliest days of the Indies trade, all goods that were not declared when the ship reached port were considered *de comiso* (contraband) and were to be confiscated and sold by the treasury officials. Had this often-repeated law been executed with consistency, smuggling would have been less common. The law, however, was partly replaced by a custom which greatly favored smugglers. Traders who declared contraband when the cargo was unloaded and who paid the tax due on it were granted a pardon. Their goods were not confiscated, and if traders themselves declared the goods, no fine was imposed. If goods were not voluntarily declared by the merchants but were denounced by treasury officials or by another party, offenders might also pay a fine. Even in this instance, the fine was fairly low: one-fourth more in 1595 and one-seventh more than the value of the goods in 1614. While the pardon was being arranged, the merchant might either keep the goods or surrender them to a person who held them in deposit. Traders were supposed to post bond for the tax payment, but tried to avoid doing so.[15]

The royal prerogative to grant pardons frequently overrode royal law. As the expert on commercial law, Joseph de Veitia Linaje, put it: "one can see the constant charity of the king towards his vassals who ship on the *carrera de las Indias* (convoys), for he has manifested it many times by dispensing with the laws and allowing pardons. . . ."[16] The frontis-piece of Veitia Linaje's treatise, indeed, depicts the monarchs as patrons of commerce as well as arms (see plate 8). Between 1590 and 1610, there were six decrees forbidding the granting of pardons. But in 1593, 1595, and 1597, there were three royal pardons given to contrabandists, and the pardon might well involve underpayment of the tax for the cargo.[17] Clearly, the whole system offered incentives to the smuggler because he usually had nothing to lose by attempting to bring in nondeclared goods.

This largesse was not one-sided, of course. Large-scale pardons of contraband were often accompanied by royal requests for loans or other favors. The *almojarifazgo* pardon of 1608 illustrates how the system worked. On March 6 of that year the king promulgated a decree again forbidding the granting of pardons and ordering the confiscation and sale of contraband. When treasury officials began this unpopular policy, the merchants petitioned the viceroy for suspension and appealed to the *audi-encia*, and the *audiencia* reached an agreement with the *consulado*. The merchants would pay 70,000 pesos for the taxes on the nonregistered goods. Viceroy Velasco, however, considered the high court too lenient. After further negotiations the *consulado* agreed to pay 120,000 pesos. At this point a royal decree dated July 5, 1608, arrived to pardon the whole-salers and permit settlement. On December 17, Velasco, uncertain of what course to follow, wrote back for further instructions. The Crown then confirmed the viceroy's settlement with the *consulado*, and on May 29, 1609, Viceroy Velasco informed the king that the *audiencia* had rejected an appeal against the merchants from the *fiscal*. Meanwhile, in Janu-ary 1609, Velasco attempted to convince the merchants to buy 49,000 pesos of newly issued government annuities, a purchase the merchants promised to consider.[18] Thus, bargaining over the *almojarifazgo* was an accepted practice that gave merchants considerable freedom of action but was neither smooth nor predictable.

The Alcabala

A few years earlier, in 1593, Viceroy Velasco II had been party to a similar arrangement with regard to the sales tax. The merchants had asked that he suspend collection until they had informed the king of their needs. He agreed to postpone, if the merchants offered the Crown "algún socorro" (some assistance).[19] The *alcabala* evoked much longer resistance than had the *almojarifazgo*. The sales tax was a tax on the sale and resale of every kind of property, from mules to mortgages, and it was levied on

8. Frontispiece of *Norte de la contratación de Indias*
by Joseph Veitia Linaje, 1671.

Table 18. Sales Tax Farms of Mexico City, 1602–1708

Contract	Contractor	Years	Rate (Percent)	Rent per Year (in Pesos)
I	City	1602–16	2	77,000
II	City	1617–31	2	91,000
III	City	1632–33	4	180,000
	City	1634–38	4	194,800
	City	1639–43	6	254,800
	Guild	1644–46	6	254,800
IV	Guild	1647–61	6	270,275.5
V	City	1662–72	6	273,000
	Guild	1673–76	6	273,000
VI	Guild	1694–1708	6	260,000

Source: Robert S. Smith, "Sales Taxes in New Spain, 1575–1770," *Hispanic American Historical Review* 28 (1948): 7.

both credit and cash transactions. Between 1575 and 1631, the rate was 2 percent; from 1632 to 1638 it was 4 percent; and from 1639, it was 6 percent (table 18). Decreed for New Spain in 1558, it was not actually collected until 1575 and in the 1590s, the colonists were still trying to eliminate the tax. In 1593, the *cabildo* and *consulado* called for its revocation, claiming that shipping from Spain would diminish if it were imposed, causing the Crown to lose more money through the drop in *almojarifazgo* revenues than it would gain through the collection of *alcabala*.[20]

The difficulty of collection was one of the reasons the Crown decided to farm the sales tax. In the early sixteenth century the Crown had placed more taxes *en administración* in the Indies than it had in Spain, but from the 1590s, the trend was reversed. From 1575 to 1602, the sales tax was collected by treasury officials; from 1602 to 1753 (except between 1676 and 1694), it was farmed by either the *cabildo* or the *consulado*. Although the system was criticized for alienating royal authority and putting the public at the mercy of the farmer, it did bring in at least some of the tax proceeds as well as the credit that the farmer was supposed to provide, and it saved some administrative costs.[21] It was believed that collection *en asiento* created a psychological climate more conducive to payment among taxpayers. Autonomy was thought to promote compliance. The tax farming system was a typical instance of the seventeenth-century trend toward greater de facto independence of the colonists on matters of implementation—although not formulation—of royal policy.

The colonists were forced to accept the *alcabala*, but by manipulating the due process of the imperial judicial system they minimized its impact. Negotiations for the first *alcabala* farm of 1602 were protracted and complex; each party knew that conditions initially agreed upon would become the precedent for subsequent farms. For the farms contracted from 1602 to 1676, the trend for the Crown was to increase the amount of sales tax owed, which suggests increasing royal exploitation. However, each increase was accompanied by concessions on the jurisdiction of the Mexico City farm (the territory around the city from which the farmers could collect), reductions of payments when the fleets or the Manila galleons did not arrive, and the percentage of proceeds farmers could retain for administrative expenses. These technical changes, and the reductions and postponements obtained, explain why taxes on silver rather than taxes on sales sustained public revenues at high levels in the seventeenth century.[22]

The negotiations for the 1602 sales tax farm lasted from July 1598 to April 1601, almost three years. Three parties were involved, or, to put it differently, two levels of negotiations. The best-known was that between the Crown, represented by the viceroy and the *junta de hacienda*, and the taxpayers, represented by the *cabildo* and the *consulado*. The less-well-known negotiation was between the merchants and the other taxpayers. Usually, these two latter groups were termed *mercaderes cargadores* and *vecinos*, respectively, even though most of the *mercaderes cargadores* were themselves *vecinos*. The history of the *alcabala* farm in the seventeenth century clearly reveals the antagonism between these two groups. The first two farms were from 1602 to 1631; the third farm (1632–46) is part of the history of the fiscal crisis of the 1630s.

For the 1602 farm, the government proposed a lump *alcabala* payment of 200,000 pesos a year for the short duration of five years. The area to be included in the Mexico City farm was the whole viceroyalty, making the Mexico City farmers collectors for the whole kingdom. The *cabildo* and *consulado* accepted the suggested area, but not the rest of the proposal. The *cabildo* offered only 100,000 pesos a year for forty years, while *consulado*, more realistically, suggested 130,000 pesos for twenty years. The outcome was an assessment of 77,000 pesos; the area to be comprehended would be Mexico City alone, that is "within the canals"; and the period covered would be fifteen years. The other cities of the kingdom would make their own contracts with the government for lump sum payments.[23] On the whole, the city groups did well in this first showdown with the Crown.

For the second farm (1617–31) the sum owed was raised from 77,000 pesos to 91,000 pesos. In exchange for the increase, the viceroy extended the jurisdiction of the Mexico City farm to the *ejidos* (city common lands) surrounding it. This provision benefited the taxpayers of Mexico City at the expense of farmers from other cities of the viceroyalty. Livestock and grain sold on the city's outskirts, formerly under the jurisdiction of other farms and providing those provincial cities with sales tax income, now filled the quota of the capital. According to investigations of the 1630s, under the post-1617 arrangement, the persons from provincial towns came to the *ejidos* and reached agreements with the *alcabala* collectors of Mexico City to pay less than the 2 percent for which they were liable. In 1635, the investigation found, don Prudencio de Armenta and doña María de Gordejuela, his wife, paid the subcontractor for the tax on small livestock for Mexico City only 800 pesos of the 2,900 pesos due from a sale of forty thousand sheep. Another provision of the first two farms also favored Mexico City collectors at the expense of the provincial farmers. If sales of real estate located elsewhere in the kingdom took place in the capital, the *alcabala* was paid to the collector in Mexico City. The subcontractors of the capital were accused of undertaxing such sales to encourage them to be made there.[24] The territory encompassed by the *alcabala* farm of Mexico City continued to expand in the third and fourth sales tax farms.

In addition to these provisions, the 1617 contract permitted a reduction of one-half in *casos fortuitos* such as fire, depopulation, or another disaster but did not include the failure of fleets to arrive. Finally, the colonists were permitted administrative expenses of 5,875 pesos, that is, 7.6 percent of the sum due. The assessments of the amount of *alcabala* each group or individual had to pay was made by a committee of six: the *corregidor* of Mexico City, two *regidores*, and three merchants. It also had to be approved by the viceroy and the *oidores*.[25] Thus, the taxpayers' representatives were intimately involved in the assessment and collection procedures of the *alcabala*.

As with the *almojarifazgo*, taxpayers legally could appeal their assessments, which they often did, through several avenues. Members of a guild, such as the *consulado*, could first appeal to the head of their guild. In 1635, for example, Francisco de Haro, merchant from the calle de San Agustín, objected to the assessment of 200 pesos of *alcabala*. He asked his guild officer to reduce it because his shop contained only petty wares made in Mexico, such as *huipiles, naguas* (petticoats made and worn by

Indian women), and other items of small value. Moreover, in 1633 and 1634, he had only been assessed 140 pesos each year. If this appeal was not successful, he could go to the *audiencia*. In 1631, the merchant Pedro Deza, alleging that the *consulado* had maliciously assessed him too much, took this course.

Another type of appeal occurred when the guilds themselves, or persons who did not belong to a guild and paid as individuals, appealed their payment to the *corregidor* or deputies of the *cabildo* within six days of notification of the sum due. Two "honest men" would be appointed to review the assessment, and if no agreement were reached, the taxpayer was to pay at the assigned rate for two years, with a reappraisal made at the end of that time. If this were not satisfactory, the party could appeal to the *audiencia* as the *consulado* did in 1612.[26] Delaying payment through appeals was a continuation of what had occurred when the tax was collected *en administración* by royal officials. In 1594, Viceroy Velasco II referred to suits in the *audiencia* over the 2 percent charged and ordered merchants to pay first and appeal later, but this was not observed.

Legal proceedings were expensive and time-consuming for both sides, and a compromise was often preferred. In 1618, the *cabildo* sued the merchant Fernando Matías de Rivera for nonpayment of 180 pesos due from the sale of slaves and tools from the mint, where his deceased brother, Juan Luis, had been treasurer. It pronounced a sentence of auction against Juan Luis's estate. Fernando Matías first appealed to the *audiencia* but then concluded that to avoid lawsuits and trouble, he was willing to pay half of what he owed as a compromise. His proposal was accepted.[27] Others simply refused to pay, and some officials believed it cost more to force them than the tax was worth. Thus, evasion was permitted. Reductions also were granted or noncompliance overlooked because of the view that it was risky to push taxpayers too far, and that to proceed rigorously at law against them was to make them debtors of even greater amounts without the means to pay. Thus, the *cabildo* remarked, "It is necessary to collect gently so as not to destroy the contributors."[28]

The tug-of-war between the royal government and taxpayers was the first of the conflicts involving the sales tax. The second was that among the taxpayers themselves. The two antagonists were the professional merchants and the rest of the *vecinos* of Mexico City. The bargain struck by the Crown and the colonists over payment of this unpopular tax involved acceptance of the general principle that persons selling goods on their own account pay as small a share as possible, whereas persons acting as commission agents pay the bulk of the tax. This was supposed to make the tax more palatable to the majority of *vecinos* so the rent would be more secure.[29] The tax assessments were made, therefore, according to the seller's relationship to what he or she was selling. There were three categories of relationships: *forastería*, when the seller was an agent for a nonresident merchant; *vecindad*, when the seller was acting on his own account; and *viento*, when certain types of goods were sold, regardless of whether the seller was an agent. From the first sales tax farm, it was assumed that *forastería* would comprise the bulk of the tax. One merchant might well pay *forastería*, *vecindad*, and *viento* all in a given year. It would depend on what he sold and whether he sold it as an *encomendero* or on his own account. The division of sellers into these three categories enabled the tax farmer to favor the payers of *alcabala de vecindad* by assessing them at a lower rate.[30]

The distinction made among these types of sales was based on the common view that there was a difference between professional merchants and other colonists. During the negotiations for the 1617 farm, *regidores* of landowning background expressed their opinion that the merchants constituted a different type of trader. Don Francisco de Trejo, of first-settler descent, for example, urged that the payers of *vecindad* be taxed at the lower rate "since the majority of this republic is poor and its business is small, while those who trade in large amounts are recently arrived, rich merchants who only come to these far away kingdoms to carry off what little the *vecinos* have."[31] The spokesmen for the merchants, Salvador de Baeza, Diego Matías de Vera, and Alonso Ortiz, proposed that all sales by merchants who were *vecinos* of Mexico City, even when the sales were on commission, be classified under *alcabala de vecindad*. But, in the January 28 meeting of the *cabildo*, the *regidores* rejected this proposal. Don Pedro Núñez de Prado y Córdoba asserted that merchants sold goods for gain, while *vecinos* only sold possessions and other things when absolutely necessary! Merchants, for their part, also acknowledged the negative views held of their group. In 1612, the *consulado* complained that its share of *alcabala de vecindad*, the tax paid by merchant-*vecinos* when they sold goods on their own account, was too high at the 2 percent rate. Thus, each side felt that the other was not paying its full share.[32]

The crucial role of the *consulado* in the collection of the sales tax exacerbated the tension between professional and nonprofessional traders. For the first (1602–16) and second (1617–31) farms, the *cabildo* was the contractor, but it subcontracted collection of the different branches of the tax to other groups. The *consulado* was the largest subcontractor, for it collected all of *forastería* and the *consulado*'s share of *vecindad* as well. In 1602, the *consulado* paid 52,000 pesos of the 77,000 pesos due, or 76.5 percent of the tax; in 1632, it paid 113,000 pesos of 180,000 pesos due, or 62.7 percent of the tax. The *consulado* was accused of making its assessments at less than the stipulated rate of 2 percent and forcing the other taxpayers to pay at the stipulated rate.[33]

Thus, the system of sales tax collection both reflected and aggravated antagonism between the professional merchants and those persons who traded "out of necessity," and between their respective institutional representatives, the *consulado* and the *cabildo*. When the sales tax was increased in the late 1620s and 1630s, the conflict became more intense between Crown and colony—and among the colonists themselves.

THE FISCAL CRISIS OF 1628–36

The Unión de Armas *(1628–32)*

From the 1620s, Spain entered a period of high taxation caused primarily by increasing military costs incurred in European wars. Unwaveringly committed to a foreign policy of refusing to recognize complete Dutch independence, in 1621, Spain resumed an extraordinarily expensive war against the United Provinces, which lasted until 1648. Subsequent campaigns in northern Italy and the Holy Roman Empire brought additional expense, culminating in the costs of the war against France (1635–59). The principal new defense measures were the *Unión de Armas*, decreed in 1626 and gradually put into effect, and the *Armada de Barlovento*, decreed in 1635 after many years of discussion. In addition to the usual royal requests for loans and the seizure of privately owned bullion from the Indies fleet, these meant the introduction of new taxes and increases in existing imposts. Intended to last fifteen years, the *Unión de Armas* was to comprise twelve warships and three support vessels; four warships and one support ship were to escort the vessels of the convoy, while the rest were to be used in the North Atlantic. The architect of this plan, the Count-Duke of Olivares, intended to finance it by requiring the various kingdoms of the Empire to bear a larger proportion of defense costs than they had previously. New Spain was assessed 250,000 ducats (343,750 pesos) and Peru, 350,000 ducats (481,250 pesos). The rest of the Indies was to pay 50,000 ducats, for a total of 600,000 ducats from the American kingdoms. For Olivares and his reformist officials and social critics, the *Unión de Armas* formed part of a larger effort to strengthen the position of the monarch in his own kingdoms and rationalize his financial base, which would, in turn, allow the king, Catholicism, and Spain to regain dominance in world affairs. The *Unión* was, therefore, a moral as well as fiscal and military program.[34]

As in the past, the Crown suggested to the American viceroys a number of methods of raising revenues, and the viceroys were to use their discretion in proposing certain taxes to the *cabildos* and to other local bodies and soliciting suggestions from them. But the *Unión de Armas* levy was the first relatively permanent defense tax of this magnitude, and the colonists of New Spain (and Peru) were loath to accept it, as were the subjects of the king's other realms. They employed their customary methods of debate, delay, and requests for favors in exchange for funds but this time buttressed their claims with reference to political philosophy, illustrating the existence of a self-conscious political culture.

The *cabildo* of Mexico City delayed payment of the city's share for more than four years. When on October 12, 1628, the colonists finally heard the unwelcome news of the *Unión de Armas*, the timing of the decree could hardly have been worse. On September 7, the Dutch under Piet Heyn had seized 8,000,000 pesos returning on the fleet to Spain; locally, 100,000 pesos had just been budgeted for flood repairs in the Valley of Mexico. Of the 343,750 pesos due from New Spain, Viceroy Cerralvo stated that the city pay a rather substantial share: 130,000 pesos (38 percent), 100,000 pesos from the city itself (including the *ejidos*) and 30,000 pesos from the surrounding five leagues.[35]

The timing and unprecedently large sum stimulated colonists' claims for an expanded political role. They made explicit their view that a contract existed between king and subjects, but they endowed this position with a more recent, regalist interpretation. On November 18, referring to his degrees in civil and canon law, don Fernando Angulo Reynoso stated that it was well known that a *contrato de justicia* existed that required the king to protect and defend his vassals and they, reciprocally, to obey and provide funds to him. He then emphasized, however, the subjects' obligation to pay taxes rather than the ruler's obligation to obtain the subjects' consent. The formation of the *Unión*, he stressed, clearly was a just cause which would benefit the colonists and which they should support. Even if this were not apparent, the mere word of the king was sufficient because he incarnated justice. Angulo placed the colonists' requests to the King in the context of being necessary to promote the economic well-being that would enable the colonists to offer more money, rather than being justified in themselves.

Alguacil mayor Marcos de Guevara took another, bolder tack. He asked that the cities of the viceroyalty first meet to determine how much each would contribute to the *Unión*, thus demonstrating a familiarity with current practice in Spain, where royal demands for higher taxes reinvigorated the *Cortes*, even in Castille.[36] But, even Guevara did not question the reason for the taxes, the Crown's military policy, and when Viceroy Cerralvo rejected his suggestion that representatives of the cities assemble, the matter was closed for the time being.

The city also put forward its requests for royal concessions in the customary manner and delayed proposing taxes until it received a response. One of the few *regidores* who was also a merchant, Juan Francisco Vertiz, asked that the trades with Peru and the Philippines be opened without any limitation whatsoever, for, if not, "with 350,000 pesos removed from the kingdom each year. . . . only the echo of the wealth that has left for Spain and the Philippines will remain."[37] Don Diego de Monroy made other proposals: one-half of all civil and ecclesiastical posts should go to native sons, and *encomiendas* should be perpetual or, at least, for three lives. In April 1629, the *regidores* added the request that sales tax farm be renewed after its expiration in 1631, at the same rate of 91,000 pesos a year, for twenty years, and the territory covered be extended to five leagues outside the city. Cerralvo's unwillingness to do more than consider this request postponed a settlement once more, and the catastrophic flood of September 1629 delayed the debate still further.[38]

Only on August 8, 1630, did the members of the city council comply and specify the means by which to raise the 130,000 pesos the city was assessed. Three taxes were proposed: a 1 percent raise in *alcabala*, provided the territory under Mexico City's jurisdiction was increased by the five leagues; a 2 or 3 real increase on each deck of playing cards, which were currently selling at 5 reales each deck; and a tax of 20 pesos (about 8 percent) on the salary of the *alcaldes mayores*. Of these three taxes, the viceroy approved an even greater increase in *alcabala*, bringing it to a total of 4 percent of sales (100 percent more due); and a lesser, 1 real increase on playing cards, whose production was a government monopoly, so that they now cost 6 reales the deck (20 percent more due). He rejected the taxation of the *alcaldes*, most of whom were his appointees.[39]

The burden fell, therefore, on merchants and consumers of nonessential goods. Suggestions by individual *regidores* that the clergy be assessed, or by one *vecino* that agriculturalists contribute, were not accepted by the rest of the *regidores*, who continued to exempt these groups. As part of the tax increases of the 1630s, the royal government did impose the *media anata* and *mesada* on ecclesiastics and bureaucrats and collected the *composiciones de tierras* (tax on legal title to land and/or water) more rigorously. The first, however, was not very onerous, and the second was collected for only a short period. Tax-free groups essentially maintained their previous status. As in Peru, the most privileged members of society were not to be charged for the *Unión de Armas*.

None of the major policy changes proposed by the city council were accepted by Viceroy Cerralvo. He opposed the colonists' view that granting of funds obligated the king to accede to their requests. They did obtain changes in the conditions of the sales tax farm, introduced to compensate for the higher rate after 1631. The council's most successful action, however, was the traditional one of not collecting the tax increases to which they had agreed. They seem to have complied with the card tax increase reasonably well after an initial delay. The current farmer of the card tax, the merchant don Francisco de la Torre, did state that he could not pay the new 20,000 pesos yearly and refused to continue his farm. Collection awaited the assumption of his contract by a fellow merchant, Mateo Barroso, in February 1633. Barroso completed de la Torre's term and contracted for a new card farm at 150,000 pesos per year from 1634 to 1640. Until 1637, Barroso probably met most of his obligations, but the increase of 50,000 pesos on cards could not by itself meet the quota of 130,000 pesos that the city had to fill.[40]

The sales tax farm, on the other hand, from 1632 to 1648 entered a notable crisis. The third farm required the colonists of Mexico City to pay 180,000 pesos a year from 1632 to 1633 and 194,800 pesos from 1634. The latter sum was more than twice the amount due only three years before. In exchange, the 1632 contract between the city and the royal government offered new advantages to the *cabildo*. The jurisdiction of the Mexico City farm was extended even further, to eight leagues surrounding the capital, and the city was allowed reductions should the ships from Spain or the Philippines fail to arrive. In the past, reductions had only been permitted in the case of local disasters.[41] Despite these benefits, the *alcabala* deficit reached 171,286 pesos by December 1636, an amount in excess of previous arrears (table 19). One official claimed that since 1632, the tax had fallen short by 40,000 pesos a year. Thus, Viceroy Cerralvo had written to the king on December 18, 1634, that "the balance [of the *Unión de Armas*] will have to come from more sensitive sources."[42]

Thus, seven years after the *Unión* had been decreed, it had not brought

Table 19. Debits of the *Alcabala* Farm at Different Periods, 1606–59

Date	Amount of Debit (in Pesos)	Source
1606	32,800	AC 16:409
1615	28,146	AC 21:20
1616	67,000	AC 21:175–76
1617	9,861	AC 21:296–97
1632–36	40,000 per year	AGI, Aud Méx 330
1636	171,286	AGI, Aud Méx 34
1637 (Mar.)	63,550	AGI, Aud Méx 330
1637 (Nov.)	43,100	AGI, Aud Méx 34
1640	5,762 [a]	AC 32:65–66
1641	67,867	AC 32:259
1642	175,000	AC 33:422
1643	450,000	AC 33:492
1648	580,000	AGI, Aud Méx 38
1651	724,404	AGI, Aud Méx 4
1659	No debits	AGI, Aud Méx 38

[a] Another source states that 72,279 pesos was owed by the *cabildo* for the third farm at this time. Manuel Álvarado Morales, *La ciudad de Mexico ante la fundación de la armada de Barlovento: Historica de una encrucijada (1635–1643)* (México: El Colegio de México–Universidad de Puerto Rico, 1983), 192.

in the revenues to which the colonists agreed, even though they received some concessions in the third *alcabala* farm. By the time-honored legal methods of delaying agreement to taxes and manipulating the judicial system, and by outright evasion, the colonists expressed their opposition. The antagonism between professional merchants and other *vecinos* also increased, leading to unsuccessful efforts to remove the *consulado* from its key role in the collection of the tax.

The Armada de Barlovento *(1636–38)*

After 1635, the military commitments of the monarchy expanded further. Among other measures, a battle squadron of sixteen warships and two or three support craft, termed the *Armada de Barlovento*, were to be assembled for defense of the Caribbean. The squadron was to escort the fleet coming from Spain to the mainland ports and then to Havana for the return voyage; it was then to patrol the Lesser Antilles and the Tierra Firme coast, wintering in Puerto Rico. To finance the squadron, the Crown requested the sum of 600,000 ducats (840,000 pesos) from the Circum Caribbean regions, including New Spain, Guatemala, New Granada, and the Captaincy of Venezuela.[43] The Crown suggested that Mexico City pay 200,000 pesos annually, a considerably larger sum than the 130,000 pesos requested for the *Unión de Armas* and representing 24 percent of the total.

This time the viceroy pushed the consultative process as quickly as possible and obtained approval of the levy and designation of new taxes by the city in ten months. On March 8, 1636, Viceroy Cadereita informed the *cabildo* of the founding of the *Armada* and of the 840,000 pesos required to maintain it. On December 23 the *cabildo* entered the writ of agreement in its records. Thus, within a year the colonists had accepted a massive new fiscal burden, "which [Viceroy Cadereita wrote to the king] had seemed impossible."[44] However, there was a long step from agreement to implementation. The *Armada de Barlovento* only functioned between 1641 and 1647, usually with five to seven ships. It made three trans-Atlantic voyages and never patroled the Caribbean as stipulated. Between 1647 and 1667, it ceased to exist.[45]

This debacle was due to interconnected causes which reflected the relationship of State to society at the mid-century. The Crown refused to offer the concessions the colonists requested in exchange for money and added insult to injury by diverting the funds that were collected and ships that were built to European needs. The colonists did not provide the sums to which they agreed because they were accustomed to underpaying, postponing, or evading taxes. Finally, the economic downtown of the 1640s and 1650s, which will be discussed in the Conclusion, made the increases more burdensome. In addition, the *Armada* suffered because its officers and crew sold equipment for profit, as well as from delays in shipbuilding and jurisdictional quarrels between viceroys and admirals.

The city's alacrity in agreeing to taxes was based on the expectation that the viceroy and the Crown would grant long-standing requests despite the disappointing response of 1628 to 1630. From 1636 to 1638, the *cabildo* aggressively asserted that such concessions were due in exchange for the 200,000 pesos and threatened not to pay until the requests were promised. The king, however, reminded Viceroy Cadereita that the *mercedes* desired by the city "not be treated as conditions for an agreement . . . since *mercedes* must never be treated as conditions but rather the expression of the grandeur and generosity of the King. Nothing will be accomplished if it is necessary for a condition to be met before the resolutions [regarding new taxes] are implemented, for many of these requests require careful study before they can be granted and others should not be granted at all."[46] Philip IV expressed the same view in his relations with the Castillian *Cortes*, which in the 1630s lost several tax battles to the Crown, as well as the right of representatives to consult constituents before voting approval.[47] In 1636, Viceroy Cadereita rejected the city council's claim that it could impose conditions in exchange for funds, but he did not believe it politic to offer no hope and so encouraged the council to believe that he supported the substance of the conditions.

The 1636 list of requests for the viceroy and Crown to consider was the work of the *cabildo* and *consulado;* many had been raised for years with no result. Frequently, interests by the two bodies were in accord, but not always. Reflecting the influence of the merchants was the *cabildo*'s inclusion of the demand that trade between Acapulco and Lima be reopened, even if on a limited basis, and the long-standing request that the *permiso* to the Philippines, the maximum value of cargo allowed shipped, be enlarged.

There were other common objectives. One of these was the health of the mining industry, which depended both on a network of adequate credit to miners and an adequate labor supply. "As mines declined, so did the trade which depended on them." The city council suggested either legalizing credit from the *alcaldes mayores* or encouraging wealthy persons to lend to the miners, which would have ratified the existing structure of merchant credit. The *cabildo* also asked that 500 slaves a year be imported to work in the mines and on haciendas suffering from the end of agricultural *repartimiento*, adding the proviso, suggestive of merchant influence, that the *cargadores* (merchants) who violated the limit on slave imports pay only twice the taxes they would owe. Self-governance was of lively interest to both merchants and landowners. The *cabildo* sought to buy back the office of *corregidor*, a viceregal appointee, while the *consulado* opposed the Crown's projected sale of the notaryship of the *consulado*, seeking to appoint that person itself. Both bodies were also interested in royal patronage.

The *consulado* was very much at odds with the city council, however, over the administration of the *alcabala* and over legal jurisdiction. The guild insisted on first-instance hearing of all creditors' suits, including criminal suits over debtors hiding their assets. It was also uniquely concerned about retailer competition. It asked for a royal decree forbidding the unattractive and "harmful" *cajones* (wooden stalls) that retailers occu-

9. Inscription forbidding the construction of wooden market stalls next to *portal* belonging to Convent of San Agustín, 1671.

pied on the central plaza. The wholesalers wanted to confine trade to their own, more dignified, cut-stone *portales* along the west side of the plaza! Even the convent of San Agustín obtained an order prohibiting the placing of market stalls in front of a *portal* it owned (see plate 9). Certain other of the twenty-six requests presented by the city council on July 21, 1636, reflected primarily the wishes of the landowners and local officials who comprised the majority of its members.[48]

All these requests had to be approved first by the viceroy and the *junta general*, consisting of the *junta de hacienda* and representatives of the *cabildo*, *consulado*, clergy, and *audiencia*, and then, definitively by the king. Patronage relating to supplying the *Armada* and the Philippine regiments and appointing officers for them was within the viceroy's authority, and in his reply of September 11, 1636, he conceded these *mercedes* to the city. He also implied agreement with the requests that the Peru trade be reopened, the Philippine *permiso* enlarged, and one-half the bureaucratic appointments be given to native sons, but when the *junta* concluded its review on December 19, 1636, it made no further concessions and passed the bulk of the requests on to the king and Council of the Indies.[49]

Meanwhile, the colonists were considering how to raise the 200,000 pesos a year that the city owed. The debates about taxes indicate how colonists could influence politics in a legal manner at the secondary level, that of implementation. A majority of the *cabildo* and consulting bodies, for example, chose an increase in existing sales and import-export taxes over new taxes on cochineal and cacao. The tax debates again show how fiscal policy reflected social structure. Merchants and Hispanicized consumers with some discretionary income were fair game, whereas on the low end of the social scale, Indians and "poor people" were to be exempt and, on the high end, clergy and bureaucracy were touched lightly if at all because of their "nobility." Contemporaries also thought of products themselves as hierarchically ordered. Subsistence items (grains, livestock and meat, fuel and building materials, Indian clothing, fresh fruits, and vegetables) were supposed to be exempt, whereas nonessential goods (wine, sugar, cochineal, and cacao) were legitimately taxed.[50] In this case, the luxury goods, handled by merchants, were liable.

New taxes were imposed in 1636, 1638, and 1642, as officials became increasingly desperate. Initially, the viceroy hoped to raise revenues by diverting royal income allotted to military garrisons, the Veracruz tax on wine for the *desagüe*, the *cabildo*'s purchase of the office of *corregidor*, and other sources to the *Armada*. It was necessary, however, for the colonists to contribute specifically. In July 1636, the city made four recommendations to the viceroy: the extension of the tax on the retail sale of wine in the capital to the rest of the viceroyalty (estimated to provide 75,000 pesos); an additional 2 reales on each deck of playing cards, bringing the price to 8 reales the deck (estimated to provide 40,000 pesos); an additional 2 percent on the import-export tax at Veracruz and Acapulco (50,000 pesos); and 1 real on each mark of silver minted in Mexico City (50,000 pesos). Viceroy Cadereita rejected the tax on minted silver as an infringement on royal sovereignty and the extension of the wine tax as an unfair, although typical, attempt of Mexico City to force the provinces to pay more than their share. Then, on September 20, 1636, the city proposed a tax on the cloth produced in the city and rest of the *audiencia*, a tax on hides, and a tax on the coinage of silver plate and on gold. On November 3, 1636, Viceroy Cadereita and the *junta general* ratified the first two measures and rejected the third.[51] Thus, playing cards, imported goods, hides, and domestic cloth bore the brunt of the new taxes.

The Increase in the Import-Export Tax: 1636, 1640. Wholesalers had come in for a particularly heavy share of the imposts. It was they who would pay the additional *almojarifazgo*, they who exported hides to Spain; they also had a role in the production and marketing of playing cards and *obraje* cloth. Although they failed in their effort to prevent the import-export tax increase from being imposed,[52] they did maneuver around it with considerable success. First, they persuaded the viceroy to collect at only 1 percent at each port, a reduction which lasted until April 1640. The Mexico City wholesalers and the factors of the Philippine trading community, also argued that the Acapulco increase was unfair because the *Armada* did not protect the Manila trade. This led to a postponement of collection at Acapulco until the viceroy was persuaded in 1639 that the Pacific traders were also beneficiaries and that the high profits of the Philippine trade were better able to withstand a new imposition than those of Castille. While the Pacific traders paid only a 2 percent *avería* to the Crown, the Atlantic paid at 30 percent. Nevertheless, wholesalers obtained the significant concession that all silver bar and coin, the bulk of the cargo, exported from Acapulco was to be free of the 2 percent increase. They had also defeated *regidor* don Diego de Barahona's proposal that an unprecedently high tax of 20 percent be imposed on the 4 or 5 percent commissions that merchants received as agents.[53] Finally, the merchants smuggled on a wide scale, disembarking goods at Old Veracruz, Tampico, Tabasco, and the Río de Álvarado at Resascoya, as well as at San Juan de Ulúa. In August 1637, the *regidores* asserted it was common knowledge that although 4 million pesos' worth of unregistered merchandise had arrived on the four galleons of the Marqués de la Cardeñosa, the royal treasury officials had no record of it because it was disembarked at these coastal rendezvous points. Indeed, the sums collected from this rent were sporadic and small, never more than 6,704 pesos in a year.[54]

The Increase on Playing Cards: 1636–40. Meanwhile, although the playing card farm was supposed to be one of the most secure of royal rents, it was staggering under its new cost of 8 reales the deck. In this case, too, the affected parties fought the increase. They were the tax farmer, a wealthy merchant named Mateo Barroso, who went to court, and the consumers, who bought fewer cards (chapter 4). Barroso first tried to have the *audiencia* uphold his original 1634 contract, which stipulated that the cards be sold at 6 reales the deck and that Barroso pay 150,000 pesos annually. Failing, Barroso withdrew from his contract, but in October 1637, Álvaro Paz, an associate who concealed the connection, successfully bid for it at the new price of 8 reales the deck, with 195,000 pesos owed annually. It seemed that the city could now count on 45,000 pesos from this source, but the playing card farm went bankrupt in the fall of 1639. Paz and Barroso attributed it to a drop in demand due to the rise in price. The *cabildo* roundly denied this explanation and pinned the collapse on the tax farmers' maladministration, *accidentes de tiempo*, and the failure of the farmers to prosecute counterfitters. As shall be seen, the truth lay with Paz and Barroso.[55]

The mopping-up operations were prolonged and complicated. Paz had given insufficient bond, only 112,500 pesos for a farm of 195,000 pesos; in 1643, the farm had a debt of 434,456 pesos. The debt could be repaid only by "composing" it, that is, reducing it to 121,585 pesos. Even so, it proved impossible to return to the status quo. The city council tacitly accepted the limitations of the market when, in April 1640, it decreed the abolition of the 2 real increase, substituting for it the additional 1 percent increase in *almojarifazgo* at San Juan and Acapulco. No one was willing to take the farm at the 150,000 pesos of Barroso's 1634–37 contract. The rigor with which Paz and Barroso's bondsmen were prosecuted made potential backers leary, and interim administration by the *cabildo* brought in only 60,000 pesos total a year. Only in 1643 did two other entrepreneurs, the merchant's son Nicolás de Salcedo backed by his brother-in-law Antonio Urrutia de Vergara, also a merchant, and his nephew-in-law Antonio Flores, offer a bid, and this of only 90,000 pesos. Thus, from 1636 to 1660 the playing card farm did not fund the *Armada*.[56]

Cacao and Cochineal: 1638. On October 16, 1637, the *regidor* and trader Leandro Gática told his colleagues that they would be lucky to see 70,000 pesos that year, far from the 200,000 pesos owed by the city.[57] In addition to the failure of sufficient income from *almojarifazgo* and playing cards, the collection of the hides tax was riddled with difficulties. As for the tax on cloth, neither Puebla nor Tlaxcala, two major producing centers, had made contracts for the tax, nor had the *alcaldes mayores* of other cloth towns responded in adequate numbers. What was to be done? Among the king's suggestions to the viceroy was a tax on cacao. This was a profitable but ticklish business, Cadereita replied, which he postponed because of the resistance it was sure to provoke, not only from traders but also from the clergy and the Indians, well-known aficionados of the beverage.

Cacao had been the object of official attention well before the *Armada*. In 1624 and in 1628, the Mexico City *cabildo* favored prohibiting entry to Venezuelan and Guayaquil cacao, a step actually taken by the *audiencia* of Guatemala in 1628. The new imports were considered inferior to the Guatemalan and Mexican products, less healthful and more bitter, so when they were mixed with the preferred and sold at the higher price, the public was cheated. The *cabildo* had also addressed the problem of monopoly. In 1635, it had attacked "a few rich *vecinos* of this city" for buying up cacao at the ports and hoarding it to raise prices. In 1636, it drew up the ordinances for an *alhóndiga* (public supply) to halt the rise in prices of that summer and to prevent mixing of inferior beans. Four to six persons were accused of hoarding cacao.[58]

"The *alhóndiga* was essential," wrote Viceroy Cadereita, "because otherwise, no matter what judicial and extrajudicial means are taken, it would not be possible to learn the quantity of cacao. . . ."[59] With an eye to the next step, a tax, the viceroy pressed on, and the *alhóndiga* was inaugurated in January 1638. Six months later Cadereita reported to the king that he had wasted a year trying to get the cacao tax underway. In September 1638, the city council, spurred by the realization that it had collected only 103,000 pesos of the 200,000 pesos due that year, decided to reconsider the cacao tax. The tax rate proposed was 2 pesos per *carga* of Maracaibo cacao, and 3 pesos per *carga* of Guatemalan cacao, or 23 to 19 percent because the former was estimated at 13–16 pesos the *carga* and the latter at 22 pesos the *carga*. The impost was expected to raise 70,000 pesos annually, a very substantial sum.[60]

The predicted clamor arose. Merchants inside and outside the *cabildo* protested. "What the merchants dislike," the *cabildo* declared, "is not being allowed to keep the cacao in their houses and freely use it as security or payment on account since there is no other method in this city. . . ,"[61] a statement which was a considerable exaggeration. Therefore, instead of storing the cacao in an *alhóndiga*, it should simply be registered in an *aduana* (customs house), where records of the amount, owner, and destination could be kept. Granted some control was necessary for "there are few persons in whom one can have confidence, especially when it is a question of goods which are difficult to verify when hidden."[62] The establishment of an *aduana* in Mexico City and four subsidiary houses at Acapulco, Veracruz, Puebla, and Guanajuato, seemed a good compromise, and the Mexico City *aduana* was instituted in June 1640. Merchants and consumers succeeded having the tax rejected, however. In October, Cadereita and the *junta general* turned it down. In 1643, when again there were high prices, the *cabildo* complained that there was no *alhóndiga* functioning.[63]

Another tax proposed in September 1638 was a levy on cochineal. The efforts of the Crown to profit from the cochineal trade had a long history. Like cacao, cochineal was potentially remunerative but difficult to tax, first because of the ease of hiding the product and second because it was grown by Indians and so trade was decentralized. Now desperate, however, the *regidores* revived an earlier suggestion of 5 pesos the *arroba*. Since an *arroba* sold at between 115 and 130 pesos, this was a 4 percent tax that the council estimated would raise 15,000 pesos from the 3,000 *arrobas* of cochineal exported at Veracruz. Registration would also occur at Mexico City, Puebla, and Oaxaca. The *regidores* were not concerned about ill effects on Indian growers, rather, they referred to the "zeal of the *alcaldes mayores* in remedying the laziness of the Indian." In addition, the council proposed a small tax on soap.[64] Again bowing to pressure from traders and others, however, the October *junta general* also rejected the proposed tax on cochineal.

That left the *alcabala*. In the fall of 1638, when the viceroy concluded a new farm with the city council, the amount due from Mexico City was raised by 60,000 pesos, from 194,800 pesos to 254,800 pesos. The king observed to Cadereita that even at the new rate of 6 percent, the traders of New Spain were paying less than the 10 percent charged in Castille.[65] This was slight consolation to the merchants, who now applied their customary strategies of manipulation and evasion.

The Sales Tax Increase of 1639. The history of the *alcabala* between 1636, when the *Armada* imposts were first confirmed, and 1644, when the whole *alcabala* farm was awarded to the *consulado* for the first time, saw turmoil in this rent: mounting deficits, frank hostility between *cabildo* and *consulado*, frustrated attempts by the viceroy to make collection more efficient, and provincial opposition to payment.

From 1639, the *cabildo* was responsible for raising a total of 254,800 pesos yearly for the *alcabala* farm. The deficits of 1632 through 1636 had led both city council and viceroy to conclude that the sum due could be raised by improving management, especially by reducing the role of the *consulado* in collection. The terms of the third farm (1632–46) had stipulated that contrary to provisions of previous contracts, the *alcabala de forastería* could not be subcontracted to the same body as the *alcabala del gremio de los mercaderes*, which made up the bulk of the *alcabala de vecindad*. In other words, the *consulado* could collect the sales tax for its own guild (*vecindad*), but it could not also collect the sales tax for the sales on commission (*forastería*).

The *cabildo* had insisted on the inclusion of this novel provision because it blamed its past failures to meet payment, with some justification, on the machinations of the merchants. It identified two types of abuses which the *consulado*'s role as subcontractor of the major portion of the tax made possible. First, the *consulado* did not compel the payers of *forastería*, persons who sold goods on commission, to pay at the full 4 percent of their transactions. These persons were supposed to pay in full so that the payers of *vecindad* would only have to pay at 2 percent or less. Instead, the *consulado* shifted the burden to the *vecindad*, forcing the guilds of the city to pay more than their share. In 1632, the *cabildo* had ordered an inventory of the warehouses, shops, and the writs of sale of the city's merchants to see what *forastería* really amounted to. The *cabildo* at that time concluded that *forastería* alone could pay all of the 113,000 pesos due from both *forastería* and from the merchant's *vecindad* toward the 180,000 pesos owed by the city. In other words, commission merchants were grossly underpaying *forastería*.

Second, the merchants did not even pay the 2 percent they owed for *alcabala de vecindad*, the tax paid by the *consulado* when merchants sold goods on their own behalf. If the accountant of the sales tax audited the records, the *cabildo* asserted, he would find that forty of the richest traders in the city did not even pay one-half of 1 percent of tax. This forced the other guilds to pay at the full 4 percent. Wholesalers were not meeting their obligations even as members of the *vecindad* category. Nonetheless, in 1633, the *cabildo* had been forced to back down in its effort to loosen the *consulado*'s grip on collection in order to get the merchants to subcontract *any* part of the tax. In the city council's agreement with the *consulado* of that year, it specifically revoked clause 29 of the third farm, the clause which had prohibited the *consulado* from subcontracting both *forastería* and *vecindad*.[66] It was impossible to deny the reality of merchant fiscal power.

Nevertheless, a new attempt was made in 1636, shortly after the arrival of Viceroy Cadereita, when he had *oidor* Iñigo de Argüello Carvajal bring suit against the *consulado* for violating the terms of the third farm, even though the city had agreed to the revocation of the terms. Cadereita's attack on the privileged position of the merchant guild was part of a larger effort to tighten fiscal administration which reached even the provincial cities. In 1639, for example, the viceroy forced his appointee *alférez real* don Juan Francisco de Ayala on the taxpayers of Villa de Carrión instead of allowing the town's taxes to be collected by the *cabildo* or the *alcalde mayor* as in the past. Cadereita also tried to replace the royal treasury officials who had overseen administration of the sales tax which had not been compounded (*alcabalas no encabezadas*) with an accountant and assistants of the viceroy's own choosing.[67]

In legal terms the attack on the position of the merchant guild was successful. The viceroy ordered the *cabildo* to replace the *consulado* as subcontractor of *forastería*, and the *consulado*'s appeal to the *audiencia* this time failed. This was less a defeat for the *consulado* than the city council had desired, since the *cabildo* actually petitioned the viceroy to dissolve the *consulado* itself.[68] The merchants withstood these assaults on their key fiscal role, however, because it soon became obvious that the *cabildo* could not manage the sales tax farm by itself. Deficits mounted rapidly, and soon exceeded previous arrears (table 19). In 1641, the sales tax owed 67,867 pesos; in 1642, 175,000 pesos; and in 1643, 450,000 pesos. Salvatierra refers to it as bankrupt. The *cabildo* blamed the irregularity of the fleets, reduced assessments and postponments obtained by merchants, and smuggling at the new customs' houses. All that it omitted was its own maladministration.

The case of Álvaro de Lorenzana, one of the wealthiest merchants of the city, illustrates the accuracy of the *cabildo*'s charges. In 1640, Lorenzana supposedly realized sales worth 28,330 pesos; at the 6 percent rate, therefore, he owed 1,098 pesos. He was actually taxed at 1,000 pesos, which was then reduced to 698 pesos. In 1641, a similar attrition occurred. He allegedly realized 4,800 pesos' worth of sales; at 6 percent he owed 288 pesos. He was assessed 192 pesos, but this was reduced to 25 pesos. Why the reductions? The goods, he claimed, were partly for his personal use, not for sale and, therefore, not taxable. Some of his cloth was to be sold outside the jurisdiction of Mexico City and so should pay the sales tax there. Other pieces were to be given to a convent. And so on. The *cabildo* brought suit against Lorenzana and sought an auction of his property for the full amount of all taxes. In 1645, the *audiencia* ordered him to pay but at only 360 pesos of the 724 pesos he owed. Smuggling, of course, continued, too. The Ordinances for the Mexico City *aduana* of June 1640 provide a lively account of methods used. Goods were unloaded at the shores of Lakes Mexicaltzingo and San Cristóbal, placed in canoes, covered with tax-free cargoes of firewood or sugar, and shipped into the capital.[69]

While the merchants distinguished themselves by obtaining judicial redress and evading the sales tax, the *regidores* became notorious for their inefficient collection. By the terms of the writ of agreement to the *Armada* signed in December 1636, the *cabildo* acted as the farmer general for all *Armada* funds from the Viceroyalty of New Spain. Its record was so poor, however, that in mid-1638, Viceroy Cadereita insisted on the removal of the administrator, Leandro de Gática, who had yet to prepare an account of his administration. Although prodded again by Cadereita in that December, and again a year later, to reduce *Armada* arrears, the *cabildo* procrastinated.[70] By this time, royal refusal to offer the proposed *mercedes* was known. In July 1638, the *cabildo* had learned that the king confirmed the section of the writ of agreement promising taxes but declined to approve the section which listed the requests. Although the city again threatened not to pay, the king held firm and the colonists had to back down.[71]

Proposals of 1642. The *Armada* had yet to patrol the Caribbean or cross the Atlantic. In 1641, nine vessels were assembled to convoy the fleet to Havana but were wrecked or damaged and returned to Veracruz. Another round of fundraising suggestions occurred, which reflected official recognition that Mexico City interests had succeeded in obstructing existing taxes. Thus, although the chief spokesman for the new measures, Viceroy Palafox, included new taxes on the *géneros nobles* of cochineal, indigo, sugar, and, especially, tobacco (which were not imposed), most of his suggestions involved implementing existing savings, seeing that the provincial cities and other regions paid their share, and winning the cooperation of the colonists by offering them positions in the *Armada* and giving them more contracts to build and provision it. Significantly, he also urged that the *alcabala de viento* and the other branches that "belonged to" the *consulado* be returned to it because the merchant guild was better able to come up with the payment.[72] *Regidor* Valero supported this suggestion, "since the members of the city council do not know how to manage these matters of trade."[73]

In 1644, Viceroy Salvatierra and the *junta de hacienda* cancelled the city's contract to farm the sales tax over the *cabildo*'s objections. Salvatierra plied the merchant guild with favors in order to get it to assume collection for all three branches—*forastería, vecindad,* and *viento*—of the tax. He reminded the merchants that they could expect reductions in their assessments only if they assumed this responsibility. He promised to raise the issue of the reopening of the Peru trade and to urge the cancellation of part of a large fine levied on the consulado by the *visitador* Pedro de Quiroga in 1635 (600,000 pesos) and 1636 (300,000 pesos).[74] The merchants' administration of the sales tax subcontract no doubt had been corrupt, but it was the lesser of the two evils. In a society organized by corporate bodies, the merchants, the chief payers of the sales tax, were more likely to cooperate with a member of their own group than with administrators appointed by the State.

The merchants came out of the fiscal wars of the 1630s and early 1640s scarred but triumphant. In 1647, for the first time, the contract for the entire sales tax farm was let to the *consulado*, which outbid the unrepentant *cabildo* by offering bond of 135,000 pesos instead of the 100,000 pesos offered by the city council. The merchants also agreed to pay 35,000 pesos of the bond immediately and provide the characteristic advance, 50,000 pesos of the 270,275.5 pesos due.[75] The merchants simply had more cash on hand. The guild continued to enjoy viceregal favor in the 1650s. Under Viceroy Alva de Liste (1650–53), the officials of the *consulado* had excellent relations with the *visitador* Pedro de Gálvez. Consul Simón de Haro bragged that the *visitador* came to his summer house to eat and relax, and prior Pedro de Soto López asserted that Gálvez was "so much his creature that he collected his fees and paid his expenses."[76]

By the terms of the fourth contract, the *consulado* assumed all previous debts of the sales tax, which pushed the arrears to dangerous heights. In 1648, they climbed to 580,000 pesos, and in 1651, to 724,404 pesos. The government simply could not force the traders to pay more. Viceroy Albuquerque (1653–60) wined and dined *consulado* officials to pressure them to pay sales tax debts, but combined his wooing with the threat (made good) to put them under house arrest if all else failed. Even Albuquerque, however, wrote to the king to inquire whether or not he should proceed as *tibiamente* (cautiously) in his relations with the merchants as had his viceregal predecessors.[77] The only way to break the impasse was through the State's established method of legalizing opposition to its demands: *composición*. By negotiating a reduction in the arrears in exchange for an agreement by the merchants to pay the lower sum, the viceroy could inform the king in 1659 that all *consulado* debts to the sales tax were paid. As table 18 indicates, the *alcabala* farm was increased again during the fourth farm (1647–61) to 270,275.5 pesos a year, but the increase was offset by a number of concessions to the *consulado*, among them the addition of a group of *alcalde mayor* districts to the jurisdiction of the Mexico City farm.[78] The alcabala deficit crisis was over.

By spring 1640, after four years of jockeying and debate, only two taxes existed that were destined specifically for the *Armada:* the 2 percent increases in import-export tax and the sales tax. A combination of social groups forced the rejection of the proposed imposts on cacao, cochineal, and soap; approved but abandoned those on hides and cloth; and drove the playing card rent into bankruptcy and the sales tax close to it. Minority proposals to expand the tax base by assessing landed proprietors, civil bureaucrats, or the Church were rebuffed. Nor did Mexico City meet the quotas for either of the taxes to which it had assented. The total for the taxes specifically destined for the *Armada* was an annual average of 78,631 pesos for the period from 1636 to 1660, a sum considerably less than the 200,000 pesos owed by Mexico City. A significant portion of revenues had to come from existing royal rents such as *composiciones de tierras*, sale of salt, reduction of garrisons, or from taxes previously accepted by the colonists and which the Crown diverted to the *Armada*, such as one-half of the wine tax at Veracruz.[79]

Had the Crown been willing to grant some of the *mercedes* requested, Mexico City would have been more cooperative because the colonists believed that concessions should accompany the payment of new taxes. Likewise, Mexico City believed that its compliance was legally contingent on the other cities and regions paying their share. Puebla, which owed 25,000 pesos annually, had refused to send its assessment. By 1642, of the regions outside New Spain, only Guatemala had paid and that, half its share. The 40,000 due from Yucatán, 30,000 from Nueva Galicia and Nueva Vizcaya, 40,000 from Cartagena, and sums from the Caribbean, as well as the balance of 18,000 from Guatemala were still outstanding.[76] Colonial resistance was also based on royal misuse of the funds collected. In 1636, only a quarter of the 200,000 pesos sent by Cadereita from various sources were used by the Crown for the *Armada*. In 1655, the viceroy recognized the justice of this complaint when he refused to ask the *consulado* for additional *Armada* funds.[80]

It was only after 1677 that *Armada* funds attained stability, in part because of taxation of pulque from 1672, which annually brought in an average of 134,135 pesos, or 44 percent of the revenues provided by Mexico City; the other large contributor was the sales tax, which produced 87,672 pesos, or 36 percent. The slow but definite revival in mining and trade from the 1670s, and the continued administration by the *consulado* of the sales tax farm, chiefly accounted for the change in the sales tax. The fiscal structure, however, had not changed: trading and consuming groups still bore the brunt of the tax. Although the king continued to divert *Armada* income to other sources, Guatemala, Cartagena, and Havana made more frequent and substantial payments, and the *Armada* squadron was in fairly regular operation, with five to six vessels through the end of the century.[81] Under these circumstances, the failure of Mexico City either to obtain certain policy changes or to obtain royal recognition of the right to receive them as parties to a contract receded in importance.

THE CAMPAIGN TO LIBERALIZE THE PACIFIC TRADE

Lobbying for Legislative Change

The trade between New Spain, the Philippines, and Peru was an extremely lucrative enterprise which lured investors from the 1570s onward. The high quality of Far Eastern goods, their cheapness relative to European imports of similar types, and the dominant role of the Mexico City merchants in their relations with Manila merchants all combined to make Pacific commerce highly attractive. Until recently, the contribution of the Pacific trade to capital gains of the elite and to the development of New Spain's economy was overlooked because of the emphasis on the Atlantic convoys. Research has demonstrated the significance of this branch of the colonial economy.[82] Certainly, its importance was readily accepted by the colonists, who tried repeatedly to shape royal policy relating to the galleon trade, as it was also called.

The legislation governing Pacific commerce, which developed chiefly between 1582 and 1634, was the subject of much city council, *consulado*, and viceregal correspondence. No issue preoccupied the merchant guild more than the royal restrictions imposed on this traffic, and other authorities were also frequently concerned. The crux of the debate was that colonists desired to have the trade as free as possible, while the Crown wished to limit it as much as possible. On the whole, the colonists failed in their attempts to attain their objectives. Between 1593 and 1609, they achieved a few successes, but from 1620 to the early eighteenth century, their efforts were in vain. They reverted, therefore, to manipulating the legal system in their favor. More frequently than in the case of tax paying, they also relied on outright disobedience: smuggling.

The characteristic pattern of royal actions and colonial reactions developed in the 1590s. The first group of restrictions appeared in 1582 and 1583, when the royal attitude to the Philippine commerce was formed and from which there was little subsequent deviation. There were four basic restrictions. First, the Crown imposed a limit on the number of ships, their tonnage, and the amount of cargo they were to carry. In 1593, the year when most of the laws were promulgated, the king declared that two vessels, of up to 300 tons, were to voyage each year, with one additional vessel to remain at Acapulco for repairs. The investors were allowed to place a maximum of 250,000 pesos' worth of goods on the galleons from Manila to Acapulco and to receive a maximum of 500,000 pesos' worth on the galleons returning from Acapulco to Manila. This maximum was termed the *permiso*.[83]

Second, the trade was to benefit the residents of Manila, not those of New Spain or other regions. Only Philippine residents were to trade with New Spain, and they were not supposed to be the agents of Mexico City merchants. Lading space permits, were to be divided among the *vecinos* of Manila according to the value of their estates, with due regard for those in need. Third, direct trade between Manila and Lima, Tierra Firme, Guatemala, or any other region except Japan was prohibited, and China goods could not be reexported between New Spain and any other region. The only legal trade was between Manila and Acapulco. Fourth, the trade was subject to import-export taxes, the admiralty tax, and the sales taxes, just as any other trade.[84]

The comprehensive regulations of 1593 immediately provoked a response from New Spain. Viceroy Velasco II—and soon after, Viceroy Monterrey—noted that the new restrictions could not be enforced and suggested that the authorities apply them laxly. The *cabildo* emphasized the importance of imports from the Philippines to the economy.[85] The king did not back down on any of the new measures but helped prevent the complete closure of the galleon trade, a course of action urged on the Crown by the Seville *consulado* from the earliest days of the trade. The merchants were supported by Spanish manufacturers of fine cloths and by wine and olive oil exporters who disliked the New Spain–Peru leg of the commerce. As early as 1585, the Seville *consulado* complained of a glut of Chinese fabrics at Veracruz, and in 1586, it called for suppression of the galleons. In the 1590s, the king again seriously considered complete closure.[86] The loss of silver bullion to the Far East, where it was used to finance Spain's enemies the Dutch and Portuguese, and the damage allegedly done to Spain's industry and trade, were persuasive arguments. Religious, military, and prestige considerations outweighed them, however.

The second royal offensive against the Manila trade occurred between 1604 and 1609 and provoked a similar chorus of opposition. In 1604, a new limitation was introduced. Only three ships of up to 400 tons were allowed to sail between New Spain and Peru; they could carry only domestic products. No China or Philippine goods could be sent south, and no Peruvian silver could return north. The tonnage permitted the two Manila galleons was reduced to 200 tons. The Mexico City *cabildo* and the *consulado* called for revocation, especially of the prohibition of trade in silver. They pointed out that Peru had nothing that Mexico needed but silver, and there was much clothing in the viceroyalty which lacked a market and was needed in Peru. Moreover, Peruvian silver was used to dispatch the fleet to Spain.[87]

The issue remained controversial, and in 1609, the *consulado* asked for an increase of one-fifth of 1 percent in the convoy tax to pay for a representative to argue against the prohibition of silver imports from Peru. The royal government relented to the point of allowing the ships coming from Peru to carry 200,000 ducats of silver (280,000 pesos), but it reduced the vessels to two annually, with a maximum of 200 tons. This victory was regarded as insufficient, however. Aware of continuing local opposition to the restrictions, in 1610, Viceroy Velasco II urged the king to enlarge the 200,000 ducat limit on silver imports—but to no avail.[88] Rather than liberalize the commercial legislation, from 1619 to 1621 and again from 1631 to 1635, the Crown added new constraints.

The royal government could have benefited directly from the flourishing Pacific trade in the first half of the seventeenth century. By allowing it to expand and taxing the proceeds, the Crown could have obtained badly needed revenue to support its military and ecclesiastical establishment in the Philippines and its defense needs elsewhere. Instead, however, it tried to raise more capital in Spain itself by bowing to the wishes of the merchants, agricultural exporters, and textile producers there. In 1618, the Seville *consulado* launched the most systematic attack on the galleon trade to date. It refused to sign a new contract for the collection of the *avería* unless the king promulgated a new decree restating the *permiso* to the Philippines. The Crown obliged and issued a new batch of decrees intended to strengthen royal control over the allocation of lading space, appointment of ships' officers, and inspection of cargo. The most obnoxious provision was the stipulation that no Peruvian wine could be imported into New Spain on the two legal annual vessels. Because wine was, with silver, Peru's chief means of paying for China goods, this decree struck a new blow to the trade. The usual requests followed for revocation by the *cabildo* and *consulado* in Mexico City. In 1622, the *consulado* attributed a slowdown in local trade, a decline in the galleon trade, and high prices in the viceroyalty to the new restrictions on traffic from Peru. It called fruitlessly for the "reopening" of the Acapulco-Lima route.[89]

The climax of the attack occurred in the 1630s. In 1631, the royal government closed the Peru trade entirely on a temporary basis, and in 1634 the trade was ended for five years, subject to renewal. Its reopening was one of the issues raised in 1636, when Mexico City bargained with the king over the imposition of taxes for the *Armada de Barlovento*. Neither this request nor the request that the *permiso* be raised another 250,000 pesos were granted. Despite the annual recommendations of Viceroy Cadereita and the repeated petitions of the *cabildo*, the *consulado*, the representative of Manila, the governor of the Philippines, and the *audiencia* of New Spain, the king remained adamant.[90] Colonial efforts to change Pacific commercial policy were very strong in the mid-1630s, but they also continued for many years afterward. And Viceroys Villena, Conde de Liste, Albuquerque, and Salvatierra seconded these efforts.[91] The Crown was too wedded to local Spanish pressure groups to reconsider, however.

Circumventing the Permiso

Understandably, the colonists had recourse to their other strategy, manipulating and, if necessary, disobeying the law. Here they enjoyed considerable success. From the letters of Viceroy Velasco II in the 1590s and onward, the viceroys insisted on their inability to enforce the *permiso*, the limit on the Peru trade, and the quota on the number of military going to Manila. Mercantile defiance dated from the late sixteenth century and not only from the 1630s. Viceroys Monterrey in 1603, Montesclaros in 1604, Velasco II in 1609, Gelves in 1622, Cerralvo in 1634, and Cadereita in 1638 all reported that they could not enforce the rules. The terms of office of Viceroys Gelves and Archbishop Palafox were cut short, in part because they attempted to enforce the unenforceable.[92] The dangerous riot of 1624 was provoked to some extent by Gelves's seizure of Philippine contraband and rigorous tax collection. And the mere repetition of laws regarding the *permiso*, the prohibition of reexport of China goods, and the inspection procedures offer additional evidence of successful flaunting of the commercial legislation.

The viceroys objected to commercial restrictions in part because their inability to implement them was frustrating and in part, in some cases, because they themselves were illegally trading to the Philippines. There were several good reasons to expand the Pacific trade: Velasco II and Monterrey stressed the income the Crown would gain from taxes on it and also

Table 20. Remittances of Privately Owned, Registered Silver
to the Philippines, 1591–1700

Decade	Amount for the Decade (in Pesos)
1591–1600	578,170
1601–10	3,516,513
1611–20	5,048,118
1621–30	5,423,822
1631–40	3,509,871
1641–50	1,759,706
1651–60	2,015,681
1661–70	1,726,151
1671–80	2,230,883
1681–90	876,528
1691–1700	171,954

Source: John J. TePaske, "New World Silver, Castile, and the Far East (1590–1750)," in
Precious Metals in the Later Medieval and Early Modern World, ed. John Richards (Durham: Carolina Academic Press, 1982), table 3. The figures are based on the *almojarifazgo*
receipts from the *caxa de Acapulco.*

the necessity of converting the Chinese and Japanese to Christianity. They
also noted that the consumers of New Spain needed the cheaper Chinese
silk. Montesclaros and Velasco in his second term made the same arguments, Velasco also asserted that the Pacific trade was *safer* and returned
profits *more quickly* than the Atlantic, that the American economies were
producing goods such as wine and soap that would lower the demand from
Spain regardless of the Philippine trade, and that capital invested in the
Philippine trade was only one-tenth of what was sent to Spain, an exaggeration but not a complete falsehood. Velasco also claimed that fraud
was less prevalent in the Pacific, a questionable assertion (tables 20 and
21). Cadereita noted the need to keep prices lower in New Spain and to
enable the *manileños* to earn a living, thus permitting the continuation of
the Philippines as a Spanish base. Many viceroys suggested that rather
than restrict the trade, the Crown should raise taxes on it.[93]

In addition to the testimony of these authorities, the import tax receipts
at Acapulco indicate that the restrictive legislation was not effective. The
periods of intense royal legislation were 1589–1593, 1604–1609, 1619–
1621, and 1631–1634. How did the Philippine trade fare after these periods of increased legislative restrictions? Most of the limits were in place
by 1609. According to the receipts of import-export tax, the trade in pri-

Table 21. Estimates of the Private Acapulco-Manila Cargo, 1593–1655

Year	Value of Cargo (in Pesos)	Source
1593	942,101	AGI, Aud Méx 22, 25 February 1593
1601	2,500,000	Schurz, *Manila Galleon*, p. 189
1602	2,400,000[a] and 3,000,000	AC 15:47
1603	2,000,000	AGI, Aud Méx 325, 27 May 1603
1603	2,700,000	AGI, Aud Méx 25, 21 March 1603
1605	2,000,000+	AC 16:207
1618	1,000,000 to 2,000,000	AGI, Aud Méx 29, 18 July 1618
1629	1,500,000 to 2,000,000	AGI, Aud Méx 30, 20 January 1629
1630s	4,000,000	AGI, Aud Méx 330
1636	2,000,000	AGI, Aud Méx 34, 12 July 1638, referring to 1636
1637	6,000,000[b]	AGI, Aud Méx 33, 12 July 1637
1638	4,000,000	AGI, Aud Méx 34, 12 July 1638
1655	800,000+ [c]	AGN, Tierras, 1272

[a]The source states that 12,000,000 pesos were sent *over the five-year period* from 1597 to 1602 and that usually 3 million pesos were sent to the Philippines.
[b]The source states that 3 million pesos of goods were sent from the Philippines, which would mean approximately double that amount returning there. An often-cited estimate of 8,500,000 pesos in the 1630s is not reliable, because it comes from an opponent of the Manila trade, who tried to prove it drained large amounts of silver to the Far East.
[c]This amount was removed from a damaged galleon.

vate silver prospered in 1601–1610, increased in 1611–1620, and went to its greatest heights in 1621–1630, the years after the new restrictions on the Peru wine trade. True, there appeared to be a relative decline in the 1630s, when the Peru trade was closed altogether and the *visitador* Pedro de Quiroga levied heavy fines upon—and confiscated the merchandise of—traders on the galleon. Factors other than legislation may have contributed to the decline, however. The Dutch began a new, effective offense against the trade and against Portuguese and Spanish territories in the Far East. In the 1640s, the new Ming dynasty was hostile toward the silk export trade.[94] Finally, the relative decline in volume in the 1630s may not have been as great as appears if what also occurred was that the crackdown prompted more smuggling and postponments of tax payments. (Public silver exported to the Philippines remained at the same level between 1631 and 1640 as from 1621 to 1630; it declined from 1640 on.)

The Pacific trade was notorious for its frauds against the royal exchequer. The tax receipt figures from Acapulco are considered less reliable than those from Veracruz, and the greater weakness of administrative machinery in the Pacific makes this understandable. More reliable estimates of the value of the Philippine trade come from the viceroys, *cabildo, consulado,* and *visitadores;* table 21 presents these estimates from 1593 to 1655. All are nearly 1 million pesos or much more. In other words, because the legal amount shipped from Acapulco to Manila was 500,000 pesos, all estimates put fraud at least 100 percent. Significantly, the highest figures, those which put the value of the Acapulco to Manila cargo at 4 to 6 million pesos, occur after 1630, the period when tax receipts showed a relative decline. On the galleon of 1646, a year in the decade when receipts were their lowest since the 1590s, an investigation revealed that the silver chests of the merchants contained six, eight, or even fourteen times the amounts declared.[95] Therefore, it is quite possible that even during the administrative pressure of the 1630s, commercial restrictions had little impact on the trade.

Thus, the core restriction of the galleon trade, the limitation of the value of cargo to 500,000 pesos from Acapulco, was consistently and flagrantly violated. The discrepancy reached incredible proportions in the years when 3 or 4 million pesos were sent to the Far East. Contrary to the stereotypical view of the relationship between law and reality, however, colonists were not content simply to violate the law. With the help of almost all the viceroys of that era, they tried to revoke or emend the damaging decrees. In part to obtain greater security and profits from their operations and in part because they preferred to be in accord with the law if possible, they repeatedly requested that the Pacific trade be liberalized and achieved a few notable successes. They prevented its complete closure, which Spanish interests urged, and obtained permission for the importation of Peruvian silver from 1609 until 1631. On all other counts, however, they failed dismally. The impotence of the colonists to change policies opposed by metropolitan interests is strikingly demonstrated by this chapter of seventeenth-century politics.

CONCLUSION

The reaction of merchants and other colonists to the fiscal and commercial demands of the Crown is an important theme in the history of the first two-thirds of seventeenth-century New Spain. Certainly the notions of a somnolent or nonpolitical century can be dismissed. Moreover, politics were not merely wrangling over petty matters of precedence and honors as they have sometimes been depicted.

Colonist-metropolitan friction was a constant in the imperial relation-ship. Merchant responses in the 1590s and 1600s to the *almojarifazgo*, *alcabala*, and limits on the Philippine and Peru trades indicate the ex-tent of their opposition and the forms it took. Antagonism became overt, first with the riot of 1624 and then with the large, new impositions for the *Unión de Armas* and the *Armada de Barlovento* and the limits on, then clo-sure of, the Peru trade in the 1620s and 1630s. The colonists threatened to withhold funds unless they received royal concessions and buttressed their position with a particular interpretation of political theory. These events led some historians to conclude that royal control of New Spain was slipping away, but such an opinion underestimates the colonists' attach-ment, both idealistic and self-interested, to the Crown. Amid their peti-tions opposing particular measures or officials, we find no questioning of the fundamental imperial objective of maintaining a strong Spanish and Catholic presence in Europe, Asia, and the New World. Considering the economic and military stresses of the 1640s and 1650s, it is striking that there was not more political disturbance in New Spain.

Colonial adherence to the status quo was also the result of considerable integration among elite groups. Here their political cooperation was noted, illustrated by the agenda of 1636. The merchant experience indicates that the "peninsular" versus "settler" dichotomy as generally understood is too neat; wholesalers straddled both groups, as did many public officials. Born, for the most part, in Spain, merchants kept close personal and com-mercial ties there, but they also identified with many settler demands and invested in the local economy. However, the "tax wars" of the period from 1590 to 1660 also show that merchants were not fully accepted into the creole elite and retained a distinct social and fiscal standing. In some ways they were penalized, in others they profited, but they did occupy a special position.

Political conflicts between elites and urban popular groups were rare. Rioting occurred once, but more typical was consumer opposition to buy-ing playing cards at the higher price or the guilds' refusal to pay the sales tax at the higher rate. The prospect of a cacao tax brought sufficient popu-lar agitation that the viceroy forbid the clergy to preach sermons about it, and indeed, the viceroy rejected this impost. Ignoring government de-mands, as occurred with the tax on cloth, was another nonviolent action taken. The official policy of exempting basic foodstuffs and fuel from taxation contributed to the relative social calm in the capital.

A growing colonial political independence would have been a fitting complement to the economic independence gained in certain areas. If by political independence is meant the ability to shape public policy, not much was accomplished. The colonists did prevent the closure of the Philippine–New Spain trade and obtained the continued inclusion of silver in the Peru–New Spain trade until 1631, but otherwise their repeated and strenuous efforts to change the curbs on the galleon trade failed. They succeeded in influencing the types of taxes to be imposed, but they could not affect the overall amount requested from New Spain, nor did they attempt to alter royal priorities. Nevertheless, their campaigns against certain aspects of Crown policy are important demonstrations of tenacity and vitality, and their arguments are a reflection of the political culture.

What merchants and other colonists did dramatically affect was the manner in which policy was implemented. If by political independence is understood the management of public life on a routine basis, there is no doubt that the colony became more autonomous in the seventeenth century. The entry of more creoles and long-resident Spaniards into the bureaucracy contributed, as did the imposition of unpopular royal policies which were naturally going to provoke resistance. The most striking instance was the huge frauds in the Philippine trade; more ships than before the prohibition sailed between New Spain and Peru. Less well known but equally important was the colonists' long failure to pay in full the *almojarifazgo*, the *alcabala*, and the various taxes imposed for the *Unión* and the *Armada*. Fiscal arrears were greater in the 1630s and 1640s, but they had existed in the 1590s. However, the colonists also achieved de facto independence because the imperial system furthered it. Law and custom provided accepted channels for resistance, as when merchants appealed tax assessments in court or were pardoned for importing contraband when they paid a fine. They were masters at manipulating these provisions. The constant bargaining for money and favors gave a decidedly mercantile cast to metropolitan-colonial relations. Partial compliance with the law, in addition to outright defiance of it, was a key element in the longevity of the Empire despite its undeniably exploitative character.

One question remains unaddressed thus far; If the Crown had conceded the policy changes and bureaucratic appointments the colonists so anxiously sought, would they have been able to pay the higher taxes of the 1630s and later? The Conclusion will begin by considering the economic context of the political debates described here. First, however, we will look at the intergenerational history of some prominent merchant families.

CHAPTER VI

Progeny and Property

Colonial Mexico was an explicitly hierarchical society in which custom and law sanctioned the preservation of the status quo. From the time of conquest, however, there was a degree of mobility which varied in frequency and extent for each social group. In the first two-thirds of the seventeenth century such mobility did not challenge the existing social categories, but it did allow certain individuals to enter (and to leave) these categories. Wealth and education, marriage to a higher-status or lighter-skinned person, acquisition of a title, and political influence were the building blocks of upward mobility; loss of income, marital mésalliances, and scandalous conduct were the descending steps of downward mobility. The purpose of this chapter is to place the Mexico City wholesalers within colonial social structure, to show how they attempted to transmit their wealth to and confer higher social status upon their children and grandchildren, and, finally, to assess their success. What was the respective influence of economic, demographic, and social factors in affecting their prospects for success? Does the often-cited proverb which claims the impermanence of high station, "padre comerciante, hijo caballero, nieto pordiosero" (merchant father, gentleman son, beggar grandson), apply to these men and their families?

Merchants occupied an ambiguous position in the colonial social scheme. On the one hand, they were as wealthy or wealthier than the most respected landowner or bureaucrat families. They used their fortunes to maintain an aristocratic style of living centered in the *casa principal* staffed by slaves and servants in the heart of the capital. They purchased public office and land for themselves and for their children. They placed a high proportion of their children in the clergy. Undoubtedly, the wholesalers of the capital belonged to the colony's socioeconomic elite, broadly conceived. Their inclusion testifies to the importance of wealth in this birth-conscious society. On the other hand, as a class, no matter how rich, the merchants did not belong to the highest social echelon. In the seventeenth century most wholesalers did not even use the honorific "don." As chapter 1 describes, the majority did not marry into aristocratic families (table 5), and as chapter 4 indicates, the offices they purchased were generally in the lower ranks of government. Being a public merchant still carried a social stigma in the seventeenth century, and the influx of Portuguese *conversos* from the 1580s may have strengthened it. One indication of the merchants' acceptance of the depreciation of their profession is that they chose nonmercantile careers and spouses for many of their children. There were other reasons for this choice, but protecting their children from the socially undesirable calling of public merchant was one of them. There were limits to what wealth could buy; the wholesalers accepted this fact of social life.

FAMILY SIZE AND FAMILY WEALTH

Quite a few merchants succeeded in using their fortunes to obtain a financially secure and socially respected place for all their children. They employed the same strategies to preserve the family's assets which other elite families did, such as the *mexora* (larger share of inheritance) granted to a favored child, but they also enjoyed certain advantages which made it easier to perpetuate their fortunes. First was their great wealth, which was more likely to include cash. Second, in one-third of the merchant families studied, one of the children became a professional merchant, and even in the other families the children sometimes continued the trading activity of their parents unofficially. Continuation of commerce was by no means a guarantee of wealth, but in many cases it did contribute to maintaining the family's prosperity. Families manifested economic stability and social instability, the latter in a positive sense.

To appreciate the economic power of the wholesaler elite and their offspring, we must first define what wealth meant in this society. In chapter 1 merchants' annual investments in trade were compared with the annual legal income of other occupational groups. Here we are concerned with the merchants' total assets at a given time. Chroniclers in seventeenth-century Mexico City considered it worthwhile to report estates of "over 50,000 pesos" left by the secretary of the Viceroy Alba de Liste and the 150,000 peso estate of the pulque contracter Alonso de Narváez.

Among the historians, Chevalier considered 80,000 pesos a "fabulous sum," while Israel placed Francisco Texoso among the leading merchants with an estate of 70,000 pesos.[1] In this period, therefore, if a person were worth 10,000 to 25,000 pesos, he or she was well-to-do; if 25,000 to 50,000 pesos, wealthy; and more than 100,000 pesos made a person the equivalent of a millionaire. Where did Mexico City's wholesalers fit in this classification? The majority (75 percent), although not all, of wholesalers whose estates were analyzed were rich (table 22). They fell in the categories of wealthy, very wealthy, millionaires, billionaires, and "described as wealthy." To return to the topic of intergenerational mobility, what was the effect of this state of affairs on the children and grandchildren of merchants? Brading has suggested that mercantile fortunes were susceptible to decline, in part because of the large number of children and in part because of the legal requirement that the estate, with some exceptions, be divided equally among all the children.[2] We can call this the demographic-legal interpretation of downward social mobility. An analysis of wholesaler families shows, however, that while the presumption of matrimony for most merchants is correct, the belief that most had large families is not.

Wholesalers shared fully in the Hispanic aspiration to found a family and perpetuate the line. Transoceanic travels and treks to provincial markets in their youth postponed marriage, but eventually the majority wed, some more than once. Information about the exact number of children is available for sixty-nine merchant families. (Forty-two other families are known to have had at least one child.) Of the sixty-nine, 20 percent had no surviving children at all, 6 percent had no surviving legitimate children (table 23). Only legitimate children had claim to their parents' estate. A parent might choose to bequeath a sum to his or her natural children but was not obliged to do so, and such legacies were usually smaller than the portions granted to legitimate children.[3] The other merchants had families of widely varying sizes. Thirty-six percent had four or fewer children; 25 percent had five or six children; and 13 percent had seven or more children.

Thus, from the history of all 111 families, we can conclude that childless merchant couples existed (and had a significant influence on philanthropy) but were a distinct minority. From the history of the sixty-nine families, it is apparent that nearly two-thirds had four or fewer legitimate offspring, a conclusion consistent with recent research on elite family size in colonial New Spain. In seventeenth-century Guadalajara, of seventy-

Table 22. Value of Merchants' Estates, 1602–60

Value of Estate	Number of Merchants	% of Merchants
Under 1,000 pesos (poor):		
Benavides, F.		
Bribiesca Roldán, M.		
Brizuela, P.		
Cárdenas Jaramillo, J.		
Fernández, M.		
Galarreta, A.		
Total	6	7.8
1,000–9,999 (modest):		
Ossorio Soto, Lope		
Rodríguez Acevedo, A.		
Total	2	2.6
10,000–24,999 (well-to-do):		
Cabeza de Vaca, F.		
Chavarría, M.		
Fuente, T.		
Munabe, A.		
Pacheco Maldonado, J.		
Saco de Frías, G.		
Sánchez Arías, L.		
Sánchez Olivera, P.		
Santos Corral, T.		
Serralde, D. "the elder"		
Torres, Jacinto		
Total	11	14.4
25,000–49,999 (wealthy):		
Arlanzón Güemes, F.		
Baeza del Río, A.		
Ossorio Soto, Lucas		
Pardo de Agüero, J.		
Rodríguez León, J.		
Rossal, A.		
Santillana, G.		
Urrea, T.		
Total	8	10.4
50,000–99,999 (very wealthy):		
Alzega, M.		
Gutiérrez Gil, G.		
León Castillo, G.		

Table 22—*Continued*

Value of Estate	Number of Merchants	% of Merchants
López Erenchun, M.		
López Zarate, J.		
Rivera, F. M.		
Rodríguez Figueroa, A.		
Ruíz Oca de Ahumada, P.		
Termiño, G.		
Total	9	11.7
100,000–499,999 (millionaires):		
Arellano Sotomayor, F.		
Bonilla Bastida, C.		
Bribiesca Roldán, M.		
Caballero, D.		
Castellete, F.		
Castillo, F.		
Cuéllar, M.		
Enríquez, S.		
Esquivel Castañeda, F.		
Guerra Chacón, M.		
Haro, S.		
López Páramo, F.		
López Páramo, G.		
Medina Reynoso, F.		
Millán, A.		
Montemayor Herrera, J.		
Moreno Monroy, L.		
Ortiz Arevalo, A.		
Rivera, J. L.		
Ruíz Orduñana, P.		
Salcedo, G.		
Sánchez Herrera, G.		
Terreros, M.		
Toledo, P.		
de la Torre, F.		
Vaéz Sevilla, S.		
Valdés, C.		
Vásquez Medina, J.		
Vásquez Medina, L.		
Vera, D. M.		
Zuleta, C.		
Total	31	40.2

Table 22—*Continued*

Value of Estate	Number of Merchants	% of Merchants
500,000–1,000,000 (billionaires):		
Lorenzana, A.		
Molina Mosquera, E.		
Rodríguez Ríos, B.		
Soto López, P.		
Total	4	5.2
Described as Wealthy:		
Barainca, D.		
Cantabrana, D.		
Martínez Guadiana, F.		
Medina Orozco, L.		
Rodríguez Vado, A.		
Zuaznavar y Aguirre, T.		
Total	6	7.8
Totals	77	100.0

Sources: AHH, Consulado; AJud.; AGI, Audiencia de México, Escribanía de Cámara, Contratación; AGN, Vínculos, Civil, Bienes Nacionales, Real Fisco, Tierras; AN; AEA; Guijo, *Diario*; Robles, *Diario*; and Villaseñor y Villaseñor, *Los condes*. Sources include the following types of documents: seventeen are inventories of the estate taken at the time of death or afterward; nine are chroniclers' summaries of such inventories; twenty-four are detailed wills written shortly before death; five are inventories or wills of the wife, child, or brother, which include the merchants' assets; four are foundations of entail or other information about property; and eighteen are from the declarations of wealth of 1622.

three *español* families, the mean number of children was 3.5. Sixty-three percent of the families had four or fewer children. Even in mid-eighteenth-century Mexico City, when infant mortality rates were probably lower, the mean size of upper-status households was only 6.6 persons.[4] While large nuclear families of five or more children were present, therefore, they were not as common among the upper classes as previously thought.

What effect does this conclusion have on the transmission of wealth from the first to the second generation? Broadly speaking, a comparison of table 22 with table 23 suggests that mercantile fortunes could accommodate substantial legacies to the four or fewer children often present in the wholesalers' families. More than half of the men whose assets are included in table 22 had estates of 100,000 pesos or more. Assuming the children received half the estate, 50,000 pesos in a family of four would

Table 23. Number of Children in Merchant Families

Number of Children	Number of Families	Percent
None	14	20.3
Illegitimate only	4	5.8
1–2	10	14.5
3–4	15	21.7
5–6	17	24.6
7–8	4	5.8
9–11	5	7.2
Total	69	100.0

Source: AGN, Inquisición, and sources listed for table 22.

start each child off with 12,500 pesos, definitely placing him or her in the well-to-do category in colonial society. (And, the bulk of the mother's share would probably later pass to the children.) If we consider specific families, a similar picture appears.

Children generally received their inheritance on specific occasions. When the child married, took religious vows, or came of age at twenty-five, he or she was provided with the means considered necessary to be established in accordance with the family's station. Then, when a parent died, the child received his or her share of the parent's estate, called the *legítima*. Property given to the child on the first occasion was added back to his or her share of the estate on the second occasion, so that the *legítima* represented the total amount granted to the child by the parent during the parent's lifetime. The inheritances received by children in twenty-six merchant families are presented in table 24. These sums represent the division of the net assets of the merchants' estate, that is, the sum remaining after all debts were paid. Of these families, seven bequeathed estates of less than 10,000 pesos to their children; eight bequeathed estates of 10,000 to 25,000 pesos; and eleven bequeathed estates of more than 25,000 pesos. The majority of children in these families, therefore, received legacies which placed them in the well-to-do, wealthy, or more wealthy categories in colonial society. Inevitably, the sums received by the children had to be smaller than the sum held by their parents. In this sense, there was a decline of economic position from the first to the second generation, as Brading first pointed out. But if we consider these legacies by the standards of the time, it is clear that many merchants' children received substantial inheritances. The decline was relative, not

Table 24. Inheritance Patterns of Selected Merchants, 1602–60

Amount Inherited by Children[a]	Number of Families	Percent
Under 5,000 pesos:		
Baeza del Río, A.		
Benavides, F.		
Cárdenas Jaramillo, J.		
De la Barrera		
Total	4	15.4
5,000–9,999 pesos:		
Arellano Sotomayor, F.		
Ossorio Soto, Lucas		
Rodríguez de Acevedo, A.		
Total	3	11.5
10,000–14,999 pesos:		
López Olaiz, J.		
Termiño, G.		
Total	2	7.7
15,000–19,999 pesos:		
Toledo, P.		
Torres, J.		
Total	2	7.7
20,000–24,999 pesos:		
Montemayor Herrera, J.		
Guerra Chacón, A.[b]		
Rodríguez León, J. (San Agustín)[b]		
Vásquez Medina, L.		
Total	4	15.4
25,000–29,999 pesos:		
Alzega, M.		
Total	1	3.8
30,000–49,999 pesos:		
León Castillo, G.		
Rivera, F. M.		
Total	2	7.7
50,000 pesos or above:		
Bonilla Bastida, C.		
Gutiérrez Gil, G.		
Medina Reynoso, F.		
Millán, A.		
Molina Mosquera, E.		

Table 24—*Continued*

Amount Inherited by Children[a]	Number of Families	Percent
Rodríguez de los Ríos, B.		
Salcedo, G.		
Vera, D. M.		
Total	8	30.8
Totals	26	100.0

Sources: See table 22.

[a] If the family contained a "favored" child, who received a larger legacy than his or her siblings, the legacy of the siblings is what is included here, in order to present the amount most of the children received.

[b] In these cases the wife predeceased the merchant husband, so that the inheritance represented both paternal and maternal property.

absolute. Moreover, the children could use their legacies to improve their position further. They could make economically advantageous marriages and invest in income-producing properties.[5]

In addition, the law allowed the wholesaler to grant one child more than his or her share of the estate under certain circumstances. The favored child received the *mexora*, which usually meant the balance of one-fifth of the estate plus one-third of what remained after the fifth was deducted. As Ladd describes, the estate was thought of as divisible into fifteen shares. One-fifth (three of fifteen shares), called the *quinto*, was set aside to pay the testator's funeral expenses, bequests, and debts. If there was a sum left over from the *quinto* once these expenses were paid, that amount (the *remaniente*) was granted to the favored child. Once the *quinto* had been deducted, the estate consisted of twelve shares. The favored child might also receive a third (four of twelve shares), called the *tercio*. Then the balance of the estate (eight of twelve shares), called *bienes libres*, was divided between the children and the wife. The property of the favored child might be converted into an entail, formed from the *remaniente del quinto* and the *tercio*. Alonso Ortiz de Arevalo founded entails for two of his six children out of a 300,000 peso estate. One was for his daughter doña María, the wife of don García de Legaspi, Albornoz y Acuña, and was worth 120,000 pesos. The other was destined for Doctor Alonso Ortiz Oraá, his eldest son. Martín Bribiesca Roldán entailed 135,000 pesos' worth of houses and shops in Mexico City for his two sons, who were to maintain their four sisters from the rents of the entail.[6]

As these examples indicate, entail was not limited to one child nor to males. Entails were not used that extensively, however. It was more common for merchants simply to favor a particular child with a larger share of the estate than to take the step of founding an entail on the larger share. De la Peña estimates that there were fifty entails in mid-seventeenth century New Spain, eleven founded by merchants and the rest by first settlers, bureaucrats, clerics, and mineowners.[7] Albi Romero notes that the second or third generation of conquistadors frequently founded entails. Even a simple *mexora*, however, allowed a large proportion of the family property to pass intact from one generation to the next.

Any discussion of the economic position of the second generation must also consider the impact that children who entered the Church had on the inheritance of their siblings who remained laypersons. Since the choice of a clerical career reflects social and religious as well as economic aspects of family history, however, it is necessary to turn first to the social position of the second generation.

SOCIAL POSITION OF THE SECOND GENERATION

The wholesalers were quite successful in bettering the social position of the family through their children. All merchants' sons used the "don." Their occupancy of such offices as *regidor, secretario de la cámara real*, or *corregidor* or, in the case of daughters, their marriage to such officials, indisputably represented upward mobility, as did the entry of sons and daughters into the monastic institutions or, in the case of sons, the secular clergy. While scholars have noted the trend of upward mobility for traders' offspring, they have not yet documented it for this period, and one purpose of this discussion is to present data which supports this assertion. The second purpose, however, is to show that although a shift in occupational identity occurred from trade to office (clerical and civil) across the generations, the break between the professions of parents and children was not complete. Occupational instability was common but it was not universal. Children did become merchants, and those who did not retained connections with their commercial pasts. An interesting and hitherto neglected dimension of intergenerational continuity was the close social and business ties among the second and third generations of merchant families, even when they were no longer professional traders.

A noteworthy feature of the second generation was occupational diversification. Unlike the generation of the founding fathers, when several brothers and brothers-in-law were associates in wholesale trade, the sec-

Table 25. Occupational Distribution of All Merchant Children

Sons			Daughters		
Occupation		Number	Occupation		Number
Public office		41	Married public official		35
Clergy			Clergy		
Secular	33				
Regular	20		Regular	41	
Total	53	53	Total	41	41
Merchant		14	Married merchant		17
Landowner		4	Married landowner		5
Total		112			98

Source: AC; AGI, Contaduría, Audiencia de México, including Registro de oficios; GSU, Parroquia de Asunción Sagrario, Mexico City, Españoles: Amonestaciones, Matrimonios, and Entierros; AGN, Inquisición and sources listed in table 22; Hoberman, "Merchants"; Muriel, *Conventos.*

ond generation was spread out among trade, civil officeholding, clergy, and rural landownership. (For the purposes of this analysis, landowner is a residual category for an individual who does not have a commercial, government, or ecclesiastical identity. Of course, traders, clerics, and officials might well own land also). This diversification was common among colonial families and clearly was beneficial to the family interest. There were basically three occupational patterns for the second generation in seventy-six families. Either all children became ecclesiastics or became, or married, public officials (66 percent); or they followed these careers but included a sibling who became, or married, a professional merchant (25 percent); or they all became, or married, merchants (9 percent). The movement into civil and clerical office is striking. Another way to view the occupational patterns of the second generation is to look at the total number of children rather than at the total number of families (table 25). Of 210 offspring, ninety-four (45 percent) became ecclesiastics, and seventy-six (36 percent) became or married public officials. Therefore, 81 percent of the children joined the civil or ecclesiastical bureaucracies. Thirty-one (15 percent) chose merchant careers or spouses.

The strong interest of these families in civil posts was due to the financial security many offered, the prestige, and the possibility of using political influence, even if in a limited fashion. Had there not existed an extensive bureaucracy whose posts were sold, the careers of the second generation would have been different. Although merchants did not necessarily have the political connections to secure an office by appointment, they usually did have the means to secure one by purchase. Some merchants had, of course, bought office for themselves, but more children than fathers held posts. The ranks occupied by the children were similar to those held by the fathers, although a few offspring rose to the heights. The daughters of García León Castillo and Gonzalo Gutiérrez Gil married *oidores*, Andrés de Rossal's sons became treasury officers, and Domingo de Cantabrana and Toribio Fernández de Celi's daughters married treasury officers. These were the exceptions, however. In part because the sons could inherit their father's posts of *receptor* or *regidor* upon payment of the renunciation fee, in part because of the stiff competition for the high-level judgeships, lucrative *corregidor* posts, and treasury offices, wholesalers' children clustered in their fathers' valuable but middle- and low-ranking positions. Antonio de Millán bequeathed his regidorship to his son Félix, as did Leandro de Gática to his son Juan. Martín López Erenchun passed his office of *balansario* in the mint to his son Martín. Or, the merchant could buy an office for his son but hold it himself until the boy reached his majority, as did Francisco Medina Reynoso and Diego Matías de Vera. An office might also pass from older to younger brothers.[8]

Merchant Riches and the Church

Entering the clergy was motivated by a more complex combination of causes than was becoming (or marrying) an official. The high proportion of children who joined the Church is one of the most salient characteristics of merchant family history, especially when contrasted with families of the late eighteenth century.[9] In mid-seventeenth century Mexico City, sons and daughters entered the clergy in 91 percent of merchant families. The ecclesiastical life offered many of the attractions of government employment. It was respected, economically secure, albeit at a low level for priests dependent on small endowments, and, to the extent that the children became canons, priests in important urban parishes, or abbesses, it conferred some political power. More important, destining children to the religious life expressed the piety of the child and the parents in a society which placed high value on religious feeling. As with the adornment of chapels, the founding of schools and hospitals, and the endowment of masses, the choice of ecclesiastical careers for children was one form that spiritual concerns took in this era. Perhaps merchants felt the need to demonstrate their religiosity more acutely because of a residue of guilt about engaging in activities whose limits were still set by the Church (chapter 1).[10]

Finally, it is possible that some merchants gave weight to general economic considerations in placing their children in the religious life. It might be easier to obtain a loan from a religious order in which one's child had professed. Also, children who became monks or nuns usually returned the bulk of their inheritance portion to their siblings, allowing the lay members of the family to inherit more of the estate than they would have otherwise. Clerical careers for some of the children had the effect of preventing the equal division of the family's property.[11]

The laws governing profession were such that whether the child entered the regular or the secular clergy, his or her portion (in the case of the regulars) tended to remain under the family's control. Monks and nuns were obliged to contribute an endowment upon entry into a religious order. The endowment came from their *legítima* but often did not entirely consume it. Monastic dowries of merchants' children were generally 3,000 to 4,000 pesos in the seventeenth century, with often another 2,000 to 3,000 pesos for the purchase and furnishing of a cell and for expense money. These sums were considerably smaller than the portions of many merchant daughters (table 24). In such cases, therefore, there was a surplus. The religious could bequeath the surplus to his or her convent or could "renounce" it back to the parental estate to be divided among the siblings. No instances have been found of the former practice, whereas the latter was common. The secular priest, for his part, did not have to contribute principal in the form of an endowment, but rather only income from interest from a chantry fund whose principal remained part of his family's estate. He retained his right to his inheritance portion, which he could bequeath to members of his family, to other persons, or to pious works.[12]

For example, the merchant Juan de Montemayor Herrera and his first wife, doña Leonor de Bañuelos, had seven children. The eldest son, don Joseph, was favored not only in the *tercio* and *remaniente del quinto* but he also received the *legítimas* of his three nun sisters and his two monk brothers, once their endowments had been paid. Each nun's *legítima* was 12,035 pesos. Of this amount, 4,000 pesos went for the dowry, 2,500 pesos for a cell, and the balance reverted to don Joseph. His total share was 68,018 pesos (one child's occupation is not known). The Montemayor Herrera were a large family, but such arrangements also occurred in small families. The wholesaler Diego Serralde had three children. Don Agustín joined the Franciscans and received an income of 100 pesos a year plus 200 pesos for his studies; his sister, madre Clara de San Francisco, a nun in the convent of San Juan de la Penitencia, had an income of 150 pesos a year, which was to revert to her siblings upon her death. Both children renounced the balance of their inheritance portions to their brother Diego, who became a merchant. In the family of Alonso Guerra Chacón, the two sons, Miguel and Alonso, who became monks received 1,250 pesos each, while their three lay siblings received paternal portions of 9,716 pesos each.[13]

One common family pattern was for one child to become, or to marry, a public official while the other children entered the Church. In Juan González Fuente's family, don Juan, the son, became an *alférez* while his four sisters entered the convent of San Gerónimo. There were nine children in the family of Toribio Fernández de Celi. Of the two daughters, the one old enough to marry at the time of his death had wed Gordián Casasano, *contador* of the Mexico City treasury office and owner of a sugar plantation in Cuautla Amilpas. Six of her brothers entered the Church, three as seculars, two as Dominicans, and one as a Mercedarian. The two other children were minors at the time of their father's death. Of the five offspring of Antonio de Millán, one became an official, one a priest, one a nun, and the other two married officials.

It is possible that the inheritance portions renounced by the religious in such families contributed to the purchase price of the lay sibling's office or, in the case of the daughters, to wedding dowries. On the other hand, children were motivated to become religious for a number of noneconomic reasons, and their choice should not be oversimplified as a strategy in family estate planning. There were households, for example, of only one child, such as that of the merchant Esteban Molina Mosquera, where with a fortune at her disposal to make a brilliant match, the daughter became a nun instead. All of Tiburcio de Urrea's three children joined the Church despite their father's estate of nearly 50,000 pesos. Whatever the motive, however, almost all merchant families had at least one child who became an ecclesiastic.[14]

The piety of the wholesaler group could find fullest expression among couples who had no children. In such cases there was no obligation to conserve wealth for offspring, and large donations were made to ecclesiastical institutions of different kinds. Here the demographic factor did have a direct relation to the transmission of wealth. But if childlessness made large donations to the Church legally possible, religious feeling and social acceptance made them probable. Of the fourteen wholesalers who had no children at all, eight either founded religious institutions or left large legacies to them, three left their estates to wives or relatives, one died in debt, one had his property seized by the Inquisition, and one disposed of his estate without leaving a record.

Although those who bequeathed their property to the Church may appear to have been favoring the Church at the expense of their relatives, this was often not the case because the merchant donors expected their relatives to enter the religious orders which they supported. For example, the wholesaler Diego de Caballero and his wife doña Inés de Velasco founded the Convent of Santa Inés for poor girls without dowries and for his nearest relatives. (He imposed *censos* on his urban and rural property to support the convent.) He also established eight *capellanías* ranging from 2,000 pesos to 4,500 pesos each, possibly for his young male relations.[15] Other merchants set up *capellanías* for the same reasons. The founder of a religious house usually became its patron and was granted a number of privileges, which included the continuation of the patronage in his family and the burial of the patron and his wife in the order's chapel. Caballero and his architect discussed at length the statue of Caballero to be placed over his grave in the Convent of Santa Inés. Molina Mosquera, whose daughter became a nun in the Carmelites of San Joseph, left 400,000 pesos to that order. The father, as patron and builder, was buried in its chapel and his daughter later used the rest of the family's great wealth to found another convent, Santa Teresa la Nueva.[16] Thus, pious works were linked in several ways with the donor's family, who could retain a close association with the religious house.

The transfer of capital from lay to clerical hands, nevertheless, was impressive. Álvaro de Lorenzana, the childless merchant banker of the 1640s and 1650s, donated more than 160,000 pesos to build a new church and convent for the nuns of La Encarnación, which was begun in 1639 and finished in 1648. He gave 40,000 pesos to build the infirmary at the Monastery of San Francisco, 20,000 pesos to the Convent of La Merced, and made donations to other convents as well. Lorenzana also bequeathed 20,000 pesos to endow eight cathedral prebends and 10,000 pesos to provide dowries for orphans. Lorenzana's division of his estate among different religious orders and for different purposes was typical of other wealthy childless merchants.[17]

A variant on the perpetuation of the patronage of a religious house in the same family was the case of the Convent of Limpia Concepción, whose patronage passed from one merchant to another. The wholesaler Tomás Zuaznavar y Aguirre and his wife doña Isabel de Estrada y Álvarado began the new church of the convent, having foundations laid and walls partially built. They became patrons in 1643. In 1646, doña Isabel, now a widow, renounced the patronage of the new church, and it passed to Simón de Haro and his wife, a childless merchant couple. Haro spent 160,000 pesos to finish the new church by 1655, when he died. He also placed 100,000 pesos' worth of *censos* to support it. Among the bequests of Haro and his wife was 15,000 pesos to the Jesuit College of San Pedro and San Pablo. Doña Isabel herself founded the Convent of San Felipe de Jesús.[18]

Merchants who founded religious houses were active in the early seventeenth century when orders were still establishing themselves. In addition to Diego Caballero, Andrés de Acosta founded the Hospital de la Misericordia and spent 20,000 pesos to repair the Convent of Jesús María, while Alonso Rodríguez del Vado and his wife founded the Convent and Hospital of Espíritu Santo for the poor. Juan Luis Rivera established the Jesuit Casa Profesa and appointed a nephew as patron. His wife, doña Juana, left a 20,000 peso *censo* to the Casa. Such activities were by no means limited to the early years of the century, however, as the examples of the Molina Mosquera and Haro families indicate. The Jesuits came in for their share of childless merchant legacies. Juan de Castellete, the wholesaler who financed sugar mills and produced textiles in the 1620s and 1630s, offers one instance. He left an estate of 180,861 pesos, half of which he bequeathed to the Discalced Carmelites and to the payment of his funeral expenses and charitable legacies, and half of which he bequeathed to his wife. Doña Beatriz Marquesa de Amarilla, in turn, left her share to the Jesuits. Merchants also made donations to their *cofradías*, such as San Pedro Mártir, the religious brotherhood of the Inquisition, to which belonged familiars and other Inquisition personnel. While by no means the only wealthy pious donors of the time, the wholesalers left their mark on the proliferation of ecclesiastical orders and architecture of the seventeenth century.[19]

Ties Among Merchants' Descendants

Among childless families the mercantile traditions came to an end with the first generation. In many commercial families, however, such traditions were continued by the children who carried on their father's business, either as public merchants or, more likely, in combination with a

10. Church of the *cofradía* of San Pedro Mártir, Mexico City, 1659.

different profession. Among the families studied, both sons and daughters helped perpetuate the fathers' contacts and skills: fourteen sons became professional merchants, while seventeen daughters married merchants. Juan Ruíz Portillo, mint merchant and large lender to the Crown from 1623 to 1632, was following the same occupations as his father, Rodrigo Ruíz.[20] Gonzalo Sánchez de Herrera, Gerónimo López Páramo, and Tiburcio de Urrea were other merchant sons who did the same. Each of these sons who continued their fathers' occupations bore their fathers' Christian names. Thus, sons did carry on the family business. Marriages of two merchant daughters to the two sons of another merchant were another interesting feature of family relationships in the group. The Valdés–Medina Orozco, Picazo Hinojosa–Vásquez Medina, and Contreras-Ansaldo matches were of this type. Certainly, in these families mercantile traditions were carried on vigorously in the second generation. Thus, merchant dynasties existed, even though they were not the dominant type of second-generation family.

Intermarriage among merchants' children or grandchildren was another form of merchant solidarity that has sometimes been overlooked. The offspring were not necessarily professional merchants or married to them, but they continued the social ties of their forefathers. For the purpose of this discussion, families linked in the second generation will be termed *clusters*. The term denotes three or more merchant families linked in the second generation through real or fictitious kinship. One such cluster was the Fernández de Sigura–Saco de Frías–Pacho–Valdés–Medina Orozco families. There were at least nine such clusters, and they included forty different families whose first-generation members had been merchants and whose second generation intermarried.

In addition to intermarriage of offspring, *compadrazgo* linked the first generation of traders with the more occupationally diverse second generation. Baptismal records faithfully record these relationships. In the decade from 1590 to 1600, wholesalers served as godparents two to four times a year, both to their colleagues' children and to the children of other social groups. Seven clusters of merchant families related by *compadrazgo*, which included thirty-one different families, were found during this time. One cluster comprised nine families: the Rodríguez Soltero, Astudillo, Bribiesca Roldán, Tamayo, Sánchez de Herrera, Díaz de la Barrera, Torres Loranca, Hervas, and Rodríguez Figueroa.[21]

The vertical linkages effected by *compadrazgo* illustrate the merchants' interclass relationships in a most interesting fashion. The wholesaler Diego López Flandes illustrated downward linkage by acting as godfather to the son of the clothes dealer Antonio de Trento. Gonzalo Sánchez de Herrera, a merchant, typifies upward linkage as *padrino* (godfather) to the first-settler families of Sebastián Vizcaíno and Rafael de Trejo. The wholesaler Clemente de Valdés was godfather to the children of the secretary of the Inquisition, Pedro Sáenz de Mañozca and of the *escribano de registros* in Acapulco. Of course, it is easier to document the merchants' ties with the politically and socially powerful members of society in the baptismal records. There is no doubt that *compadrazgo* furthered, and sometimes initiated, these useful connections. It should be remembered, however, wholesalers were *padrinos* to the children of more humble individuals, parents with common Christian names, only one surname, and no titles, which makes them difficult to identity.[22]

"PADRE COMERCIANTE, HIJO CABALLERO, NIETO PORDIOSERO?"

The dynamics of upward and downward mobility have full play in the case histories of ten merchant families. In most cases it is possible to trace progeny and property into the third generation and to suggest the place of these merchant families in colonial society over time. This is the first such analysis of seventeenth-century families who were not nobles or descendents of first settlers and includes previously unknown information about the families' wealth.

Certain characteristics are common to all the families. All children started their adult lives in a secure economic position, whether they had few or many siblings. The children enjoyed a higher social status than their parents, and many grandchildren maintained the social position of *their* parents. Socially, there was not one instance of "clogs to clogs in three generations," because the families held onto their offices and titles. Economically, the adage was more applicable, for some fortunes were clearly in decline at the end of the second generation. Even so, there was considerable variety in the financial standing of the third generation.

The Financially Successful Families: Bonilla Bastida, Salcedo, Zuaznavar y Aguirre, Vera, and León Castillo

The first five families to be discussed represent those who were more economically resilient. The merchant Cristóbal Bonilla Bastida, his children, and his grandchildren exemplify the social heights which the offspring could scale and the successful transmission of wealth, indeed its increase, into the third generation and beyond. Cristóbal distributed his seven surviving children among occupations in the classic fashion. The son, don Nicolás, received the family real estate and the office of *alguacil mayor de corte* which his father had purchased for him with the loan from a colleague, Álvaro de Lorenzana. Five daughters entered convents; one, madre María de San Lorenzo, even became an abbess. The sixth daughter married a merchant-*político, maestre de campo* don Antonio Urrutia de Vergara. Because the rest of the children were ecclesiastics, the history of this family in the second generation revolves around the lives of don Nicolás and his married sister, doña María.

Fortunately, it is possible to compare the real property which the father, merchant Cristóbal, declared he owned in 1622 with the property the son, don Nicolás, offered as security for bond in 1661, nearly forty years later. Don Nicolás kept his paternal inheritance and added slightly to it with the houses he owned behind the Church of Santa Clara and with the hacienda he purchased in San Agustín de las Cuevas. The lesser importance of urban landed property versus public office in his case may be seen from the fact that the houses he inherited were declared worth 30,500 pesos, while the office had cost 70,000 pesos. Don Nicolás also obtained rent from houses on the central plaza of Veracruz, which he had inherited from his first wife. This income, however, went to repay a debt of 15,230 pesos owed his brother-in-law, don Antonio Urrutia de Vergara. Also of economic importance, don Nicolás unofficially continued the mercantile activities of his father.[23]

In addition, don Nicolás contracted two extremely prestigious marriages that produced four children. The first was to doña María Sáenz de Mañozca, sister of the Inquisitor of the Inquisition. Their three surviving children were don Cristóbal, don Joseph, and doña Gertrudis. The second marriage was to Inés de Estupiñan y Flores, daughter of Cádiz merchant, town magistrate, and admiral don Bartolomé de Estupiñan, and widow of the Mexico City wholesaler Francisco de Solarte. (She was also a relation, possibly the sister, of don Antonio Estupiñan, a member of the order of Santiago and *alcalde mayor* of the mining town of Pachuca.) The couple had one surviving child, don Bartolomé.

But what of don Nicolás's four children? His son, don Cristóbal, put the final feather in the social cap when he married doña Ana de Villanueva Cervantes, a descendant of first settlers and as aristocratic a lady as could be wished. The match was more a social than an economic triumph, for although doña Ana was the holder of an extensive entail including rental

11. Heraldic crest of don Nicolás Bonilla Bastida, 1632.

properties in Mexico City and wheat haciendas in Toluca, the entail was
the source of prolonged litigation and its final disposition unclear. What
is certain is that the entail did not permanently enter the Bonilla family.
This did not adversely affect the fortunes of the family, however, since it
was already well provided for. The two other sons, don Joseph and don
Bartolomé, probably entered the clergy, for after their father and brother
died, the office of *alguacil mayor de corte* and the other family properties
passed to their sister doña Gertrudis. She brought this wealthy estate to
her marriage in 1659 with the notable, don Juan de Fonseca, a member of
the military order of Alcántara.[24]

The history of merchant Cristóbal's other line, through his daughter doña María, is also the history of don Antonio Urrutia de Vergara, the millionaire wholesaler, banker and adviser to Viceroy Cerralvo, and political broker. The Bonilla Bastida benefited socially and financially from this marriage. Don Antonio was bitterly criticized by some, but he could not be accused of humble birth or behavior. His father was a *hidalgo* (gentleman) from Vergara in Guipúzcoa, who held such posts as general paymaster of the *Armada de la Guardia de las Indias* and who passed the family farm on to his son. In addition to his various military titles, the Mexico City merchant don Antonio was *alcalde mayor* of Tacuba and one of the few wholesalers to be admitted to the military order of Santiago. Although both the Bonilla Bastida and Urrutia de Vergara families were commercial, therefore, the latter enjoyed a higher social status at the time of the marriage. By doña María's death, the position of the Bonilla Bastida had improved even more. She had brought don Antonio a dowry of 32,000 pesos, and when she died in 1675, her estate was more than 500,000 pesos.[25]

The position of doña María's children was even better. She and don Antonio had two daughters. Doña Juana married don Nicolás de Vivero y de Jaso, the third Count of the Valle of Orizaba. Her entail was founded on a complex of mills, houses, wheat lands, and garden plots at Chapultepec, Tacubaya, and Santa Fe. In 1649, don Antonio had purchased this property for 91,500 pesos; in 1666, it was worth more than 115,000 pesos. To this *mayorazgo* was later added two wheat haciendas at Pachuca, bought for 12,000 pesos. Because this couple had no children, the entail passed to her sister, doña Ana.

Doña Ana, one of the grandchildren of merchant Cristóbal Bonilla Bastida, also married well. Her husband was don Antonio Flores de Valdés, a Spaniard, who held an entail and for whom his father-in-law had purchased the office of *contador mayor de la cruzada*. Doña Ana was an extraordinarily wealthy woman. In addition to her share of her mother's and sister's estate, doña Ana had two entails of her own. Because they illustrate the diversified investments of a successful wholesaler, they are described in detail.

Entail Number 1:

Type of Property	Value in pesos
House and lot in Spain	Unknown
Casas principales on Alguaciles Mayores	40,000
Contador mayor office	80,000
2 haciendas and sugar mills, Michoacán	145,000

House and garden, Tacuba	15,000
Gifts from Viceroys Cerralvo, Alva de Liste, and Salvatierra	Unknown
Censo on fire extinguishing equipment	1,500
Capellanía	13,000
Total	294,500 pesos+

Entail Number 2:	
Casas principales, their shops, and rental units on Tacuba	17,000
Wheat hacienda, Malacatepec	3,200
2 fulling mills and hacienda, Texcoco	10,500
Hacienda with license to build fulling mill, Texcoco	Unknown
6 *caballerías* of farmland	Unknown
Assorted jewels	Unknown
Total	30,700 pesos+

The annual income from some of these properties is also given. It is interesting to note that the rent from the office of *contador mayor de la cruzada* was 4,963 pesos annually, whereas the rents from the shops and apartments totaled 850 pesos and that of the wheat hacienda, 160 pesos.

The two entails originally founded for doña Ana and the third entail which passed to her children after her sister's death amounted to well over 400,000 pesos in value. And, this did not include her husband's *capital*, nor the joint increase during their marriage. Therefore, even though the Flores–Urrutia Bonilla couple had six children, they could be well provided for.[26] Thus investment in diverse types of landholding, public office, and continuation by some family members in trade enabled the Bonilla Bastida family to prosper into the third generation and to make socially prestigious marriages. It was one merchant clan that succeeded in meshing with the highest ranks of colonial society and whose wealth was so extensive that it was not undermined by the risks of agriculture and trade or by an aristocratic style of life.

The Salcedo family offers another example of high social ascent and continued financial well-being. The wholesaler García del Salcedo had six children. His three children by his first wife, doña Juana de Abezia, entered the clergy, and he inherited some of her property. His three children by his second wife, doña Beatriz de León, received a splendid legacy. One girl, doña Isabel, predeceased her siblings before their majority and her share of the family estate reverted to them. The son, don Nicolás de Salcedo inherited a fortune. He was favored in the *tercio* and the *remaniente del quinto* by both mother and father, so that he received 310,405 pesos. His sister, doña Tomasina, inherited 102,942 pesos. The two children made excellent matches with a branch of the first-settler Samano Turcios family. Doña Tomasina wed don Juan de Samano Salamanca, heir to the entail founded in 1626 on haciendas in Toluca and a house on Encarnación in Mexico City. Her father had previously supplied funds to the founder of the *mayorazgo*, don Juan de Samano Medinilla, who still owed him 1,278 pesos when García del Salcedo died. Don Nicolás married doña Francisca de Samano Salamanca, his sister-in-law.[27]

Don Nicolás was an example of the merchant's son who did not continue as a public wholesaler but still engaged in the types of activities in which they were involved. He was the farmer of the playing card tax from 1643 to 1651, with don Antonio Urrutia de Vergara and Urrutia's son-in-law Antonio Flores. To obtain this farm, Salcedo had to present bond of 90,000 pesos. He himself was a bondsman of the meat contracter in Zinacantepec, his relation don Nicolás de Peralta, and of Juan Astudillo Masuelo, the *alcalde mayor* of Pachuca. (Salcedo's wife's entail was located in the jurisdiction of Zinacantepec.) Through his wife, however, he could be considered a member of the landed elite. When the division of don Nicolás's estate was made in 1633, his social position was higher and his wealth was roughly equal to that of his father when he had died in 1619.

The third generation of the Salcedo maintained the social status of their parents. Doña Tomasina's son, don Carlos, for a time held the Samano *mayorazgo*, which was still in the family in 1755. One of don Nicolás's sons, don José, was *maestre de campo* in 1670, while another son, don Andrés de Salcedo Coronel y Samano, administered the entailed estate for a period and also inherited a 10,000 peso *censo* that his mortgage-holding grandfather had placed on the *propios* of Mexico City.[28] While the economic standing of the third generation of the Salcedo is not available in detail, it is probable that with these titles and occupations it was, at least, respectable.

Unlike the Bonilla Bastida and the Salcedo, the third family to be considered here did not continue to trade after the first generation. The wholesaler Tomás de Zuaznavar y Aguirre, the Basque-born supporter of Viceroy Gelves, experienced considerable upward mobility in his own lifetime, being one of the few merchants to be called *don*. By virtue of marriage to doña Catalina Márquez de Amarilla, his first wife, he entered the wealthy Fernández de la Higuera–González de Amarilla landowners of Puebla and Jalapa. His father-in-law, don Francisco, had founded the sugar plantation in Jalapa, which was estimated worth 350,000 pesos and brought in annual gross revenues of 50,000 pesos. The estate supported entails for two of don Francisco's children. But don Tomás did even better with his second marriage to doña Isabel Estrada y Álvarado. Now he joined a clan of first-settler families: the Villanueva, Altamirano, Samano, Cervantes, and Pacheco Córdoba y Bocanegra. Doña Isabel received an entail placed on houses on Doncelles Street.[29] Don Tomás's children could hardly improve on this situation and, in fact, the second generation concentrated on managing the landed property acquired by the first.

The elder son, don Juan, married, like his father, into the highest social class. He wed doña Leonor de Vivero y Mendoza, sister of the third Count of the Valle of Orizaba and one of the few noble families of seventeenth-century Mexico. Doña Leonor brought a dowry of 14,000 pesos. Don Juan inherited his father's office of *alguacil mayor* of the Inquisition and managed his father's plantation, San Pedro Mártir in Izúcar. In 1666, nine years after his father's death, don Juan successfully defended a water-sharing agreement of thirty units, which his father had reached with the town of San Luis Chalma, against the challenge of a neighboring *trapiche* owner, doña Teresa Pérez del Gallo, who had wanted to divert the water to her mill. The other son, *licenciado* don Salvador, became a priest and administered his father's haciendas in the Valley of México. In 1649, for example, he delivered 605 *cargas* of irrigated wheat to the mill of his father's merchant colleague, Juan de Alcocer. The third child, doña María, married *licenciado* Pedro de Vega Sarmiento.[30]

The third generation of this family experienced the demographic pattern which tended to concentrate property rather than to disperse it. Don Juan and his wife had no children. His disposition of his paternal property, the office and sugar mill, is not known, but his wife, in the fashion typical of the childless parent, established two *capellanías* and left the remainder of her estate to the Convent of Santa Clara. The other son, don Salvador, of course had no legitimate offspring, leaving only the descendents of the daughter, doña María, to inherit. Although the history of her line has left no trace, it should have been in a good economic position due to the estates of the uncles.

A similar demographic situation prevailed in the fourth merchant family, the Vera. The role of the State in this family's financial position makes this history particularly interesting. The prosperity of the second generation was linked to the office of director of the mint. The Crown had first made possible the family's continued prosperity by selling this lucrative office, but the Crown then undercut the Vera's economic and social position by challenging their ownership of it.

Diego Matías de Vera and doña Ana de Ureña had three children, none of whom entered the Church. They founded an entail for their eldest son, don Melchor de Vera, on the office of the director of the mint, which they bought for 250,000 pesos' cash in 1607, the highest known price paid for a public office at that time. Diego Matías, a merchant, added 16,500 pesos to the price to make the post proprietory, with the right to renounce to his descendants. In addition to the *mexora* with which the entail was created, don Melchor was entitled to 75,836 pesos.[31] His brother, don Juan, received a second *mayorazgo* founded on the family's Hacienda de Miraflores in Tecamachalco. Both sons were minors when the mint post was purchased, so the first occupant was their brother-in-law, Cristóbal de Zuleta, who held it until 1617. Sister doña Ana brought Cristóbal, who was a professional merchant, a dowry of 12,600 pesos in household furnishings and 57,400 pesos in reales, while he provided an *arras* of 20,000 pesos.[32] Certainly, the second generation of the Vera family got off to a princely start.

However, there was no third generation in this family; none of the three children had heirs. The centerpiece of the family fortune—the directorship of the mint—became an object of dispute when don Juan, who succeeded his brother, died in 1663. There were three claimants to the entail, all distant relatives: don Juan Ansaldo de Vera, whose father had married the merchant Diego Matías de Vera's sister Sebastiana in 1600; don Juan Francisco Senteno de Vera, whose grandfather had married Diego Matías's sister Gerónima; and Diego Mexia de Vera, a cousin of Diego Matías and the grandson of his uncle, Gaspar Mexia. If this were not sufficiently complicated, the dispute also involved seven other parties, the shareholders in the ownership of the mint office. In 1629, when don Juan began occupancy of the mint directorship, he owed the crown one-half of the value of the proprietary post, 137,500 pesos. Whether to free his capital for other purposes or whether due to inability to raise the capital from his own funds, don Juan sold shares in the office to seven partners, most of whom were merchants. The agreement was that these investors would put up the cash and divide the income from the mint directorship with don Juan. Between 1629 and 1663, don Juan and the shareholders had been dividing the proceeds evenly. By 1663, however, the identity of the share-holders had changed in a manner which reflected the transformation of the second generation of merchant families into a more diverse class and the transfer of some commercial wealth to the Church. In 1663, the majority share (50,000 pesos) was held by the Convent of La Encarnación; the other six shareholders were a merchant (10,000 pesos), a merchant's son (20,000 pesos), two merchant widows (20,000 pesos and 10,000 pesos, respectively), and two persons with university degrees (20,000 pesos and 10,000 pesos, respectively) who were probably the sons or nephews of the original merchant shareholders. The total paid out was 140,000 pesos, rather than the 137,500 pesos payable to the Crown.

Finally, the lawsuit was made more difficult to resolve because of the Crown's wish to disentail it altogether so that it would revert to the Crown and be resold. If this were to occur, the Crown had to take into account not only the distant Vera relations, but also the heirs of the wholesalers of Mexico City who had invested in the post. The arguments made by all parties were voluminous and disengenuous. The final decision declared that the rightful successor was Juan Francisco Senteno de Vera but that the office was disentailable and resaleable. It was auctioned to doña Isabel Picazo de Hinojosa, the widow of wholesaler Juan Vásquez Medina, for 300,000 pesos, for her son Capitán don Francisco Antonio de Medina Picazo. She paid 160,000 pesos to the Crown right away and 140,000 pesos to the shareholders. Senteno de Vera was compensated by a share of the income from the office.[33] Thus, due to a demographic mishap, the bulk of the Vera fortune passed out of the immediate family; part returned to the family's point of origin, the Seville branch, part passed to a new merchant dynasty, and part was adjudicated to the heirs of the merchant colleagues of the founder, Diego Matías.

The fifth family to be discussed is the León Castillo. The merchant Juan had married doña Francisca de Ureña, the sister-in-law of the wholesaler Diego Matías de Vera. The couple had three children. Son Juan attained a high position in the Church. He held a doctorate, which was not common for clergymen in the seventeenth century, and obtained the very desirable post of canon of the Cathedral Chapter of Mexico City. Son García carried on the family business, first as his father's agent in the Philippines and later as the stationary trader in Mexico City. By the 1620s, he was an elector of the *consulado*. García made a good marriage to doña María Rodríguez de Villegas, daughter of an *oidor* of the *audiencia* of Mexico City and sister of the *oidor* of the *audiencia* of Manila. The third child, doña Luisa, wed *regidor* Juan de Carbajal, a descendant of the conquistador Antonio de Carbajal. When García died, his estate was worth more than 50,000 pesos and, given the position of his two siblings, it is likely that their economic standing was also good.[34]

The third generation continued the social and economic standing of their parents. Son García had two children. His son, also called García, entered the secular clergy, obtained a doctorate like his uncle Juan, held desirable rural benefices at Zumpango and Tepotztlán, and then, following the typical upper-class *asenso* (pattern of career advancement), entered the Cathedral Chapter of Mexico City. He was also associated with the Inquisition, as familiar and *juez ordinario*, and held estates in the Valley of Atlixco. The daughter, doña Francisca, married an *oidor*, don Juan González de Manjares, of the *audiencia* of Guatemala. She brought a large dowry of 38,120 pesos to the marriage, and at her death, her estate was worth 43,130 pesos, making her a wealthy woman. The other grandchild of the merchant Juan León Castillo did well also. Daughter doña Luisa and her husband don Juan de Carbajal produced one daughter, doña Francisca, who became the third wife of Cristóbal de Zuleta, a rich merchant and interim director of the mint. The León Castillo were shareholders in the company which in 1629 helped purchase the post for Zuleta's first brother-in-law, don Juan de Vera. This is another instance of intermarriage among merchant families continuing into the third generation. Cristóbal de Zuleta, who had started out as a ship's *maestre*, successively wed three wholesalers' daughters. When he took doña Francisca as his third wife, Cristóbal was renewing the commercial connections of the León Castillo family.[35]

Only in the fourth generation do signs of economic slippage appear in the family of doña Francisca, who had an interesting history. She outlived her two husbands, first the *oidor* of the *audiencia* of Guatemala and second, the *relator* of the same *audiencia*, Capitán don Agustín de Ceballos y Ayala, and supported herself, in part, by moneylending in amounts of 500 to 1,000 pesos. She had four children, for whom she provided well. Socially, they attained good positions. One daughter, Teresa, married the *factor* of the treasury of Zacatecas, don Luis de Bolívar y Mena; another daughter, doña Catalina, wed *secretario* don Pedro de Arteta. (Although the body to which he was attached is not identified, the don indicates he had respectable social status.) The only son, don Francisco, was destined for the clergy but died one year after his mother. The fourth child, doña Juana, was a minor at her mother's death.

Doña Francisca was able to bequeath substantial inheritance portions to her children, but they were not as large as that she had received from her father, and part of the family estate had to be sold to finance them. For reasons not explained, daughter doña Teresa renounced her claim to most of her mother's property. The other three children were to receive 13,703 pesos each, but due to brother Francisco's early death, sisters Catalina and Juana actually received 17,086 pesos and 19,107 pesos, respectively. To raise this sum, doña Francisca's household goods were sold and the *casas principales* were auctioned to the Convent of Santa Catalina de Sena in Mexico City, which held a 6,000 pesos *censo* on the houses.[36] On the one hand, therefore, the fourth generation of León Castillo inherited less money than had their parents and grandparents. On the other hand, inheritance portions of more than 17,000 pesos and good marriages show that the family was in a strong position even in the fourth generation.

Economic Decline at the End of the Second Generation: Esquivel Castañeda and Millán

The sixth and seventh families to be considered, the Esquivel Castañeda and the Millán, represent families with large numbers of children who nevertheless began their adult lives in a strong economic position. Unlike the five families considered previously, however, they manifest a decline in prosperity by the end of the second generation. Both families remained active in trade, but while the Esquivel Castañeda children either were professional merchants or were married to them, the Millán children entered diverse occupations in the manner more typical of the second generation.

Founder Francisco de Esquivel Castañeda had nine children, three by his first wife, doña Antonia Cifuentes Argüelles, and six by his second wife, doña Margarita Covarrubias. Of Francisco's first group of children, one, don Antonio, became a priest and professor. Between 1621 and 1625, he obtained a bachelor's degree in canon and civil law and was then elected to the chair in this subject at the university. In 1640, he became a prebend of the Cathedral Chapter of Mexico City. Don Antonio maintained his mercantile traditions, however; in 1639, he and the merchant Bernardino Paredes were trading with the wholesaler Diego de Castroverde. A second son, Francisco, followed his father's calling. He started at the lower level of shopowner in Mexico City, but in 1646, now called *alférez*, he was able to buy at auction 20,000 pesos' worth of merchandise which the Inquisition had confiscated from the *converso* magnate Simón Váez Sevilla. The third son was a miner in Cuautla, where his grandparents were *vecinos*.[37]

The second group of children included more merchants. The only son, don Joseph, obtained a bachelor's degree and became a priest. In addition to income from a *capellanía*, he owned a house. One of the daughters became a nun, madre Ana de San Diego, in the Convent of San Gerónimo. She derived income from a *censo* of 7,600 pesos. The other four daughters all married men with mercantile connections. Doña María wed Cristóbal de Pastrana, the Valley of Atlixco planter, merchant and *obrajero*, whose activities were described in chapter 3. Doña Juana married Francisco de Salcedo; doña Margarita, Juan Crespo Carrillo; and doña Lorenza, the wealthy *converso* Sebastián Báez Acevedo. Parents' and children's business activities were intertwined. When their mother died in 1644, all her merchant sons-in-law owed her money, the debts ranging from 2,000 pesos to 5,000 pesos.[38] Thus far the history of this family demonstrated a consolidation of its existing position and some diversification (the children who entered the clergy) within the usual limits. While primarily still mercantile, the second generation included offspring with more prestigious occupations and more formal education than had the first. Aside from doña Lorenza's divorce, there were no signs of financial difficulties.

In the third generation, however, one line showed clear financial straits. Francisco and doña Juana de Salcedo Esquivel had eleven children. They were well provided for but the effort exhausted the inheritance and the joint estate. One son, Juan, became *secretario de cámara* of the *audiencia* in Mexico City. Five other children entered the regular and secular clergy. Three of the daughters married although to men of no title or particular distinction. This was accomplished by the religious renouncing their portions to their parents and by some children predeceasing their siblings. Another daughter was to profess, but her mother had already spent the 500 pesos which her grandmother had given for her nun's dowry, and the history of the eleventh child is unknown. By doña Juana's death in 1689, her husband's store had been robbed and she could not even pay two bakers who had provided bread for her family.[39] In this branch of the third generation, therefore, respectable placement of a large family had brought the parents to reduced circumstances.

The sons and daughters of the merchant Antonio de Millán got off to a very good financial start indeed. By the time of their deaths, however, the chief family property, the sugar mills of Pantitlán and Amanalco, had been sold because of economic problems. Millán and doña Juana de Covarrubias had five children: don Félix, don Nicolás, doña María, doña Juana, and doña Francisca. They were distributed among the usual occupations and spouses. Don Nicolás became a priest and was a prebend of the

12. Heraldic crest of don Félix Millán, 1661.

Cathedral Chapter of Mexico City by the time he died in his early thirties. His inheritance then passed back to his siblings. Doña Francisca became a nun in the Convent of Regina Celi. She received a 8,000 peso inheritance, 4,000 pesos for her nun's dowry and 4,000 pesos for expenses. She renounced the rest of her *legítima* to her siblings. Thus, these children held prestigious positions in the Church. Sister Juana and brother Félix both married the children of their father's merchant colleagues. She wed Capitán Joseph Montemayor, a *secretario* in the *audiencia* of Mexico City; he married doña María de Contreras, daughter of Tomás de Contreras, the Tacubaya *obrajero* and Mexico City merchant, who brought him a large dowry of 64,822 pesos. The third daughter, doña María, wed Francisco de Escoto, *factor* of the treasury of Acapulco.[40]

Capitán don Félix was the favored child. He received the *tercio* and *remaniente del quinto* from both his parents, who died in 1661 and 1662: 90,941 pesos. His siblings received 61,345 pesos each. Don Félix assumed ownership of the sugar mills, paying his siblings a percentage of the annual income they produced. In addition, he took over his father's regidorship, became *alcalde ordinario* in 1661, and is described as farmer of the playing card and *cruzada* taxes. Finally, don Félix continued to trade, at least for a while. His mother stated that she gave him the *mexora* in her estate because of his good care of her and his assistance to his father in his commercial activities. At some point he apparently stopped trading, however, for no merchandise is mentioned in his inventory of 1692. At that time his property consisted of *casas principales* on señor don Juan Manuel, the two sugar mill complexes, fifteen slaves, and household goods.

Unfortunately for the Millán family, by 1696, the mills were heavily encumbered. Of an impressive yearly income of 11,950 pesos, all but 1,717 pesos was consumed in paying interest of different kinds, 2,600 pesos to the Millán family but the rest to several *capellanías* (held by individuals who do not seem to have been close relatives), the mortgage owed to the Inquisition for the mills' purchase, and *censos* imposed to finance the maintenance of the mills. Thus, four years after don Félix died, the properties were sold to the Aranda family. His widow's lawyer spoke of the decline of the mills, which he attributed to bad times and poor administrators.[41]

The merchant Antonio de Millán had helped his children in their careers. His son don Joseph owed him 12,586 pesos for past accounts when his father died; he had posted bond for his son-in-law, the *factor* at Acapulco. Don Félix was less family-minded. In 1696, his nieces and nephews brought suit against his estate for misusing the portion of his father's estate, of which he was the executor, that should have passed to his siblings. He was accused of "trading with the inheritance portions of his brothers and sisters, as is public knowledge, earning profits both in trade, administration of the *cruzada* and playing card farms and *avio* to sugar mills, all with the capital of his siblings . . . always postponing presenting his account of the executorship and the division of the property. . . ."[42] They asked that don Félix's estate pay 5 percent interest on the part of their portions which he had retained for his own purposes. In addition, he was said to have engaged in accounting tricks such as charging to his expense a *capellanía* he had never founded and lawsuits he had never brought, and to have granted himself extra commissions. Certainly, don Félix's management of the estate had not produced good economic results.

The decline of important family assets occurred too late to hurt the marriage prospects of the third generation of the Millán, however. Don Félix's daughter doña Andrea married the *contador de cuentas* don Nicolás del Rossal y Ríos, son of merchant Andrés del Rossal, while his daughter doña Sebastiana entered the Convent of San José de Gracia with 5,250 pesos, which she renounced after her lifetime. Daughter doña Antonia did a bit less well socially, as the wife of the merchant Capitán Domingo de Cantabrana, but economically she was very well off because her husband was one of the financial powers of his era and held the office of *tesorero de la pruebas* of the Inquisition. Don Félix had two sisters. Doña Juana married one daughter, María Teresa, to Juan Esquivel Salcedo, *secretario de cámara* and grandson of merchant Francisco Esquivel Castañeda. Another daughter, Gertrudis, seems to have become a nun. Don Félix's other sister, doña María, had only one heir, doña Andrea Escoto y Millán, who married her uncle, Capitán Fernando Bustos de Mendoza, member of a family which held a *mayorazgo* and occupied a local governorship. All these third-generation Milláns were each to receive a 4,000 peso endowment from their grandmother, doña Juana de Covarrubias, in addition to what they received from their parents and, in the case of the women, their office-holding husbands.[43]

Another member of this generation was doña Juana's son, Capitán Antonio de Millán, who became administrator of Uncle Félix's mill San Nicolás Pantitlán and of the San Nicolás Tolentino mill as well. The former was sold, and the latter did not do well under Capitán Antonio. When his contract for the latter position was discussed, his ability to pay the 20,000 peso rent was questioned because he lacked any real property and already had the burden of paying the rent for the Pantitlán mill to his uncle. His opponents accused him of being an incompetent and cruel administrator.[44] For Capitán Antonio, at least, the prosperity of his grandfather's and father's days had diminished.

Commerce had propelled the Esquivel Castañeda and Millán families to prominence and wealth and enabled three generations to live well. Signs of financial trouble, however, appeared in some lines of these families by the end of the second generation's lifetime. For one branch of the Esquivel Castañeda, trade did not generate enough income to provide for a large family. For the Millán, the decline of profits from agriculture due to indebtedness and the cessation of trade by most of the children were responsible. Still, there was no dramatic decline in either of these families.

Families in Trouble: Medina Reynoso, Barrera, and Vásquez Medina

The Medina Reynoso and the Barrera, eighth and ninth families, present a picture which conforms to the stereotype of downward mobility in the second and third generations. The merchant Francisco Medina Reynoso was one of the most prominent traders of his day. In 1622, his net estate was 284,430 pesos, and he had only three children. The hard times which were to befall his offspring could hardly have been expected from the provision he made for them. His son, don Fernando Angulo Reynoso, was favored in the *tercio* and *remaniente del quinto* of the estate and received a *mayorazgo* and two offices from his father. The entail was founded on the *casas principales*, some smaller houses near them, and a house and garden in Tacuba, together worth 41,000 pesos. In addition, don Fernando first held a regidorship for which his father paid 11,000 pesos, and then occupied the office of *receptor general de penas* of the *audiencia*, which was purchased for 80,000 pesos. He was also elected *alcalde ordinario* of the Mexico City *cabildo* in 1623. In accordance with his wealth and status, don Fernando married doña María Altamirano Guevara, the daughter of Miguel Rodríguez de Guevara, *alguacil mayor* of Puebla, and doña María Altamirano de Guzmán, of first-settler stock. Doña María was also the granddaughter of the merchant Baltasar Rodríguez de los Ríos. She brought a dowry of 25,000 pesos: 3,500 pesos in houses, 5,800 pesos in jewels and household goods, and 8,000 pesos in cash.[45]

Don Fernando did not rely solely on income from urban rental property and fees from office. He continued his father's commercial activities, using part of his father's estate for this purpose as well as part of his own funds. He continued to work with his father's associates such as his relations Jorge de Reynoso and Pedro de Vertiz. In 1629, he sent 80 *arrobas* of Oaxaca cochineal, 1,500 leather hides, and a number of boxes of indigo to Vertiz in Spain; he also traded to Manila. With the merchant Esquivel Castañeda, don Fernando imposed two *censos* on the slaughterhouse and *propios* of Mexico City. Active in potentially lucrative civic affairs, don Fernando was paymaster of the wine tax funds, a commissioner of the work on the Santa Fe aqueduct, and commissioner of public order under both Viceroys Guadalcazar and Gelves, overseeing as many as 3,000 Indians who were opening the clogged canals of the city and repairing the channel of the Río de Azcapotzalco. Just before his death he requested a military habit and an office of justice or finance in the government.[46]

Don Fernando's two siblings were not as politically prominent but were well established and well off. His sister doña Isabel married *hacendado* and once *alcalde mayor* of Huachinango don Álvaro de Acevedo, son of the merchant. Her dowry was a very high 50,000 pesos. She also received her balance of her portions from her parents. Don Diego became a monk in the Convent of San Francisco and received a 4,000 peso *capellanía*.

Despite the spectacular start, don Fernando's fortunes rapidly declined, and because he died young at age thirty-one, he did not have the chance to revive them. After his death in 1629, his estate was valued at 82,494 pesos, with 63,829 pesos in debits, so that the balance was only 18,665 pesos. To explain his unenviable situation, in his will don Fernando refers to the fact that his and his wife's joint assets did not increase due to the many losses in trade, especially from the fleet seized by Piet Heyn in 1628, and to his uncollectable credits. His father's debts were part of his problem, including 47,141 pesos to Jorge. Doña Isabel, for her part, also had financial problems. Only 10,000 pesos of her promised dowry was actually paid in 1622, and although her *legítima* was large, it may have later been reduced by her husband's business setbacks. His haciendas in Huachinago, after all, were nearly sold to enable him to repay the merchant Martín de Chavarría in 1647.[47] Thus, even a very distinguished and wealthy family could suffer reverses in the second generation, because of severe commercial losses, poor administration of rural property, and inability to collect the credits which formed part of the inheritance.

The de la Barrera suffered a more marked and equally surprising downward slide. Family size was clearly a factor in one line, whose reduced wealth could not provide for all the children. The de la Barrera hung on to one important source of income, the post of *correo mayor*, but only through a lucky remarriage. Founder Alonso Díaz de la Barrera was a prominent trader at the turn of the century. In 1600, he paid taxes on 10,900 pesos shipped to Manila, and in 1606, on 39,370 pesos. In 1604, he bought at auction the office of *correo mayor* and the regidorship attached to it for 58,000 pesos; he held both until his death in 1615. Alonso had at least three children. Don Juan became a canon of the Cathedral Chapter of Mexico City, and doña Mariana married *licenciado* Pedro Gallo de

Escalada. The best-known heir, don Pedro, inherited his father's offices in the city council. He married doña Ana Bastida y Hermosillo, a niece of merchant Cristóbal Bonilla Bastida, from whom he received a 16,000 peso dowry.[48]

Despite the fact that don Pedro derived income from trade and office, the two most lucrative possibilities of that time, when he died in 1651, his estate was not large. The chronicler Guijo describes him as poor, and his inventory bears this out. His assets were about 68,000 pesos, while his debts were 46,409, not counting the expenses of his funeral. Most of his assets lay in his office and his urban real estate. His largest debt was the interest due on *censos* placed on his houses, not the position in which one would expect to find the *correo mayor* of Mexico City.[49]

To make matters worse, don Pedro had a large family. His inventory mentions nine children, while Guijo attributes eleven to him. Naturally, the inheritance portions were small, about 2,000 pesos each. Of his offspring, two were minors in 1651, two were nuns, one (don Francisco Alonso) inherited the office and had been receiving one-half of its yearly income of 2,000 pesos. Don Pedro established four *capellanías*, two at 1,600 pesos and two at 2,000 pesos, which may have gone to his other sons. Finally, two other sons, don Juan and don Alonso, received 3,900 pesos of their portions.

Despite this unpromising situation, the de la Barrera managed to retain the offices, even though the executor of don Pedro's will spoke of the possibility of their sale. In 1654, don Francisco Alonso managed to pay the 19,586 pesos owed the Crown to occupy, and he held onto the posts through the 1690s. By 1658, don Pedro's widow had married the merchant and royal treasurer of Zacatecas, Capitán Francisco Gómez Rendón, and he and associates put up the bond which the executor offered for the security of the office.[50] Quite likely the fortunes of don Pedro's other children were improved by the advantageous remarriage of his widow. But the small size of his estate at his death does illustrate that merchant wealth could be greatly reduced by the end of the second generation.

The tenth and final family, that of Luis Vásquez Medina, offers an interesting variant on the theme of economic decline. Despite six children, the family had entirely died out by the end of the seventeenth century. (Luis's brother Juan's family, however, had not.) Demographically, therefore, the Vásquez Medina resembled the Vera, but unlike the wealthy proprietors of the directorship of the mint, they were in financial straits by the end of the childrens' lives. The Vásquez Medina did not continue in trade; rather, they invested in rural and urban property and encountered unrewarding results.

In 1652, Capitán Luis Vásquez Medina died a wealthy man, worth more than 300,000 pesos. He provided well for his six offspring. His eldest, Juan de Díos, despite the monastic-sounding name, received the office of *escribano de cámara* of the *audiencia*. Another son, Luis, received a 20,817 peso cash inheritance and a 10,000 peso dowry from his wife. Son Nicolás and daughters Teresa and Juana de San Miguel were endowed to enter the clergy, Nicolás becoming prior of the Convent of Santo Domingo. Agustín, a secular priest in the Archbishopric of Mexico, held a number of valuable rural and urban properties.[51]

By the third generation the size of the family and its assets had shrunk considerably. The clergy, of course, had no legitimate offspring, and the *escribano de cámara* was childless. Don Luis fathered only one son, don Joseph, before he died young in 1663. In 1695, don Joseph's daughter, doña Francisca Xaviera de Medina Cotillo, a nun in the Convent of La Encarnación, was the only descendent of the wealthy merchant Luis Vásquez Medina.

By that year also the wholesaler's legacy was reduced and channeled away from his direct descendents. The accounts of don Agustín, the priest, illustrate this process as well as some of the problems facing property owners in the mid-century, whether lay or clerical. They also show how a priest at this time disposed of his property. In 1695, don Agustín's assets totalled 34,924 pesos, but only a little more than half this sum was available for his personal use.[52] He owned two sets of houses in Mexico City, both overburdened by *censos* and both of which had to be sold when he died to pay the interest on them. One, his own residence in front of the Convent of La Encarnación, was evaluated at 6,000 pesos but carried 8,500 pesos of *censos;* it was sold to the Convent of San Bernardo for 6,300 pesos, and an additional 2,200 pesos was taken out of don Agustín's estate and paid to the convent. The other urban property was a collection of thirteen houses with stores, renting for an average of 195 pesos a year each, located at the corner of the College of San Pedro and San Pablo. Valued at 24,000 pesos, they already carried *censos* totaling 18,000 pesos, and when don Agustín bequeathed two more *censos* upon them, totaling 4,000 pesos, they were auctioned to the Convent of Santa Teresa de Jesús for 22,000 pesos. Thus, these houses passed from the Vásquez Medina family into clerical hands.[53]

Padre don Agustín also had some problems with his rural properties, but one of these did earn him a profit. Toward the end of his life, he had purchased a hacienda and ranch called San Diego in Chalco from *sargento mayor* don Francisco Lorenzo León y Leal for 4,300 pesos. The hacienda carried a 1,000 peso *censo* in favor of the Convent of San Agustín of the town of Ayotzingo. Moreover, the hacienda did not contain the houses and tools specified in the sale. The other rural enterprise was successful, however. This was the rental of the hacienda Buena Vista and ranch La Huerta, also in Chalco, which belonged to the Convent and Hospital of San Juan de Díos in Mexico City. The rental noted here dates from 1689, however; perhaps there were previous contracts.

Accounts for 1694 and 1695 show some of the reasons that rural holdings were not avidly sought by investors. Although don Agustín did well in these years, similar expenses ruined other landholders. Of the 5,120 bushels of corn the hacienda produced in 1694, 1,384 bushels (27 percent) went to pay the tithe, were given to convents, were spoiled, were used for seed, and went to pay the work force. They brought no earnings at all. Another 2,400 bushels (47 percent) were sold at a fixed price to the public granary of Mexico City, leaving 1,336 bushels of production to be sold free and clear. In 1694 and 1695, don Agustín earned a total of 12,206 pesos from the sale of his corn. His expenses for salaries, mortgage payments, tools, sacks, canoes, and lost livestock totalled 7,713 pesos, giving him net earnings of 4,493 pesos, a good income. One advantage he had over other producers was low transportation costs; the property had a wharf on Lake Chalco, and the produce glided to the city's market by canoe. As with other growers, however, his sales were reduced by drought: the 5,120 bushel harvest of 1694 dropped to 2,912 bushels in 1695.

Although padre don Agustín himself held *censos* on other properties, they earned less than the 1,575 pesos he owed in annual interest on the *censos* on his holdings, in addition to the back interest due. (He held 1,050 pesos on some houses and gardens in Tacuba, 10,000 pesos on a set of houses in Mexico City, and 4,000 pesos on a sugar mill in Las Amilpas belonging to the Order of San Hipólito, all of which earned 753 pesos a year in interest.) The profits from the Buena Vista hacienda could have been used to help retire the urban *censos*, but this was not done.[54] As a result, 14,812 pesos of the estate went to mortgage payments and debts. Another 1,665 pesos was due lawyers, leaving 18,447 pesos for personal use. Padre don Agustín spent this amount on his funeral, on masses, on donations to convents, and on providing small dowries and *capellanías* to some eighteen beneficiaries. His two family heirs, his grandniece and his sister-in-law, received only 3,488 pesos and 3,405 pesos respectively.[55]

Other children of Luis Vásquez Medina also experienced no improvement or decrease of the substantial sums their father had bequeathed them. Don Luis realized no increase on his paternal inheritance of 20,930 pesos. His son, don Joseph, did receive 14,869 pesos as his paternal inheritance. Friar Nicolás's inventory has not been found, but he relied on his brother to pay off one of his debts for vestments. The *escribano de cámara* Juan de Díos held a number of haciendas in Michoacán, but a lawsuit between him and a nephew on his wife's side over a *capellanía* founded on these properties indicates that they were encumbered. In any case, in 1713, the two remaining descendents of Luis Vásquez Medina, his daughter-in-law doña Leonor and his great-granddaughter doña Francisca Xaviera, were still disputing the annual rent of 500 pesos derived from a *capellanía* established in 1645 of 10,000 pesos on houses and stores in Mexico City. Doña Francisca unsuccessfully tried to deprive doña Leonor of her half of the interest. One party to the suit was doña Leonor's creditors.[56]

CONCLUSION

The merchant group, and the history of the ten families discussed in this chapter, present a variety of experience but include patterns. One was economic success. The conventional wisdom about the rapid rise and fall of merchant fortunes in three generations, therefore, requires modification. One-half of the families studied retained their wealth in the third generation; the other half experienced economic decline but not as dramatic a decline as the adage (from merchant to beggar) expresses.

Diversification of investments was the key to maintaining the family fortune. First, by providing different careers and sources of income for their children, merchants did their best to ensure prosperity. In almost all the case histories, the income of the second generation derived from a combination of public office, clerical endowments, urban or rural property, and trade. Second, continuation in trade contributed to economic resiliency. In the group as a whole, more than one-third of the families included a professional merchant. All but two of the families continued commercial activity (whether publicly or not) in the second generation. Trade could produce much higher profits than agriculture, but the practice of commerce was not a guarantee of financial success, as the Medina Reynoso family's decline shows. A third factor in maintaining the family fortune was the profitability and reliability of income from public office. All but one of these families bought one or more offices for their children or in-laws. The legitimate income ranged from a few hundred pesos to 12,000 pesos for the director of the mint in the late sixteenth century; then there was the additional income from tips, bribes, and influence peddling.

Finally, although in law the estate was to be divided equally among all the children, the practice was infrequent. Neither were these families especially large. In the group as a whole, nearly two-thirds of the merchants had four or fewer children who survived to adulthood to claim an inheritance. There was generally no correlation between family size and family fortunes here. Large families, such as the Bonilla Bastida, the Salcedo, and the Esquivel Castañeda, prospered, and small families such as the Medina Reynoso, declined. In part, this was because using the *mexora* and renouncing the *legítima* favored certain children economically, and in part because of the great wealth (including cash) of the merchant. The demographic factor exerted more influence when these conditions were not present, as in the third generation of the Barrera and Esquivel Castañeda families. Thus, family size played a role but a less determining one than has been thought previously.

In social terms the merchants were extremely successful in raising the status of their children and grandchildren, and in some cases, their own status as well. The proliferation of civil and ecclesiastical titles, as well as the use of the *don*, reflects this achievement. The social returns of officeholding were perhaps greater than the economic returns, and the merchant class benefited tremendously from this fact. The existence of a highly articulated structure of government was a primary mechanism of merchant upward mobility. Another advantage to officeholding was that because posts could be made proprietory and inheritable, the status they conferred was not in danger of being lost. The only exception was when the occupant could not pay the inheritance fees. Thus the purchase of many middle- and lower-ranking posts was the ideal solution to the wholesalers' social strivings.

The entry of children and grandchildren into the Church was another sign of the merchants' social success. In each generation the children flocked to profess; it was the most common career. Virtually all families included one or more children who entered the clergy. The frequency of this choice seems to represent not only the religious vocations of the individuals concerned, but also a striving for acceptance in both social and spiritual terms. Then, of course, there were the economic considerations. The social attainments of these families, therefore, endured.

A final aspect of social mobility is the fact that the second and third generations preserved ties among themselves through intermarriage and *compadrazgo*. Because the most common children's occupational pattern was to enter the civil or ecclesiastical bureaucracy, they did leave public merchant identity behind but retained a connection with their past through these continued interfamily relations.

Conclusion

NEW SPAIN'S ECONOMY

The history of the merchant elite between 1590 and 1660 yields new information that strengthens the view that the economy was dynamic until 1635 or 1640 and then suffered a contraction until the 1660s. For merchants, this downturn was significant but limited in impact. It further weakened the official transoceanic trades, lowered the overall volume of exchanges, ruined certain wholesalers, and depressed particular regions of the viceroyalty. However, it did not change the fundamental characteristics of the commercial elite of New Spain, nor did it alter the export orientation of the economy. Although the last third of the century lies beyond the scope of this study, secondary sources on mining and trans-Atlantic trade indicate that these years saw a slow and erratic improvement. This recovery built on the financial and commercial practices which had propelled the viceregal economy in its prosperous years and which persisted in a narrower scope through the years of contraction.

Continuity and Change in the Export Trade

In 1666, a lawsuit over ownership of the directorship of the mint led to the presentation of records which showed the income from a commission of 1.04 percent on silver coined between 1630 and 1663. These personal accounts substantiate the trend of mid-century decline manifested in official records of viceregal silver production. (The absolute amounts are lower because the director's accounts refer only to silver coined). As Figure 4 (p. 88) shows, there was sharp decline in average income from the 1630s to the 1640s and the 1650s. There were sharper fluctuations in the first two decades; the 1650s were more stable. The director's annual average from 1630 to 1639 was 26,110 pesos, with a high of 36,893 pesos in 1630. From 1640 to 1649, his annual average income was 20,442 pesos, representing a drop of 22 percent; from 1646 to 1648 were particularly bad years, with a low of 15,999 pesos in 1647. In the 1650s, the director received an annual average of 21,226 pesos, marking a 4 percent increase over the previous decade but indicating coinage continued at a level much lower than in the 1630s. The few years available for the 1660s show an additional decline.[1]

Less silver meant a drop in the overall volume of trade. The question is, How far did it fall and with what effect? The official figures show sharp declines. In the Atlantic trade, the number of registered inbound and outbound Indies sailings declined 26 percent from 1631–40 to 1641–50 and then 43 percent to 1650–59. The registered Philippine trade declined 50 percent from 1631–40 to 1641–50 and only rose 15 percent in the following decade. In the Caribbean, the attacks of the Dutch in the 1620s and 1630s and the bucanneers in the 1650s and 1660s are indisputable evidence of the interruption of trade. Yet, the Mexico City merchant elite as a whole does not show the devastation official statistics suggest.

The length of mercantile careers for three generational cohorts for which a span of trade data is available is shown in table 26 and depicts both continuity and change. The generation of 1590 were merchants who became electors in the last decade of the sixteenth century; the generation of 1620 became electors in the 1620s and 1630s; and the generation of 1640 became electors in the 1640s and 1650s. (The abundance of records from the 1590s led to the choice of that decade as a starting cohort). In all cohorts, merchants stayed in business a considerable length of time. First, of the three cohorts, from 30 to 42 percent were in business for eleven to twenty years; another 44 to 58 percent were in business twenty-one to forty or more years. Second, the distribution of wholesalers among the "length of time in trade" categories showed very little change, whether in the 1590s cohort, the 1620s cohort, or the 1640s cohort. The pattern was similar across time. (These figures represent a minimum number of years in trade because not every commercial transaction can be traced.)

The size of the 1640 group of merchants, however, was notably smaller than the two preceding groups. And, in accord with this conclusion, the cohort of 1640 is underrepresented among the great fortunes of Mexico's merchant elite (table 22). There were fewer wealthy men from the 1640 cohort than from the 1620 and 1590 cohorts. Additional evidence of concentration in commerce comes from the official Atlantic trade records, the

Table 26. Length of Time in Trade for Three Cohorts of Merchants (in Years)

	1	2–5	6–10	11–20	21–30	31–40	More than 40	Total
Cohort of 1590	2	2	5	28	19	8	2	66
		(13.6%)		(42.4%)		(44.0%)		(100%)
Cohort of 1620	1	4	3	20	23	8	7	66
		(12.1%)		(30.3%)		(57.6%)		(100%)
Cohort of 1640	2	1	4	17	12	8	1	45
		(15.6%)		(37.7%)		(46.7%)		(100%)

libros de registro. The 1630s was a watershed decade in the organization of the trade. The total number of investors decreased, dropping from 400 in 1625 to 169 in 1630 and 138 in 1639. The number of large investors, persons lading more than 7,000 pesos' worth of bullion and merchandise, dropped from fifty-two or more people before 1630 to twenty-three or fewer in 1630 and 1639 (table 1). The *number* of investors shrank more rapidly than the *value* of cargo.[2] Therefore, per-capita investment increased in the Atlantic trade in the 1630s, as fewer people shipped more money. The trend toward greater concentration in the Atlantic can also be seen by comparing the ratio of the tonnage of returning vessels to the number of shippers; fewer investors laded on more tons (appendix A).

The difficult economic conditions of the 1640s and 1650s accelerated the concentration of productive resources in the viceroyalty which had been underway in important sectors since the late sixteenth century. One finding of the research for this volume was the pervasiveness of a monopolistic structure which permitted a small number of traders, proprietors, or creditors to exercise a disproportionate influence on a particular activity. In the Pacific trade, the trend appeared earlier. The total number of shippers to Manila decreased from 246 or 247 in 1590–1610 to 85 or much fewer subsequently. The number of large investors dropped from forty-three in the 1590s to twenty-six in the 1600s, and it continued near or under the lower figure to 1660 and probably beyond. Likewise, the *number* of investors shrank more rapidly than the *value* of the cargo, for if tables 3 and 4 are compared, it can be seen that, regardless of fluctuations in the total investment in different decades, per-capita investment rose after the 1610s. It peaked in the 1620s and 1630s; in the 1640s and 1650s, it fell somewhat but was still much higher in the mid-century than in the early seventeenth and late sixteenth century. Fewer people shipped more money.

The State and some members of the public criticized this situation, particularly when entrepreneurs were hurt by tight credit, or consumers by artificial shortages. However, because the State was itself wedded to the credit provided by merchants who favored a monopoly trade, and because it acted as a monopolist itself in its sale of salt, mercury, and other products, there was no sustained effort to foster a more open, competitive system. Thus, the mid-century contraction furthered a process inherent in the colonial economy. The Mexico City mint, which so influenced the supply of specie in New Spain, offers another instance. The mint was managed by only four officials, who usually came from the group of merchant financiers in the capital. The providers of coin to the mint were also a small group of ten or fewer men, the mint merchants, who between them were coining 3,438,977 pesos a year in the early seventeenth century (see table 10). In the 1630s their number fell to six or seven, and in the 1650s to four or fewer.[3] The size of the pool of persons lending money to the Crown also diminished. In the 1640s and 1650s, there were some years when only two individuals provided all the money borrowed in that year. The institutional lenders who had been important early in the century also had dropped out.

The survivors of hard times were not only fewer, but also somewhat different in composition from their predecessors. The major change was the expulsion of the *converso* merchants. From 1620 and 1640, the Seville-based commercial associates of Portuguese bankers in Lisbon and Madrid had been key components of the Spanish mercantile elite. Between 1640 and 1660, however, some of these firms withdrew or were forced out by the Inquisition allied with certain politicians and Old Christian merchants. Their confiscated capital and merchandise was partly shared among these groups in the peninsula and the Indies; the rest was spirited off to Northern Europe, especially to the Netherlands, and to the Caribbean, particularly Curaçao and Barbados, from which points it subsequently reentered the viceregal economy as contraband goods and slaves. Nevertheless, in the 1640s and 1650s, important Spanish-Mexican trade networks were disrupted, and some capital lost to the viceroyalty. Although the Portuguese regrouped in Castile after 1647 around a new generation of bankers, it was a smaller group operating at a lower volume of payments. The Genoese continued their role, while the Dutch and English supplanted the Portuguese to a considerable extent. The locus of commercial power increasingly gravitated toward Cádiz, where foreign firms were even more influential than they had been in Seville. Illustrating the resulting new distribution of nationalities, in the 1670s in Cádiz, there were eighty-seven leading firms. Twelve were Spanish, seventeen were Genoese, eleven French, ten British, seven Hanseatic, and twenty Flemish or Dutch.[4] Another shift in the regional origin of merchants was the advance of the Basques, who appear more frequently in the 1640 cohort of Mexico City merchants than in earlier cohorts, a harbinger of the influx of Basques into the Seville *consulado* in the 1670s, which broke the Andalusian dominance of the Seville guild. Mexican-born wholesalers were also represented in the 1640 cohort. The few traders born in New Spain almost all appear at the mid-century, due to the number of merchant offspring who continued their fathers' careers in trade. Nevertheless, the great majority were still *peninsulares* who, although deeply enmeshed in Mexican society, maintained close ties to Spain.

Warfare, the fall in silver production, and royal monetary policies (sequestrations and devaluations) contributed to a decline in almost all overseas trade in the second third of the seventeenth century. The Introduction discusses the interplay of these negative factors in the Atlantic and Caribbean, the Pacific, and the north-south inter-American trades. The inability of the government to collect higher taxes for the *Unión de Armas* and the *Armada de Barlovento* from 1632 onward also reflected the commercial distress of those years. There was, however, a sufficient level of legal and, especially, contraband trade for a reduced merchant elite to survive and prosper relative to other groups in the viceroyalty. In the Caribbean, for example, the routes and foreign traders were in place for the reexport of smuggled goods and slaves to New Spain, even though the volume was lower than earlier or later years. In the 1610s and 1620s, the Portuguese and their creole confederates reexported slaves to Veracruz through Cartagena and the Greater Antilles. In 1636, the prominent *converso* trader, Sebastián Báez Acevedo, remarked on the large number of slave ships waiting in Spanish Jamaica to learn of market conditions in New Spain.[5] The cacao trade through Caracas, which flourished except for a slump from 1664 to 1675, was another entrée to New Spain for contraband. In the 1640s, the Dutch supplanted the Portuguese and made their colony at Curaçao the entrepôt of illegal Caribbean commerce; next in line, from the 1660s, were the English at Barbados. Although these islands were not the closest to Veracruz, by transshipments through other ports, they supplied the viceroyalty to a limited extent.[6]

On the fleets, smuggling skyrocketed after convoy taxes went up in the 1630s and the Crown confiscated more private silver in the 1640s. In 1636, the *contador* of the Mexico City treasury asserted that of the 3 million pesos of goods usually imported on the fleet from Spain, two-thirds were smuggled in. Between 1641 and 1645, Dutch, Portuguese, and English merchants exported an average of 3,014,000 pesos of contraband Indies bullion a year to Northern Europe. During this time, registered bullion imports at Seville were an average of 3,180,679 pesos a year. In 1671, likewise, an estimated 49 percent of the bullion coming from the Indies was transferred directly onto French vessels at Cádiz.[7] Because it is unlikely that the royal government strengthened its control of trade between the 1640s and the 1670s, it is likely that much smuggling occurred then also. Thus, Atlantic and Caribbean contraband helped keep the volume of trade at a lower, but viable, level in the second third of the century.

Other characteristics of the wholesalers also persisted through the crisis years. Wholesalers continued to serve as commission agents for Spanish, Portuguese, or North European houses based in Seville or Cádiz throughout the period. The value of transactions which were carried out by commission in the Atlantic trade actually increased from 1620 onward and reached 77 percent of merchants' cargo in the fleet of 1639. The Mexico City sales tax contracts for three different periods in the seventeenth century also indicate the continued importance of the merchants' role as *encomenderos*, selling imported goods. Although the amount of the total owed climbed from 77,000 pesos in 1602 to 180,000 pesos in 1632, and reached 273,000 pesos in 1662, the proportion owed on *forastería* (imports sold on commission) stayed at 44, 41, and 44 percent, respectively. The proportion owed for *gremio de consulado* (imported and domestic goods sold by members of the merchant guild on their own account) was stable at 23 and 22 percent.[8] A few merchant inventories from the post-1630 years also suggest the importance of European and Chinese wares; goods from Europe and China made up the majority of the stock-in-trade of these merchants, as opposed to goods from New Spain and other American regions (table 27). The American products comprise a significant portion of the inventory, but they are still a minority category. This is quite consistent with the lower per unit value of most American

Table 27. Provenance of Goods in Four Merchant Inventories, 1631–69

Name	Spain	China	Mexico	America	Not Known	Total
Alzega	5,276	9,640	3,828	8,096	963	27,803
	(19%)	(35%)	(14%)	(29%)	(4%)	
Guerra Chacón	13,516	2,009	3,027	629	1,693	20,874
	(65%)	(10%)	(15%)	(3%)	(8%)	
Montemayor	4,160	789	1,792	—	—	6,741
	(62%)	(12%)	(27%)			
Toledo y Mendoza	22,710	5,715	2,649	5,580	8,139	44,793
	(51%)	(13%)	(6%)	(12%)	(18%)	

Source: AJUD.

products (chapter 3). Thus, although merchants acted autonomously in their mining and agricultural investments within New Spain, when it came to trade with Europe, many continued as commission agents. Apparently, they still needed or preferred to use European capital.

In all years studied, the Mexico City traders also continued to maintain their close relationship to the mining sector, as financiers and purchasers of silver. Silver-dealing was the common denominator of the Mexico City traders. In every year of the Atlantic trade studied, all men exported bullion, whereas only certain individuals exported cochineal or hides. The Pacific commerce was, of course, chiefly a silver trade. More merchants invested in mining than in other sectors, whether their involvement took the form of providing bond to public officials in mining centers, goods to provincial merchants, or credit to miners. Profits generated by mining (due to local factors such as labor availability and ore quality as well as to international factors such as private and state credit and mercury) were reinvested in mines and trade; used to expand local agriculture and manufacturing; placed in state office and state enterprise (defense); and directed toward consumption.

Other Sectors of the Economy

Thus far, the history of the merchant elite indicates that there was a serious contraction from 1635 or 1640 to 1660 or later, but that a reduced group of traders survived it. What does the persistence of international trade during the crisis years suggest about the domestic economy? While new information on other sectors is less definitive than that for trade, it does show that two trends were in effect simultaneously. There was an increase in local production of clothing and certain foods. New Spain, however, still had an export-led economy and relied on Europe and the Far East for many goods.

Production for local markets grew in some sectors and regions but declined in others. Manufacturing increased throughout the first two-thirds of the century. In 1602, the annual value of *obraje* production was estimated at more than 400,000 pesos. In 1612, Viceroy Guadalcázar remarked on the increase of Puebla textiles, to the extent that Spanish manufacturers complained of the competition in supplying the Indies, a complaint which continued. In 1636, viceregal output was evaluated at 670,000 pesos a year and may have been even higher. Growth continued from the 1640s into the 1690s because *obrajes* in the Valley of México and Querétaro expanded, even though those in Puebla declined. Half of the Coyoacán *obrajes* were established between 1640 and 1679.[9] In the case of fine and low-grade woolen textiles, therefore, the economic downturn fostered self-sufficiency. Yet, New Spain continued to purchase much fine-quality cloth and clothing, as well as other artisanal products such as paper, glass, iron, complex tools, elaborate furniture, and books from Europe and the Far East. The viceroyalty was capable of making high-quality cloths. Puebla produced taffetas and damasks in the 1630s, and merchants imported raw silk from China to have it woven and made up into luxury articles. Consumers who could afford it continued to desire imported goods, however.

Agriculture presents a more complex and incomplete picture than manufacturing. We can generalize on one point: there was no unrelieved "great depression" during which commercial farming collapsed. Sugar is a case in point. During the mid-century, some mills grew in size. The plantations of San Pedro Mártir Casasano, San Hipólito, and the Jesuit mill of Jalmolonga expanded, the latter doubling in area between 1620 and 1661. New mills were founded. Licenses to establish new mills continued to be issued from 1630 to 1670, but there were fewer than before.[10] The production figures from the San José also fit a trend of continuing productivity at a lower level. From 1620–29 to 1630–39, the mill increased output 46 percent producing an average of 14,017 *arrobas* a year in the latter decade. Then it declined 28 percent in 1640–49, producing 10,062 *arrobas* on the average; it rose slightly to 10,652 in 1650–51. In absolute terms, however, the mill was still certainly productive. Given that 1630 through 1670 was a time of stagnation and decline for the Morelos plantations, perhaps newer mills such as the San José in Puebla allowed viceregal production as a whole to remain stable or even increase.

Scattered information suggests very diverse development for basic foodstuffs agriculture. Official inventories of 1622 contained many references to improvements made on haciendas and ranches and to the establishment of new enterprises. Did these cases continue? The approach of the seventeenth-century property owners studied herein was to borrow, expand production, and accumulate more debts. This outlook bespeaks a confidence in the market. Yet, merchants showed less interest in lending to *hacendados* than to other groups. More preferred to invest in urban buildings, whose value in the capital increased from 1607 to 1635 and probably more thereafter. Did local sources of capital make up for the lack of Mexico City funds, or was there a dearth of credit for basic food cultivators? The slow shift of wheat production from the older, more encumbered farms of Puebla to newer farms in Toluca and the Bajío might indicate credit problems. As for labor, in 1647, the Mexico City *cabildo* called for the reinstatement of agricultural *repartimiento* to ease a shortage.[11] Previous evidence of scarce farmworkers came only from the 1630s, when flood works competed with agriculture for hands, but apparently the problem persisted.

Price data would help clarify the state of agriculture and ranching. To the little that is known about price movements, we can add a little more, which again points to variety by sector and region. From 1636 through the 1650s, known sugar prices ranged between 4 to 9 pesos the *arroba* wholesale, somewhat higher than previously believed.[12] Likewise, a study of the price of maize shows it increasing at 2.2 percent a year until 1661 and growing only 0.5 percent a year after that date,[13] a conclusion which differs with the earlier view that basic food prices rose in the late sixteenth and early seventeenth century and probably stablized after that. The prices of cochineal and indigo do fit that model, however. Cultivated cochineal destined for export was 149 pesos the *arroba* in 1614, fell to 110 pesos the *arroba* in 1620, rose somewhat to 125 pesos the *arroba* in 1625, and fell to 115 pesos the *arroba* in 1630 and 1639. Production reached between 3,000 and 4,000 *arrobas* a year and remained constant for the first third of the century. Indigo declined and then stabilized also. At 34 pesos the *arroba* in 1614, it dipped to 22 pesos in 1620, 24 pesos in 1625, and 23 in 1630. In 1639, it was 20 pesos the *arroba*.[14] The price of wool, neither an export nor a *género noble*, fell from 7 to 8 reales the *arroba* in 1580 to 4 to 5 reales the *arroba* in 1636.[15]

One area of the economy for which we have conclusive information is the value of public office. Although not a type of production, it does reflect income from fees and fines, which are indirect indicators of productivity. Table 15 presents the prices of 21 purchaseable offices in the mint, tribunals, and city council of Mexico City for the years before and after 1625. Of these offices, eight increased in value, eight decreased in value, and five lack comparable data. Quantitatively speaking, the values point to an overall stability. However, if types of office are considered, it is noteworthy that all four offices of the mint, the posts most closely connected to silver production, rose in value. Among the salaried posts, the wages of the *contador mayor de cuentas* and the *contador de tributos y azogues* (accountant for tribute and mercury) increased between 1626 and 1666. The salaries of the *oidores, alcaldes de crimen, oficiales reales de hacienda* remained the same. We can posit that in a depressed economy prices paid for public office would manifest a marked decline, as they did in Zacatecas after the end of the first mining boom. In Mexico City, the cost of brokerage licenses rose from 1598 to 1623 and remained fairly constant from then to 1640.[16]

Falling or rising prices, declining or expanding regions or enterprises, point to a viceregal economy in the middle third of the seventeenth century which cannot be easily characterized. Even the evident regional diversification which occurred had contradictions. Areas previously devoted to subsistence agriculture acquired specialities, became integrated into new trade networks, and gained some autonomy from the capital. One instance was the development of trade in southern New Spain, reflected in the growing importance of the *camino nuevo*, the alternate route to the coast which passed from Mexico City to Puebla to Orizaba and then to the new site of Veracruz. Goods shipped up from Guatemala or Oaxaca could now pass to the port without going through Mexico City at all.[17] Nevertheless, the northern route from the capital through Jalapa continued to be more important. Regional growth did not necessarily mean greater autonomy. In the Mixteca, for example, livestock production and trade increased in the seventeenth century, but at the same time the proportion of capital invested in the region from Puebla and Mexico City increased, too.[18] Likewise, "American"-oriented routes such as the Pacific exchange of clothing, furniture, and hardware from New Spain for Peruvian mercury, wine, oil, and silver, as well as cacao from Guayaquil and indigo from Central America illustrate the diversity of the New World economies, but the bulk of this commerce was still in imported goods and silver.

CONCLUSION

The smaller commercial and financial class reflected the contraction in the mid-century economy caused by international and local factors. Since the silver trade was the source of credit for many enterprises, these necessarily suffered, too. Because the mining decline was not catastrophic, however, they did not collapse. Depending on the amount of outside capital needed and its availability from other sources, some domestic enterprises prospered, whereas others failed. Neither an era of self-sufficient prosperity, nor a great depression, the mid-century economy, as a whole, can be described as a time of regional variations within an overall viceregal downturn. This situation in some ways resembles that of seventeenth-century Europe, where a few regions were productive, while others remained stable or declined.[19]

Placing the Mexican merchants of the period from 1590 to 1660 in the context of dependency and world systems analysis highlights the complex nature of the wholesaler group. Traditional traders in many respects, they were sufficiently innovative in some areas to challenge interpretations which dismiss them as conservative and parasitic. Furthermore, in social terms they were not that different from many of their contemporary European colleagues; both sought to merge with the aristocracy to some degree.[20] These cross-regional similarities substantiate the critics of the world systems school, who believe that sharp differences among the core, semiperiphery, and periphery were not yet present in the sixteenth century. They assert that the capitalist world economy may have been in gestation during the sixteenth century but only truly appeared in the eighteenth.[21]

In their business practices, Mexican wholesalers were quite traditional, carrying on the methods initially developed by Italian medieval traders and still widespread in sixteenth-century Europe.[22] Their short-term partnerships, commission arrangements, and reliance on family members were the pre-modern forms of association. Allocation of more business capital to such moveable items as inventory and credits than to such fixed items as buildings, foundries, or textile workshops was the common practice. The uncertain conditions of transoceanic trade and transport within the viceroyalty, along with legal protection for debtors which made collections difficult, led to high transaction costs and sharply fluctuating trade investments. Credit was provided by bills of exchange, letters of obligation for short-term loans, and *depósitos* and *censos*. Legally, interest was only 5 percent on *depósitos*, but merchants tried to circumvent these limits. Particularly traditional were the Mexican merchants' attachment to monopoly and their efforts to subject more decentralized types of distribution to monopolistic ones. Their control of the mint and manipulation of money supply exemplifies this monopoly.

However, a few aspects of business practice foretold a more open, modern, commercial system. Businesses were more permanent than it might seem, since company agreements were renewed and profits reinvested. The length of time elite merchants spent in trade was a surprising finding of this study. Also, trading profits were not as high as those realized by merchants of an earlier era (as well as some in the sixteenth century), even though they were higher than those realized in other types of activities, and it took a longer time to build up capital and contacts than previously thought. On balance, however, if we consider trading practice alone, the dependency view of merchants as conservative is correct. For historians who believe the business techniques of the thirteenth century were capitalistic, seventeenth-century Mexican merchant practices were capitalistic; for those who reserve that term for the methods of eighteenth century traders, the Mexican wholesalers' methods were definitely premodern. And their role as commission agents and close ties to Spanish and other European traders do make them fit the world system model of entrepreneurs on the periphery being strongly influenced by their counterparts in the core region.

If we look at merchant investments in other sectors, the "conservative merchant" characterization is less apt. There is no doubt that Mexico City wholesalers were primarily silver traders, and that they preferred to invest in export or high-cost-per-unit domestic goods, as well as urban real estate and public office. As some dependency scholars have argued, however, silver did stimulate local markets, and merchants also invested in, and owned, enterprises which supplied these markets. Selling in larger volume for lower per-unit prices, they fostered the commercialization of sugar, cacao, and wheat; they employed, or financed the employment of, wage workers of different races in mines, plantations, *obrajes*, and haciendas. Thus, merchants and other owners of capital began to break down the barriers to a free labor force which slave, convict, and indigenous forced labor systems erected. These rural workers joined urban groups and the elites in a domestic market, which some writers claim accounted for more demand than the international market.[23] In Mexico, the geographical dimension of commercialization was the greater influence of Mexico

City and cities in general, but this was compatible with greater regional specialization.

The existence of a dynamic, domestic economy stimulated by local conditions must, therefore, be taken into account, but without exaggerating its importance. Its share of wealth relative to the export economy, influenced by decisions in the core regions of Europe, will be debated for some time. The case of textiles in Mexico from 1590 through 1660 is illustrative. Merchants sponsored domestic production in many ways, including hiring non-guild artisans and financing *obrajes*. Some *obrajes* were located in the countryside on haciendas, which might suggest a movement toward the cottage industry of Europe. However, the traditional practice of merchant financing of guild artisans was more prevalent, and *obrajes* were not a high-priority investment for the wholesalers. Moreover, wholesalers continued to import textiles even during the economic contraction.

Nevertheless, the fact that merchants were modern in some ways, argues for a theoretical framework which recognizes the colonial merchant as a distinct type. He applied traditional techniques to enterprises with modern elements, and he cannot be dismissed as a parasite on the peripheral economies.

POLITICS AND THE STATE

The politics of the first two-thirds of the seventeenth century in New Spain differed from those of the early colony in two major respects: creoles entered the government in unprecedented numbers and the colonists were subjected to unprecedented fiscal pressure from Madrid as the Crown relinquished more functions to them.

The Creole Century

From the 1590s, the Crown alienated its power in a variety of ways in order to gain revenue for its military expenses in Europe, America, and the Far East. By selling an increasing number of offices, some created expressly to be sold, the Crown made possible an hereditary class of officials. From the 1620s, even corregidorships and other high offices which included judicial functions were sold illegally. In 1636, the governor of the Philippines asserted that viceroys received 140,000 pesos a year selling such offices.[24] Some scholars believe that this loss of royal power to the colonists was accompanied by the decline in the power of the Council of the Indies and the rise of that of the *juntas especiales*, which sold the posts in question.[25] The Crown's diminishing control over its servants reached a climax in 1654, when the *cédula de medios* was promulgated. This decree declared that all posts sold since 1626, both existing and future vacancies, be again put up for sale to obtain the best price; it also confirmed the sale of treasury and accounting posts. Financially, this drastic measure was a failure, and it further weakened royal authority in the Indies. Attempts to curb the autonomy and corruption of officeholders through *residencias* and, in the 1660s and 1670s, a broad *visita* were also unsuccessful. Offices were not the only expressions of royal power alienated in the seventeenth century. Royal pardons, entails, titles of nobility, membership in military orders, titles to land, and the right of an *encomendero* to have his grant renewed three or four times were also exchanged for the desperately desired funds. The Crown did try to limit the damage. For example, in 1660 it revoked the 1654 *cédula* and removed appointments of local governors from the viceroys, but these were tentative reforms which did not halt the thrust of royal policy to barter away much patronage to the colonists and Indies' authorities.[26]

Merchants took advantage of this state of affairs to purchase offices which enabled them to dominate the mint and to wield some influence in the *cabildo* and the lower ranks of the Inquisition. They also purchased lower-level police and clerical posts in all five branches of government, thus affecting the execution of legislative and judicial decisions. Theoretically, they were excluded from corregidorships and from treasury offices, whose occupants were not allowed to trade, but some wholesalers occupied these as well. Due to competition from other colonists for the same posts and to social prejudice, however, they were prevented from buying even more offices and translating economic power into political power to the fullest. This situation was typical of the merchant elite in ancien regime societies.

The "creolization" of the colonial bureaucracy took place from the bottom up, since the highest posts, such as high court judge, were the last to be sold. And it was the highest officials who influenced the formation of policy regarding the Indies. Even the top-ranking ministers in the Americas had a limited impact on metropolitan legislation, however. Thus, it was extremely difficult for the colonists to translate their presence in government into determination of governmental policy.

The history of new commercial and fiscal measures imposed by Spain on the Indies illustrates the gap between presence and influence when it came to policy. The mother country's catastrophic military and economic crisis led to demands for money from the colonies which were unprecedented in the metropolitan relationship. Fiscal and commercial issues were by no means the only topics of political debate in this far from quiescent period. The disposition of Indian labor and the jurisdiction of the regular clergy also provoked conflict. However, fiscal and commercial matters assumed a prominence they had not had in the sixteenth century. The object of restrictions on interregional trade between New Spain and Peru, Central America and Tierra Firme, or the Philippines was to strengthen Spain's slipping position as commercial center of the Empire, to redress the balance of economic power which was tilting toward the Indies. Such an attempt was, in the long run, futile, but the colonists had no success in trying to convince the king and Council of the Indies of the injustice or the inefficacy of their position. Despite years of petitions and protests, the *cabildo, consulado*, and viceroys of New Spain who sympathized with the colonists' needs were unable to persuade the Crown to revoke the hated restrictions.

The colonists had more success resisting the new defense taxes, which comprised the *Unión de Armas* and the *Armada de Barlovento*. Imposts on cochineal and cacao were rejected entirely, and increases in the sales, import-export, and card taxes were only partially complied with. The colonists' behavior fell between the acquiescence which in the past historians have erroneously attributed to them during this time (the "deep sleep" syndrome) and the rebelliousness which revisionist historians have perhaps overestimated. Colonists preferred to work for their immediate objectives by manipulating the due process of the imperial judicial system. They also exploited favorable customs such as postponement of tax payments. For the hundreds of creole and long-resident Spaniards in New Spain to have challenged the entire system of government would have been foolish, however, and a decisive blow to their own supremacy in the Indies.

Importance of the State

The formal government helped provide the public order which made the elites' position possible. By appointing the *alcaldes mayores* at all major centers of settlement, for example, the government established a network of representatives who could be relied upon to dispense justice, offer commercial contacts, and maintain order. The provincial clergy similarly contributed in the ecclesiastical sphere. In the capital, the royal mint helped the economy function by standardizing the chief medium of exchange and supervising the final stages of its manufacture.

The resilience of the colonial government was what made bureaucratic careers attractive to colonists. Officeholding provided a secure income, although the amount varied considerably depending on the office. It conferred prestige and constituted a reliable indication of a family's social standing. Public office was a very important investment for merchants and their children. In addition to offering a salary or fees, a bureaucratic post paved the way for other types of income. Tax farming, for example, provided a commission specified in the original contract between government and farmer, but it also conferred opportunities for trading through provincial agents and for patronage.

The political theorists of the seventeenth century envisioned a role in politics for interest groups outside the government, but this role was not well defined.[27] Merchant activities illustrated how legitimate and illegitimate power operated. In addition to serving as contractors for the outfitting of fleets and lending money to the royal treasury as the law permitted, merchants evaded taxes and intimidated judges to obtain favorable rulings, behavior which the law condemned. Despite the wide impact of private interests, nevertheless, it was the existence of a stable, prestigious government which created the tension between formal and informal power. One was the foil for the other. In the first two-thirds of the seventeenth century, the center of gravity shifted toward informal influences, but the shift was not as drastic as it has sometimes been depicted.

SOCIAL MOBILITY VERSUS SOCIAL CHANGE

Of the not very numerous scholars who have written about seventeenth-century New Spain, one of the most compelling is Irving Leonard, who developed a synthesis of the age which linked the social characteristics of the period with the style of the Baroque in literature, architecture, and art. Baroque society was a rich tapestry of diverse colors, behaviors, occupations, and statuses. Tradition was exalted and innovation held suspect. Tradition prescribed luxury and power for the elites, suffering and dependence for the masses, and a heavenly reward for the deserving. A positive side to the elites' lifestyle was their splendid buildings and public processions, living manifestions of the artistic conventions of the erudite treatises of the time. The potential for large-scale violence was omnipresent, but it rarely developed because of the strength of custom and the sublimation of aggression into religious fervor. Rather, the tensions flared up between individuals. The piety of the age was one of its most striking features.

Support for the Church in its various institutional forms was a hallmark of all social classes. Thus Baroque society was complex, compartmentalized, and tension-ridden. Its diverse and antagonistic components hung together in magnificent but uneasy balance.[28]

Should we accept as accurate this esthetically satisfying vision of seventeenth-century society in New Spain? On the whole, yes. In this case a picture drawn chiefly from literary and artistic sources does coincide with a picture based on social and economic data from the archives.

Social Distinctions

Seventeenth-century society was undoubtedly more complex than post-conquest society. The growth of racially mixed populations, unanticipated in the early colony, added new categories to the original bipartite division between the Republic of Spaniards and the Republic of Indians. Within the elite, well-to-do families who had in the early sixteenth century gained their income from Indian tributes and office now derived wealth from a combination of different types of rural properties, mines, officeholding, and, in some cases, trade. A larger and more diverse population became, in turn, more concerned about social distinctions. By the seventeenth century the majority of the guilds and religious orders of colonial Mexico had been established. The founding of the consulado in 1594 was the last such event until the late eighteenth century, when institutional representation was extended to the army, the miners, and to provincial traders. The hypersensitivity to social differences that the corporate system promoted affected the choice of marriage partners and business associates, the dress, and the self-image of all social groups.

For the wholesalers, two parameters bounded their sense of identity. On the one hand, they were whites and members of the Republic of Spaniards, as well as often well-to-do or rich. On the other hand, persons who "traded in public, as acknowledged merchants" were not part of the highest social echelon, even though certain individual merchants—through marital or political alliances—did enter this restricted circle. The merchants' place in the colonial social structure was, therefore, special.

The treatises of the time recognized the social usefulness of a trading class but placed its status below such groups as clerics and government officials. To what extent did the wholesalers themselves accept this subordinate position? They, like other members of the elite, respected tradition and, in the seventeenth century at least, put forward no challenges to the social order. They knew they gained many economic advantages from the status quo. They pursued their goal of following the lifestyle of the aristocracy in kind, if not always in degree: they dressed luxuriously, sought the same honors, and chose the traditional upper-class careers of Church and bureaucracy for the majority of their children. The merchants had a strong sense of their own group identity, however, a sense which included pride in their achievements and contributions to the Republic. We catch glimpses of this in the accounts a few offered of their economic ascent. More than two-fifths of first-generation merchants married merchants' daughters and lived out their lives in a commercial milieu in the same prosperous neighborhood and as members of the same guild. They did not retire to landowner standing when they could have afforded it and continued as associates in many successful ventures. Wholesalers remained primarily a mercantile and financial group.

The compartmentalization of colonial Mexican society also showed itself in wholesalers' superior attitude toward retailers, provincial merchants, and other lesser members of the commercial community. Just as blue-blooded landowners of first-settler descent sought to maintain the social distance between themselves and upstart immigrant traders, the securely established wholesalers did the same with the less affluent and lower-status types of businessmen. They excluded them from the *consulado* of Mexico City and from their marital circles; attempted to force them to pay more than their share of the sales and extraordinary taxes, and attempted to evict their market stalls from the *plaza mayor*. As long as the distinction between wholesalers and retailers was preserved, the former might help the latter by serving as godparents or providing financial assistance on an individual basis. But the wholesalers held tenaciously to the distinction. Similarly, there was a division between the Old Christian and New Christian merchants, who practiced Judaism, although in reality, there were business and, occasionally, marital ties between them.

A Pious Century

Religious observance fulfilled spiritual, social, and sometimes economic functions, and the cross-class ties which such religious bonds such as *compadrazgo* fostered helped to counteract the racial and social tensions of colonial society. The merchants' behavior corroborates the assertion that the seventeenth century was an intensely pious one. Every wholesalers' family included parents whose wills made generous provision for masses and alms, and in every family at least one child became a religious. Families with children were obliged to limit their largesse to one-fifth of the estate. Childless couples could give without restraint, however, and these merchants spent thousands of pesos to found religious houses and hospitals and to adorn existing chapels and facades of monasteries. The seventeenth century saw the increasing acquisition of property by the clergy as individuals and by the Church as a group of institutions. To this trend, the wholesalers made a notable contribution. Scholars have often emphasized how ownership of, or mortgages on, rural property passed to ecclesiastical hands. The same was true of urban holdings and public office.

How Much Social Mobility?

One of the striking features of Leonard's canvas of seventeenth-century society is that although the various parts are in motion, the picture as a whole is static. He portrays intense activity in small, circumscribed spheres but rigidity in the overall universe.[29] This is an accurate representation of the social dynamics of the period, except that Leonard overemphasizes the lack of opportunity for change. The *sociedad de castas* did discourage changes in the position occupied in the social hierarchy by such groups as artisans or merchants, but it permitted upward (and, of course, downward) mobility for particular families.

In the history of the merchants throughout the period from 1590 to 1660, the first generation was a community of peninsular immigrants. For the Spanish- and Portuguese-born sons of provincial merchants, estate managers, or artisans, attainment of *mercader* standing in Mexico City might mean a rise in income, status, or both. For the sons of merchants already established in Seville or Lisbon, it signified the continuation of the family's position in Europe. The second generation, the children of the Mexico City wholesalers, in most cases further improved the family's social position; in the majority of families they became ecclesastics or became or married bureaucrats. Still, one-third of the families included a child who carried on the father's commercial career, so that social transition from trader family to priest-official family was by no means complete.

How enduring were these social advances? The history of ten seventeenth-century merchant families for three generations indicates that it was easier to retain a higher social position than it was to retain the family fortune, but that, even so, half of the families were still fairly prosperous in the third generation. The other families declined, but most did not fall back to the position occupied two generations previously, thanks chiefly to their possession of public office. Large families could prosper and small families could decay, suggesting that demography must be combined with such topics as types of investments to understand the group's social dynamics. Investment in many different enterprises helped preserve the family's estate. Public office in particular earned prestige and provided modest but reliable revenue. However, there were no guarantees. The great fortunes which were the hallmark of Baroque society were attained by many prosaic business decisions and had to be carefully tended by the stewards of each family's wealth.

Appendixes

A. ATLANTIC TRADE

Methodology for Analyzing the Ships' Manifests

Tables 1 through 4 are based on the *libros de registro,* or ships' manifests, found in the section *casa de contratación* of the AGI. The libros give the *avería* payments made by individual shippers. The rates are: 6 percent for 1614, 6 percent for 1620, 7 percent for 1625, 31 percent for 1630, and 22 percent for 1639. These years were selected because they were approximately five years apart and/or because more registers are preserved for these years than for others. The *avería* rates are given in the documents. Each shipper laded one or more boxes, and each box was assessed separately. There are no summary totals for a particular individual nor for the total shippers in the manifests. To arrive at the values in tables 1 and 2, each shipper's tax payments were totaled.

The *libros de registro* contain more information about all the individuals participating in the trans-Atlantic trade than any other source. In particular, they provide valuable serial information, which other sources lack. Because not all the manifests are extant for every vessel, however, it was necessary to devise a system which took the non-extant registers into account. Fortunately, the system used by the shippers themselves aided in this endeavor. The study of the manifests revealed that most of the shippers laded on the three largest vessels because these were the most capacious and the best defended. Again to protect against loss, investors spread the rest of their cargo among the smaller vessels. Finally, in each fleet the *capitana* (admiral's ship) and the *almiranta* (vice-admiral's ship), which usually had the largest tonnages, carried most of the silver and more of the commodity cargo than any other individual vessel (García Fuentes, *El comercio,* 379; Lorenzo Sanz, *Comercio,* 2:74–76). Luckily, the registers of the three largest vessels are preserved for all the years studied. They can serve as the basis for suggesting the content of the non-extant registers.

Thus, the *libros* are especially useful for estimating the annual number of shippers; they can also provide approximate information about the distribution of cargo among large, medium, and small shippers. They are not reliable sources for the total value of the cargo in a given year, which must be ascertained from other sources.

Table 1, Column 8, Note d (p. 36)
The number of shippers listed in extant registers obviously undercounts the actual number of shippers because additional names were present in the non-extant registers. To estimate the actual number of shippers, it was necessary to identify a relationship between the extant and non-extant registers for the most complete year, which could be used as a base year. The year 1614 is taken as a base because all or part of the manifests have been preserved for all ships that year. In 1614, the registers of the three largest vessels accounted for 73 percent of the shippers listed in the manifests of all vessels. Using this ratio, the numbers of shippers were: 1614, 479; 1620, 481; 1625, 532; 1630, 232; and 1639, 189. Finally the shippers contained in the missing sections of some of the 1614 *registros* should be included. Based on the decreasing numbers of new names in each succeeding ship of this year, at the most, another fifty names appeared here. Although the total numbers would be, therefore, somewhat higher than those cited in the text and in table 1, they do not alter the conclusions about the small number of shippers in an absolute sense or relative to the *vecino* population of Mexico City.

The percentage of vessels whose registers are extant for the other years are: 1620, 49 percent; 1625, 60 percent; 1630, 43 percent; and 1639, 35 percent. However, except for 1614, these percentages have little bearing on the number of shippers because this number was not proportional to the number of vessels nor to the number of registers. The most meaningful ratio is the number of shippers on the three largest vessels to the number of shippers on all vessels.

The tonnage and number of vessels for each of the years studied are: 1614, twelve vessels, totaling 5,600 tons; 1620, fourteen vessels, totaling 6,931 tons; 1625, twelve vessels, totaling 7,070 tons; 1630, nine vessels, totaling 5,148 tons; and 1639, thirteen vessels, totaling 4,890 tons. The vessels are those returning from Veracruz with the fleet.

Table 1, Column 1, Note e

The number and proportion of "Large" and "Medium" shippers is undercounted, especially for years 1630 and 1639. Since the existing *libros* do not contain all the registers, the amounts shipped in the extant registers are too low; we know these shippers placed additional amounts in the non-extant registers. The same individuals were sending cargo on many ships in a given year. Therefore, if we had records of this additional cargo, it would push more shippers into the "Large" and "Medium" categories. Although we cannot determine exactly how many more, we have sufficient evidence of monopoly and concentration of investment from the available data.

Table 2, Column 9, Note a (p. 37)

The total value of private cargo (silver *and* merchandise) laded on each vessel by year from Veracruz to Seville is not given in the *libros*, nor in any other source. Totals for private silver from Veracruz for certain years are available, as are totals for merchandise from the Indies, but not totals of silver and merchandise from Veracruz. The totals in table 2, column 9, are the sum of the value of all the boxes listed in the extant Veracruz manifests. These totals do not account for all private cargo, however, because some registers are not extant, and sections of existing registers have been torn out. These totals can be compared to another source.

In *Séville* (Table 217A), Chaunu provides the value of private silver shipments from New Spain for certain years. Tables 672 (cochineal), 675 (indigo), and 719 (silk) provide the value of these commodity exports for some of the same years. The two were added together, and it was possible, therefore, to arrive at the following estimates. For 1614, about 3,678,202 pesos' worth of private cargo (silver and merchandise) were sent from Veracruz; for 1620, about 5,564,480 pesos' worth of private cargo were sent; and for 1630, about 3,494,468 pesos in private cargo. Figures for 1625 and 1639 are not provided.

Thus, the ships' manifests are not reliable for the total value of private cargo each year. However, they are reliable for estimating the number of shippers and the approximate distribution among types of shippers.

To obtain the ratio tonnage: number of shippers per hundred tons, the tons of the vessels whose manifests were preserved were totaled and divided by the number of shippers on those vessels. The results were: 1614, 8.2; 1620, 6.2; 1625, 5.7; 1630, 3.3; and 1639, 2.8. The trend toward increased concentration is clear.

B. PHILIPPINE TRADE

Methodology for Analyzing the Import Tax

Tables 3 and 4 (pp. 39 and 40) are based on the import tax collected at Acapulco and recorded in the *caxa de México*, cargo side, on goods imported from the Philippines. In the *contaduría* records, the tax is called *almojarifazgo de Filipinas a razón de 10%* through 1611; thereafter it is termed *islas Filipinas*, with the rate generally at 13.5 or 14.5 percent.

These records give the summary totals for the import tax on Philippine goods almost all years between 1590 and 1660, but they do not give totals for the individual shippers, whose payments are scattered through the document. The addition of the entries for each individual forms the basis for the average number of shippers and the taxes paid which appear in tables 3 and 4. The content of each year's tax records varies considerably. Some years have very small summary totals of 300 or 400 pesos, whereas other years have a summary total of more than 100,000 pesos. This variation occurred because the tax was only paid in full every two or three years. Another variation is between years in which individual payers are specified and years in which only lump-sum payments are specified. In the latter case, or where there is a mixture of accounting methods, it is not possible to analyze the investments of individual shippers. Finally, for a few years the summary totals are preserved but sections of the rest of the tax payments are missing or burned. Thus it is not possible to present a year-by-year analysis of the Pacific trade, although it is possible to present more years than for the Atlantic. In the latter case, the documents are too scanty before 1614 and after 1639 to permit analysis. They were also written in the oversize notarial script, which made it prohibitively expensive to microfilm every year between these dates; it was necessary, therefore, to select years at relatively similar intervals with which to work. In the case of the Pacific trade, it was possible to microfilm all years, but not every year provided the necessary data for the reasons described above. Although each series has its strengths and weaknesses, both fill a void in the data previously used for the study of trade.

Notes

Introduction

1 AGI, México 31, 10 January 1634, f.2.

2 Charles Gibson, "Writings on Colonial Mexico," *Hispanic American Historical Review* 55, no. 2 (May 1975): 303–14.

3 Christon I. Archer, *The Army in Bourbon Mexico, 1760–1810* (Albuquerque: University of New Mexico Press, 1977); Christiana Borchart de Moreno, "Los miembros del consulado de la ciudad de México en la época de Carlos III," *Jahrbuch für Geschichte von Staat, Wirtschaft, und Gesellschaft Lateinamericas* 14 (1977) (hereafter cited as *Jahrbuch*); D. A. Brading, *Miners and Merchants in Bourbon Mexico, 1763–1810* (Cambridge: Cambridge University Press, 1971); Hira de Gortari and Guillermo Palacios, "El comercio novohispano a través de Veracruz (1802–1810)," *Historia Mexicana* 17, no. 3 (January–March 1968); Brian R. Hamnett, *Politics and Trade in Southern Mexico, 1750–1812* (Cambridge: Cambridge University Press, 1971); John E. Kicza, *Colonial Entrepreneurs: Families and Business in Bourbon Mexico City* (Albuquerque: University of New Mexico Press, 1983).

4 Huguette and Pierre Chaunu, *Séville et l'Atlantique, 1504–1650*, 8 vols. (Paris: SEVPEN, 1955–59); Lutgardo García Fuentes, *El comercio español con América (1650–1700)* (Sevilla: Escuela de estudios hispanoamericanos, 1980); John J. TePaske and Herbert S. Klein, "The Seventeenth-Century Crisis in New Spain: Myth or Reality?," *Past and Present*, no. 90 (February 1981); Clarence Haring, *Trade and Navigation between Spain and the Indies in the Time of the Hapsburgs* (Cambridge: Harvard University Press, 1918); C. N. Guice, "The *Consulado* of New Spain, 1594–1795," Ph.D. diss., University of California, Berkeley, 1952; Robert S. Smith, "The Institution of the *Consulado* in New Spain," *Hispanic American Historical Review* 24, no. 1 (February 1944).

5 Stanley and Barbara Stein, *The Colonial Heritage of Latin America* (New York: Oxford University Press, 1970); J. I. Israel, *Race, Class, and Politics in Colonial Mexico, 1610–1670* (London: Oxford University Press, 1975); P. J. Bakewell, *Silver Mining and Society in Colonial Mexico: Zacatecas, 1546–1700* (Cambridge: Cambridge University Press, 1971); José F. de la Peña, *Oligarquía y propiedad en la Nueva España (1550–1624)* (México: Fondo de cultura económica, 1983); Stanley

Hordes, "The Crypto-Jewish Community of New Spain, 1620–1649: A Collective Biography," Ph.D. diss., Tulane University, 1980.

6　Carlos Sempat Assadourian, *El sistema de la economía colonial. Mercado interno, regiones y espacio económico* (Lima: Instituto de estudios peruanos, 1982), 61–62, 138, 282; Steve J. Stern, "Feudalism, Capitalism, and the World-System in the Perspective of Latin America and the Caribbean," *American Historical Review* 93, no. 4 (October 1988): 839–40.

7　José Carlos Chiaramonte, *Formas de sociedad y economía en Hispanoamérica* (México: Grijalbo, 1983), 169, 194; Immanuel Wallerstein, *The Modern World-System*, vol. 1: *Capitalist Agriculture and the Origins of the European World-Economy in the Sixteenth Century* (New York: Academic Press, 1974), 124–26, and vol. 2: *Mercantilism and the Consolidation of the European World-Economy, 1600–1750* (1981), 19; Robert DuPlessis, "The Partial Transition to World-Systems Analysis in Early Modern European History," *Radical History Review* 39 (1987): 25. Charles Ragin and Daniel Chirot, "The World-System of Immanuel Wallerstein: Sociology and Politics as History," in *Vision and Method in Historical Sociology*, ed. Theda Skocpol (Cambridge: Cambridge University Press, 1987), 292, 306–8 discuss Wallerstein's influence on the scholarship of several regions.

8　Stern, "Feudalism," 833–35, especially n. 11; Enrique Semo, *Historia del capitalismo en México: Los orígenes, 1521–1762* (México: Ediciones Era, 1973), 17, 248, 250; DuPlessis, "Partial Transition," 14–15. Wallerstein posits local economic growth in the seventeenth century but denies its autonomous character. *World-System* 2:156–57.

9　Assadourian, *El sistema de la economía colonial*, 303; Stern, "Feudalism," 872.

10　Sherbourne Cook and Woodrow Borah, *Essays in Population History*, 3 vols. (Berkeley: University of California Press, 1971–79), 2:197–200; Nicolás Sánchez-Albornoz, "The Population of Colonial Latin America," in *Cambridge History of Latin America: Colonial Latin America*, ed. Leslie Bethell, 2 vols. (New York: Cambridge University Press, 1984), 2:4; María de las Mercedes Gantes Tréllez, "Aspectos socios-económicos de Puebla de Los Angeles (1624–1650)," *Anuario de estudios americanos* 40 (1983): 531. Her figures for the other socio-racial groups are much lower than the other sources cited. Guy P. C. Thomson, *Puebla de los Angeles: Industry and Society in a Mexican City, 1700–1850* (Boulder: Westview, 1989), 154.

11　Cook and Borah, *Essays*, 2:197–98. John Lynch, *Spain under the Hapsburgs* (New York: Oxford University Press, 1964–69), 2:206, believes there were 35,000 blacks in 1650 and 100,000 persons of black mixed ancestry. Silva Solis, cited in Colin Palmer, *Slaves of the White God, 1570–1650* (Cambridge: Harvard University Press, 1976), 29, claimed 80,000 slaves circa 1645. Israel, *Race, Class, and Politics*, 21, believes there were 150,000 Europeans in 1650.

12　Thomson, *Puebla*, 151, 158, shows continuing growth in the province and city, including from 1681 to 1737. In *Hacienda and Market in Eighteenth-Century Mexico: The Rural Economy of the Guadalajara Region, 1675–1820* (Berkeley: University of California Press, 1981), 29–33, Eric Van Young sees a slow increase throughout the century and a rise in *vecinos* between 1637 and 1713. In *To Love, Honor, and Obey in Colonial Mexico* (Stanford: Stanford University Press, 1988), Patricia Seed believes the mixed population of Mexico City began to grow from 1650 or 1670 (25, 251 n.25). It is possible, as Lyle N. McAlister suggests in *Spain and Portugal in the New World* (Minneapolis: University of Minnesota Press, 1985), 335–37, that outside the major administrative centers, urban growth slowed after 1650, but no data are yet available for the viceroyalty as a whole. Mark A. Burkholder and Lyman Johnson, *Colonial Latin America* (New York: Oxford University Press, 1989), 104, believe smaller ships led to fewer emigrants after 1650.

13   Jorge E. Hardoy and Carmen Aranovich, "Urban Scales and Functions in Spanish America toward the Year 1600: First Conclusions," *Latin American Research Review* 5, no. 3 (1970): 67, 71; Adriaan C. van Oss, "Architectural Activity, Demography, and Economic Diversification: Regional Economies of Colonial Mexico," *Jahrbuch* 16 (1979): 118, 128, 139. There are other figures for the number of *vecinos* in Mexico City at this time. In 1629, Archbishop Francisco Manso y Zúñiga reported 20,000 white families; in 1636, the *cabildo* asserted there were 10,000 *vecinos*, and a copy of the map of Gómez de Trasmonte notes that in 1628 there were 10,000 *vecinos*. See Louisa Hoberman, "Bureaucracy and Disaster: Mexico City and the Flood of 1629," *Journal of Latin American Studies* 6, no. 2 (1974): 214.

14   Lyman Johnson, "Artisans," in *Cities and Society in Colonial Latin America*, ed. Louisa S. Hoberman and Susan Socolow (Albuquerque: University of New Mexico Press, 1986), 235–39.

15   James Lockhart, "Postconquest Nahua Society and Culture Seen through Nahuatl Sources," Readings in Colonial Nahua History, unpublished paper.

16   William Taylor, "Indian *Pueblos* of Central Jalisco on the Eve of Independence," in *Iberian Colonies, New World Societies: Essays in Honor of Charles Gibson*, eds. Richard Garner and William Taylor (Privately printed, 1986), 172–73.

17   Gibson, "Writings," 304–5; Louisa S. Hoberman, "Elites in Seventeenth-Century Mexico: A Review of the New Social History," paper presented at the Latin American Studies Association, Washington, D.C., 1982, 8.

18   D. A. Brading, "The Catholic Monarchy in the Seventeenth Century," lecture given at the University of Texas, 1989; and *Los orígenes del nacionalismo mexicano* (México: Ediciones Era, 1973), 21–23; William Taylor, "The Virgin of Guadalupe in New Spain: An Inquiry into the Social History of Marian Devotion," *American Ethnologist* 14 (February 1987): 11–12, 28, notes 18, 20.

19   Israel, *Race, Class, and Politics*, 104, 217–47; John Frederick Schwaller, *The Church and the Clergy in Sixteenth-Century Mexico* (Albuquerque: University of New Mexico Press), 82–83, 109.

20   Solange Alberro, *Inquisición y Sociedad en México, 1571–1700* (México: Fondo de cultura económica, 1988), 150–51, 210, 215.

21   Woodrow Borah, *Justice by Insurance: The General Indian Court of Colonial Mexico and the Legal Aides of the Half-Real* (Berkeley: University of California Press, 1983), 94, 119.

22   Mark Burkholder, "Bureaucrats," in *Cities and Society*, Hoberman and Socolow, 82–84; Kenneth J. Andrien, *Crisis and Decline: The Viceroyalty of Peru in the Seventeenth Century* (Albuquerque: University of New Mexico Press, 1985), 104, 123; John Parry, *The Sale of Public Office in the Spanish Indies under the Hapsburgs*, Ibero-Americana 37 (Berkeley: University of California Press, 1953), 52–53;

Horst Pietschmann, "Burocracia y corrupción en hispanoamérica colonial. Una approximación tentativa," *Nova Americana* 5 (1982): 25.

23   Lynch, *Spain*, 2:271–72, 277.

24   TePaske and Klein, "Seventeenth-Century Crisis," 133.

25   Peter Rees, *Transportes y comercio entre México y Veracruz, 1519–1910* (México: Sepsetentas, 1976), 28–30; Lynch, *Spain*, 2:177.

26   Chaunu, *Séville*, 5:368–69; Clarence Haring, *The Spanish Empire in America* (New York: Oxford University Press, 1947), 292–94; Hoberman, "Bureaucracy and Disaster," 221; François Chevalier, *Land and Society in Colonial Mexico* (Berkeley: University of California Press, 1966), 266, 270.

27   The data on total silver and gold production was provided by John J. TePaske. For Zacatecas, see Bakewell, *Silver Mining*, 242, 259, and "Mining in Spanish America," in *Cambridge History of Latin America*, ed. Bethell, 139.

28   Charles Gibson, *The Aztecs under Spanish Rule* (Stanford: Stanford University Press, 1964), 324; Chevalier, *Land and Society*, 73–74; Raymond L. Lee, "Cochineal Production and Trade in New Spain to 1600," *The Americas* 4 (1948): 459; Fernando Sandoval, *La industria del azúcar en Nueva España* (México: UNAM, 1951), 114; Rees, *Transportes y comercio*, 17, 19, 24, 35, 55.

29   Chaunu, *Séville*, 6:1:337, 474; 8:2:1:250; 8:2:2:920, 1071–72, 1176.

30   Woodrow Borah, *New Spain's Century of Depression* (Berkeley: University of California Press, 1951), 1, 3–4, 28, 32, 39.

31   Chevalier, *Land and Society*, 4, 41, 49, 52, 69, 102, 112–13, 134–38, 169, 180, 279; Lynch, *Spain*, 2:184.

32   Data provided by John J. TePaske; TePaske and Klein, "Seventeenth-Century Crisis," 124–28, 134; Richard L. Garner, "Long-Term Silver Mining Trends in Spanish America: A Comparative Analysis of Peru and Mexico," *American Historical Review* 93, no. 4 (October 1988): 902–4. Garner presents Zacatecas production as decreasing only 2.1 percent from 1623 to 1661, but that is because this cycle includes both high and low years (912 n.29).

33   García Fuentes, *El Comercio español*, 222, 409, points out that the registers he used are incomplete because they do not include illegal sailings, warships, or slavers.

34   Ibid., 211–13; Lynch, *Spain*, 2:163, 166, 192; Chaunu, *Séville*, 6:1:337.

35   K. R. Andrews, *The Spanish Caribbean: Trade and Plunder, 1530–1630* (New Haven: Yale University Press, 1978), 73–74, 154–55; Enriqueta Vila Vilar, *Hispanoamérica y el comercio de esclavos*, (Sevilla: Escuela de estudios hispanoamericanos, 1977), 158–59, 169, 172; H. Kamen, J. I. Israel, John J. TePaske, and Herbert Klein, "Debate. The Seventeenth-Century Crisis in New Spain: Myth or Reality," *Past and Present* 97 (November 1982): 156; J. I. Israel, *Empires and Entrepôts: The Dutch, the Spanish Monarchy and the Jews, 1585–1713* (London: The Hambledon Press, 1990), 211; Haring, *Trade and Navigation*, 249–50.

36   Tables 21 and 22, herein; John J. TePaske, "New World Silver, Castile, and the Far East (1590–1750)," in *Precious Metals in the Later Medieval and Early Modern World*, ed. John Richards (Durham: Carolina Academic Press, 1982) 444–45; William S. Atwell, "International Bullion Flows and the Chinese Economy circa 1530–1650," *Past and Present* 95 (May 1982): 86–90; William Lytle Schurz, *The Manila Galleon* (New York: E. P. Dutton, 1939), 90, 350, 355.

37   Murdo J. MacLeod, *Spanish Central America: A Socioeconomic History, 1520–1720* (Berkeley: University of California Press, 1973), 358, n.27; McAlister, *Spain and Portugal*, 378; Richard Boyer, "Mexico in the Seventeenth Century: Transition of a Colonial Society," *Hispanic American Historical Review* 57, no. 3 (August 1977): 463.

38   Bakewell, *Silver Mining*, 223–25.

39   McAlister, *Spain and Portugal*, 381; Israel, *Race, Class, and Politics*, 30–31; Herman Konrad, *A Jesuit Hacienda in Colonial Mexico: Santa Lucía, 1576–1767* (Stanford: Stanford University Press, 1980), 305–10. Boyer, "Mexico in the Seventeenth Century," 471, notes that Borah's assumption that Indian population decrease caused a labor shortage did not apply to the mining industry, but did help explain the reorganization of labor for agriculture.

40   Data provided by John J. TePaske; TePaske and Klein, "Seventeenth-Century Crisis," 124–27; Bakewell, *Silver Mining*, 243; García Fuentes, *El comercio español*, 211–15, 230–33, 383, 411–12.

41   John J. TePaske, "La política española en el Caribe durante los siglos XVII y XVIII," in *La influencia de España en el Caribe, La Florida, y la Luisiana, 1500–1800*, ed. Antonio Acosta y Juan Marchena (Madrid: Instituto de cooperación iberoamericana, 1983), 64–66; Stephen Fortune, *Merchants and Jews: The Struggle for British West Indian Commerce, 1650–1750* (Gainesville: University Presses of Florida, 1984), 105, 107, 114. For an excellent analysis of contraband, see MacLeod, *Spanish Central America*, 361–73; Andrews, *Spanish Caribbean*, 243–45; Lang, *Conquest*, 54; Lynch, *Spain*, 2:193; J. I. Israel, *The Dutch Republic and the Hispanic World* (Oxford: Clarendon Press, 1982), 415.

42   AGI, México 22, 30 March 1594. *Foja* numbers are not included for pages which do not have pagination or which have more than one number on each page.

43   Guice, "Consulado," 64, 168, 174, 188.

44   AGI, México 22, 30 March 1594.

45   J. Ignacio Rubio Mañé, "Gente de España en la ciudad de México, año de 1689," *Boletín del Archivo General de la Nación*, 2d ser., 7, no. 1 (January-March 1966): 5–406.

46   AC 22:97 (the number after AC refers to the book number, which does not always coincide with the volume number); Guice, "Consulado," 18, 170.

47   One hundred and seventy-seven persons called themselves wholesalers in the individual entries, Rubio Mañé, "Gente de España," 5–406; 194 are so designated in the census totals, ibid., 234–36.

48   Hordes, "The Crypto-Jewish Community," 114, 207.

49   AHH, Consulado, 791, 7 (1595–1626); 213, 12 (1635–61); and 664, 32 (1636–65). AGI, Escribanía de Cámara, 176B, *pieza* 4, and 177B, *pieza* 3; Borchart de Moreno, "Los miembros del consulado," 137; Antonio Domínguez Ortiz, *Orto y ocaso de Sevilla: Estudios sobre la prosperidad y decadencia de la ciudad durante los siglos XVI y XVII* (Sevilla: Junta de patronato, 1946). In 1566 the *casa de contratación* recognized 264 merchants trading to New Spain. Eufemio Lorenzo Sanz, *Comercio de España con América en la época de Felipe II*, 2 vols. (Valladolid: Diputación provincial, 1979), 1:119. Only eighty-two wholesalers attended the general meeting of 1787; Brading, *Miners and Merchants*, 114. John E. Kicza, "Colonial Urban Social

History: The Case of Mexico," in *1979 Proceedings of the Rocky Mountain Council on Latin American Studies Conference*, ed. John J. Brasch (Lincoln: University of Nebraska Press, 1980), 228, states that in late-eighteenth-century Mexico City there were about 200 wholesalers out of a population of about 100,000 persons. The wholesalers constituted, therefore, about 0.2 percent of the population.

50   Alberro, *Inquisición y sociedad*, 67, 421, 425, 442.

51   James C. Boyajian, *Portuguese Bankers at the Court of Spain, 1626–1650* (New Brunswick: Rutgers University Press, 1983), 43–44, 176.

52   Antonio Domínguez Ortiz, "La concesión de 'naturalezas para comerciar' en Indias durante el siglo XVII," *Revista de Indias* 19 (1959): 231. See also Hordes, "The Crypto-Jewish Community," 85–86, 207, and Alfonso Quiroz, "The Expropriation of Portuguese New Christians in Spanish America, 1635–1649," *Ibero-Amerikanisches Archiv* 11, no. 4 (1985): 412–15. Both show that the majority of Portuguese *conversos* in New Spain were not wealthy wholesalers. Stuart Schwartz, "The Voyage of the Vassals: Royal Power, Noble Obligations, and 'New Christian' Capital before the Portuguese Restoration of Independence, 1624–1640," *American Historical Review*, forthcoming, notes that in seventeenth-century Bahia, about half of the merchants were New Christians. The *converso* traders had commercial advantages over their competitors but even under the sympathetic Olivares received only sporadic state support. In *Empires and Entrepôts*, 395–97, Israel notes that in the 1640s, Portuguese *conversos* at Seville and Cádiz included numerous leading Indies merchants and that Jews then played a larger role in Dutch-Spanish trade than previously.

53   AGI, México 34, 7 November 1637, f. 120.

54   AGI, México 34, 12 August 1638, ff. 120–62; Bernard Slicher van Bath, "Economic Diversification in Spanish America Around 1600: Centres, Intermediate Zones, and Peripheries," *Jahrbuch* 16 (1979): 83; Gantes Tréllez, "Aspectos socios-económicos," 602.

55   Eric Wolf, *Sons of the Shaking Earth* (Chicago: University of Chicago Press, 1959), 3–10; Ward J. Barrett, *The Sugar Haciendas of the Marqueses del Valle* (Minneapolis: University of Minnesota Press, 1970), 4; Lee, "Cochineal Production," 464.

56   Bakewell, *Silver Mining*, 29–30, 59–61; Robert C. West, *The Mining Community in Northern New Spain: The Parral Mining District* Ibero-Americana 30 (Berkeley: University of California Press, 1949), 6.

57   Rees, *Transportes y comercio*, 36, 42–43; Alejandra Moreno Toscano, "Regional Economy and Urbanization: Three Examples of the Relationship between Cities and Regions in New Spain at the End of the Eighteenth Century," in *Urbanization in the Americas from Its Beginnings to the Present*, ed. Richard P. Schaedel et al. (The Hague: Mouton, 1978), 406; William B. Taylor, *Landlord and Peasant in Colonial Oaxaca* (Stanford: Stanford University Press, 1972), 3.

58   Ramon María Serrera Contreras, *Guadalajara ganadera: Estudio regional novohis-pano, 1760–1805* (Sevilla: Escuela de estudios hispano-americanos, 1977), 263; West, *Mining Community*, 88; Rees, *Transportes y comercio*, 70.

59   Rees, *Transportes y comercio*, p. 40; Haring, *Trade and Navigation*, 223–28; Vila Vilar, *Hispanoamérica y el comercio de esclavos*, 146, 151–52.

60   Vila Vilar, *Hispanoamérica y el comercio de esclavos*, 158, 181–82; Haring, *Trade and Navigation*, 115–18; Andrews, *Spanish Caribbean*, 70, 208; Chaunu, *Séville*,

6:2:814–48 (1590–1616), tables 576–600; 8:1:699, 702, 709, 833.

61 Schurz, *Manila Galleon*, 31–33, 69, 115, 132.

62 Ibid., 221–41, 262–63, 281.

63 Woodrow Borah, *Early Colonial Trade and Navigation between Mexico and Peru*, Ibero-Americana 38 (Berkeley: University of California Press, 1954), 30, 86–93, 123; MacLeod, *Spanish Central America*, 169; Ross Hassig, *Trade, Tribute, and Transportation: The Sixteenth-Century Political Economy in the Valley of Mexico* (Norman: University of Oklahoma Press, 1985), 167–68.

64 MacLeod, *Spanish Central America*, 82, 158, 172, 180, 276; Diego López Rosado, *Atlas histórico-geográfico de México* (México: n.p., 1940), 102.

65 Eduardo Arcila Farías, *Comercio entre Venezuela y México en los siglos XVII y XVIII* (México: El colegio de México, 1950), 22, 79–81; Chaunu, *Séville*, 8:1:1:710.

66 Manuel Romero de Terreros, *La plaza mayor de México en el siglo XVIII* (México: UNAM, 1946), 2, 5.

1 Formation of the Merchant Elite

1 Haring, *Trade and Navigation*, 136, offers the traditional view of Mexican merchants as agents of a few commercial houses in Seville. Kicza, *Colonial Entrepreneurs*, 148, 153, emphasizes the Mexican influence.

2 A figure comparable to figure 1 cannot be drawn for the Philippine trade, because the sharp decline in total investors after 1610 distorts the ratio of percentage of large shippers to percentage of investment. What looks like a more egalitarian trade simply reflects its restriction to a small number of the people who could place large investments. See tables 3 and 4.

3 Officially, the Pacific trade was limited to an export of 500,000 pesos to Manila and the tax records from Acapulco (table 20) show exports at that level or less. Approximate figures for registered private cargo can be reached for the Atlantic trade by using Hamilton's registered imports of private silver to Seville from the Indies (TePaske, "New World Silver," 441), calculating New Spain's share based on its proportion of the cargo (Chaunu, *Séville*, 6:1:374), and adding the approximate value of the merchandise (Chaunu, *Séville*, 6:1:474).

4 (Stefantoni Federegui, Florence), AGN, *ramo* Inquisición, *legajo* 286, *expediente* 8, *foja* 8 (hereafter the terms *legajo* and *expediente* will be omitted, and *foja* will be abbreviated as *f.*; not all *legajos* are subdivided into *expedientes*, not all *fojas* are paginated); Domínguez Ortiz, "La concesión," 229; (Astudillo) AGI, Inquisición, 395; Ruth Pike, *Aristocrats and Traders: Sevillean Society in the Sixteenth Century* (Ithaca: Cornell University Press, 1966), 123.

5 Antonio Domínguez Ortiz, "Comercio y blasones: Concesiones de hábitos de órdenes militares a miembros del consulado de Sevilla en el siglo XVIII," *Anuario de estudios americanos* 33 (1976): 253–54; see also (León Castillo, Medina del Campo), Inquisición, 399, 14, f.8r, and (Burgos, Flanders) Inquisición, 430, 1.

6 Ruth Pike, *Enterprise and Adventure: The Genoese in Seville and the Opening of the New World* (Ithaca: Cornell University Press, 1966), 16–19, 37, 49–50, 163 n.73.

7 Pike, *Aristocrats and Traders*, 126; Pike, *Enterprise and Adventure*, 9. For the importance of Italians and Flemish, see also Domínguez Ortiz, *Orto y ocaso*, 46-47; Chaunu, *Séville*, 4:394–95; Antonio Domínguez Ortiz, *Política y hacienda de*

Felipe IV (Madrid: Editorial de derecho financiero, 1960), 120, 129–30, 135–36; Boyajian, *Portuguese Bankers*, 5, 12.

8   Pike, *Enterprise and Adventure*, 5, 16; Albert Girard, *Le commerce français a Séville et Cadix au temps des Hapsburg* (Paris: n.p., 1932), 551.

9   (S. Baeza) Peter Boyd-Bowman, *Índice geobiográfico de 40,000 pobladores españoles de América en el siglo XIV*, 5 vols. (cards consulted in author's office), 4 (1560–79), drawer no. 1, A–F; AGI, Contaduría 585, "Relaciones, 1604–1639"; Pike, *Aristocrats and Traders*, 108; (Justiniano) Pike, *Enterprise and Adventure*, 2; Domínguez Ortiz, *Política*, 20, 96. Other well-established Seville houses were: (Jiménez Enciso) AGI, Contratación, 161, no. 3, f.41; (Medina Orozco) AGN, Inquisición, 87, 1; AGI, Contaduría 585; (Vera) AGN, Vínculos, 284, ff.53, 208.

10 Chaunu, *Séville*, 1:235; 4:396; Haring, *Trade and Navigation*, 136.

11 (Alcocer) AHH, Consulado, 213, 11; AGN, Inquisición, 351, 3, f.21 and also (Arlanzón Güemes) AGN, Inquisición, 273, 9; AHH, Consulado, 213, 11 and 791, 7.

12 (Bribiesca Roldán) AGN, Inquisición, 192, 6; and also (Díaz Posadas, Juan, Celorio) AGN, Bienes Nacionales, 315, 1, ff.3–4, 38r; (Díaz Posadas, Julián, Vivanco) AGN, Bienes Nacionales, 381, 8; (López Murillo, Benalcázar) AGN, Inquisición, 196, 1, f.1r; (Fernández de Celi, Celi) AGN, Inquisición, 195, 6, ff.1r–5r; (Cerralde, Diego, Nanclares) AN, Diego de los Ríos, 22 May 1659.

13 Examples of brothers in trade are: (López Páramo, Francisco and Gabriel) AGN, Inquisición, 659, 1; Vínculos, 32, 245, ff.71–75; (Gutiérrez Çarfate, Pedro and Diego) AGI, México 322 and AC 19:164; (Medina Orozco, Lucas and Agustín) AGN, Inquisición, 331, 18, f.1, and B. Bennassar, "Facteurs sévillans au XVIe siècle d'après des lettres marchandes," *Annales. Economies. Sociétés. Civilisations* (December 1957): 70. Bennassar characterizes the factor as not only a businessman, estimating demand and assessing creditworthiness, but also, informally, a journalist, a police inspector, and a lawyer.

14 (Solarte) AJUD, 1630–31, no. 14 (all documents in this section of the Archivo Judicial are classified by year, but not all have numbers); (Fernández Sigura) AHH, Consulado, 791, 7; (Brizuela) AGI, México 259; (Cuéllar) AGI, México 261.

15 (Zuleta) Chaunu, *Séville*, 3:416, 520, 554; 4:12; AGI, México 260; Contratación, Libros de Registro, Years 1611, 1614, and 1620; (Jiménez Enciso) AGI, Contratación, 161, no. 3, ff.41v–44r; 952, no. 4, ff.285–88, 402; Libros de Registro, Years 1620, 1625, and 1630; AGI, Contaduría, 585, Years 1605, 1618; AN, Pedro de Santillán, 3 April 1621, 4, ff.70–72r; Chaunu, *Séville*, 4:353, 386, 400, 424, 470, 548, 558; 5:18, 136.

16 (Aramburu) Chaunu, *Séville*, 5:284; AGI, Contratación, Libros de Registro, Years 1625, 1630, 1638; Contaduría, 585; AN, Pedro de Santillán, 1616; (Váez Acevedo) Chaunu, *Séville*, 4:530; 5:72; (Ormachea) ibid., 4:154; (Atienza y Navarro) ibid., 5:342; (Vertiz) AGI, Contratación, 952, 4; Contaduría, 585.

17 (Rivera, F. M.) AJUD, 1617–21, no. 76.

18 (Cuéllar) AGI, México 261; (Castillo, Francisco and Matías) AGN, Mercedes, 33, f.278v; AJUD, 1612–16, no. 65; AGI, México 149, and México, Registro de oficios y partes 1095, Libro 23:228–29; Contaduría, 722, 1619–20 (hereafter all citations to Contaduría refer to the *cargo* side unless otherwise indicated).

19 (Acosta) AHH, Consulado, 215, 6, f.5v.

20   Figures are for the electors which are the subject of this study; the figures on which tables 1, 2, 3, and 4 are based are for all shippers listed in the tax records. Because most shippers did not give their occupation, an outside source is needed to determine if a shipper was a merchant.

21   See appendix A, table 1, column 1, note e, for an explanation of why these are minimum sums. Although a "fraud factor" can be used to estimate the large annual totals, because contraband varied greatly among individuals, the unofficial individual shipments cannot be estimated in the same manner.

22   Antonio Vásquez de Espinosa, *Compendio y descripcion de las Indias occidentales* (Washington, D.C.: Smithsonian Institution Press, 1948), 264–68; AGI, México 326, 1666; Guillermo Céspedes del Castillo, *La avería en el comercio de Indias* (Sevilla: Escuela de Estudios Hispanoamericanos, 1945), 107.

23   De la Peña, *Oligarquía*, 129–30.

24   (Toledo) AJUD, 1631; Bennassar, "Facteurs," mentions markups of 100 to 120 percent in 1564.

25   Based on twelve cases, for example, John Super notes that all profits earned by merchants trading from Quito to Panama from 1580 to 1610 were less than 100 percent, and one-half were less than 50 percent, "Partnership and Profit in the Early Andean Trade: The Experiences of Quito Merchants, 1580–1610," *Journal of Latin American Studies* 11, no. 2 (November 1979): 274–76. Between 1562 and 1597, of 50 examples from Peru and New Spain, half earned little or no profit, while the majority of the rest earned 50 to 70 percent, before taxes and commissions. Lorenzo Sanz, *Comercio*, 1:458–62.

26   See chapters 3 and 4 for a full discussion of these activities.

27   Chaunu, *Séville*, 4:565; Antonio Domínguez Ortiz, "Los caudales de Indias y la política exterior de Felipe IV," *Anuario de estudios americanos* 13 (1956): 371; Joseph de Veitia Linaje, *Norte de la contratación de las Indias Occidentales*, 2d ed. (Buenos Aires: Comisión argentina de fomento interamericano, 1945), 782; Victoria Cummins, "The Church and Business Practices in Late Sixteenth-Century Mexico," *The Americas* 54, no. 4 (April 1988): 434–35.

28   (Rivera, F. M.) AJUD, 1617–21, no. 76.

29   Cummins, "The Church and Business Practices," 429–32. By the late seventeenth and early eighteenth century, however, religious institutions were offering *préstamos a interés*. Asunción Lavrin, "El Capital eclesiástico y las elites sociales en Nueva España a fines del siglo XVIII," *Mexican Studies/Estudios mexicanos* 1 (Winter 1985): 5–6.

30   Von Wobesor, Gisela, "Mecanismos crediticios en la Nueva España. El uso del censo consignativo," *Mexican Studies/Estudios mexicanos* 5 (Winter 1989): 5; Stanley J. Stein, "Prelude to Upheaval in Spain and New Spain, 1800–1806: Trust Funds, Spanish Finance, and Colonial Silver," in *Essays*, ed. Garner and Taylor, 189–90.

31   De la Peña, *Oligarquía*, 122–24.

32   (López Páramo, F.) AGN, Vínculos, 247, f.61r; (Arellano) AJUD, 1654.

33   (Ruíz de Ordunaña) AGN, Tierras, 2834, 4, f.56r. See also (Jiménez, C.) AN, Santillán, June 1621, no. 7, ff.126–28.

34   (Toledo) AJUD, 1631; AGN, Tierras, 1272, 49r–62r.

35   Companies where profits were evenly split were: (Calar de Irolo), AJUD, 1628–29, no. 6; (Haro), AGN, Bienes Nacionales, 256, 1, f.55r; (Rossales) AN, Juan Pérez de Rivera 18 May 1613, ff.76r–68v. Companies where the division was unequal were: (Carrillo Barrientos) AN, Toribio Cobián, ff.37–4, 6 June 1651; (Jiménez Enciso) AN, Santillán, no. 5, ff.96r–98r; (Jiménez, C.) AN, Santillán, no. 7, ff.126–28; (Díaz Posadas, Juan) AN, Cobián, 9 July 1651, ff.50–51; (Medina Reynoso) AN, Santillán, 27 May 1626, f.468; (Vásquez Medina, Luis) AN, Santillán, 7 January 1639, f.26v; (Valdés, Alonso) AN, Cobián, 22 February 1655; (Brizuela) AGI, México 259.

36   (Montemayor, J.) AJUD, 1648, no. 1; (Baeza del Río) AGN, Tierras, 81, ff.322r–324r, and 82, f.441r.

37   (Vásquez Medina) AN, Santillán, 7 January 1639, f.26v; (Vera), AGN, Vínculos, 284, ff.59r, 213v–219r.

38   (López Páramo, F.) AGN, Vínculos, 245, ff.75, 154r, 333–37; 247, ff.44–71, 124–63; Guillermo S. Fernández de Recas, *Mayorazgos de la Nueva España* (México: UNAM, 1965), 55, 87.

39   Compared to thirty-seven dowries received by merchants studied by Socolow in Buenos Aires from 1752 to 1808, a time when elite income levels were generally higher than in the seventeenth century, the munificence of these seventeenth-century Mexican dowries is apparent. In Buenos Aires, 35 percent of the merchants received dowries worth 10,000 pesos or more; another 32 percent received no dowry. Susan Socolow, *The Merchants of Buenos Aires, 1778–1810: Family and Commerce* (Cambridge: Cambridge University Press, 1978), table B6.

40   Asunción Lavrin and Edith Couturier, "Dowries and Wills: A View of Women's Socioeconomic Role in Colonial Guadalajara and Puebla, 1640–1790," *Hispanic American Historical Review* 59, no. 2 (May 1979): 289–95; (Cantabrana) AN, D. Ríos, 1642, ff.5–9r; see also (Munabe) AGI, Escribanía de Cámara, 175B, 1676; (Zuleta) AGI, México, 260.

41   (Alcocer) Gregorio M. de Guijo, *Diario, 1648–1664*, 2 vols. (México: Porrua, 1952), 1:60; (Millán) AGN, Inquisición, 417, 3; (Salcedo) AGN, Tierras, 1720, 6, item no. 12; Asunción Lavrin, ed., *Latin American Women: Historical Perspectives* (Westport: Greenwood Press, 1978), 34.

42   (Rodríguez León, J., calle S. Agustín) AGN, Inquisición, 351, 190; AJUD, 1611; (Cuéllar) AGI, México 261; (Munabe) AGI, Escribanía, 175B.

43   (Montemayor) AJUD, 1648, no. 1; (Díaz Posadas, Julián) AGN, Bienes Nacionales, 315, 1, ff.1–8r; (Arezti) AJUD, 1623; AGI, Contaduría, Islas Filipinas, 728 (1), 1626–27.

44   (de la Torre) AGI, México 263; Contaduría, Alcabalas, 697, 1598–99; (Alcocer) AC, 31:335; AGN, Inquisición, 351, 3, f.181r; Civil, 1835, 9, ff.1–7; Guijo, *Diario*, 1:59–60; AN, Cobián, May 1655, f.247; Chevalier, *Land and Society*, 120, 182.

45   *Cajeros* generally received 300 to 400 pesos a year in the 1630s. (Ossorio Soto) AGN, Civil, 1737, no. 31. It is not clear whether the commission was received on the wholesale or the retail value, but to calculate income the former value is utilized here.

46   Living expenses for widows with family are given in the following sources: 3,200 pesos and 2,000 pesos (Millán) AGN, Tierras, 1272, f.78r; 2,000 pesos (Castellete) AGN, Bienes Nacionales, 220, 1, f.221v; 8,000 pesos (Haro) AGN, Bienes Nacionales, 256, 1, ff.126–27v.

II   The Mexican Economy and Merchant Capital: Mining and the Mint

1   Lewis Hanke, ed., *Los virreyes españoles en América durante el gobierno de la casa de Austria*, 5 vols. (Madrid: Atlas, 1977–78), 2:145.
2   AGI, México 33, 22 July 1637, f.185.
3   In 1609, for example, it was estimated to have made up 84 percent of exports, while in 1628, the estimate was 80 percent. François Chevalier, "Les cargaisons des flottes de la Nouvelle Espagne vers 1600," *Revista de Indias* 4, no. 12 (1943): 329; AGI, México 351, Flota de Juan de Benavides, 1628.
4   Schurz, *Manila Galleon*, 189.
5   Marta Espejo-Ponce Hunt, "The Processes of the Development of Yucatán," 33–37, and John C. Super, "The Agricultural Near North: Querétaro in the Seventeenth Century," 231, note the nonmineral types of wealth in their respective regions, in *Provinces of Early Mexico*, ed. Ida Altman and James Lockhart (Los Angeles: UCLA Latin American Center Publications, University of California, 1976).
6   Bakewell, *Silver Mining*, 139; Chaunu, *Séville*, 1:773; Melvyn F. Lang, *El monopolio estatal del mercurio en México colonial, 1550–1710* (México: Fondo de cultura económica, 1977), 363.
7   Bakewell, *Silver Mining*, 132, 138; Colin M. MacLachlan and Jaime E. Rodríguez O., *The Forging of the Cosmic Race* (Berkeley: University of California Press, 1980), 170–73; Lang, *El monopolio estatal del mercurio*, 217–18; David A. Brading and Harry Cross, "Colonial Silver Mining in Mexico and Peru," *Hispanic American Historical Review* 52, no. 4 (November 1972): 567.
8   Peter J. Bakewell, "Zacatecas: An Economic and Social Outline of a Silver Mining District, 1547–1700," in *Provinces*, ed. Altman and Lockhart, 206.
9   AGI, México 263; Bakewell, *Silver Mining*, 205, and "Mining in Colonial Spanish America," in *Cambridge History of Latin America*, ed. Bethell, 2:136.
10   De la Peña, *Oligarquía*, 76; Bakewell, "Mining in Colonial Spanish America," 2:113; Lang, *El monopolio estatal del mercurio*, 209. As Bakewell pointed out, the *hacienda de minas* did not account for all silver refining activity because refining was also carried out at backyard smelters or at small Indian furnaces near the actual mine, but at Zacatecas the latter produced only small amounts of silver at this time.
11   AGI, Esribanía, 275B, ff.18–23r; Bakewell, *Silver Mining*, 197.
12   AGI, México, Registro de Oficios, 1097, Libro 28:42v; AHH, Consulado, 664, 32, f.42v.
13   Lang, *El monopolio estatal del mercurio*, 234, 363; AGI, México 37, 6 February 1651; West, *Mining Community*, 129 n.41; Capitan José Villarreal, the chief constable of Zacatecas in the 1660s, had an annual average trade worth 60,981 pesos. Bakewell, *Silver Mining*, 213.
14   AGI, México 24, 1 April 1598; West, *Mining Community*, 128 n.24.
15   AGI, México 29, 2 October 1618; Alberto Yali Román, "Sobre alcaldías mayores y corregimientos de Indias: Un ensayo de interpretación," *Jahrbuch* 14 (1977): 252–27.
16   AGI, México, Registro de Oficios, 1095, Libro 22:38; AGI, México 33, 3 June 1636, and 37, 6 February 1651, ff.21v–22r.
17   (Salcedo) AGN, Tierras, 1720, 6, ff.43v–63r; (Rivera, J. L.) AGI, Contratación, 773,

5, 1609; (Acosta) AGN, Civil, 1832, no. 9, 1621; AN, Santillán, 1 June 1615, ff. 107–8; (Arellano) AJUD, 1654, item no. 99; (López Páramo, F.) AGN, Vínculos, 247, ff. 61r–71v.

18 West, *Mining Community*, 83–84; AGI, México, 266, no. 3, f. 11v; Bakewell, *Silver Mining*, 213.

19 (Alfonso) AN, Luis Valdivieso, 9 September 1652, ff. 631r–632v; (Pérez Passos) AN, Gabriel López Ahedo, 26 October 1646, f. 77; (Salcedo) AGN, Tierras, 1720, 6, f. 48r.

20 (Ossorio Soto, Lope) AGN, Civil, 1737, no. 24, f. 34v.

21 AGI, Indiferente de Nueva España, 77, 1607.

22 AGI, México 266, no. 3.

23 (Castroverde) AN, López Ahedo, 21 February 1641, f. 13 and 9 April 1641, f. 44; (Salcedo) AGN, Tierras, 1720, 6, ff. 51r–54r; see also (Medina Reynoso) AN, Santillán, 27 May 1626, f. 468.

24 (Medina Reynoso) AN, Santillán, 1621; (Urrea) AN, 26 June 1630, ff. 3–4 and 4 July 1630, f. 8; see also (López Páramo, F.) AGN, Vínculos, 247; (Salcedo) AGN, Tierras, 1720, 6, f. 54v.

25 (Rivera, F. M.) AJUD, 1617–21, nos. 33 and 76 (with Aransemendi) AGI, México 266, no. 3.

26 AGI, México 266, no. 4 and no. 11.

27 (Urrea) AN, Cobián, 31 October 1652, f. 100; (Arellano) AJUD, 1654, no. 99; (López Páramo, F.) AGN, Vínculos, 247, ff. 55r–57v; (Garay) AN, López Ahedo, 2 September 1639, f. 130; (Medina Reynoso) AN, Santillán, 25 August 1621, ff. 113v–14r; 4 October 1621, f. 194; 29 October 1621, f. 268; 10 November 1621, f. 281; 24 November 1621, ff. 294r–295v.

28 AGI, México 266, no. 13.

29 (Salcedo) AGN, Tierras, 1720, 6, ff. 49r, 60r; (Terreros) AGN, Civil, 195, 14; AGI, Escribanía, 275A, *pieza* 3, ff. 73v–75r, 125r.

30 (Rivera, J. L.) AGI, Contratación, 773, 5, 1609; (Castellete) AGN, Bienes Nacionales, 220, 1, f. 35r; (Acosta) AN, Santillán, 1 June 1615, ff. 107–8; AGN, Civil, 1832, no. 9, 1621; (Medina Orozco, A.) AN, Juan Pérez de Rivera, 7 December 1624, ff. 20, 23; (Santos Corral) AN, de los Ríos, 23 December 1643, f. 71.

31 Miguel León-Portilla et al., *La minería en México: Estudios sobre su desarrollo histórico* (México: UNAM, 1978), 82. The office of *apartador de oro* is not included in the 1597 list of officials, but it is mentioned in the following: AGI, México 325, 4 May 1604, f. 2r and México 27, 24 May 1609, and Escribanía, 272A, *pieza* 2, f. 101.

32 Humberto F. Burzio, *Diccionario de la moneda hispanoamérica*, 2 vols. (Santiago: Fondo histórico y bibliográfico José Toribio Medina, 1956–58), 1:65, 2:394; AGI, México 23, 26 November 1597, ff. 1–3; México 27, 24 May 1609; Ismael Sánchez Bella, *La organización financiera de las Indias. Siglo XVI.* (Sevilla: Escuela de estudios hispanoamericanos, 1968), 235; AGN, Civil, 1305, 1, ff. 1–16.

33 Diego G. López Rosado, *Historia del peso mexicano* (México: Fondo de cultura económica, 1975), 20, 30; AGI, México 325, 27 May 1604, f. 1v.

34 AGI, México 23, 26 November 1597, 260–61; Contratación, 2754 and 2794; Contaduría, 722, Oficios vendibles; Registro de Oficios, 1094, book 18, 1095, book 22, and 1096, book 27; AGN, Vínculos, 284; Civil, 2849; AJ, no. 19, 1631; and

Alberto F. Pradeau, *Historia numismática de México desde la época precortesiana hasta 1823* (México: Banco de México, 1950), 45.

35   AGI, Escribanía, 168B; 272A, *piezas* 2–6, and 272B, *piezas* 7–15; México 37, 6 February 1651, and 266. In Seville, too, the *mercaderes de plata* were the most powerful men in the commercial hierarchy, Michèle Moret, *Aspects de la société marchande de Séville au debút du XVIIe siècle* (Paris: M. Rivière, 1967), 32.

36   AGI, Escribanía, 272A, *pieza* 2, ff.48–49r; f.122v.

37   AGI, Escribanía, 168B, f.148.

38   AGI, México 23, 26 November 1597, f.3r.

39   AGI, Vínculos, 284, f.459v.

40   AGI, México 261, and Escribanía, 168B, ff.213–227r.

41   (Cuéllar) AGI, México, 261; (Toledo) AJUD, Toledo, 1631; (Vera) AGN, Vínculos, 284; (Gutiérrez Gil) AGI, Escribanía, 272A, *pieza* 2, f.123r, question no. 117.

42   AGI, Escribanía, 168B, f.255, question no. 6.

43   AGI, México 325, 4 May 1604.

44   Bakewell, *Silver Mining*, 211 n.3, 245; (Rivera, J. L.) AGI, Contratación, 773, 5, 1609; (Zavala) AGI, México 263.

45   Lang, *El monopolio estatal del mercurio*, 225.

46   AGI, México 38, 24 March 1661.

47   AGI, Escribanía, 272A, (Gutiérrez Gil) *pieza* 2, f.8; (Fernández Celi) *pieza* 4; (Ruíz) *pieza* 3, f.9.

48   AGI, Escribanía, 272A, *pieza* 2, ff.121r–125r.

49   AGI, Contaduría, 708, Extraordinario, 1605–6. All citations from Contaduría are from the cargo side unless otherwise indicated.

50   AGI, Contaduría, Data, Extraordinario, all the following: 708, 1605–6; 730, 1630–31; 735(1), 1639–40; 742, 1648–49; 745, 1652–53; 751, 1659–60.

III   The Mexican Economy and Merchant Capital: Agriculture, Manufacturing, and Urban Real Estate

1   AGI, México 92, r.3, 1651.

2   Fred Bronner, "Urban Society in Colonial Spanish America: Research Trends," *Latin American Research Review* 21, no. 1 (1986): 38, notes the low returns on agriculture found at different times in the colonial period; Eric Van Young, "Mexican Rural History Since Chevalier: The Historiography of the Colonial Hacienda," *Latin American Research Review* 18, no. 3 (1983): 17 and 42 n.22, has documented the many studies which show the importance of capital flows from commerce and other sectors *to* agriculture.

3   J. Eric S. Thompson, ed., *Thomas Gage's Travels in the New World* (Norman: University of Oklahoma Press, 1958), 294.

4   Barrett, *Sugar Haciendas* 4; Chevalier, *Land and Society*, 77–78. Sandoval, *La industria del azúcar*, 51, states that forty mills were founded in New Spain in the sixteenth century.

5   Chaunu, *Séville*, 6:2:986 (table 672).

6   Adriana Naveda Chávez-Hita, *Esclavos Negros en las haciendas azucareras de Córdoba, Veracruz, 1690–1830* (Veracruz: Universidad Veracruzana, 1986), 110.

7   Chávez-Hita, *Esclavos Negros*, 96; AGN, Bienes Nacionales, 420, f.8; Cheryl English Martin, *Rural Society in Colonial Morelos* (Albuquerque: University of New Mexico Press, 1985), 38, 129; de la Peña, *Oligarquía*, 97. In early eighteenth-century Córdoba, the slave work force was the most valuable single component of the plantation. Chávez-Hita, *Esclavos Negros*, 95.

8   Martin, *Rural Society*, 28–38.

9   AGN, Tierras, 1272, f.1014; BN, 420, 7, ff.1–2; AJ, 1621–25, 1654; AN, Ríos, 15 December 1645; Jean-Pierre Berthe, "Xochimancas: Les travaux et les jours dans une hacienda sucrière de Nouvelle-Espagne au XVIIe siècle," *Jahrbuch* 3 (1966): 92; Chevalier, *Land and Society*, 94 n.2 and 95 n.3 (French ed.); de la Peña, *Oligarquía*, 96–99; Alejandro Villaseñor y Villaseñor, *Los condes de Santiago* (México: Privately published, 1901), 293–94.

10   Martin, *Rural Society*, 7, 39–40; Barrett, *Sugar Haciendas*, 110–11. Gisela von Wobeser, *San Carlos Borromeo: Endeudamiento de una Hacienda Colonial (1608–1729)* (México: UNAM, 1980), 99–116 and table 3, shows that for this *trapiche*, the *Juzgado de Capellanías* provided most of the financing.

11   Chávez-Hita, *Esclavos Negros*, 118.

12   Kicza, *Colonial Entrepreneurs*, 90; Barrett, *Sugar Haciendas*, 20; Doris M. Ladd, *The Mexican Nobility at Independence, 1780–1826* (Austin: University of Texas Press, 1976), 38.

13   Barrett, *Sugar Haciendas*, 4.

14   Sandoval, *La Industria del azúcar*, 31–32, 48; Fernández de Recas, *Mayorazgos*, 321; AGN, Bienes Nacionales, 420, 7, ff.3–4.

15   AGI, México 75, r.1; Barrett, *Sugar Haciendas*, 110; Sandoval, *La Industria del azúcar*, 98; Martin, *Rural Society*, 27–28.

16   Barrett, *Sugar Haciendas*, 110, 112; AGN, Tierras, 1272, ff.89r, 113r; Bienes Nacionales, 378, 2, f.72; Sandoval, *La Industria del azúcar*, 94, 132, 145; Martin, *Rural Society*, 29, 33, 81–82.

17   Sandoval, *La Industria del azúcar*, 129; AGI, Contaduría, 725 (1), Préstamos, 1622–23; AGN, Tierras, 109, 1, f.1v; Mercedes 39, ff.135v–136r.

18   AGN, Bienes Nacionales, 378, 2, ff.71, 264r; Sandoval, *La Industria del azúcar*, 99.

19   Berthe, "Xochimancas," 89–91; Sandoval, *La Industria del azúcar*, 103, 108–10; Cheryl English Martin, "Crucible of Zapatismo: Hacienda Hospital in the Seventeenth Century," *The Americas* 38, no. 1 (July 1981): 32.

20   Sandoval, *La Industria del azúcar*, 95, 99; Martin, "Crucible of Zapatismo," 32, 45. Martin, *Rural Society*, states that certain properties of this hacienda eventually became part of Atlihuayan, founded in 1627 by Andrés Mendes.

21   AN, Valdivieso, 28 January 1652, ff.79v–80r and 3 February 1652, ff.95v–96r; Barrett, *Sugar Haciendas*, 19–20; von Wobeser, *San Carlos Borromeo*, 80–81.

22   AGN, Tierras, 1272, f.286r; Civil, 381, 8; Bienes Nacionales, 420, 7, ff.1–7; Inquisición, 294, 1; de la Peña, *Oligarquía*, 103; Martin, *Rural Society*, 75.

23   (Esquivel Castañeda) AN, López de Rivera, 19 October 1631, ff.52–54, 72–75; (Haro) AGN, Bienes Nacionales, 256, 1; (Castellete) Ibid., 220, 1, f.47r; 220, 2; (Urrea) AGN, Tierras, 2802, 4, ff.23–24; also, (Ruíz de Orduñana) AGN, Tierras, 2834, 4, f.55; (Sánchez Cuenca) AN, Martín de Sariñana, 23 September 1641.

24   Berthe, "Xochimancas," 92; Martin, "Crucible of Zapatismo," 35, 40, 42; James

Denison Riley, *Hacendados jesuitas en México: El colegio máximo, 1685–1767* (México: Sepsetentas, 1976), 28–30; (Navarro y Atienza) AN, Valdivieso, 12 April 1652, ff.340–41.

25   AGN, Mercedes, 39, ff.135v–136r.

26   Ibid., 41, ff.22v–23r; Martin, *Rural Society*, 38–40; Berthe, "Xochimincas," 91. For San Carlos Borromeo, von Wobeser attributes indebtedness primarily to expenditure on pious works and conspicuous consumption; *San Carlos Borromeo*, 97, 118.

27   (Caballero) AGN, Mercedes, 22, ff.79–80; Bienes Nacionales, 420, 7, ff.6–7; (Zuaznavar) AGN, Mercedes, 39, ff.138r–140v, 41, ff.22v–23r; Tierras, 109, 1, ff.1–12.

28   AGI, Contaduría, 691, 708; Almojarifazgo 10 percent Filipinas, 1605–6; Azogues, 1589–90; Escribanía, 171A, ff.170–176, 208v–224r, 543r; Silvio Zavala and Maria Castelo, *Fuentes para la historia del trabajo en Nueva España*, 8 vols. (México: Fondo de cultura económica, 1939–45), 4:464.

29   AGI, Escribanía, 171A, ff.161r, 272r–274r, 373r, 1358r; AGN, Bienes Nacionales, 56, 12, nos. 40–43, 54–55; AJUD, 1636–39, no. 7.

30   AGI, Escribanía, 171A, ff.1374, 1417.

31   Ibid., f.416v.

32   Ibid., ff.778–781, 1358–1359r; Barrett, *Sugar Haciendas*, 130; Riley, *Hacendados jesuitas*, 200; Berthe, "Xochimancas," 104–5 and n.46.

33   AGI, Escribanía, 171A, ff.2, 1110–11, 1121.

34   Ibid., f.2r.

35   Ibid., ff.1369–1374r.

36   Ibid., f.412v.

37   Ibid., f.1370.

38   De la Peña, *Oligarquía*, 39–41, 44; James Lockhart, "Capital and Province, Spaniard and Indian: The Example of Late Sixteenth Century Toluca," in *Provinces*, ed. Altman and Lockhart, 105.

39   De la Peña, *Oligarquía*, 44.

40   MacLachlan and Rodríguez, *Forging of the Cosmic Race*, 157; Taylor, "Town and Country," in *Provinces*, eds. Altman and Lockhart, 82.

41   Ursula Ewald, *Estudios sobre la hacienda colonial en México: Las propriedades rurales del colegio de Espíritu Santo en Puebla* (Wiesbaden: Steiner, 1976), 108. In Oaxaca, haciendas were usually less than 28.6 *caballerías* (3,000 acres) in size; in the early eighteenth century they sold from between 7,990 to 60,000 pesos, but most were sold for about 30,000 pesos. Taylor, *Landlord and Peasant*, 135, 200.

42   De la Peña, *Oligarquía*, 220–22; these entails included urban property. Gantes Tréllez, "Aspectos socios-economicos," 385. By the late colony 846 haciendas were counted for the whole viceroyalty.

43   Enrique Florescano, "Formation and Economic Structure of the Hacienda in New Spain," in *Cambridge History of Latin America*, ed. Bethell, 176–79, 181–82; de la Peña, *Oligarquía*, 220–22.

44   AGN, Mercedes, 22, f.281; 23, f.348; 25, f.203; 31, f.219; Civil, 400, 1, f.22r; AJUD, 1622–23; and 1623–24, no. 49, items 9–12, 26, 33.

45   AN, López de Rivera, 10 June 1633, f.68; 7 July 1633, ff.73–74; 5 August 1633, ff.82–83.

46 Ewald, *Estudios*, 15; Edith Boorstein Couturier, "Hacienda of Hueyápan: The History of a Mexican Social and Economic Institution, 1550–1940," Ph.D. diss., Columbia University, 1968, 46.

47 AGN, Mercedes, 26, ff. 152v, 157; Tierras, 81, ff. 42r–47r, 68r, 135r–137v, 315.

48 AGI, México 259; Tierras, 81, ff. 68r, 120, 264r–278v.

49 AGN, Mercedes, 26, f. 157; Tierras, 81, f. 295; Bienes Nacionales, 140, 29.

50 AN, Santillán, 7 January 1619, ff. 31v–32r; 21 July 1616 to 1618, ff. 37–39.

51 Ibid., 30 June 1618, ff. 267–70.

52 Ibid., 1620, ff. 164–66.

53 AGI, Contaduría, 695A, Almojarifazgo 10 percent Filipinas, 1595–96, Data, Extraordinario, 708, 1605–6.

54 AN, López Ahedo, April 1647, ff. 27r–28.

55 AGN, Mercedes, 49, ff. 2, 128–32v.

56 (Barainca) AN, de los Ríos, 1649; (Rodríguez Acevedo) see n. 50 herein; (Ontiveros Barrera, J.) AGN, Civil, 955, 2, ff. 8, 27–28; (Puerto), AN, Valdivieso, 3 June 1652, f. 441.

57 Jacques Heers, "La búsqueda de colorantes," *Historia mexicana* 11, no. 1 (July–September 1961): 5–6; Lee, "Cochineal Production," 452, 463–64.

58 Chevalier, *Land and Society*, 72–73; Heers, "La búsqueda de colorantes," 4; MacLeod, *Spanish Central America*, 179–80; Raymond Lee, "American Cochineal in European Commerce, 1526–1625," *Journal of Modern History* 23 (1951): 224.

59 Arcila Farías, *Comercio*, 38; MacLeod, *Spanish Central America*, 70, 73, 80, 87, 242, 235–36; Chevalier, *Land and Society*, 73.

60 Chaunu, *Séville*, 6:2:980–90. Figures for exports and evaluations refer to the annual average between the two dates specified. Figures for indigo are usually given in *libras;* in the following data, *libras* have been converted into *arrobas*, at the rate of 1 *arroba* for 25 *libras.*

61 AC 30:81.

62 AGI, México 4, 2 September 1638.

63 Lee, "American Cochineal," 206.

64 AGI, México 29, 31 March 1618; 31, 18 December 1634.

65 Lee, "Cochineal Production," 463; Taylor, *Landlord and Peasant*, 94.

66 De la Peña, *Oligarquía*, 66–71; Chevalier, *Land and Society*, 72; MacLeod, *Spanish Central America*, 235–36, 241; AGI, México 73, f. 11.

67 (Urrea) AN, López Ahedo, 4 September 1639, f. 131; 18 January 1641, f. 6; (Arlanzón) AGN, Civil, 237, 5, f. 25r; (Solarte) AJUD, 1630–31, no. 14; (Bribiesca) AGN, Bienes Nacionales, 132, 39; (Treviño) Hordes, "The Crypto-Jewish Community," 99–101; (Rossales) AN, Pérez Rivera, 18 May 1613, ff. 76r–68v. Cacao was measured in *cargas* (1 *carga* equalled 12 *arrobas*).

68 AGI, México 73, f. 13.

69 AGI, México 29, 30 March 1618, ff. 1v, 25v, 27v; AC 30:81.

70 AGI, México 261; Contaduría, 721, Préstamos, 1618–19; Islas Filipinas all the following: 728(1), 1626–27; 729(1), 1628–29; 729(2), 1629–30; 732, 1631–32; Contratación, Libro de registro, year 1630.

71 AGI, México 32, 28 September 1635, ff. 645–46.

72 Lee, "Cochineal Production," 469, and "American Cochineal," 219; Chaunu, *Séville*, 4:571–72.

73   AGI, México 29, 27 May 1620; 31, 18 December 1624; Lewis Hanke, ed., *Guía de las fuentes en el Archivo de Indias para el estudio de la administración virreinal española en México y en el Perú, 1535–1700*, 3 vols. (Vienna: Böhlau Verlag Köln, 1977), 3:284; AGI, México 34, 12 July 1638; 29, 30 March 1618, f.26v.

74   Chaunu, *Séville*, 4:572.

75   AGI, México 29, 8 November 1622; *Recopilación de leyes de los reynos de Indias*, 3 vols. (Madrid: Consejo de la hispanidad, 1943), 8:23:xvii.

76   AGI, México 32, 28 September 1635, f.646; AGN, Civil, 1737, no. 32, ff.3r–9r.

77   AGI, México 318, 12 December 1602; 25, 2 April 1602; Richard J. Salvucci, *Textiles and Capitalism in Mexico: An Economic History of the Obrajes, 1539–1840* (Princeton: Princeton University Press, 1987), 149, estimates it at 1,500,000 pesos, which I consider too high.

78   Salvucci, *Textiles and Capitalism*, 13, 29.

79   David M. Szewczyk, "New Elements in the Society of Tlaxcala, 1519–1618," in *Provinces*, ed. Altman and Lockhart, 146; Gibson, *Aztecs*, 243; John C. Super, "Querétaro: Society and Economy in Early Provincial Mexico," Ph.D. diss., University of California, 1973, 70, and "Querétaro Obrajes: Industry and Society in Provincial Mexico, 1600–1810," *Hispanic American Historical Review* 56, no. 2 (May 1976): 208; Jan Bazant, "Evolution of the Textile Industry of Puebla," *Comparative Studies in Society and History* 7 (October 1964): 68; Salvucci, *Textiles and Capitalism*, 11, 15, 103, 110, 114–16, 118–19. In 1597, the average number of loom in Puebla was 6.4 per *obraje*; five had ten or more. AGI, México 26, 23 June 1597.

80   Salvucci, *Textiles and Capitalism*, 43, 48.

81   AGI, Contaduría, 722, *Alcabalas encabezadas, México*; Kicza, *Colonial Entrepreneurs*, 202.

82   AJUD, 1609–11, no. 9, February 1607; AGN, Bienes Nacionales, 220, 1, ff.31–32, 37; AGI, Contratación, Libro de Registro, 1614.

83   (Esquivel) AGN, Inquisición, 359, 3, ff.114v, 139r; AGI, Contratación, Libros de Registro 1620, 1625, 1630; (Sánchez Cuenca) AGN, Inquisición, 417, 4; AN, López Ahedo, 5 September 1639, ff.120v–121r; (López Páramo, G.) AGN, Inquisición, 352, 1, f.11v; AN, Hernando Arauz, 28 July 1630, f.14; AGI, Contaduría, 733, Islas Filipinas, 1633–34; (Brizuela) AGI, México, 259; (Toledo) AJUD, 1631.

84   (Montemayor) AJUD, 1646–48, no. 2; AGI, Contratación, Libro de Registro, 1638; (Arellano) AJUD, 1654; (P. Lara) AJUD, 1632–35, items 95 and 99; (Gutiérrez Gil) AJUD, 1623–24, no. 49, item 15.

85   Woodrow Borah, *Silk Raising in Colonial Mexico*, Ibero-Americana 20 (Berkeley: University of California Press, 1943), 33–35, 76–78; Richard Greenleaf, "The Obraje in the Late Mexican Colony," *The Americas* 22 (January 1967): 231.

86   AGI, México 26, 10 May 1604, f.1; Salvucci, *Textiles and Capitalism*, 13.

87   AGI, Contaduría, 704, *Alcabalas encabezadas*, 1602–03; Escribanía de Cámara, 172B, *pieza* 5.

88   Salvucci, *Textiles and Capitalism*, 139.

89   (Díaz Posadas) Zavala and Castelo, *Fuentes*, 8:29–41 (1662); (Contreras) AC 26:170; Zavala and Castelo, *Fuentes*, 6:538 (1631); AGI, Contaduría, 742, Alcabalas encabezadas, 1648–49; AGN, Real Fisco, 22, 3; Civil, 355, 1, f.21r; (P. Sierra) Zavala and Castelo, *Fuentes*, 6:579; AGN, *Boletín* 11 (1940): 33–117; (Ansaldo) AGN, Civil, 355, 1, f.6; Zavala and Castelo, *Fuentes*, 8:58–59 (1665).

90 AGN, Civil, 355, 1, ff.6, 28–30, 38r, 53r, 77v, 90r, 268r. Salvucci, *Textiles and Capitalism*, 76–78, discusses certain aspects of this enterprise and brings the account into the eighteenth century.

91 Julia Bell Hirschberg, "A Social History of Puebla de Los Angeles, 1531–60," 2 vols., Ph.D. diss., University of Michigan, 1976, 201; Super, "Querétaro Obrajes," 203, and "Querétaro: Society," 61.

92 In 1592, the *obraje* of Gabriel de Angulo in Puebla was worth 5,755 pesos, not including the buildings and land; the most valuable item was the Indian workers. Guadalupe Albi Romero, "La sociedad de Puebla de los Angeles en el siglo XVI," *Jahrbuch* 7 (1970): 135–36.

93 (Sierra) AGN, Tierras, 1056, 5, ff.15r–19v.

94 AC 26:170; AGN, Inquisición, 22, 3, f.61.

95 Salvucci, *Textiles and Capitalism*, 39, 51–52, 60; de la Peña, *Oligarquía*, 88.

96 AGI, México 26, 23 June 1597.

97 De la Peña, *Oligarquía*, 225.

98 (De la Barrera, P.) AC 23:134; (Rivera, J. L.) AGI, Contratación, 773, 5, 1609; (Vásquez Medina) AJUD, 1632–35; (López Zarate and Picazo Hinojosa) AN, "Persons renting stores from Hospital Nuestra Señora de la Concepción," 1619, Shop 27; AGN, Bienes Nacionales, 531, 25, f.31; AC 34:478; and books 20–27 *passim*.

99 This conclusion is based on the property of ninety-four merchants in the following sources: AC, AJUD, AGN (Civil, Real Fisco, Bienes Nacionales, Vínculos, Tierras), AGI (México, Escribanía), and Guijo and Robles.

100 (Bribiesca) AGN, Civil, 1743, 3, ff.1–7; (Rodríguez de los Ríos) AGI, México 266; (De la Torre) AGI, México 263; Alejandra Moreno Toscano, ed., *Ciudad de México: Ensayo de Construcción de una Historia* (México: SEP-INAH, 1978), 93.

101 (Rodríguez Acevedo) AN, Santillán, June 1613, f.72; (Medina Reynoso) AGI, México 260; AC 16:77; (Gutiérrez Gil) AJUD, 1623–24, no. 49; (Ortiz Arévalo) AN, Juan de Porras, 23 December 1616, f.253r; Santillán, 1619, ff.29r, 36r, 77v, 92v; 17 August 1618, f.279v; 22 October 1616, f.19, and 13 December 1615, ff.33–36; Juan López de Rivera, 9 May 1625, ff.36–41; Cobián, 6 April 1620, ff.4–5; (Rivera, J. L.) AGI, Contratación, 773, 5, 1609; (Medina Orozco) AN, Pérez de Rivera, 7 December 1623, ff.20, 23; (Pérez Gallardo) AN, Valdivieso, 23 September 1652, ff.684–86r.

102 (Castellete) AGN, Bienes Nacionales, 220, 1, ff.36v–47r; (Salcedo) AGN, Tierras, 1720, 6, f.64v. All *censos* encountered were *censos redimibles*.

103 (Medina Reynoso) AC 16:177; 23:242; (Rossas) AC 20:278, 281; (Urrea) AGN, Tierras, 2802, 4, f.59; (Ramírez Vargas) AJUD, 1642–43; (Ruíz Orduñana) AC 23:206; AGN, Tierras, 2834, 4.

104 (Ontiveros Barrera) AGN, Bienes Nacionales, 8, 1, ff.9r–12r; AGI, México, 261; (Valdés) AN, López Ahedo, 24 August 1646, ff.49, 57–60, 73–74; 1647, ff.4, 11, 51, 72; 1648, ff.4, 18–19, 38–39, 48–49; 1649, f.1; AC 23:219, 242.

105 (Rodríguez de los Ríos) AGI, México 260, 266 (his son): AEA, "Testimonio de muerte de Baltasar Rodríguez de los Ríos", 25 November 1620, ff.78–118v; (Barroso) AGN, Bienes Nacionales, 549, 11; AN, Cobián, 27 March 1650, f.24; (Sánchez Olivera) AGN, Bienes Nacionales, 498, 9, ff.1–22r.

106 Hoberman, "Bureaucracy and Disaster," 214–15; Richard E. Boyer, "Mexico City and the Great Flood: Aspects of Life and Society, 1629–1635," Ph.D. diss., University of Connecticut, 1973, 38–61.

107   AC 20:279–80; 21:227; 31:97; AJUD, 1611; AGN, Tierras, 2834, 4.
108   Asunción Lavrin, "The Role of the Nunneries in the Economy of New Spain in the Eighteenth Century," *Hispanic American Historical Review* 46 (November 1966): 376.

IV   Public Office and Private Gain

1   Karen Spalding, ed., *Essays in the Political, Economic, and Social History of Colonial Latin America* (Newark: University of Delaware, 1982), vii–ix, xiv–xv, 31–32, 54.
2   Linda Arnold, "Bureaucracy and Bureaucrats in Mexico City: 1808–1824," M.A. thesis, University of Texas, Austin, 1975, 5–53; John L. Phelan, *The Kingdom of Quito in the Seventeenth Century: Bureaucratic Politics in the Spanish Empire* (Madison: University of Wisconsin Press, 1968), 119–46 *passim* and 166–74.
3   Haring, *The Spanish Empire*, 119–20, 129–35, 141–43, 168–71, 298–302, 310.
4   Arnold, "Bureaucracy and Bureaucrats," 37.
5   For salaries: AGI, México 27, 20 June 1608; 263 (1622) and 326 (1666); Indiferente 77 (1607); AGN, Vínculos 194; Vásquez de Espinosa, *Compendio*; Hanke, *Virreyes*, 3:91; Fernando Muro Romero, "La reforma del pacto colonial en Indias. Notas sobre instituciones de gobierno y sociedad en el siglo XVII," *Jahrbuch* 19 (1982): 66.
6   Domínguez Ortiz, "Los caudales de Indias," 324.
7   AGI, México 32, 25 September 1635, f.597r.
8   In this debate D. A. Nwasike, "Mexico City. Town Government, 1590–1650: Study in Aldermanic Background," Ph.D. diss., University of Wisconsin, 1972, 50, 59, and Aurora Flores Olea, "Los regidores de la ciudad de México en la primera mitad del siglo xvii," *Estudios de historia novohispana* 3 (1970): 163–72, represent the traditional view of the Mexico City *cabildo*.
9   De la Peña, *Oligarquía*, 144–49, and Manuel Álvarado Morales, "El cabildo y regimiento de la ciudad de Mexico en el siglo XVII: Un ejemplo de oligarquía criolla," *Historia mexicana* 28, no. 4 (April–June 1979): 497, represent the revisionist view, which stresses the diverse social and economic origins of the councilmen. For the limited number of *regidor*-merchants, see Hoberman, "Merchants," 481 and 482 n.11. For Puebla, Albi Romero, "La sociedad de Puebla," 102, emphasizes the struggle of the nouveau riche *obraje* owners to enter the *cabildo* and their lack of influence on its policies at the end of the sixteenth century. Gantes Tréllez, "Aspectos socios-económicos," 551, notes the presence of industrial and commercial fortunes among the *regidores*, but does not assess their relative influence.
10   AC 9–32 (1590–1643) *passim*; AGI, México 318, 1643–60, and now published in Enriqueta Vila Vilar and Justina Sarabia Viejo, eds., *Catálogo de cartas de cabildos hispanoamericanos: Audiencia de México (siglos XVI y XVII)* (Sevilla: Escuela de estudios hispanoamericanos, 1985), 136–56. De la Peña's account is based primarily on the *cabildo* in 1622, while this analysis looks at the entire 1590–1660 period.
11   José Toribio Medina, *Historia del tribunal del Santo Oficio de la inquisición en México* (México: Ediciones fuente cultural, 1952), 393–94; Hoberman, "Merchants," 497–98; Alberro (*Inquisición y sociedad*, 54) notes 20 merchants among the 144 familiars she documents between 1571 and 1646, but many others were also

merchants, such as Francisco de Arlanzón, and apparently were not so identified in her sources.

12 (Córdoba) AGI, Escribanía, 275B, ff.28–29r, 50–52r; Guijo, *Diario*, 1:8, 95, 175; (Alcocer) AC 17:140–41, 525–28; 26:177, 184; 30:61, 135–38; 32:12, and Louisa S. Hoberman, "City Planning in Spanish Colonial Government: The Response of Mexico City to the Problem of Floods, 1607–1637," Ph.D. diss., Columbia University, 1972, 105; AGI, Escribanía, 220c, and México 28, 24 May 1617, and 36, 24 September 1646; Medina, *Historia del tribunal*, 393–95; (Acosta) AHH, Consulado, 215, 6, ff.68–69, 73, 143–44.

13 Fabian de Fonseca and Carlos de Urrutia, *Historia general de la real hacienda*, 6 vols. (México: V. G. Torres, 1845–53), 2:295, 3:264–65; AGI, México 30, 21 January 1626, f.1v.

14 AGI, México 30, 21 January 1626, ff.8, 13v; Contaduría, 724, Solimán, 1621–22, and 738, Alumbre, 1643–45.

15 AGI, México 30, 21 January 1626, ff.11r–20r.

16 AGI, Contaduría, 697, Bulas, 1598–99; 714, Bulas, 1611–12.

17 Ibid., ff.8r–21v.

18 Maldonado's predecessor also had his brother, an elector of the *consulado*, sell *cruzada* goods for him in the capital. AGN, Bienes Nacionales, 416, 11, f.58r; 381, 1, f.9r; Guijo, *Diario*, 1:130–31.

19 AGI, México 30, 21 January 1626, ff.11r–18r.

20 AGI, México 24, 20 April 1600; 28, 24 May 1617; 31, 3 November 1632; Registro de Oficios, 1096, book 27; Contaduría, 739, Naipes, 1645–46.

21 AGI, México 30, 21 January 1626, ff.23v–24r; 35, 26 July 1640, f.11v; Registro de Oficios, 1096, book 27:5v–11v; Contaduría, 719, Bulas, 1616–17.

22 AGI, Contaduría, Naipes, 696, 1596–97 and 697, 1599–1600; 744, Naipes, 1651–52; Escribanía, 169A, f.256v; México 35, 6 June 1641 and June 1643.

23 AGI, Escribanía, 169A, ff.40v, 255r.

24 AGI, Indiferente de Nueva España, 77, 1607.

25 AGI, México 263; AC 18:184; 19:88–93.

26 AGI, México 30, 21 January 1626, f.8r.

27 AGI, México 31, 3 November 1632, f.18r.

28 Ibid., f.10r.

29 Ibid., f.9v.

30 Ibid., f.14.

31 AGI, México 31, 10 January 1634; 36, 1 June 1645, f.1.

32 AGI, México, Registro de Oficios, 1096, book 27, f.14.

33 AGI, México 36, 12 April 1648, f.1.

34 AGI, Contaduría, 750, Bulas, 1657–58.

35 AGN, Civil, 1835, 9, and n.12 herein.

36 AGI, México 36, 18 May 1647 and 12 April 1648.

37 AGI, México 36, 12 April 1648.

38 Villaseñor y Villaseñor, *Los condes de Santiago*, 299; Guijo, *Diario*, 1:59–60.

39 AGN, Civil, 1757, 1, f.7r.

40 Hanke, *Virreyes*, 3:323.

41 De la Peña, *Oligarquía*, 118–19; AGN, Tierras, 1272, ff.71r, 90v; AGI, México 38,

15 November 1659, ff.1v–2r; 17 December 1659, f.1r; 19 December 1659, f.1v; 19 December 1660, f.2r.

42   AGI, Contaduría, 719, Bulas, 1616–17; Hanke, *Virreyes*, 3:23.

43   AJUD, 1611.

44   AN, Pérez de Rivera, 6 and 17 September 1630.

45   AGI, Escribanía, 220C, ff.3v, 503r; México 32, 28 September 1635, f.613.

46   AGN, Bienes Nacionales, 549, 11.

47   AGI, Escribanía, 220C, *pieza* 5, ff.134–36; México 35, 26 July 1646.

48   AGI, Escribanía, 220C, ff.1–3r.

49   Ibid., ff.3v–4r.

50   Ibid., ff.3v, 505r.

51   Fonseca and Urrutia, *Historia*, 2:305.

52   AGI, Escribanía, 220C, f.503; México 35, 6 July 1641, and June 1643.

53   Conclusions about bonding activities are based on analysis of the *azogues* (mercury) and *alcances* (money still owed to treasury) sections of *contaduría* from 1619 to 1645. AGI, Contaduría, 728 (1) azogues, 1626–27; 739, alcances de cuentas, 1645–46. For treasury officials in seventeenth-century Peru, the bond was between 20,000 pesos and 40,000 pesos. Andrien, *Crisis and Decline*, 111.

54   AGI, Contaduría, Alcances de cuentas for the following: 722, 1619–20; and 732, 1632.

55   Likewise; the merchant Miguel López de Erenchun. AGI, Contaduría, 722, alcances and azogues, 1619–20; azogues for the following: 727, 1625–26; 728(1), 1626–27; 728(2), 1627–28; 729(1), 1628–29; and 729(2), 1629–30.

56   Other examples are Felipe Navarro y Atienza, Pedro Sánchez de Olivera, Antonio Urrutia de Vergara, Juan Francisco de Vertiz, and Salvador de Baeza. AGI, Contaduría, 722, alcances; 728(1), azogues; 732, alcances; 744, azogues, 1651–52.

57   AJUD, 1611; Hanke, *Virreyes*, 4:246; AGI, Contaduría, 722, alcances, 1619–20.

58   AGI, Contaduría, 701, azogues, 1601; 722, alcances, 1619–20; 727, azogues; María de los Angeles Romero, "Los intereses españoles en la Mixteca," *Historia Mexicana* 29 (October–December 1979): 248.

59   AGI, México, Registro de Oficios, 1097, book 29:292v–294r.

60   (Rodríguez de Acevedo) AN, López Ahedo, April 1647, ff.27r–28; (Arellano) AJUD, 1654; (Rodríguez de los Rios) AEA, "Testimonio . . . ," f.92v; (Cantabrana) Hanke, *Virreyes*, 4:233; (Pérez Passos) AN, Valdivieso, 4 November 1652, f.732; AGI, Contaduría, 722, Procedido de Oficios Vendibles, 1619–20.

61   Hoberman, "Elites and the Commercial Crisis," 7–8; AGI, Contaduría, Data, Préstamos for the following: 743, 1649–50; 748, 1654–55; 749, 1655–56. There is a Data for Préstamos for 748.

62   AGI, México 32, 28 September 1635, ff.573r, 615; 29 April 1636, ff.7, 17; Hanke, *Virreyes*, 3:299; Ismael Sánchez Bella, "Visitas a la audiencia de México (siglos XVI y XVII)," *Anuario de estudios americanos* 32 (1975): 384.

63   (Zuaznavar) Israel, *Race, Class, and Politics*, 167; AGI, Patronato, 221, ff.15–16; (Rodríguez de Acevedo) Hanke, *Virreyes*, 2:301; (Vásquez Medina) Ibid., 4:178.

64   AGI, Registro de Oficios, 1096, Book 27; Hanke, *Virreyes*, 4:46–47, 151.

65   Likewise, the wholesalers Simón Soria, José de Retes, and Joseph de Quesada. Hanke, *Virreyes*, 4:220, 232, 236, 241, 243, 246.

66   AGI, Escribanía, 275B, ff.29r–43r.

67   Ibid., f.32r.

68   Ibid., ff.90–95r; 275C, f.121r; Sánchez Bella considers San Milián to have been more competent than the *visitador* under whom he served, *fiscal* Gonzalo Suárez de San Martín. "Visitas," 395.

69   Spalding, *Essays*, 65.

V   *The Mercantilist Mirage*

1   Vicente Riva Palacios, ed., *México a través de los siglos* (México: Ballesca, 1887), 2:540–41, 546–47, 570–75, 579; Manuel Rivera Cambas, *Los governentes de México* (México: Privately printed, 1872), 1:181, 194, 268; Hubert H. Bancroft, *History of Mexico* (San Francisco: Privately printed, 1883), 3:19, 29–30, 42, 44; Israel, *Race, Class, and Politics*, 33–35, 50, 269–72; Manuel Álvarado Morales, *La ciudad de México ante la fundación de la Armada de Barlovento* (México: El colegio de México), 69–70, 87–89.

2   Altman and Lockhart, *Provinces*, 39–40, 50–51; Nwasike, "Mexico City Town Government," 68.

3   Israel, *Race, Class, and Politics*, 139–40, 151–62; Noel Stowe, "The Tumulto of 1624: Turmoil at Mexico City," Ph.D. diss., University of Southern California, 1970, 16, 382–83; Rosa Feijoo, "El tumulto de 1624," *Historia mexicana* 14 (July–August 1964): 62.

4   Bakewell, *Silver Mining*, 235–36; Álvarado Morales, *La ciudad de México*, 160–61.

5   Writers who argued for constitutional or popular checks in the 1590–1660 period were Mariana, Saavedra Fajardo, Rivadeneira, and Gudiel. John Elliott, *The Count-Duke of Olivares: The Statesman in an Age of Decline* (New Haven: Yale University Press, 1986), 481; Louisa Hoberman, "Hispanic American Political Theory as a Distinct Tradition," *Journal of the History of Ideas* 41, no. 2 (April–June 1980): 205; Álvarado Morales, *La ciudad de México*, 43–44 n.81 and 141. In *Spain's Empire*, 7, 9–11, 24–25, and 38, Colin MacLachlan discusses the unconventional ideas of Mariana, as well as the tension between "original consent" and extensive royal powers.

6   J. H. Elliott, "Spain and America in the Sixteenth and Seventeenth Centuries," in *Cambridge History of Latin America*, ed. Bethell, 1:317, 332; Richard Boyer, "Absolutism versus Corporatism in New Spain: The Administration of the Marquis of Gelves, 1621–1624," *International History Review* 4 (November 1982): 477–79, 490. Boyer's discussion of the strength of corporate groups and patronage systems (501) develops his earlier emphasis on the growing political power of the local elites in the seventeenth century ("Mexico," 474–76). Elliott, *Count-Duke of Olivares*, 562.

7   Diego de Encinas, *Cedulario indiano*, 4 vols. (Madrid: Ediciones cultura hispánica, 1945–46), 3:445–49; Chaunu, *Séville*, 1:246.

8   AGI, México 22, 4 October 1593, f.1.

9   AGI, México 35, 26 February 1645, f.8v.

10   *Recopilación*, Libro 8, Tít. 16, Ley vii.

11   Encinas, *Cedulario indiano*, 3:468, 471.

12   AGI, México 22, 9 March 1591, f.2; 24, 20 April 1600; Encinas, *Cedulario indiano*, 3:471; *Recopilación*, 8:16:xvii; Antonia Heredia Herrera, *Inventario de los fondos de consulados: Archivo General de Indias*, 2 vols. (Sevilla: Escuela de estudios hispanoamericanos, 1979), 2:374; Sánchez Bella, *La organización financiera*, 191 n.224.

13   AGI, México 24, 20 April 1600; AHH, Consulado, 791, 6, 1638.

14   AGI, México 22, 2 December 1590; Heredia Herrera, *Inventario*, 1:693, 2:93; *Recopilación*, 8:15:xxvii, xviii.

15   Encinas, *Cedulario indiano*, 4:200–201.

16   Veitia Linaje, *Notre de la contratación*, Libro 2, Cáp. 7, Núm. 19.

17   Ibid., Núm. 20.

18   AGI, México 27, 6 March 1608; 17 December 1608; 21 January 1609; 29 May 1609.

19   AGI, México 22, 4 October 1593, f.1.

20   AC 11:157, 162.

21   I. A. A. Thompson, *War and Government in Hapsburg Spain, 1560–1620* (London: Athlone Press, 1976), 256–58; Sánchez Bella, *La organización financiera*, 206.

22   TePaske and Klein, "Seventeenth-Century Crisis," 135.

23   AC 13:246; 14:149, 160, 163, 324–25.

24   AC 21:42, 53; AGI, México 34, 12 July 1638, ff.117, 122, 164, 171; 33, 21 January 1632, f.483r.

25   AGI, México 24, 10 April 1601, ff.1, 3v, 6r; AC 21:28, 65.

26   AGI, México 330, 1635; 24, 10 April 1601, f.3r; Jesús Silva Herzog, ed., *Documentos relativos al arrendamiento del impuesto o renta de alcabalas* (México: Secretaría de hacienda y crédito público, 1945), 102; AC 18:363.

27   AGI, México 24, 10 April 1601, f.5r; 22, 30 March 1594, f.1; 33, 21 January 1632, ff.400v–401r, 541r; AC 21:31; 22:40, 66.

28   AC 32:260.

29   AC 14:245; 21:10, 296.

30   AGI, México 24, 10 April 1601, f.4v. The *alcabala de forastería* was paid on all goods brought into Mexico City, whether these goods came from Europe, Asia, other regions of the Indies, or New Spain outside the city limits. The agents might themselves be residents or nonresidents. The important point was that they were not acting on their own account. The *alcabala de vecindad* was paid by persons assumed to be *vecinos* selling on their own account most local or imported goods. It was divided among all the guilds within the city (*consulado*, silkweavers, shoemakers) and also paid by individual taxpayers who did not belong to a guild. The *alcabala de viento* was paid by persons selling such goods as silk worked up in the capital or lengths of other kinds of cloth which had not already been included in *forastería*, livestock and meat, mortgages and real estate, auctioned goods, slaves, wine and vinegar sold in taverns, and wares sold on the street.

31   AC 14:244.

32   AC 14:363; 18:363.

33   Robert S. Smith, "Sales Taxes in New Spain, 1575–1770," *Hispanic American Historical Review* 28 (February 1948): 1; Silva Herzog, *Documentos*, 14.

34   Fred Bronner, "La unión de armas en el Perú: Aspectos políticos-legales," *Anuario de estudios americanos* 24 (1967): 1134; Israel, *Race, Class, and Politics*, 179; AC 26:358; Elliott, *Count-Duke of Olivares*, 65–66, 90–93, 105, 193.

35   AC 26:369.

36   AC 27:7–14; Elliott, *Count-Duke of Olivares*, 96–97, 149, 159–60.

37   AC 26:380–81.

38   AC 27:3–21, 95, 105; AGI, México 30, 26 January 1630, f.4.

39   AC 27:266; AGI, México 31, 3 November 1632, f.1.

40   There is no record of arrears for the 1633 through 1637 period in the later lawsuits against Barroso. The *contaduría* accounts are not extant for August 1632 to June 1636, and the November 1636–July 1637 entry shows income of 123,424 pesos from the card tax in the Mexico City treasury. John J. TePaske, *La real hacienda de Nueva España: La real caja de México (1576–1816)* (México: Instituto nacional de antropología e historia, 1976), 5731, 5733.

41   Silva Herzog, *Documentos*, 15.

42   AGI, México 31, 18 December 1634, f.1.

43   AC 30:170; Bibiano Torres Ramírez, *La Armada de Barlovento* (Sevilla: Escuela de estudios hispanoamericanos, 1981), 1–34, 37–38, 57, 71–73. In the late sixteenth century, in 1646, and again after the English occupation of Jamaica in 1655, the *Armada* was also to patrol the Greater Antilles. Torres Ramírez's study is based on official correspondence and *consultas* (reports) of Spanish officials and on the treasury account totals, whereas that by Álvarado Morales uses principally the Mexico City *cabildo* records. This analysis draws on the *cabildo* records, viceregal correspondence, lawsuits and internal fiscal records, and it emphasizes the role of the merchants, as opposed to the Crown and *cabildo*.

44   AGI, México 31, 2 May 1636, f.18; AC, 30:216–17, 251–54, 266.

45   Torres Ramírez, *Armada de Barlevento*, 37–38, 43–68.

46   AGI, México 31, no month, 1636.

47   Elliott, *Count-Duke of Olivares*, 439–40, 481, 538–39. A minority of *regidores*, led by *procurador* Andrés Balmaceda, continued to oppose the taxes chosen.

48   AC 30:191–92; 175; 215; AHH, Consulado, 213, 13, nos. 1, 5, 9.

49   AGI, México 31, 1636; AC 30:263–65.

50   Álvarado Morales, *La ciudad de México*, 46, 169, 251–52. On 30 January 1636, Fernando Carrillo had proposed ending the wine/oil subsidy to clergy, estimated to bring in 50,000 pesos.

51   Torres Ramírez, *Armada de Barlovento*, 222; AC 30:207–17, 239–42, 251–54.

52   AGI, México 33, 23 February 1638, f.121r; AC 30:217; 31:25–26, 233.

53   AC 30:241; 31:264, 32:40; AGI, México 34, 12 July 1638, f.238.

54   AC 31:28–29. John J. TePaske and Herbert Klein, *Ingresos y egresos de la Real Hacienda de Nueva España* (México: INAH, 1986), Acapulco, S897–906A, Veracruz, S884B–887.

55   AGI, México 31, 3 November 1632, f.1; 10 January 1634; 33, 27 July 1637; Escribanía 220c, *pieza* 5 (25 January 1641), ff.2v, 502v; Hanke, *Virreyes*, 3:279; AC 32:21–25.

56   AGI, México 35, 6 July, 6 December 1641; AC 32:40, 61.

57   AC 31:96.

58 AGI, México 33, 22 July 1637, ff. 113v–114r; MacLeod, *Spanish Central America*, 242, 441 n.24; AC 25:204 and 26:343; 30:195–202, 266.

59 AGI, México 34, 12 July 1638.

60 AGI, México 33, 23 February 1638, f. 121v; 34, 12 July 1638; 75, ramo 4, 2 September 1638, f. 190; AC 31:49–57, 207, 263–65.

61 AC 31:266.

62 Ibid., 265.

63 Ibid., 357; 33:466.

64 AGI, México 29, 27 May 1620; AC 31:267–68; Álvarado Morales, *La ciudad de México*, 166, 108.

65 AGI, México 35, 14 September 1639, f. 1.

66 AC 31:282; AGI, México, 330, f. 19r; Silva Herzog, *Documentos*, 11, 17.

67 AGN, Civil, 11 October 1639, f. 21v; AGI, México 33, 21 January 1632, ff. 371v, 394v.

68 AC 30:181–82; 31:383, 331, 334–35; 32:245, 259; AHH, Consulado, 685, 2.

69 AC 32:69–74; 33:245, 259; AGN, Bienes Nacionales, 209, 26.

70 AC 30:213; 31:238, 258, 319; AGI, México 33, cuadro II, 23 February 1638, f. 122r; 35, 7 December 1639; 35, 28 March 1643, f. 6v.

71 AGI, México 33, 19 July 1638, ff. 194–98; AC 31:15–16, 242, 249.

72 Hanke, *Virreyes*, 4:64; Torres Ramírez, *Armada de Barlovento*, 44–46, 228–32; AC 32–33:383.

73 Álvarado Morales, *La ciudad de México*, 203.

74 Hanke, *Virreyes*, 76; AC 33:488, 494; AGI, México 75, r.4, f.2r.

75 AHH, Consulado, 213, 12, 1635–66, f.3r; see also, Silva Herzog, *Documentos*, 3r.

76 AGI, México 37, 14 November 1653.

77 Ibid.

78 AGI, México 38, 21 May 1659; Silva Herzog, *Documentos*, 95 (s f.6r in document).

79 These figures are the total of the following taxes: *caxa de México: Armada de Barlovento; Armada de Barlovento y seno mexicano;* 2 percent of *alcabalas encabezadas;* 2 percent of *la real Armada de Barlovento; consulado de México;* 2 percent of *del consulado de México para Armada de Barlovento;* 2 percent of *alcabalas de 4 cabezón; caxa de Veracruz* and *Acapulco:* 1 percent of *Armada de Barlovento.* The first two categories include both the 2 percent sales tax increase from Mexico City and various other funds. TePaske, *Real hacienda*, S734–49; and TePaske and Klein, *Ingresos y egresos*, Acapulco, S897–906A; Veracruz, S884A–887. Torres Ramírez, *Armada de Barlovento*, 233, 236–37, estimates that *Armada* proceeds from all Circum Caribbean regions totaled about 100,000 pesos annually from 1636 to 1642 and about 141,494 pesos annually for 1647 through 1655, the latter increase due to the receipt of funds from previously delinquent regions.

80 Torres Ramírez, *Armada de Barlovento*, 71, 229, 235.

81 Ibid., 239–43; AGI, México 36, 2 October 1645; 33, 22 July 1637, f. 113v; 35, 28 March 1643, f.3v; 35, 21 February 1645, f. 1r; Gantes Tréllez, "Aspectos socioseconómicos," 109–13.

82 Schurz, *Manila Galleon*, stood alone until the 1960s, when Chaunu, *Les Philippines et le Pacifique des Ibériques* (Paris: SEVPEN, 1960) appeared. TePaske, "New World Silver," 433–39; TePaske and Klein, "Seventeenth-Century Crisis," 131–34; and Hoberman, "Merchants," 490–93, also stress the impact of the Philippine trade.

83   Schurz, *Manila Galleon*, 155; TePaske, "New World Silver," 10; *Recopilación*,
     9:45:6 and 15; Antonio José Álvarez de Abreu, *Extracto historial del expediente . . .*
     sobre la forma en que se ha de hacer y continuar el comercio de los texidos de China . . .
     (Madrid: Juan de Ariztia, 1736), 1v.

84   *Recopilación*, 9:45:1, 5, and 66. Álvarez de Abreu, *Extracto historial*, 1v, 2v;
     Borah, *Early Colonial Trade*, 118–19; Schurz, *Manila Galleon*, 180–81.

85   AGI, México 22, [25 February] 1593; 23, 4 August 1597; 24, January 1598; AC
     11:177, 13:88.

86   Heredia Herrera, *Inventario*, 2:121; Chaunu, *Séville*, 3:366, 4:346; Schurz, *Manila
     Galleon*, 405–6.

87   AC 16:212–13; Borah, *Early Colonial Trade*, 126; Israel, *Race, Class, and Politics*,
     100; AGI, México 26, 28 October 1606, f.4.

88   Guice, "Consulado," 45–46; AC 17:342; *Recopilación*, 9:45:78; Borah, *Early Colo-
     nial Trade*, 127; AGI, México 28, 1 September 1610.

89   TePaske, "New World Silver," 35–38; Chaunu, *Séville*, 4:541; Céspedes del Cas-
     tillo, *La avería*, appendix 3, 168; Álvarez de Abreu, *Extracto historial*, 15v; Borah,
     Early Colonial Trade, 127; AC 25:58, 296 and 26:254; AGI, México, Registro de
     Oficios, 1095, book 22:67.

90   AGI, México 318, April 1634, and 1635; AC 30:208; AHH, Consulado, 213, 73; AGI,
     México 33, 1 December 1636; 22 July 1637, f.19v; 34, 12 July 1638, ff.301–302r;
     México, 4(1636); Juan Grau y Monfalcon, "Relación del procurador general de la
     ciudad de Manila . . . 1635," *Colección de documentos inéditos relativos al descu-
     brimiento . . .*, 42 vols. (Madrid: Ministro de ultramar, 1864–84), 6:413; Vila Vilar
     and Sarabia Viejo, *Catálogo de cartas*, 132.

91   AC 32:171, 33:448; AHH, Consulado, 213, 12; AGI, México 4, 12 March 1642; 36,
     10 August 1651; 36, October 1645; 76, r.3, 1645; 322, 1655.

92   AGI, México 25, 21 March 1603, ff.1–4; 26, 9 January 1604; 27, 24 May 1609,
     ff.2v–3r; 28, 25 May 1616; 29, 16 June 1622; 31, 10 January 1634; 34, 12 July
     1638; Hoberman, "Merchants," 489.

93   AGI, México 22, 10 March 1592; 24, January 1598; 27, 24 May 1609; 34, 12 July
     1638, ff.308–309r; Hoberman, "Merchants," 491.

94   Schurz, *Manila Galleon*, 350, 355–56.

95   Hoberman, "Merchants," 490.

VI   Progeny and Prosperity

1   Guijo, *Diario*, 1:169, 197; 2:21; Antonio Robles, *Diario de sucesos notables, 1665–
     1703*, 3 vols. (México: Porrua, 1972), 1:241; Chevalier, *Land and Society*, 179;
     Israel, *Race, Class, and Politics*, 127 n.64. The fortunes of Viceroy Velasco's son-
     in-law, *contador* don Alonso Camargo, and Archbishop Manso are discussed in
     Hoberman, "Elites in Seventeenth-Century Mexico," 18, as well as that of Nicolás
     Villanueva (Albi Romero, "La sociedad de Puebla," 112).

2   Brading, *Miners and Merchants*, 102.

3   (Sánchez Arías) AGI, Contratación, 1627; (Sánchez Olivera) AGN, Bienes Nacio-
     nales, 498, 9; (Cerralde) AGN, Inquisición, 517, f.65.

4   Thomas Calvo, "Familles mexicaines au XVIIe siècle: Une tentative de reconstitu-

tion," *Annales de démographie historique* (1984): 169; Hoberman, "Conclusion," in *Cities and Society*, 327.

5   See Bonilla Bastida, Salcedo, and Vera in "Financially Successful Families," pp. 241–45, 247–49.

6   Ladd, *Mexican Nobility*, 73; (Bribiesca Roldán) AGN, Civil, 1743, 3, f. 1; (Ortiz de Arevalo) Villaseñor y Villaseñor, *Los condes de Santiago*, 212. The entrails of Baltasar Rodríguez de los Ríos (AGI, México, 260; AEA, "Testimonio," nos. 26, 31–34, 38–41) and Urrutia de Vergara (Villaseñor y Villaseñor, *Los condes de Santiago*, 292) are other examples.

7   De la Peña, *Oligarquía*, 220; Albi Romero, "La sociedad de Puebla," 112.

8   (León Castillo) AN, de los Ríos, 10 July 1646, f. 94; (Gutiérrez Gil) AJUD, 1623–24; (Rossal) Robles, *Diario*, 1:177 and 2:11; (Cantabrana) Fernández de Recas, *Mayorazgos*, 325; (Fernández Celi) AGN, Bienes Nacionales, 547, 2, ff. 51–54r; (Millán, F.) Guijo, *Diario*, 1:143; Robles, *Diario*, 1:3, lists Félix as elected *alcalde ordinario*, a post previously held by his father, Antonio, who was also *regidor* (Guijo, *Diario*, 2:129, 131); (Gática) Vila Vilar and Sarabia Viejo, *Catálogo de cartas*, 151, 154; (López Erenchun) AGI, México, Registro de Oficios, 1085, book 22:127–30; (Medina Reynoso) AGI, México, 147 (son Fernando).

9   Socolow, *Merchants of Buenos Aires*, 103.

10   AGI, México 27, 24 May 1609, f. 1v.

11   Hoberman, "Elites in Seventeenth-Century Mexico," 18; Bronner, *Urban Society*, 38, notes the studies which discuss how inheritance laws could be circumvented (one approach was to direct children into the Church); Paul Ganster, "La familia Gómez de Cervantes: Linaje y sociedad en el México colonial," *Historia mexicana* 31 (October–December 1981): 208; John Frederick Schwaller, "Tres familias mexicanas del siglo xvi," ibid., 175.

12   Lavrin, "Role of the Nunneries," 374–75; Paul Ganster, "Churchmen," in Hoberman and Socolow, *Cities and Society*, 146.

13   (Montemayor) AJUD, 1646–48; (Cerralde, viejo) AN, de los Ríos, 22 May 1659: (Guerra Chacón) AJUD, 1669.

14   (González Fuente) AGN, Bienes Nacionales, 420, 22; (Fernández Celi) Hoberman, "Merchants," 501; (Millán) AGN, Tierras, 1272, ff. 118–127; Bienes Nacionales, 381, 1, f. 16r; (Molina Mosquera) Asunción Lavrin, "Female Religious," in Hoberman and Socolow, *Cities and Society*, 170; (Urrea) AGN, Tierras, 2802, 4.

15   (Caballero) AGN, Bienes Nacionales, 420, 7, ff. 1, 14r; John Frederick Schwaller, *The Church and Clergy in Sixteenth-Century Mexico* (Albuquerque: University of New Mexico Press, 1987), 112, 126.

16   Lavrin, "Female Religious," 170.

17   (Lorenzana) Josefina Muriel de la Torre, *Conventos de monjas en la Nueva España* (México: Editorial Santiago, 1946), 1:86, 89; Guijo, *Diario*, 1:4; AGN, Bienes Nacionales, 221, 8 and 221, 9.

18   (Zuaznavar) AC 32:471–73; (Haro) Guijo, *Diario*, 2:36; AGN, Bienes Nacionales, 256, 1, ff. 118–20 and 658, 5.

19   (Acosta) AHH, Consulado, 215, 6, ff. 68–69, 118–19; (Rodríguez del Vado) Bienes Nacionales, 269, 9; AC 17:204, 18:415–16; (Rivera, J. L.) AGI, Contratación, 773, 5, 1609; (Castellete) Hoberman, "Merchants," 502; Richard Greenleaf, "The In-

quisition Brotherhood: Cofradía de San Pedro Mártir of Colonial Mexico," *Americas* 40 (October 1983): 172.

20   (Ruíz) AGI, Contaduría, 726, 1624–25; 727, 1625–26; 732, 1632–33; all Extraordinario.

21   The data about offspring marriage partners comes from GSU, Marriage Information, 1624–75; Marriages, 1621–25; and Deaths, 1671–79; as well as from the sources listed in table 22. Information about *compadrazgo* comes from GSU, Baptisms: 1590–1602. All GSU material is from registers of Spaniards, Iglesia Catedral, Parroquía de Asunción Sagrario.

22   GSU, Baptisms of Spaniards, Catedral, (López Flandes) 8 September 1591; (Sánchez Herrera) 3 May 1590, 27 February 1592; (Valdés) 7 October 1601, 24 September 1602.

23   AGI, México 75, 29 July 1632, and 260; AGN, Vínculos, 194, ff.238r, 250r. The charge by his brother-in-law that don Nicolás spent his entire inheritance refers to cash and is probably exaggerated. Alberro, *Inquisición y sociedad*, 66.

24   AGN, Inquisición 417, f.380r; Vínculos, 194, ff.28v–48, 94, 174v; Robles, *Diario*, 1:243; Villaseñor y Villaseñor, *Los condes de Santiago*, 10, is incorrect when he states that don Cristóbal and doña Gertrudis were don Nicolás's only children; AGN, Inquisición 417, f.380v.

25   Villaseñor y Villaseñor, *Los condes de Santiago*, 292–307.

27   AGN, Tierras, 1720, 6, f.83; Bienes Nacionales, 518, 6, ff.2, 83, 86–93; AN, López Ahedo, 31 January 1648, ff.2–3.

28   AGI, Contaduría, 744, Naipes, 1651–52; Registro de Oficios, 1096, book 27; Fernández de Recas, *Mayorazgos*, 219–20; Robles, *Diario*, 1:87; AEA, Hacienda. Censos, 1, 2, ff.120–24.

29   AGN, Inquisición, 294, 1, f.6; 589, 5, ff.170–71.

30   AGN, Vínculos, 229, f.348r; Tierras, 109, 1, ff.1v–12r.

31   AC 16:451; AGN, Vínculos, 284, ff.23v and 242r.

32   AGI, México 260.

33   AGN, Vínculos, 284, ff.259r, 362, 456v; Fernández de Recas, *Mayorazgos*, 23; AGI, Contaduría, 2794.

34   AGN, Inquisición, 399, 14, ff.8r, 25v, 36r; AJUD, 1602–5; AHH, Consulado, 791, 7; AGI, Contaduría, Almojarifazgo 10 percent Filipinas, 709(1), 1606–7; AN, López Ahedo, 29 April 1643, ff.37–40; Schwaller, *Church and Clergy*, 130, 213, 216, 219.

35   AGN, Real Fisco, 30, 1; AN, de los Ríos, 10 July 1646, f.94.

36   AGN, Bienes Nacionales, 387, 5, ff.1–11, ff.14v–35, 95, 215v, 370v, 383r, 389r.

37   AGN, Inquisición, 359, 3, ff.11, 102r, 125.

38   AJUD, 1636–39, no. 7; AGN, Bienes Nacionales, 56, 12, nos. 35, 39–44, 47–55.

39   AGN, Bienes Nacionales, 381, 17.

40   AGN, Bienes Nacionales, 381, 1, f.16r; Tierras, 1272, ff.126r, 139r, 159r, 253r.

41   AGN, Tierras, 1272, 1, ff.61, 125v, 136–37, 159r, 285–86, 296, 542–43; Bienes Nacionales 381, 1, f.17.

42   AGN, Tierras, 1272, 1, f.137r.

43   Ibid., ff.126r, 159r, 221.

44   AGN, Bienes Nacionales, 378, 2, part 1, f.71; part 2, f.80.

45   AGI, México 260; AJUD, 1629–30, no. 1; University of Texas, Castañeda Collection, Fundación del mayorazgo que impusieron don Francisco de Medina Reynoso y doña Juana de Angulo, su legitima mujer, 1638, ff.119–20; AGI, Registro de Oficios, 1095, book 22:27–28.
46   AJUD, 1629–30, no. 1; AC 25:141; AGI, México 147.
47   AN, Santillán, January 1619, ff.5–7; AGI, México 260; AJUD, 1629–30, no. 1; Fernández de Recas, *Mayorazgos*, 171.
48   AGI, Contaduría, Almojarifazgo 10 percent Filipinas, 695B, 1592–94; 697, 1599–1600; 708, 1605–6; Indiferente de Nueva España, 77; AC, 20:217–21, and 21:194–98; AGI, México, Registro de Oficios, 1095, book 2:131; AJUD, 1656–59; AN, Cobián, 31 January 1655, f.228.
49   AJUD, 1656–59; AC 32:441; Guijo, *Diario*, 1:165.
50   Guijo, *Diario*, 1:165; AGI, México, Registro de Oficios, 1098, book 31:295r–298r; Contaduría, 750, Bulas, 1657–58; AJUD, 1656–59.
51   Guijo, *Diario*, 1:198; AGN, Tierras, 108, 2, f.2v; Tierras, 162, 1, f.4r.
52   AGN, Tierras, 162, 1, f.196r.
53   Ibid., ff.143v, 187r–188r.
54   Ibid., ff.151r–163, 201v–202r.
55   Ibid., ff.171r–196v.
56   AGN, Tierras, 108, 2, f.2v, 90r; Tierras, 141, 1; Tierras, 162, 1, 4r, 330r–332v, 434r; Tierras, 141, 1.

Conclusion

1   Figure 4 (p. 88) covers income from 1634 to 1660, because 1631 to 1632 and 1661 to 1662 were not available and the graph presents a two year moving average.
2   This can be seen by comparing the number of investors in table 1 (p. 36) with the value of the cargo in appendix A, table 2, column 9, note a, second paragraph. For the reasons discussed there, the total value of trade in table 2 is undercounted, especially for the 1630s. The per capita data refers to all the shippers, not just the merchant electors.
3   See chapter 2, n.35.
4   Henry Kamen, *Spain in the Later Seventeenth Century, 1665–1700* (London: Longman, 1980), 131, 145; Boyajian, *Portuguese Bankers*, 99, 133–38, 163, 179.
5   Vila Vilar, *Hispanoamérica y el comercio*, 170 n.48.
6   Ibid., 158–59, 169, 172, 181; TePaske, "La politica española," 65–66; Fortune, *Merchants and Jews*, 27, 105–10; Arcila Farías, *Comercio*, 52–55; Cornelius C. Goslinga, *The Dutch in the Caribbean and on the Wild Coast, 1580–1680* (Assen: Van Gorcum, 1971), 345–62.
7   Boyajian, *Portuguese Bankers*, 145, states that 11 million ducats (15,070,000 pesos at 1.375 pesos to the ducat) were exported from the Iberian peninsula above the total amount of official bullion receipts registered in Seville during the same period; TePaske, "New World Silver," 441 (table 1); Álvarado Morales, *La ciudad de México*, 109; Kamen, *Spain*, 138–39; MacLeod, "Spain and America: The Atlantic Trade, 1492–1720," in *Cambridge History of Latin America*, ed. Bethell, 1:370.

8   Smith, "Sales Tax"; Silva Herzog, *Documentos*, 11; AGI, México 34, 7 November 1637; Escribanía de Cámara, 176B, *pieza* 4.

9   AGI, México 318, 12 December 1602; 28, 11 June 1612; 32, 3 November 1636; Salvucci, *Textiles and Capitalism*, 146, 150.

10   Riley, *Hacendados jesuitas*, 33. The Chicomocelo mill doubled in area between 1668 and 1690; Sandoval, *La industria del azúcar*, 48–51, 62, 78–85; Chevalier, *Land and Society*, 79.

11   Vila Vilar and Sarabia Viejo, *Catálogo de cartas*, 144.

12   AGI, Escribanía, 171A, ff.2, 1374r; Álvarado Morales, *La ciudad de México*, 102; Berthe, "Xochimancas," 103. Chevalier states that in comparison with the late sixteenth century, sugar prices fell or stabilized at between 2.5 and 5.0 pesos to the *arroba* in the seventeenth century; *Land and Society*, 78.

13   Richard Garner, "Price Trends in Eighteenth-Century Mexico," *Hispanic American Historical Review* 65, no. 2 (May 1985): 286.

14   These were the prices for *grana del marquesado*. *Grana mixteca* sold for higher prices but followed the same pattern. *Grana silvestre* sold for much less and was rarely exported. AGI, Contratación, Libros de Registro.

15   Albi Romero, "La sociedad de Puebla," 96; Álvarado Morales, *La ciudad de México*, 66 n.42.

16   There were usually twenty brokers in any year between 1623 and 1640, and the cost of a license ranged between a maximum of 2,900 pesos (1623) to 2,500 pesos (1640). AC 24:372; 25:225; 27:37; 31:325; 32:16. In 1598, there were eighteen brokers, who apparently paid only 300 pesos for the license. AC 13:253.

17   Rees, *Transportes*, 24, 27, 58.

18   Romero, "Los intereses españoles," 243–50.

19   Wallerstein, *Modern World-System*, 2:7, 25, 33.

20   Fernand Braudel, *The Mediterranean and the Mediterranean World at the Age of Philip II* (New York: Harper Torchbook, 1975), 2:725–33; Jan de Vries, *The Economy of Europe in an Age of Crisis, 1600–1750* (Cambridge: Cambridge University Press, 1976), 215–20, 234.

21   Wallerstein, *Modern World-System*, 2:7; DuPlessis, "The Partial Transformation," 21.

22   Robert Lopez, "The Trade of Medieval Europe: The South," in *Cambridge Economic History of Europe* (Cambridge: Cambridge University Press, 1952), 2:330; C. H. Wilson, "Trade, Society, and the State," in ibid. (1967), 4:491; Pierre Jeanin, *Merchants of the Sixteenth Century* (New York: Harper and Row, 1972), 35.

23   Assadourian, *El sistema de la economía colonial*, 291.

24   Fernando Muro Romero, "El 'beneficio' de oficios públicos con jurisdicción en Indias," *Anuario de estudios americanos* 35 (1978): 31–32.

25   Ibid., 27; Fred Bronner, "Tramitación legislativa bajo Olivares: La redacción de los arbitrios de 1631," *Revista de Indias* 41, no. 165 (July–December 1981): 424.

26   Muro Romero, "El 'beneficio,'" 40–41, and "La reforma," 55, 58; Sánchez Bella, "Visitas," 396; Domínguez Ortiz, "Comercio y blasones," 221.

27   Hoberman, "Hispanic American Political Theory," 201.

28   Irving Leonard, *Baroque Times in Old Mexico*, 2nd ed. (Ann Arbor: University of Michigan Press, 1966), 32, 37, 45.

29   Ibid., 51.

Glossary

All Spanish words are translated the first time they appear in the text. The glossary contains only those words of particular importance for merchants, trade, and taxation.

alcabala de forastería: sales tax paid by agents of nonresident merchants

alcabala de vecindad: sales tax paid by persons selling on their own account

alcabala de viento: sales tax paid by persons selling certain types of goods

alcalde de las cárceles secretos: officer of the prison of the Inquisition

alcalde mayor: district governor and magistrate, see *corregidor*

alguacil mayor desta corte: senior constable of the high court

almojarifazgo: import-export tax

apartador de oro: assayer of gold

Armada de Barlovento: squadron of twelve warships and two to three support craft to patrol western Caribbean

arroba: unit of dry measure equalling twenty-five pounds

audiencia: high court

avería: convoy tax

avío: credit, cash, or goods provided to an enterprise

balansario: official who weighed silver bar at mint and had quinto removed

braceaje: mint director's tax on coined silver

bulas de santa cruzada: papal indulgences sold to support war against infidels, collected for Crown

caballería: approximately 105 acres of farmland

cabildo: city council

cajero: manager for, apprentice of, a merchant

cajonero: owner of a wooden store or market stall with straw or shingle roof; retailer

capellanía: chantry fund, a type of pious work established by a private party in a church; interest from a mortgage imposed on the donor's property supported the cleric.

capital: property husband has at time of marriage

carga: unit of dry measure equalling 300–330 pounds

cargadores: merchants trading overseas, reputed to be agents of peninsular traders

casa de contratación: house of trade

casa de fundición: foundry

casa de moneda: mint

casas principales: chief residence, mansion; sometimes place of business on lower floors

censo: long term loan secured by a lien imposed on real property; could be redeemable or perpetual

compadrazgo: ritual co-parenthood

consulado: merchant guild

contador: accountant of royal treasury or other organization

contador mayor de cuentas: senior accountant in the tribunal of accounts

converso: recent convert to Christianity; sometimes a secret Jew

corregidor: district governor and magistrate

correo mayor: postmaster general

criado: salaried manager for a merchant

cruzada: see bulas de cruzada

depositario general: public trustee and member of city council

depósito: short-term loan

desagüe: drainage canal of the valley of México

diezmo: royal tax of one-fifth on silver paid by miners; ecclesiastical tithe

dueño de tienda: shopowner

ejidos: city common lands (forest and pasture)

en administración: a tax collected by royal treasury officials

en asiento: a tax collected by a corporation or private individual

encabezamiento: lump-sum payment of a tax by a corporation

encomendero: merchant's agent receiving a commission; recipient of a royal grant of Indian tributes

en reales: cash

ensayador y fundidor: assayer of silver bar who brought it to correct fineness

escribano: notary

escribano mayor de cámara de lo civil: chief notary of the civil division of the high court

factor: merchant's salaried agent; also, business manager of royal treasury office

familiar: informer for the Inquisition

fiador: bondsman

fiscal: Crown attorney

género noble: luxury trade good

hacienda de minas: mining enterprise

huipil: overblouse, made and worn by Indian women

indultos: royal pardons

ingenio: water-powered sugar mill

intereses: profits from a tax farm

junta de hacienda: finance council composed of the viceroy, senior *oidor* and *fiscal*, treasury officials, and senior accountant of the tribunal of accounts

junta general: junta de hacienda plus representatives of the *consulado, cabildo,* and clergy

libra: unit of dry measure equalling one pound

libranza: letter of credit

libro de registro: ship manifest

legítima: child's share of parents' property

maestre: supercargo

mantas: cloaks, usually cotton, woven by Indians

mayorazgo: entailed estate

mayordomo: administrator, often of a rural property

mercader: wholesaler

mercader de plata: merchant who sold silver bar to the mint for coining; merchant who coined silver at the mint

mercader viandante: traveling merchant

merced: royal grant, usually of land or office

mesillero: person selling wares from small table

mexora: larger share of inheritance: the *remaniente* plus one-third of the rest of the estate

ministro: high-level post

obraje: large workshop producing textiles and other goods

oficial: lower-level post

oficial mayor: post sold by provision of king

oficial menor: post sold by provision of viceroy

oficial real: royal official, usually treasury official

oidor: high court judge

paño número 24: highest-quality woolen cloth

partida: entry of a shipment in official records

permiso: maximum value of cargo allowed shipped from Manila

portales de los mercaderes: masonry buildings containing shops with arcades in front, along west side of Plaza

premio de albaceazgo: commission received by the executor of an estate

prometido: cash advance to treasury by tax farmer

quintal: unit of dry measure equalling 101 pounds

quinto: royal tax of one-fifth on silver paid by middlemen; three of the fifteen shares of the property set aside to pay testator's funeral expenses, bequests, and debts

real de minas: mining town

receptor: treasurer or collector of funds or fines

receptor de azogues: officials receiving the royal mercury allotment

receptor general de penas de cámara, estrados y gastos: general manager of the high court's fines and expenditures

regidor: alderman

relator: person who prepares reports and summaries of cases for court proceedings

remaniente: balance of the *quinto* (three of fifteen shares) of the parents' property once expenses paid

repartimiento: forced labor draft of Indians; apportionment of a tax among payers

repartimiento de comercio: forced sale of goods to Indians

rescatador: creole middlemen dealing in contraband in the Caribbean; person buying unrefined silver ore directly from the mineowner

secretario: secretary, usually to a government agency

secretario de entradas de la cárcel de la ciudad: secretary of the income of the municipal jail

señoreaje: royal minting tax

servicios: grants of money to the Crown

sociedad de castas: system of social stratification based on socially defined racial categories

tallador: official who stamped silver bar with royal die

tesorero: treasurer of royal treasury or other organization *tesorero de la casa de moneda:* chief administrator of foundry and mint in Mexico City

tianguis: Indian market

trapiche: animal-driven sugar mill; smaller version of *obraje*

Unión de Armas: squadron and other measures to be funded jointly by the kingdoms of Spain

vecino: householder; citizen of a city

Bibliography

Archival Sources

Unlike scholarly works based on a central corpus of material, such as hacienda records, this study relies on widely scattered documents. This seems typical of research on the seventeenth century, a period which has not been very generous with concentrated data. For example, merchants' inventories, one of the most valuable sources for information on credit networks, family structure, and investments were found one by one in almost every section of the archives consulted; pursuing these inventories was quite an adventure.

In Spain, in the Archivo General de Indias (AGI), the most useful sections were Contaduría, Contratación, Audiencia de México, and Escribanía de Cámara. Audiencia de México (Méx) contained correspondence from the diverse bodies of government and from private individuals which included information on officials' commercial activities, tax collection, appointments to office, and the enforcement of royal policies. The letters of the viceroys, which were the most detailed, were particularly helpful. Parts of the following *legajos* were used: 3 and 4 (*consultas* of the Council of the Indies); 22–38 (correspondence of the viceroys); 73, 75, and 76 (letters of the *audiencia*); and 92 (letters of *visitadores*); 112, 138, 147, 149, 153, and 155 (letters of private secular persons); 272 and 274 (petitions of the *Audiencia*); 318, 320, 322, 325, and 326 (letters of the *cabildo, tribunal de cuentas, consulado, oficiales reales*); 330 (acts regarding *alcabalas*); 351, 2771, and 2794 (*casa de la moneda*). In addition, *legajos* 265 and 266 contained the records of the *residencia* of Viceroy Albuquerque. *Legajos* 259–63, the declarations of wealth by officials in 1622, the major source for de la Peña's study, were used, but I relied more on merchant inventories which were not drawn up for official purposes. Finally, the *registro de oficios y partes, legajos 1095–1098*, gave information about bureaucratic appointments and disputes relating to them. Lewis Hanke's *Guía de las fuentes* and J. Israel's "Bibliographic Essay" were extremely useful in approaching Audiencia de México.

Contaduría provided a great deal for this study. Kenneth Andrien, Peter Bakewell, Herbert Klein, Richard Garner, and John TePaske have used these records for their studies of regional economic trends, taxation, and expenditure in the seventeenth-century empire. They have focussed more on the summary totals of the different branches of the treasury accounts. My approach here was to cull information about individual payments from within selected branches of the accounts. I used *legajos* 691 (1590)–753 (1660) of the *caxa de México, cargo* side. Almost all *legajos* were consulted for the following branches, and about half contained usable information because the amount of detail about individuals contained within each branch varied considerably from year to year. The most useful were: *almojarifazgo* 10%, *mercadurías de Filipinas*, and *islas de Filipinas* (names of persons and value of their cargo imported from the Philippines); *azogues* (*alcaldes mayores* of mining towns and their backers); *bulas de santa cruzada* and *naipes* (tax farmers, their agents, and arrears); *extraordinario* (merchants who minted coin for the Crown) and *préstamos* (lenders and amounts). Also helpful were: *alcabalas encabezadas de México* (guild and town payments, some individual payments), and *composición de tierras* (land ownership, probably assessed at false value, so not good for value of holdings). A few *legajos* were used from *alcances de cuentas* (bondsmen); *almojarifazgo nuevo and viejo* (coastal traders); *alumbre, oficios vendibles, ropa filipinas*, and *solimán*. For *data, extraordinario* and *préstamos* enabled me to trace the repayment of loans by the treasury. John TePaske's *La real hacienda de Nueva España . . .* was invaluable in managing this unwieldly (and occasionally charred) body of material. In addition to the treasury accounts, *Contaduría* 230 (fines imposed in San Luis Potosí). 570 (lists of Seville merchants and the value of cargo, 1641–75), and 585 (the same for 1604–39) were important.

Contratación offered additional perspectives on the merchants. This wide-ranging section of the AGI included lawsuits regarding particular shipments, taxes owed, debts to be collected, wills of merchants who died at sea, and foundations of charitable works in Spain. The *legajos* used here were: 161, 184, 188, 267, 346, 371, 439, 536, 597, 753, 764, 765, 773, 794, 822, 944, 952, 955, and 960. In addition, the *libros de Registro* (*legajos* 1796, 1809, 1823–29, 1859–63, 1880–84, 1896–99, and 1926–28) provided the lists of *avería* taxes paid by the shippers on the return voyage to Spain. This data was invaluable and fascinating.

Escribanía de Cámara contained much diverse and useful information. This section is divided by region and then according to whether documents were *pleitos, residencias*, or *visitas*. The *pleitos, legajos* 168b, 169a, 171a and b, 172a, 175b, 176b, and 177b, were the most helpful. They included lawsuits over a company, fees paid to the *ensayador* of the mint, the ownership of the San José mill, disputes over wills, and *alcabala* payments. The *residencias* in Escribanía de Cámara were most fruitful for the Viceroys Gelves, Cadereita, Escalona, and Albuquerque; I concentrated on the latter two, since the first two were more extensively analyzed by Israel. Finally, there were two informative *visitas:* that begun by Landeras de Velasco and continued by Vilella from 1606 to 1611 (*legajos* 272a and b, 273 a and b) and that begun by Valles, continued by Calancha Valenzuela and then by San Milián from 1664 to 1670 (*legajos* 275a and b). Finally, Indiferente General, *legajo* 77 on the Landeras investigation, and Patronato real, *legajo* 221, on Carrillo Alderete's *visita* were utilized.

In Mexico City, the Archivo General de la Nación (AGN) was a rich source. Inquisición was excellent for information about social background, family ties, and positions in the Holy Office occupied by merchants. It also contained a few suits over property. *Legajos* 86, 87, 192, 195, 196, 204, 216, 273, 286, 294, 314, 323, 327, 331, 346, 347, 351, 352, 259, 379, 399, 417, 428, 434, 442, 446, 454, 457, 489, 504, 509, 561, 570, 572, 589, 591, 592, and 659 were used. (By *legajos* here and elsewhere is meant one or more *expedientes* in these *legajos*). Of equal importance was Bienes Nacionales, which contained data chiefly about *capellanías* and other *obras pías*, the property on which they were founded, and the beneficiaries. It also included some disputes relating to the *cruzada* tax as well as a few wills. *Legajos* used were: 11, 34, 56, 60, 78, 87–88, 102, 108, 130, 132, 140, 195, 206, 220, 256, 259, 268, 310, 315, 339, 356, 378, 381, 387, 416, 420, 489, 493, 494, 498, 518, 531, 545, 547, 549, 554, 565, 604–5, 617, 630, 634, 644, and 658. Fewer merchants were found in *Tierras*, but those whose landed property was recorded here brought with them a great deal of information. Legajos used were: 74, 81–82, 85, 108, 109, 142–43, 151, 162, 1056, 1272, 1056, 1273, 1720, 2692, 2742, 2834, 2865, and 2892. Mercedes were helpful for seeing who benefitted from the wave of land grants in the late sixteenth and early seventeenth centuries. It was then possible from other sources to trace the subsequent development of some of these grants. Volumes 21–28, 30–35, 39–40, 42, and 45 were consulted. Another excellent source for real estate, urban and rural, was Vínculos y mayorazgos, *legajos* 194, 220, 229, 245, 247, 268, and 284. In all these *ramos* wives and children of merchants were traced whenever possible.

Civil provided a wide range of information, including about powers of attorney, *censos, capellanías, obrajes*, suits over debts, rental houses, and guardianships. *Legajos* used were: 2–4, 74–76, 86, 237, 319, 355, 400, 882, 899, 919, 955, 1386, 1488, 1546, 1606, 1660, 1737, 1743, 1832, 1835, and 1839. Real Fisco *legajos* 21, 22, and 30 provided information about the debts owed to the Inquisition by its officials or by other parties to them. Also useful were Casa de Moneda, 383, and Censos, 2–4.

Housed in the AGN, the Archivo Histórico de Hacienda, Consulado, was, of course, helpful, especially for the lists of merchants who were electors of the guild (*legajos* 132, 213, 664, and 791). In addition, occasional reports about freight charges, consulado expenses, complaints about taxes, challenges to elections, loans, and smuggling appear in these *legajos* and in 215 and 218. On the whole, Consulado has little on the seventeenth century, however; bankruptcy records, for example, begin with 1782. The bibliography of Guice's dissertation on the *consulado* was a valuable introduction to this *ramo*.

The other archives of Mexico City which were relied on were, first, the Archivo de Notarías del Departamento del D.F. Certain notaries specialized in merchants' business, and these contain many powers of attorney and bills of sale for merchandise, cattle, or other goods. Both types of documents illustrate the wholesalers' credit networks throughout the viceroyalty, and the bills of sale also give information about their scale of business. This archive also includes a number of loans, some dowries and wills, and a few *obras pias* and company agreements. The following are only the notaries whose records turned out to be useful. The years beside the name indicate the years read for this study. In some cases, the notary's records covered a longer period; for Bernal and Valdivieso, only that one year was available. Little remained from before 1620. Esteban Bernal, 1629; Toribio Cobían, 1649–53; Gabriel López Ahedo, 1630, 1639–50; Juan López de Rivera, 1630–39; Andrés Moreno, 1600–01, 1629–30; Juan Pérez de Rivera, 1613–15; 1621–36; Diego de los Ríos, 1642–45; Pedro Santillán, 1614–44; Luis Valdivieso, 1652. Another excellent Mexican archive was the Archivo Judicial del D.F. y Territorios Federales, Civil. This was best for inventories and wills but also provided companies, disputes over sales, and powers of attorney. *Legajos* are grouped by years and then erratically subdivided by numbers; many, especially the shorter pieces, are not numbered. Years "1593–1600" to "1668–69" were used. Finally, the Archivo del Ex-Ayuntamiento contained few but helpful items, in *Censos*, vol. 1 and *Testamentos*. The most informative material from this municipal archive was the Actas de Cabildo which, though used in the past for institutional history, contain valuable information on social and fiscal history too.

In the United States, the Genealogical Society of Utah provided some indispensable vital statistics. All parish records consulted were from Iglesia Catedral, Parroquía de Asunción Sagrario, Españoles. The *bautismos* (1590–1602) were excellent for *compadre* relations, which were usually not available elsewhere, while the *amonestaciones* (1624–1653) and the *matrimonios* (1621–25) sometimes added data about spouses, birthplaces, and names of parents, but often this was available elsewhere. Finally, *entierros* (1671–79) provided a few spouses, heirs, places of residence, and the notary who took the will (but these notarial records did not necessarily survive). The *amonestaciones* began with 1624, the *matrimonios* with 1621, and the *entierros* with 1671; there were no earlier records preserved for Spaniards of this central parish for these registers. The most detailed register, therefore, was for baptisms, and more years could have been read from this, but I felt that the point had been sufficiently made with the material from the late sixteenth and early seventeenth centuries. Finally, at the University of Texas Benson Manuscript Collection were two items of interest; the seventeenth century does not figure prominently in this collection.

Published Works

This list is limited chiefly to works cited in the text. Other works consulted about *conversos*; migration from Spain; social history of other groups or of merchants in other regions and periods; taxation, trade, and bureaucracy in the eighteenth century are unlisted.

I. Primary Sources

Álvarez de Abreu, Antonio José. *Extracto historial del expediente que pende en el consejo real . . . de las Indias a instancia de la ciudad de Manila.* Madrid: Juan de Ariztia, 1736.

Colección de documentos inéditos relativos al descubrimiento, conquista, y organización de las antiguas poseciones españoles de América y Oceania. 42 vols. Madrid: Ministro de ultramar, 1864–84. Vol. 6.

Díez de la Calle, Juan. *Memorial y noticias sacras y reales de las Indias Occidentales.* Madrid: Privately printed, 1646.

Encinas, Diego de. *Cedulario indiano.* 4 vols. Madrid: Ediciones cultura hispánica, 1945–46.

Fernández de Recas, Guillermo S. *Mayorazgos de la Nueva España.* México: Biblioteca nacional de México, 1965.

Guijo, Gregorio M. de. *Diario, 1648–1664.* 2 vols. México: Porrua, 1952.

Hanke, Lewis, ed., with Celso Rodríguez. *Los virreyes españoles en América durante el gobierno de la casa de Austria.* 5 vols. Madrid: Atlas, 1977.

México. Archivo General de la Nación. *Boletín* 11 (1940).

México. City. *Actas del ayuntamiento constitucional de México.* 54 vols. México: Aguilar y hijos, 1889–1910.

Robles, Antonio de. *Diario de sucesos notables (1665–1703).* 3 vols. México: Porrua, 1972.

Silva Herzog, Jesús, ed. *Documentos relativos al arrendamiento del impuesto o renta de alcabalas de la ciudad de México y distritos circundantes.* México: Secretaría de hacienda y crédito público, 1945.

Spain. *Recopilación de leyes de los reynos de Indias.* 3 vols. Madrid: Consejo de la hispa-
    nidad, 1943.

TePaske, John J. *La real hacienda de Nueva España: La real caja de México (1576–1816)*
    México: Instituto nacional de antropología e historia, 1976.

——— , and Herbert S. Klein. *Ingresos y egresos de la Real Hacienda.* México: Instituto
    nacional de antropología y historia, 1986.

Thompson, J. Eric. S., ed. *Thomas Gage's Travels in the New World.* Norman: University
    of Oklahoma Press, 1958.

Vázquez de Espinosa, Antonio. *Compendio y descripción de las Indias occidentales.* Wash-
    ington, D.C.: Smithsonian Institution Press, 1948.

Veitia Linaje, Joseph de. *Norte de la contratación de las Indias occidentales.* Buenos Aires:
    Comisión argentina de fomento interamericano, 1945.

Vila Vilar, Enriqueta, ed., with Juana Sarabia Viejo. *Catálogo de cartas de cabildo:
    Audiencia de México, siglos XVI y XVII.* Sevilla: Escuela de estudios hispanoameri-
    canos, 1985.

Zavala, Silvio, and María Castelo. *Fuentes para la historia del trabajo en Nueva España.*
    8 vols. México: Fondo de cultura económica, 1939–45.

II. Secondary Sources and Guides

Aiton, Arthur. "The First American Mint." *Hispanic American Historical Review* 11, no. 2
    (May 1931).

Alberro, Solange. *Inquisición y sociedad en México, 1571–1700.* México: Fondo de cultura
    económica, 1988.

Albi Romero, Guadalupe. "La sociedad de Puebla de los Angeles en el siglo XVI."
    Jahrbuch für Geschichte von Staat, Wirtschaft, und Gesellschaft Lateinamericas (here-
    after cited as *Jahrbuch*) 7 (1970).

Altman, Ida, and James Lockhart, eds. *Provinces of Early Mexico: Variations of Spanish
    American Regional Evolution.* Los Angeles: University of California Latin American
    Center, 1976.

Álvarado Morales, Manuel. "El cabildo y regimiento de la ciudad de México en el
    siglo XVII: Un ejemplo de la oligarquía criolla," *Historia mexicana* 28 (April–
    June 1979).

——— . *La ciudad de México ante la fundación de la armada de Barlovento: Historia de
    una encrucijada (1635–1643).* México: El colegio de México–Universidad de Puerto
    Rico, 1983.

Andrews, Kenneth R. *The Spanish Caribbean: Trade and Plunder, 1530–1630.* New
    Haven: Yale University Press, 1978.

Andrien, Kenneth. *Crisis and Decline: The Viceroyalty of Peru in the Seventeenth Century.*
    Albuquerque: University of New Mexico Press, 1985.

Anna, Timothy. *The Fall of Royal Government in Mexico City.* Lincoln: University of
    Nebraska Press, 1978.

Archer, Christon I. *The Army in Bourbon Mexico, 1760–1810.* Albuquerque: University
    of New Mexico Press, 1977.

Arcila Farías, Eduardo. *Comercio entre Venezuela y México en los siglos XVI y XVII.*
    México: El colegio de México, 1950.

Assadourian, Carlos Sempat. *El sistema de la economía colonial: Mercado interno, regiones y espacio económico.* Lima: Instituto de estudios peruanos, 1982.

Atwell, William. "International Bullion Flows and the Chinese Economy circa 1530–1650." *Past and Present,* no. 95 (May 1982).

Bakewell, Peter J. "Mining in Colonial Spanish America." In *Cambridge History of Latin America,* ed. Leslie Bethell. New York: Cambridge University Press, 1984.

————. *Silver Mining and Society in Colonial Mexico: Zacatecas, 1546–1700.* Cambridge: Cambridge University Press, 1971.

Bancroft, Hubert H. *History of Mexico,* vol. 3. San Francisco: Bancroft, 1883.

Barrett, Ward J. *The Sugar Haciendas of the Marqueses del Valle.* Minneapolis: University of Minnesota Press, 1970.

Bazant, Jan. "Evolution of the Textile Industry of Puebla, 1544–1845." *Comparative Studies in Society and History* 7 (October 1964).

Bennassar, B. "Facteurs sévillans au XVIe siècle d'après des lettres merchandes." *Annales, Economies, Sociétés, Civilisations* 12 (1957).

Berthe, Jean-Pierre. "Xochimancas: Les travaux et les jours dans une hacienda sucrière de Nouvelle-Espagne au XVIIe siècle." *Jahrbuch* 3 (1966).

Bethell, Leslie, ed. *Cambridge History of Latin America.* Vols 1–2. New York: Cambridge University Press, 1984.

Borah, Woodrow. *Early Colonial Trade and Navigation between Mexico and Peru.* Berkeley: University of California Press, 1954.

————. *Justice by Insurance: The General Indian Court of Colonial Mexico and the Legal Aides of the Half-Real.* Berkeley: University of California Press, 1983.

————. *New Spain's Century of Depression.* Berkeley: University of California Press, 1951.

————. *Silk Raising in Colonial Mexico.* Berkeley: University of California Press, 1943.

Borchart de Moreno, Christiana. "Los miembros del consulado de la ciudad de México en la época de Carlos III." *Jahrbuch* 14 (1977).

Boyajian, James C. *Portuguese Bankers at the Court of Spain, 1626–1650.* New Brunswick: Rutgers University Press, 1983.

Boyer, Richard. "Absolutism vs. Corporatism in New Spain: The Administration of the Marqués de Gelves, 1621–24." *International History Review* 4, no. 4 (November 1982).

————. "Mexico in the Seventeenth Century: Transition of a Colonial Society." *Hispanic American Historical Review* 57, no. 3 (August 1977).

Brading, D. A. *Miners and Merchants in Bourbon Mexico, 1763–1810.* Cambridge: Cambridge University Press, 1971.

————. *Los orígenes del nacionalismo mexicano.* México: Ediciones Era, 1973.

————, and Harry E. Cross. "Colonial Silver Mining: Mexico and Peru." *Hispanic American Historical Review* 52, no. 4 (November 1972).

Braudel, Fernand. *The Mediterranean and the Mediterranean World at the Age of Philip II.* New York: Harper Torchbook, 1975.

Bronner, Fred. "La unión de armas en el Perú: Aspectos políticos-legales." *Anuario de estudios americanos* 24 (1967).

————. "Tramitación legislative bajo Olivares: La redacción de los arbitrios de 1631." *Revista de Indias* 41 (1981).

————. "Urban Society in Colonial Spanish America: Research Trends." *Latin American Research Review* 21 (1986).

Burkholder, Mark A. "Bureaucrats." In *Cities and Society in Colonial Latin America*, ed. Louisa S. Hoberman and Susan M. Socolow. Albuquerque: University of New Mexico Press, 1986.

————, and D. S. Chandler. *From Impotence to Authority: The Spanish Crown and the American Audiencias, 1687–1808*. Columbia: University of Missouri Press, 1977.

————, and Lyman Johnson, *Colonial Latin America*. New York: Oxford University Press, 1989.

Burzio, Humberto F. *Diccionario de la moneda hispano-americana*. 2 vols. Santiago de Chile: Fondo histórico y bibliográfico José Toribio Medina, 1956–58.

Calvo, Thomas. "Familles mexicaines au XVIIe siècle: Une tentative de reconstitution." *Annales de démographie historique* (1984).

Céspedes del Castillo, Guillermo. *La avería en el comercio de Indias*. Sevilla: Escuela de estudios hispanoamericanos, 1945.

Chaunu, Huguette, and Pierre Chauna. *Séville et l'Atlantique, 1504–1650*. 8 vols. Paris: SEVPEN, 1955–59.

Chaunu, Pierre. *Les Philippines et le Pacifique des Ibériques*. Paris: SEVPEN, 1960.

Chevalier, François. *Land and Society in Colonial Mexico*. Berkeley: University of California Press, 1966.

————. "Les cargaisons des flottes de la Nouvelle Espagne vers 1600." *Revista de Indias* 4, no. 12 (1943).

Chiaramonte, José Carlos. *Formas de sociedad y economía en Hispanoamérica*. Mexico: Grijalbo, 1983.

Clayton, Lawrence A. "Trade and Navigation in the Seventeenth-Century Viceroyalty of Peru." *Journal of Latin American Studies* 7 (May 1975).

Cook, Sherbourne, and Woodrow Borah. *Essays in Population History*. 3 vols. Berkeley: University of California Press, 1971–79.

Cross, Harry E. "Commerce and Orthodoxy: A Spanish Response to Portuguese Commercial Penetration in the Viceroyalty of Peru, 1580–1640." *The Americas* 35, no. 2 (October 1978).

Cummins, Victoria. "The Church and Business Practices in Late Sixteenth-Century Mexico." *The Americas* 54, no. 4 (April 1988).

DeVries, Jan. *The Economy of Europe in an Age of Crisis, 1600–1750*. Cambridge: Cambridge University Press, 1976.

Domínguez Ortiz, Antonio. "Los caudales de Indias y la política exterior de Felipe IV." *Anuario de estudios americanos* 13 (1956).

————. "Comercio y blasones: Concesiones de hábitos de ordenes militares a miembros del consulado de Sevilla en el siglo XVII." *Anuario de estudios americanos* 33 (1976).

————. "La concesión de 'naturalezas para comerciar' en Indias durante el siglo XVII." *Revista de Indias* 19 (1959).

————. *Orto y ocaso de Sevilla: Estudios sobre la prosperidad y decadencia de la ciudad durante los siglos XVI y XVII*. Sevilla: Junta de patronato, 1946.

————. *Política y hacienda de Felipe IV*. Madrid: Editorial de derecho financiero, 1960.

DuPlessis, Robert. "The Partial Transition to World-Systems Analysis in Early Modern European History." *Radical History Review* 39 (1987).

Elliott, John. *The Count-Duke of Olivares: The Statesman in an Age of Decline.* New Haven: Yale University Press, 1986.

————. "Spain and America in the Sixteenth and Seventeenth Centuries." In *Cambridge History of Latin America*, ed. Leslie Bethell. New York: Cambridge University Press, 1984.

Ewald, Ursula. *Estudios sobre la hacienda colonial en México: Las propriedades rurales del colegio de Espíritu Santo en Puebla.* Wiesbaden: Steiner, 1976.

Feijoo, Rosa. "El tumulto de 1624." *Historia mexicana* 14 (July–August 1964).

Fernández de Recas, Guillermo S. *Aspirantes americanos a cargos del Santo Oficio.* México: Porrua, 1956.

————. *Mayorazgos de la Nueva España.* México: Biblioteca nacional, 1965.

Flores Olea, Aurora. "Los regidores de la ciudad de México en la primera mitad del siglo XVII." *Estudios de historia novo-hispana* 3 (1970).

Florescano, Enrique. "Formation and Economic Structure of the Hacienda in New Spain." In *Cambridge History of Latin America*, ed. Leslie Bethell. New York: Cambridge University Press, 1984.

Fonseca, Fabian, and Carlos de Urrutia, eds. *Historia general de la real hacienda.* 6 vols. México: V. G. Torres, 1845–53.

Fortune, Stephen A. *Merchants and Jews: The Struggle for British West Indies Commerce, 1650–1750.* Gainesville: University Presses of Florida, 1984.

Ganster, Paul. "La familia Gómez de Cervantes: Linaje y sociedad en el México colonial." *Historia mexicana* 31 (October–December 1981).

Gantes Tréllez, María de las Mercedes. "Aspectos socios-económicos de Puebla de Los Angeles (1624–1650)." *Anuario de estudios hispanoamericanos* 40 (1983).

García Fuentes, Lutgardo. *El comercio español con América (1650–1700).* Sevilla: Escuela de estudios hispanoamericanos, 1980.

Garner, Richard. "Long-Term Silver Mining Trends in Spanish America: A Comparative Analysis of Peru and Mexico." *American Historical Review* 93, no. 4 (October 1988).

————. "Price Trends in Eighteenth-century Mexico." *Hispanic American Historical Review* 65 (May 1985): 286.

————, and William Taylor, eds. *Iberian Colonies, New World Societies: Essays in Honor of Charles Gibson.* Privately printed, 1986.

Gerhard, Peter. *A Guide to the Historical Geography of New Spain.* Cambridge: Cambridge University Press, 1972.

Gibson, Charles. *The Aztecs under Spanish Rule.* Stanford: Stanford University Press, 1964.

————. "Writings on Colonial Mexico." *Hispanic American Historical Review* 55, no. 2 (May 1975).

Girard, Albert. *Le commerce français a Séville et Cadix au temps des Hapsbourg: Contribution à l'étude de commerce étranger en Espagne au XVIe et XVIIe siècles.* Paris: Published privately, 1932.

Gortari, Hira de, and Guillermo Palacios. "El comercio novohispano a través de Veracruz (1802–1810)." *Historia Mexicana* 17, no. 3 (January–March 1968).

Goslinga, Cornelius Ch. *The Dutch in the Caribbean and on the Wild Coast 1580–1680.* Assen: Van Gorcum, 1971.

Greenleaf, Richard. "The Obraje in the Late Mexican Colony." *The Americas* 22 (January 1967).

————. "The Inquisition Brotherhood: Cofradía de San Pedro Mártir of Colonial Mexico." *Americas* 40 (October 1983).

Guthrie, Chester L. "Riots in Seventeenth-Century Mexico City: A Study of Social and Economic Conditions" in *Greater America* . . . Berkeley, 1945.

Hamnett, Brian R. *Politics and Trade in Southern Mexico, 1750–1812.* Cambridge: Cambridge University Press, 1971.

Hanke, Lewis, ed. *Guía de las fuentes en el Archivo de Indias para el estudio de la administración virreinal española en México y en el Perú, 1535–1700.* 3 vols. Wien: Böhlau Verlag Köln, 1977.

Hardoy, Jorge, and Carmen Aranovich. "Urban Scales and Functions in Spanish America Toward the Year 1600: First Conclusions." *Latin American Research Review* 5, no. 3 (1970).

Haring, Clarence. *The Spanish Empire in America.* New York: Oxford University Press, 1947.

————. *Trade and Navigation between Spain and the Indies in the Time of the Hapsburgs.* Cambridge: Harvard University Press, 1918.

Hassig, Ross. *Trade, Tribute, and Transportation: The Sixteenth Century Political Economy of the Valley of Mexico.* Norman: University of Oklahoma Press, 1985.

Heers, Jacques. "La búsqueda de colorantes." *Historia mexicana* 11, no. 1 (July–September 1961).

Heredia Herrera, Antonia. *Inventario de los fondos de consulados.* 2 vols. Seville: Escuela de estudios hispanoamericanos, 1979.

Hoberman, Louisa S. "Bureaucracy and Disaster: Mexico City and the Flood of 1629." *Journal of Latin American Studies* 6, no. 2 (1974).

————. "Hispanic American Political Theory as a Distinct Tradition." *Journal of the History of Ideas* 41, no. 2 (April–June 1980).

————. "Merchants in Seventeenth-Century Mexico City: A Preliminary Portrait." *Hispanic American Historical Review* 57, no. 3 (August 1977).

————, and Susan Socolow, eds. *Cities and Society in Colonial Latin America.* Albuquerque: University of New Mexico Press, 1986.

Hordes, Stanley. "The Inquisition as Economic and Political Agent: The Campaign of the Mexican Holy Office Against the Crypto-Jews in the Mid-Seventeenth Century." *The Americas* 39 (July 1982).

Israel, J. I. *The Dutch Republic and the Hispanic World.* Oxford: Clarendon Press, 1982.

————. *Empires and Entrepôts: The Dutch, The Spanish Monarchy, and the Jews, 1585–1713.* London: The Hambledon Press, 1990.

————. *Race, Class, and Politics in Colonial Mexico, 1610–70.* London: Oxford University Press, 1975.

Jeannin, Pierre. *Merchants of the Sixteenth Century.* New York: Harper and Row, 1972.

Kamen, Henry. *Spain in the Later Seventeenth Century, 1665–1700.* London: Longman, 1980.

Kamen, H., J. I. Israel, John TePaske, and Herbert Klein. "Debate. The Seventeenth-Century Crisis in New Spain: Myth or Reality?" *Past and Present* 97 (November 1982).

Kicza, John E. *Colonial Entrepreneurs: Families and Business in Bourbon Mexico City.* Albuquerque: University of New Mexico Press, 1983.

————. "Colonial Urban Social History: The Case of Mexico." In *1979 Proceedings of the*

Rocky Mountain Council on Latin American Studies Conference. Lincoln: University of Nebraska Press, 1980.

Konrad, Herman W. *A Jesuit Hacienda in Colonial Mexico: Santa Lucía, 1576–1767.* Stanford: Stanford University Press, 1980.

Ladd, Doris. *The Mexican Nobility at Independence, 1780–1826.* Austin: University of Texas Press, 1976.

Lang, James. *Conquest and Commerce: Spain and England in the Americas.* New York: Academic Press, 1975.

Lang, Melvyn F. *El monopolio estatal del mercurío en México colonial, 1550–1710.* México: Fondo de cultura económica, 1977.

Lavrin, Asunción. "The Role of the Nunneries in the Economy of New Spain." *Hispanic American Historical Review* 46, no. 4 (November 1966).

————. "El Capital Eclesiástico y las Elites Sociales en Nueva España a fines del siglo XVIII," *Mexican Studies/Estudios mexicanos* 1 (Winter 1985).

————, ed. *Latin American Women: Historical Perspectives.* Westport: Greenwood, 1978.

————, and Edith Couturier. "Dowries and Wills: A View of Women's Socioeconomic Role in Colonial Guadalajara and Puebla, 1640–1790." *Hispanic American Historical Review* 59, no. 2 (May 1979).

Lee, Raymond. "American Cochineal in European Commerce, 1526–1625." *Journal of Modern History* 23 (1951).

————. "Cochineal Production and Trade in New Spain to 1600," *The Americas* 4 (1948).

Leonard, Irving. *Baroque Times in Old Mexico.* 2d ed. Ann Arbor: University of Michigan Press, 1966.

León-Portilla, Miguel et al. *La minería en México: Estudios sobre su desarrollo histórico.* México: UNAM, 1978.

Lockhart, James. "Social Organization and Social Change in Colonial Latin America." In *Cambridge History of Latin America*, ed. Leslie Bethell. New York: Cambridge University Press, 1984.

————, and Stuart Schwartz. *Early Latin America.* Cambridge: Cambridge University Press, 1983).

Lopez, Robert, "The Trade of Medieval Europe: The South." In *Cambridge Economic History of Europe.* Vol. 2. Cambridge: Cambridge University Press, 1952.

López Rosado, Diego G. *Atlas histórico geográfico de México.* México: N.p., 1940.

————. *Historia del peso mexicano.* México: Fonda de cultura económica, 1975.

Lorenzo Sanz, Eufemio. *Comercio de España con América en la época de Felipe II.* 2 vols. Valladolid: Diputación provincial, 1979.

Lynch, John. *Spain under the Hapsburgs.* 2 vols. New York: Oxford University Press, 1964–69.

McAlister, Lyle N. *Spain and Portugal in the New World* (Minneapolis: University of Minnesota Press, 1985).

MacLachlan, Colin. *Spain's Empire in the New World: The Role of Ideas in Social and Institutional Change.* Berkeley: University of California Press, 1988.

————, and Jaime E. Rodríguez O. *The Forging of the Cosmic Race.* Berkeley: University of California Press, 1980.

MacLeod, Murdo J. "Spain and America: The Atlantic Trade, 1492–1720" and "Aspects of the Internal Economy of Colonial Spanish America. In *Cambridge History of Latin America*, ed. Leslie Bethell. New York: Cambridge University Press, 1984.

————. *Spanish Central America: A Socioeconomic History, 1520–1720*. Berkeley: University of California Press, 1973.

Martin, Cheryl English. "Crucible of Zapatismo: Hacienda Hospital in the Seventeenth Century." *The Americas* 38, no. 1 (July, 1981).

————. *Rural Society in Colonial Morelos*. Albuquerque: University of New Mexico Press, 1985.

Medina, José Toribio. *Historia del tribunal del Santo Oficio de la Inquisición en México*. 2d ed. México: Ediciones fuente cultural, 1952.

Moreno Toscano, Alejandra. ed. *Ciudad de México: Ensayo de Construcción de una Historia*. México: SEP-INAH, 1978.

————. "Regional Economy and Urbanization: Three Examples of the Relationship Between Cities and Regions in New Spain at the End of the Eighteenth Century." In *Urbanization in the Americas from Its Beginnings to the Present*, eds. Richard Schaedel et al. The Hague: Mouton, 1978.

Moret, Michèle. *Aspects de la société marchande de Séville au debút de XVIIe siècle*. Paris: M. Rivière, 1967.

Muriel de la Torre, Josefina. *Conventos de monjas en la Nueva España*. México: Editorial Santiago, 1946.

Muro Romero, Fernando. "El 'beneficio' de oficios públicos con jurisdicción en Indias." *Anuario de estudios americanos* 35 (1978).

————. "La reforma del pacto colonial en Indias: Notas sobre instituciones de gobierno y sociedad en el siglo XVII." *Jahrbuch* 19 (1982).

Palmer, Colin A. *Slaves of the White God: Blacks in Mexico, 1570–1650*. Cambridge: Harvard University Press, 1976.

Parry, John H. *The Sale of Public Office in the Spanish Indies under the Hapsburgs*. Berkeley: University of California Press, 1953.

Parker, Angelika Ertinger. *San Mateo Huiscolotepec a Piedras Negras: Historia de una hacienda Tlaxcalteca, 1580–1979*. México: Costa Amic editores, 1979.

Peña, José de la. *Oligarquía y propiedad en la Nueva España (1550–1624)*. México: Fondo de cultura económica, 1983.

Phelan, John Leddy. *The Kingdom of Quito in the Seventeenth Century: Bureaucratic Politics in the Spanish Empire*. Madison: University of Wisconsin Press, 1968.

Pietschmann, Horst. "Burocracia y corrupción en hispanoamérica colonial: Una approximación tentativa." *Nova Americana* 5 (1982).

Pike, Ruth. *Aristocrats and Traders: Sevillean Society in the Sixteenth Century*. Ithaca: Cornell University Press, 1972.

————. *Enterprise and Adventure: The Genoese in Seville and the Opening of the New World*. Ithaca: Cornell University Press, 1966.

Pradeau, Alberto F. *Historia numismática de México desde la época precortesiana hasta 1823*. México: Banco de México, 1950.

Quiroz, Alfonso. "The Expropriation of Portuguese New Christians in Spanish America, 1635–1649." *Ibero-Amerikanisches Archiv* 11, no. 4 (1985).

Ragin, Charles, and Daniel Chirot. "The World-System of Immanuel Wallerstein: Sociology and Politics as History." In *Vision and Method in Historical Sociology*, ed. Theda Skocpol. Cambridge: Cambridge University Press, 1987.

Rees, Peter. *Transportes y comercio entre México y Veracruz, 1519–1910*. México: Sepsetentas, 1976.

Riley, James Denison. *Hacendados jesuitas en México: El colegio máximo San Pedro y San Pablo, 1685–1767.* México: Sepsetentas, 1976.

Riva Palacio, Vicente, ed. *México a través de los siglos.* Vol. 2. México: Ballesca, 1887.

Rivera Cambas, Manuel. *Los governantes de México.* Vol. 1. Mexico: Privately printed, 1872.

Romero, María de los Angeles. "Los intereses españoles en la Mixteca." *Historia mexicana* 29, no. 2 (October–December 1979).

Romero de Terreros, Manuel. *La plaza mayor de México en el siglo XVIII.* México: UNAM, 1946.

Rubio Mañé, Jorge Ignacio. "Gente de España en la ciudad de Mexico año de 1689." *Boletín. Archivo general de la nación.* 2d series, 7, no. 1. (January–March 1966).

Salvucci, Richard J. *Textiles and Capitalism in Mexico: An Economic History of the Obrajes, 1539–1840.* Princeton: Princeton University Press, 1987.

Sánchez-Albornoz, Nicolás, "Population of Colonial Latin America." In *Cambridge History of Latin America,* ed. Leslie Bethell. New York: Cambridge University Press, 1984.

Sánchez Bella, Ismael. *La organización financiera de las Indias: Siglo XVI.* Sevilla: Escuela de estudios hispanoamericanos, 1968.

————. "Visitas a la audiencia de México (siglos XVI y XVII)." *Anuario de estudios americanos* 32 (1975).

Sandoval, Fernando. *La industria del azúcar en Nueva España.* México: UNAM, 1951.

Schurz, William Lytle. *The Manila Galleon.* New York: Dutton, 1939.

Schwaller, John Frederick. *The Church and Clergy in Sixteenth-Century Mexico.* Albuquerque: University of New Mexico Press, 1987.

————. "Tres familias mexicanas del siglo XVI." *Historia mexicana* 31 (October–December 1981).

Seed, Patricia. *To Love, Honor, and Obey in Colonial Mexico: Conflicts over Marriage Choice, 1574–1821.* Stanford: Stanford University Press, 1988.

Semo, Enrique. *Historia del capitalismo en México: Los orígenes, 1521–1762.* México: Ediciones Era, 1973.

Serrera Contreras, Ramón. *Guadalajara ganadera: Estudio regional novohispano, 1760–1805* Sevilla: Escuela de estudios hispanoamericanos, 1977.

Smith, Robert S. "The Institution of the Consulado in New Spain." *Hispanic American Historical Review* 24 (1944).

————. "Sales Taxes in New Spain, 1575–1770." *Hispanic American Historical Review* 28 (1948).

Socolow, Susan. *The Merchants of Buenos Aires, 1778–1810: Family and Commerce.* Cambridge: Cambridge University Press, 1978.

Spalding, Karen, ed. *Essays in the Political, Economic, and Social History of Colonial Latin America.* Newark: University of Delaware Press, 1982.

Stein, Stanley J. "Prelude to Upheaval in Spain and New Spain, 1800–1880: Trust Funds, Spanish Finance and Colonial Silver." In *Iberian Colonies, New World Societies: Essays in Honor of Charles Gibson,* ed. Richard Garner and William Taylor. Privately published, 1986.

————, and Barbara H. *The Colonial Heritage of Latin America: Essays on Economic Dependence in Perspective.* New York: Oxford University Press, 1970.

Stern, Steve J. "Feudalism, Capitalism, and the World-System in the Perspective of Latin

America and the Caribbean." *American Historical Review* 93, no. 4 (October 1988).

Super, John C. "Partnership and Profit in the Early Andean Trade: The Experiences of Quito Merchants, 1580–1610." *Journal of Latin American Studies* 11, no. 2 (November 1979).

———. "Querétaro Obrajes: Industry and Society in Provincial Mexico, 1600–1810." *Hispanic American Historical Review* 56, no. 2 (May 1976).

Taylor, William. *Landlord and Peasant in Colonial Oaxaca*. Stanford: Stanford University Press, 1972.

———. "Indian *Pueblos* of Central Jalisco on the Eve of Independence." In *Iberian Colonies, New World Societies: Essays in Honor of Charles Gibson*, ed. Richard Garner and William Taylor. Privately printed, 1986.

———. "The Virgin of Guadalupe in New Spain: An Inquiry into the Social History of Marian Devotion." *American Ethnologist* 14 (February, 1987).

TePaske, John J. "New World Silver, Castile, and the Far East (1590–1750)." In *Precious Metals in the Later Medieval and Early Modern World*, ed. John Richards. Durham: Carolina Academic Press, 1982.

———. "La política española en el Caribe durante los siglos XVII and XVIII." In *La influencia de España en el Caribe, la Florida, y la Luisiana, 1500–1800*, ed. Antonio Acosta and Juan Marchena. Madrid: Instituto de cooperación iberoamericana, 1983.

———, and Herbert Klein. "The Seventeenth-Century Crisis in the Spanish Empire: Myth or Reality?" *Past and Present* 90 (February 1981).

Thompson, I. A. A. *War and Government in Hapsburg Spain, 1560–1620*. London: Athlone Press, 1976.

Thomson, Guy P. C. *Puebla de los Angeles: Industry and Society in a Mexican City, 1700–1850*. Boulder: Westview, 1989.

Torre Revello, José. "Merchandise brought to America by the Spaniards." *Hispanic American Historical Review* 23 (1943).

Torres Ramírez, Bibiano. *La Armada de Barlovento*. Sevilla: Escuela de estudios hispano-americanos, 1981.

Van Oss, Adriaan C. "Architectural Activity, Demography, and Economic Diversification: Regional Economies of Colonial Mexico." *Jahrbuch* 16 (1979).

Van Young, Eric. *Hacienda and Market in Eighteenth-Century Mexico: The Rural Economy of the Guadalajara Region, 1675–1820*. Berkeley: University of California Press, 1981.

———. "Mexican Rural History since Chevalier: The Historiography of the Colonial Hacienda." *Latin American Research Review* 18, no. 3 (1983).

Vila Vilar, Enriqueta. *Hispanoamerica y el comercio de esclavos*. Sevilla: Escuela de estudios hispanoamericanos, 1977.

Villaseñor y Villaseñor, Alejandro. *Los condes de Santiago*. México: N.p., 1901.

Von Bath, Slicher. "Economic Diversification in Spanish America around 1600: Centres, Intermediate Zones, and Peripheries." *Jahrbuch* 16 (1979).

Von Wobeser, Gisela. *San Carlos Borromeo: Endeudamiento de una hacienda colonial (1608–1729)*. México: UNAM, 1980.

———. "Mecanismos crediticos en la Nueva España. El uso del censo consignativo." *Mexican Studies/Estudios mexicanos* 5 (Winter 1989).

Wallerstein, Immanuel. *The Modern World-System*. Vol. 1, *Capitalist Agriculture and the Origins of the European World-Economy in the Sixteenth Century*. New York: Academic Press, 1974. Vol. 2, *Mercantilism and the Consolidation of the European World-Economy, 1600–1750.* New York: Academic Press, 1974.

West, Robert C. *The Mining Community in Northern New Spain: The Parral Mining District.* Berkeley: University of California Press, 1949.

Wolf, Eric. *Sons of the Shaking Earth.* 3rd printing. Chicago: University of Chicago Press, 1962.

Yali Román, Alberto. "Sobre alcaldías mayores y corregimientos de Indias: un ensayo de interpretación." *Jahrbuch* 9 (1972).

Yuste López, Carmen, *El comercio de la Nueva España con Filipinas, 1590–1785.* México: INAH-DIH, 1984.

III. Unpublished Secondary Sources

Arnold, Linda J. "Bureaucracy and Bureacrats in Mexico City: 1808–1824." Master's thesis, University of Texas, Austin, 1975.

Boyd-Bowman, Peter. "Indice geobiográfico de 40,000 pobladores españoles de América en el siglo XVI," 1580–1600, on notecards, 1978.

Boyer, Richard E. "Mexico City and the Great Flood: Aspects of Life and Society, 1629–1635." Ph.D. diss., University of Connecticut, 1973.

Brading, D. A. "The Catholic Monarchy in the Seventeenth Century." Lecture given at the University of Texas, 1989.

Couturier, Edith Boorstein. "Hacienda of Hueyápan: The History of a Mexican Social and Economic Institution, 1550–1940." Ph.D. diss., Columbia University, 1968.

Guice, C. N. "The Consulado of New Spain, 1594–1795." Ph.D. diss., University of California, Berkeley, 1952.

Hirschberg, Julia Bell. "A Social History of Puebla de los Angeles, 1531–1560." Ph.D. diss., 2 vols. University of Michigan, 1976.

Hoberman, Louisa S. "City Planning in Spanish Colonial Government: The Response of Mexico City to the Problem of Floods, 1607–1637." Ph.D. diss., Columbia University, 1972.

———. "Elites in Seventeenth-Century Mexico: A Review of the New Social History." Paper presented at the Latin American Studies Association, 1982.

———. "Elites and the Commercial Crisis in Seventeenth-Century New Spain." Paper presented at the American Historical Association, 1980.

Hordes, Stanley. "The Crypto-Jewish Community of New Spain, 1620–1649. A Collective Biography." Ph.D. diss., Tulane University, 1980.

Lockhart, James. "Postconquest Nahua Society and Culture Seen Through Nahuatl Sources." Readings in Colonial Nahua History, unpublished paper.

Nwasike, D. A. "Mexico City Town Government, 1590–1650: A Study in Aldermanic Background and Performance." Ph.D. diss., University of Wisconsin, 1972.

Schwartz, Stuart. "The Voyage of the Vassals, Royal Power, Noble Obligations, and 'New Christian' Capital before the Portuguese Restoration of Independence, 1624–40." *American Historical Review*, forthcoming.

Stowe, Noel J. "The Tumulto of 1624: Turmoil at Mexico City." Ph.D. diss., University of Southern California, 1970.

Super, John C. "Querétaro: Society and Economy in Early Provincial Mexico." Ph.D. diss., University of California, 1973.

Index

"Gracious gift and loan," 176–77
Gremio de consulado, 269
Guadalajara, 26, 78, 80, 81, 96, 112
Guadalcázar, Viceroy, 77, 178
Guanajuato, 24, 25, 80, 112, 175
Guatemala City, 25, 119, 122
Guayaquil, 15, 22, 29, 119, 126–27, 273
Guemez, Juan Bautista, bondsman for
    alcaldes mayores, 175
Guerra Chacón, Alonso, estate, 236
Guerrero, Juan, *licenciado*, 117
Guevara, Marcos de, *alguacil mayor*, 198
Guild: functions of, 18–21; merchant
    undermining of, 131; military orders,
    43; and *obrajes*, 129; woolen cloth
    standards, 138; workers and mer-
    chants, 276. See also *Consulado*
Gutiérrez Çarfate, Pedro, mint mer-
    chant, 92
Gutiérrez Gil, Gonzalo: building owner-
    ship, 141; *hacendados*, 62, 112–13,
    117; minter, 91
Guzmán Carabeo, Isabel, debt reduc-
    tion, 62

Hacienda de minas, 74, 76
Hacienda Hospital, 100, 101, 102
Haciendas, 14, 15, 110–18
Haro, Francisco de, tax appeal, 193–94
Haro, Simón de: Atlantic trade, 52;
    dowry, 68; public banker, 102, 177;
    and religious patronage, 238
Havana, 26, 213
Herrera, José de, companies, 63–64
Herrera y Baeza, Lorenzo, *relator*, 114
Herrera y Baeza, Rafaela, dowry, 114
Hidalgo, Alonso, sugar plantation, 82
Higuera Matamoros, Sebastián de la,
    sugar mill, 102, 141
Homeowners, and landlords, 139–42
Hospital de la Misericordia, 238
House swapping, 144
Huejotzingo, 119

Illegal activities: merchants in govern-
    ment, 154; partnerships, 179; punish-

ment of, 148, 188; silver contraband,
    81, 83, 90–91, 93; smuggled goods,
    188, 210, 219–20, 268; viceroys, 178
Import-substitution, 138
Income: comparison of, 53; mint officials,
    84, 87–89; *obrajeros*, 133
Indian: labor prohibition, 96; villages and
    social change, 7–8
Indies trade, and profits, 55, 60
Indigo, 119, 120, 123, 126
Indulgences, payment for. See *Bulas de
    cruzada*
Informal groups, 148, 174–80, 182, 279
Ingenios, 95; Nuestra Señora de Con-
    cepción, 102; of Guajoyuca, 101; San
    Francisco, 102; San José, 103–110,
    271; San Pedro Mártir Casasano, 100,
    102, 106; Santa Inés Las Amilpas, 99,
    100, 101, 102–3
Inheritance patterns, 225–32, 235–36
Inquisition, 10; and commerce, 150;
    confiscation of property, 100; and
    conversos, 21; and merchant employ-
    ment, 158. See also *Trapiches*
Interest, and church doctrine, 59, 60–61
Intergenerational, inheritance and
    mobility, 225–32
International economy: structure of,
    33–41; trading ties to, 26–32
Interoceanic trade routes, 28
Inventories, four merchant and prove-
    nance of goods, 269–70
Investment: agricultural risk, 114–15; and
    Atlantic and Pacific trade, 36–41, 51–
    53; patterns of, 146; specialty crops,
    126; threats to, 143–44; urban real
    estate, 139–43
Italians, and trade, 41–43

Jalapa, 24, 25, 29, 98, 175, 273
Jamaica, 15, 17, 268
Jérez, Pedro de, merchant, 79
Jesuits: Casa Profesa, 238; and merchant
    patronage, 238; and social change, 10;
    and sugar mills, 101, 102, 107
Jiménez Enciso, Diego, *ventiquatro*, 46

Illustration Credits

Louisa Schell Hoberman is a Lecturer at the University of Texas, Austin. Author of several articles about bureaucracy, technology, and political theory in colonial Mexico, she is also contributor to and coeditor of *Cities and Society in Colonial Latin America*. She has served on the faculties of George Mason University, Wesleyan University, and Pomona College. She has conducted research as an independent scholar and was a Bunting Institute Fellow at Radcliffe College.

Library of Congress Cataloging-in-Publication Data
Hoberman, Louisa Schell, 1942–
Mexico's merchant elite, 1590–1660 : silver, state, and society /
Louisa Schell Hoberman.
Includes bibliographical references and index.
ISBN 0-8223-1134-8
1. Merchants—Mexico—History—17th century.   2. Mexico—
Economic conditions—1540–1810.   3. Elite (Social sciences)—
Mexico—History—17th century.   I. Title.
HF3235.H63 1991
305.5'56—dc20   90-20659 CIP